Study Guide
Theory and Problems

for

Principles of
Money, Banking, and
Financial Markets

Study Guide
Theory and Problems

for

8th Edition

Lawrence S. Ritter
William L. Silber

Principles of
Money, Banking, and
Financial Markets

Gabriel Hawawini

INSEAD (The European Institute of Business Administration),
Fontainebleau, France

Paul Warner

State of Oregon

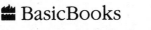 BasicBooks
A Division of HarperCollins *Publishers*

Cover design: Gene Crofts
Cover photo: Background photo copyright © by Will & Deni McIntyre, Photo
Researchers, Inc.; inset photos copyright © by Superstock, Inc.
Copyright © 1980, 1983, 1986, 1988, 1990, 1993 by BasicBooks, Inc.
ISBN: 0–465–06369–1
Printed in the United States of America
     95 96 CC/ML 9 8 7 6 5 4 3 2

contents

preface

This study guide was written in the hope that it will aid students and instructors of money, banking, and financial markets. By assigning chapters in the study guide to students, the instructor should be able to devote more classroom time to discussions, the students having acquired the basics through their own study and review. Although designed to accompany the eighth edition of *Principles of Money, Banking, and Financial Markets* by Lawrence S. Ritter and William L. Silber, the scope and structure of the study guide is such that both students and instructors using other textbooks will find it a useful tool.

To the student: How to use this study guide

The purpose of this book is to help you understand the material covered in the textbook and to test the knowledge you have acquired. It is not a substitute for the textbook. You should not attempt to answer the questions in this study guide before a serious reading of the relevant chapters in the textbook.

These chapters of this study guide are divided into these sections:

CENTRAL THEMES AND MAJOR POINTS
NEW TERMS
ESSAY QUESTIONS AND PROBLEMS
SELF-TESTS
    Completion questions
    True and false questions
    Multiple-choice questions

In order to obtain the maximum benefit from this book you should follow these five steps:

STEP ONE

Begin with a thorough reading of the assigned chapters in your textbook. Review your class notes.

STEP TWO

Read the section titled "Central Themes and Major Points" in the study guide. It is not a sum-mary of the chapter. The reading of this section is no substitute for the reading of the relevant chapter in the textbook. The purpose of this section is to highlight the objectives of the chapter and to give you a brief review of the basic issues raised in the chapter. It also ties in the material with topics covered in earlier chapters. Only major conclusions are summarized.

STEP THREE

Review the basic terms in the second section. Make sure that you know the exact meaning of these words or concepts. You should realize that your inability to comprehend some of the material covered in the textbook is often due to the fact that you are not familiar with the technical terms employed by the authors. A good understanding of these terms will enhance your overall comprehension of the chapter.

The definitions are not given in the study guide. If you are unable to define or explain a term, return to the textbook and look up the term in the appropriate chapter.

STEP FOUR

Answer the essay questions and problems in the third section. Essay questions are directly related to the material covered in the relevant chapter of the textbook. If you have understood the material in the chapter, you should not have any difficulty in answering the essay questions. To help you determine the topic the question deals with, most questions are captioned.

If you cannot answer an essay question, go back to the relevant chapter in the textbook. With the question in mind, carefully reread the chapter. You should then be able to answer the question. *Those few essay questions that do not have an answer in the textbook are marked with an asterisk. You will find the answers to these questions in the solution section at the end of this study guide.*

Detailed solutions to all the numerical questions and problems are given in the solution section. These questions and problems are identified by an asterisk. Do not refer to the solution of a problem before you attempt to solve it. The effort (and frustration) expended in your attempt to answer a question is an integral part of the learning process.

STEP FIVE

You can now test yourself with the completion, true and false, and multiple-choice questions. There are about ten completion, twenty true and false, and twenty multiple-choice questions per chapter. Answers to all these questions are available in the solution section at the end of this study guide.

Do not guess when you answer true and false or multiple-choice questions. In the case of true and false questions, if the answer is "false" try to see if the statement can be modified to make it correct.

If you can answer 90 percent or more of the questions correctly, you are in good shape. A score of 70 percent or less means that you still have some work to do on the chapter. Try to determine why your answers were wrong and make sure that you understand why the given answers are the correct ones. You may want to read the chapter again and discuss with your instructor any points that are still obscure.

part I

The Basics

chapter 1

Introducing Money

Central Themes and Major Points

In this chapter the concept of money is defined and its influence on economic activity is examined. It is shown how the quantity of money *(the money supply)* available for current spending affects the performance of the economy.

There is no unique definition of money. Various definitions are presented (*M1, M2, M3*) and related to the concept of *liquidity*. The definition of money most widely used is M1, the sum of *currency* (coins and dollar bills) outside banks, *demand deposits* and other *checkable deposits* at *commercial banks* and *thrift institutions,* and traveler's checks. We will see in the next chapter that money in the form of demand deposits is created when banks extend loans and/or buy securities from the public. It is destroyed when loans are repaid and securities are sold to the public (more on this in Chapters 2 and 14). This important bank activity is performed in conjunction with and under the supervision of the *Federal Reserve,* the central bank of the United States (more on this in Chapters 13 and 15).

The importance of money is illustrated by the problems encountered in a *barter economy*—an economy without money—and by the contribution of money to economic growth. In the former case money facilitates exchange, and in the latter, money allows the separation of the act of *saving* from the act of *investing*. These two characteristics of money have the effect of increasing the rate of economic growth.

But too much money in circulation in the economy may create rapid price inflation, which reduces the *value of money* (a reduction in the quantity of goods one can buy with one unit of money). It is therefore necessary to control the growth of the money supply. This important task is performed by the Federal Reserve. The key question, then, is: How much money should there be around? Too little may prevent healthy economic growth; too much may create rapid *inflation*. A first answer to this challenging question is given in the next chapter.

New Terms

Define and/or explain the following terms introduced in this chapter:

Currency (coins + dollar bills)

Demand deposits = checking accounts

Negotiable order of withdrawal (NOW) accounts†

Money market deposit accounts†

Money market mutual funds†

Passbook savings deposits

Time deposits

Certificates of deposit (CDs)

Commercial banks

Thrift institutions:†
Savings and loan associations
Mutual savings banks
Credit unions

Financial instruments
   Securities
   Financial assets
Money supply as M1,
   M2, M3
Liquidity of assets
Central Bank
Federal Reserve
   System
   (the Fed)

Barter economy
Savers
Borrowers
Value of money
Monetary economy
Financial markets
Financial
   intermediaries†
Hyperinflation

†More on these terms in Chapter 4.

Essay Questions and Problems

1. **Functions of money**
   a. What are the functions performed by money? Define each function and explain why any "item" should perform these functions in order to qualify as money.
   b. How and why does price inflation prevent money from performing its functions?

2. **Definitions of the money supply**
   a. What are the components of the money supply defined as M1, M2, and M3?
   b. What is the relationship between the four definitions of money and the concept of the liquidity of a financial asset?
   *c. Which function of money is emphasized by the money supply as M1?

3. **Components of the money supply**
   *a. Why is currency in commercial banks excluded from the definition of the money supply?
   b. Explain why it is the public that ultimately decides what proportion of the money supply will be in the form of currency.
   *c. How could you explain the fact that the government has been unsuccessful in its attempt to place a new $2 bill in general circulation?

4. **Barter economies**
   a. What is a barter economy, and what are the problems encountered in this type of economy?
   b. Explain how the introduction of money can solve these problems.
   *c. Can saving and investment take place in a barter economy? Explain your answer with an illustrative example.

5. **Money, financial markets, and economic growth** Money is a major contributor to economic growth and development.
   *a. Why and how do money and financial mar-

kets stimulate investment in productive facilities, which in turn spur economic growth? Compare this kind of economy with a barter economy.
   b. Explain how financial intermediaries such as thrift institutions, insurance companies, and pension funds stimulate investment in productive facilities beyond the level that would be attained in an economy with money and financial markets but without these financial intermediaries.
   c. The two preceding questions have illustrated the advantage of an economy with money over a barter economy. Is money always a blessing? What are the ill effects of money, and under what conditions will they appear?

*6. **Definitions of the money supply** Assume that in the United States, at the end of a given year, $100 billion worth of currency circulates outside the banking system, which has $300 billion in demand deposits, $400 billion in small-denomination time deposits and savings deposits, and $300 billion in large-denomination time deposits. Thrift institutions have $50 billion in demand deposits and $600 billion in small-denomination time deposits and savings deposits. Also, money market mutual funds have shares outstanding worth $200 billion, and money market deposit accounts amount to $200 billion. There are no traveler's checks outstanding and no repurchase agreements. Answer the following questions.
   a. Determine the value of the money supply as M1, M2, and M3.
   b. Determine the *direct* and *immediate* effects on the money supply as M1, M2, and M3 of the following transactions:
   (1) The public deposits $1 billion in currency at commercial banks.
   (2) The public withdraws $2 billion in currency from demand deposits at commercial banks.
   (3) The public transfers $10 billion from its savings deposits at commercial banks to (small-denomination) time deposits at thrift institutions.
   (4) The public transfers $10 billion from (small-denomination) time deposits at commercial banks to demand deposits at commercial banks.
   (5) The public transfers $10 billion from demand deposits at commercial banks to money market mutual funds.

SELF-TESTS

Completion Questions

Complete each of the following statements by entering the missing words and/or choosing the best alternative proposed.

1. Money is used as a _____, a _____ _____, and a _____.

2. A _____ economy is one without a _____ _____.

3. In the United States the central bank is the _____ _____ created by _____ _____ in 1913. It consists of 12 district _____ _____ and a _____ in Washington.

4. _____ policy involves regulating the money supply and conditions in _____, whereas _____ policy involves changing government spending and _____.

5. People hold money not because it has any _____ _____ but because it can be _____ for things that increase their satisfaction.

6. *(Liquidity/Money)* is a continuum, ranging from _____ and _____ at the top to a variety of "frozen" assets at the bottom.

7. Financial _____ provide savers with a way to lend their _____ to _____, thereby increasing the volume of both saving and _____. This mechanism encourages economic _____.

8. _____ permit the *(join-ing/separation)* of the act of _____ from the act of ____ _____.

9. Financial instruments such as _____ and _____ _____ are devices through which _____ can gain access to the surplus funds of _____.

10. If left uncontrolled, money can cause _____, which reduces the _____ of money.

True and False Questions

For each of the following statements, circle the letter T if it is correct or the letter F if it is *partially* or totally incorrect.

T F   1. A barter economy is one without a medium of exchange but with a unit of account.

T F   2. Financial instruments are utilized as devices with which borrowers can tap the surplus funds of savers.

T F   3. The value of money is directly related to the average level of all prices.

T F   4. Currency withdrawal from demand deposits at commercial banks initially decreases the money supply as M1.

T F   5. A currency withdrawal from time deposits at commercial banks initially decreases the money supply as M2.

T F   6. A currency deposit in passbook savings accounts at commercial banks initially increases the money supply as M2.

T F   7. The Federal Reserve System consists of twenty district Federal Reserve banks and a Board of Governors in New York City.

T F   8. Saving and investment cannot take place in an economy without a financial market.

T F   9. The fundamental purpose of money is to provide a means of payment.

T F   10. Barter can take place only if there exists a "double coincidence of wants."

T F   11. In periods of inflation the price of money declines, because its purchasing power is reduced.

T F   12. The narrowest definition of money is referred to as M1.

T F   13. In recent years, the Federal Reserve has used the M1 measure of the money supply as the basis for policy decisions.

T F   14. Money is the most liquid of all financial assets.

T F   15. You can find information on the current value of the money supply in the latest issue of the monthly Federal Reserve *Bulletin*.

T F   16. It is primarily the Federal Reserve that determines the size of M1, but it is the holders of M1 who decide how much of that total will be in demand deposits and how much in currency.

T F   17. If the monetary gold stock of the United States is approximately $11 billion and the money supply (M1) is approximately $440 billion, one may properly say that there is 4¢ of gold backing each dollar of the money supply.

T F   18. People will accept whatever is being used as the medium of exchange only if they are certain that they will be able to dispose of it.

T F   19. The various definitions of money in the United States are cumulative: broader definitions of money include all assets counted in narrower definitions of money.

T F   20. The economy would be better off without financial intermediaries, because they pay the savers from whom they receive funds lower interest rates than they collect from borrowers to whom they provide funds.

Multiple-Choice Questions

Answer the following multiple-choice questions by circling the best alternative.

1. In the United States the money supply
   a. is backed by approximately $11 billion worth of gold held by the government
   b. is controlled by Congress according to a law passed in 1913
   c. is under the supervision of the U.S. Treasury
   d. none of the above
   e. both (a) and (c)

2. Which one of the following items is a generally accepted medium of exchange in the United States?
   a. credit cards
   b. Canadian dollars
   c. paper money
   d. checking accounts
   e. both (c) and (d)

3. The money supply (M1) is made up of
   a. mostly coins and dollar bills
   b. mostly demand deposits
   c. mostly currency
   d. 50 percent currency and 50 percent demand deposits
   e. none of the above

4. Financial intermediaries are institutions
   a. that act as middlemen in transferring funds from ultimate lenders to ultimate borrowers
   b. that borrow funds from investors in productive facilities

c. that lend funds to small savers
d. all of the above
e. none of the above

5. Borrowers can gain access to the surplus funds of savers
   a. by issuing securities to savers
   b. through financial intermediaries
   c. by purchasing securities such as stocks and bonds
   d. all of the above
   e. both (a) and (b)

6. If the price level doubles, the
   a. value of the money supply falls by one-half
   b. money supply also doubles
   c. the velocity of money increases by 50 percent
   d. GDP falls by one-half

7. The Federal Reserve is particularly concerned with the fraction of the money supply that is in the form of
   a. demand deposits
   b. currency
   c. coins and dollar bills
   d. checking accounts
   e. none of the above

8. Which of the following items is a financial instrument?
   a. bonds
   b. stocks
   c. mortgages
   d. all of the above
   e. none of the above

9. Money in the form of demand deposits is created by
   a. the Federal Reserve System
   b. commercial banks
   c. the Bureau of Engraving and Printing
   d. both (a) and (c)
   e. both (a) and (b)

10. A flow of currency from the public to commercial banks initially leads to
    a. a decrease in the currency outside banks and an equal increase in the vault cash of commercial banks
    b. an equal exchange of currency in circulation for deposits with commercial banks
    c. a decrease in the money supply
    d. all of the above
    e. both (a) and (b)

11. Which of the following assets is most liquid?
    a. passbook savings deposits
    b. time deposits
    c. U.S. government savings bonds
    d. stocks in American Telephone and Telegraph
    e. high grade corporate bonds

12. Which of the following accounts possesses check-writing privileges?
    a. large denomination CDs
    b. small denomination CDs
    c. money market deposit accounts
    d. overnight repurchase agreements

13. A major policy issue facing the Federal Reserve is
    a. how to prevent the money supply from growing
    b. how to create sufficient money
    c. what the size of the money supply should be
    d. what the composition of the money supply should be
    e. both (c) and (d)

14. Which item among the following is not the same as the other four?
    a. financial assets
    b. securities
    c. financial instruments
    d. gold
    e. stocks and bonds

15. The money supply as M1 may not be a perfect measure of how much means of payment is in existence because
    a. it excludes traveler's checks
    b. it excludes demand deposits at thrift institutions
    c. it excludes passbook savings deposits at commercial banks
    d. it excludes money market mutual fund shares against which checks can be written
    e. all of the above

16. Money increases economic growth by facilitating transfers from
    a. investors to consumers
    b. investors to borrowers
    c. savers to investors
    d. consumers to producers

17. Money in the form of demand deposits is destroyed whenever
    a. commercial banks extend loans to the public
    b. loans are repaid to commercial banks
    c. commercial banks buy securities from the public
    d. commercial banks sell securities to the public
    e. both (a) and (c)
    f. both (b) and (d)

18. The money supply should be large enough to enable the public to buy, at current prices, all
    a. the goods and services the economy has produced over a given period of time
    b. the goods, services, and financial assets the economy has produced over a given period of time

c. the goods and services the economy is able to produce over a given period of time

d. the goods, services, and financial assets the economy is able to produce over a given period of time

e. none of the above

19. To qualify as a medium of exchange, an item should be characterized by

a. low uncertainty over its value in trade

b. high exchangeability

c. good value in store

d. all of the above

e. only (a) and (b)

20. A necessary condition for saving and investment to take place is that

a. money must be used as a medium of exchange

b. financial markets must exist

c. financial assets other than money must be highly liquid

d. borrowers must be present in the market

e. none of the above

chapter 2

Money, the Economy, and Inflation

Central Themes and Major Points

The previous chapter provided a definition of money and showed how the money supply is measured. It also discussed the importance of money as a contributor to economic growth. This chapter provides preliminary answers to several questions related to money and its influence on economic activity.

First, how is money created? Money in the form of *demand deposits* is created whenever a bank makes a loan to the public or buys securities from the public. Demand deposits are destroyed (and the money supply reduced) whenever loans are repaid and securities are sold to the public (more on this important mechanism in Chapter 14). But a bank cannot expand indefinitely its demand deposits by making loans or buying securities. It is shown in this chapter how the *Federal Reserve* controls the ability of banks to create money in the form of demand deposits.

Second, how large should the money supply be? There should be enough money circulation to enable the public to buy all the goods and services the economy can produce at full employment and stable prices. The economy's performance is usually measured by its *Gross Domestic Product,* or GDP. When the economy performs poorly, the government is expected to intervene to bring GDP in line with a potential GDP that represents full employment with stable prices. This goal of national economic policy can be achieved by varying the size of the money supply *(monetary policy).*

Unfortunately, it is not a simple task to ensure that the right amount of money circulates in the economy. For example, an increase in the money supply, if held unspent by the public, will not affect GDP. The link between the level of GDP and the money supply is the *velocity of money.* The economy's GDP equals the velocity of money multiplied by the money supply. The effectiveness of monetary policy in influencing GDP will depend greatly on the stability and predictability of the velocity of money.

Finally, what is the relationship between money, GDP, and inflation? When an ever-increasing amount of money is chasing a limited amount of goods, prices will skyrocket out of sight and the value of money will plunge practically to zero. This is the case of runaway *hyperinflation.* The remedy is simple: money creation must be halted at once. But the inflation that has prevailed in the United States in this century is of a much milder form and of a different nature. It is likely to remain so as long as the Federal Reserve maintains a high degree of independence. The causes of this type of inflation are examined in Chapters 23 and 24.

What is the relationship between money and inflation? In the short run the money supply can increase without generating any inflationary pressure. Also, inflation may occur even if the money supply does not change. But inflation in any form cannot persist over the long run unless it is accompanied by an increase in the money supply.

New Terms

Define and/or explain the following terms introduced in this chapter:

Gross Domestic
  Product (GDP)† =
  flow of spending
Monetary policy
Countercyclical
  monetary policy
Bank reserves
Reserve requirement
Vault cash

Excess reserves
Loaned up bank
Easy and tight money
Portfolio adjustments
Real assets
Investment spending
Velocity of money
Creeping inflation

†More on this and how it is measured in the Appendix to Chapter 19.

Essay Questions and Problems

1. **Economic performance and economic policy**
   a. How do we generally measure the performance of the economy?
   b. What is the major goal of national economic policy?
   c. How can this goal be achieved?

2. **Optimal size of the money supply**
   a. How large should the money supply be in order to ensure economic prosperity? Explain.
   b. What is meant by countercyclical monetary policy as a tool of economic control?
   c. Explain why tight or easy money is not really a matter of increases or decreases in the money supply in an absolute sense but rather increases or decreases relative to the demand for money.

3. **Effects on GDP of a change in the money supply** An increase in the money supply should eventually affect the economy's GDP.
   a. Describe the transmission mechanism of monetary policy from an initial increase in the money supply to its final impact on GDP.
   b. Why is the concept of portfolio readjustment so crucial in the transmission of monetary policy?
   c. In light of the transmission mechanism just described, what difficulties do you expect a central bank to encounter in carrying out its monetary policy?

4. **The velocity of money**
   a. How is the money supply related to the level of GDP? Define this link.

   b. Why is it necessary for this link to behave in a stable and consistent manner in order for monetary policy to be effective?
   c. "A rather wide range of potential spending could conceivably flow from any given stock of money." Explain this statement.

*5. **The effect of a change in the money supply on GDP** Assume that currency outside banks is $80 billion and demand deposits at commercial banks and thrift institutions are $320 billion. The velocity of money is stable and equal to 4, and potential GDP at full employment and stable prices is estimated to equal $1,680 billion. Answer the following questions.
   a. What is the value of actual GDP?
   b. What change in the money supply would bring actual GDP to its potential value?
   c. Show that the percentage change in GDP is equal to the percentage change in the money supply. How important is the assumption of a stable velocity for the equality you have just shown?

Note: You can defer your answer to this question until you get to Chapter 19.

*6. **The effects of inflation** Inflation is usually considered a painful matter. It is said, however, that certain people may benefit from it.
   a. Evaluate this statement in reference to (1) creditors, (2) debtors, and (3) businessmen.
   b. When we say that some people may benefit from inflation, which type of inflation do we have in mind—runaway hyperinflation or milder forms of inflation?

7. **Runaway inflation**
   a. What do we mean by runaway hyperinflation? Cite a historical example of this type of inflation. Are there any countries experiencing this type of inflation today?
   b. What is the classic explanation of hyperinflation? What would be the effect of inflationary expectations in this case?
   c. How could runaway hyperinflation be halted?

8. **Money supply and inflation**
   a. Under what conditions would a once-and-for-all increase in the money supply not lead to a rise in the price level?
   b. Suppose that the increase in the money supply goes on uninterrupted. Is it then possible for the price level not to rise? Explain your answer.

SELF-TESTS

Completion Questions

Complete each of the following statements by entering the missing words and/or choosing the best alternative proposed.

1. Banks create money when they extend _____ or _____ securities. They destroy money when their _____ _____ are repaid or when they _____ securities.

2. Bank reserves must be held either in the form of _____ _____ or as a _____ with the Federal Reserve.

3. A bank with no more _____ is said to be loaned up.

4. An increase in the money supply implies that the public is more _____ _____ than formerly. This increase in _____ should lead to more spending on either _____ _____ (such as cars) or _____ _____ (such as bonds).

5. Lower securities prices mean *(lower/higher)* interest rates. The *(fall/rise)* in interest rates may induce *(more/less)* spending on housing and on plant and equipment. This, in turn, should *(reduce/increase)* the rate of growth in GDP.

6. The _____ of money can be calculated by dividing the economy's GDP by the economy's _____ supply.

7. The classic explanation of inflation is that too much _____ is chasing too _____.

8. If inflation is categorized according to the speed with which prices are rising, then _____ describes a state in which prices are sky-rocketing out of sight and the _____ of money is plunging practically to zero, and _____ inflation describes a state in which prices are rising at a nonaccelerating rate of up to 5 or 6 percent per year.

9. If _____ falls, increases in the money supply will not raise prices.

10. More money *(always/often)* leads to inflation.

True and False Questions

For each of the following statements, circle the letter T if it is correct or the letter F if it is *partially* or totally incorrect.

T   F   1. A multiple increase in GDP could result from an initial increase in the stock of money.

T   F   2. The velocity of money is the speed with which it can be converted into a liquid asset.

T   F   3. If the velocity of money is constant, any percentage change in the money supply should lead to an equal percentage change in GDP.

T   F   4. An increase in the velocity of money will increase the flow of spending (GDP), even if the money supply remains the same.

T   F   5. The liquidity of an asset is directly related to its velocity.

T   F   6. Higher securities prices stimulate investment in productive facilities.

T   F   7. Underlying the effectiveness of monetary policy is its impact on the liquidity of the public.

T   F   8. The economy would be better off without financial intermediaries, because they pay the savers from whom they receive funds lower interest rates than they collect from borrowers to whom they provide funds.

T   F   9. As long as an increase in the money supply produces an increase in the liquidity of the public, the increase in the money supply will increase the public's spending for goods and services.

T   F   10. The Federal Reserve has one set of tools through which it controls the supply of money and another set through which it controls the velocity of money.

T   F   11. Money may be tight if the money supply grows at a faster rate than the demand for money.

T   F   12. If a bank has deficient reserves it must somehow get additional reserves. Otherwise it will have to call in loans or sell securities.

T   F   13. Inflation is objectionable because it makes everyone worse off.

T   F   14. Inflation is best defined as a sustained increase in the price of most goods and services.

T   F   15. Inflation generally favors lenders at the expense of borrowers.

T   F   16. Inflation is particularly painful for those people whose incomes are more or less fixed.

T   F   17. Compared with 1970, current consumer prices are about three times greater.

T   F   18. Germany in 1923 and Bolivia in 1985 are good examples of hyperinflation.

T   F   19. In periods of inflation the purchasing power of the dollar drops.

T   F   20. Over the long run, an increase in the money supply is a necessary condition for inflation.

Multiple-Choice Questions

Answer the following multiple-choice questions by circling the best alternative.

1. Demand deposits are created when banks
   a. extend credit
   b. buy securities
   c. make loans
   d. all of the above
   e. none of the above

2. Which of the following will reduce the money supply?
   a. The public buys securities from banks.
   b. The public sells securities to banks.
   c. The public gets a loan from the banking system.
   d. Banks extend credit to the public.
   e. only (c) and (d)

3. A bank cannot always expand its checking account liabilities because
   a. of self-imposed limits on loan extension
   b. the Federal Reserve would prevent the bank from doing so
   c. it is required by the Federal Reserve to hold reserves against its checking deposits
   d. it is illegal for the bank to do so
   e. monetary policy would be ineffective

4. If a bank has $100 million of demand deposits and the reserve requirement ratio is set at 20 percent, then the bank must hold reserves equal to
   a. no more than $120 million
   b. at least $20 million
   c. no more than $20 million
   d. exactly $20 million
   e. exactly $120 million

5. The current reserve requirement ratio against demand deposits is about
   a. 10 percent
   b. 20 percent

   c. 2 percent

   d. 50 percent

   e. none of the above

6. Bank reserves must be held in the form of
   a. securities
   b. vault cash
   c. deposits in their regional Federal Reserve Bank
   d. all of the above
   e. only (b) and (c)

7. A bank has $100 million of demand deposits and $10 million of reserves, and the reserve requirement ratio is set at 12 percent. The bank has
   a. $2 million of excess reserves
   b. $2 million of deficient reserves
   c. a reserve requirement of 10 percent
   d. to increase its reserve requirement
   e. both (c) and (d)

8. The bank described in question 7 must
   a. get $2 million of additional reserves
   b. call in some of its loans outstanding
   c. sell securities to the public
   d. all of the above
   e. only (b) and (c)

9. A bank has $100 million of demand deposits and $11 million of reserves, and the reserve requirement ratio is set at 10 percent. In order to bring its deposits in line with its reserves the bank should
   a. extend credit up to $1 million
   b. buy $1 million worth of securities
   c. sell $1 million worth of securities
   d. increase its reserve requirement ratio to 11 percent
   e. both (a) and (b)

10. A bank has $100 million of demand deposits and $12 million of reserves. The reserve requirement ratio is set at 12 percent. The bank
    a. is loaned up
    b. can create no more than $12 million of additional demand deposits
    c. has more than $12 million in deposit at its regional Federal Reserve Bank
    d. must extend loans to the public
    e. must buy securities from the public

11. If a bank has $100 million of demand deposits and $10 million of reserves, the reserve requirement ratio
    a. is equal to 10 percent
    b. is more than 10 percent
    c. is less than 10 percent
    d. is too low
    e. cannot be determined from the above information

12. Money is easy when
    a. the money supply grows at a faster than average rate
    b. the money supply grows at a faster rate than the demand for money
    c. the money supply grows at a slower than average rate
    d. the money supply grows at a slower rate than the demand for money
    e. either (a) or (b)

13. An increase in the money supply implies that
    a. the public is more liquid than it was formerly
    b. the public is wealthier than it was formerly
    c. the composition of the public's portfolio of total assets has not changed
    d. the velocity of money has increased
    e. both (a) and (b)

14. The effectiveness of monetary policy depends on
    a. the stability of the velocity of money
    b. the spending behavior of the public
    c. the public's demand for liquidity
    d. all of the above
    e. only (a) and (b)

15. Spending on financial assets
    a. will drive up the price of securities
    b. will lower the level of interest rates
    c. may induce investment spending on productive facilities
    d. all of the above
    e. only (a) and (b)

16. If GDP is $3,000 billion and the money supply is $600 billion, then the velocity of money
    a. is equal to 5
    b. is equal to 6
    c. is more than 5
    d. is less than 5
    e. cannot be determined from the above information

17. The flow of spending is determined by
    a. the money supply
    b. the economy's GDP
    c. the Federal Reserve System
    d. the velocity of money
    e. both (a) and (d) taken together

18. If the velocity of money is equal to 5, then the money supply should be increased by $10 billion in order to
    a. raise GDP by $2 billion
    b. reduce GDP by $50 billion
    c. raise GDP by $50 billion
    d. reduce GDP by $2 billion
    e. either (b) or (c) depending on the state of the economy

19. Over which of the following does the Federal Reserve have the least influence?

a. the velocity of money
b. the money supply as M1
c. the behavior of commercial banks
d. the rate of growth in M1
e. the level of interest rates

20. Which of the following would be considered a central problem of monetary policy?
    a. What is the best method available to change the money supply?
    b. What are the determinants of the behavior of the velocity of money?
    c. How should the Federal Reserve System and the commercial banking system be organized to make monetary policy more effective?
    d. What are the effects of bank mergers on competition in the banking industry?
    e. none of the above

chapter 3

Financial Instruments and Markets

Central Themes and Major Points

This chapter explains how financial markets operate and provides a general description of the structure of the U.S. financial markets and the securities that are traded in them.

The function of financial markets is to facilitate the transfer of surplus funds from *ultimate saver-lenders* to *ultimate borrower-spenders* who use these funds to undertake real investment.

In exchange for the funds received, ultimate borrowers issue *primary* securities. This transfer may take place directly between savers and spenders (investors); in this case it is referred to as *direct finance*.

Most funds, however, are transferred from savers to spenders (investors) through *financial intermediaries:* in this case the transfer is called *indirect finance* (see Figure 1 in Chapter 3).

"New" securities (also called *primary securities*) are issued in the *primary market,* the market for "newborn" securities. After they are issued they become part of the *secondary market,* that is, the market in which "old" securities are traded.

The different securities that are issued and traded in the financial markets are surveyed in this chapter. First, there is a general description of bonds, stocks, and mortgages, as well as so-called *derivative* financial instruments such as *options* and *futures contracts*. This is followed by a description of specific markets and instruments. A distinction is made between short-term debt instruments issued and traded in the *money* markets (money market instruments) and all other financial claims issued and traded in the *capital* markets (bonds with an original maturity in excess of one year and stocks).

New Terms

Define and/or explain the following terms introduced in this chapter:

Ultimate saver-lenders	Zero-coupon bonds
Ultimate borrower-spenders	U.S. savings bonds
	Face value
Primary securities	Tax-exempts
Direct finance	Corporate stocks
Indirect finance	Dividends
Primary market	Equities (shares)
Secondary market	Preferred stock
New York Stock Exchange	Common stock
	Capital gains
Over-the-counter market	Standard and Poor's 500 Stock Index
Corporate bonds	New York Stock Exchange Composite Index
U.S. government bonds	
Municipal bonds	Dow Jones Industrial Average
Consols	Bull market
Bond principal	Bear market
Coupon securities	

Mortgages
Amortization
FHA-VA mortgages
Variable-rate mortgages
Fixed-rate mortgages
Mortgage prepayments
Mortgage pools
Government National Mortgage Association (Ginnie Mae)
Pass-through securities
Derivative financial instruments
Options contracts
Future contracts
Chicago Board Options Exchange
Chicago Board of Trade
Call option
Put option
Strike price
Capital market
Money market
Money market instruments (Negotiable bank CDs, U.S. Treasury bills, commercial paper, bankers' acceptances)

Essay Questions and Problems

1. **Financial markets** How do savers and borrowers benefit from participating in financial markets? How do savers and borrowers participate in financial markets? How do inefficient financial markets affect borrowers and savers?

2. **Bonds versus stocks** Most financial instruments can be classified into two broad categories: debt instruments (bonds) and stocks (equity).
   a. What are the major characteristics of debt instruments?
   b. What are the major characteristics of common stocks?
   c. Which type of instrument is generally more risky? Why?
   d. How does one classify instruments such as preferred stocks and convertible bonds? Are they debt instruments or equity?

*3. **Government versus municipal bonds** Since municipal bonds are of lesser quality than U.S. government bonds, they should have a higher return than U.S. government bonds in order to induce investors to hold them. The return on municipal bonds, however, is generally *lower,* not higher, than the return on U.S. government bonds. How could this be explained?

4. **Mortgages** Mortgages are debt instruments issued by borrowers in order to buy land or buildings. What makes them different from other debt instruments is that the land or the buildings serve as security or collateral for the lender.
   a. Mortgages can be classified according to the nature of the underlying real estate. What are the three types of mortgages classified that way?
   b. Mortgages can also be insured or conventional. What are these two types of mortgages?
   c. The maturity date of a mortgage is uncertain to the lender, because homeowners usually prepay their mortgages if they move to a new location or if interest rates fall. What recent developments have helped to reduce some of this prepayment uncertainty?

5. **Options and futures contracts** Options and futures contracts are often called *derivative financial instruments.*
   a. Why are they given this name?
   b. What features do these two types of securities have in common?
   c. What are the major differences between these two types of securities?
   d. Why do people buy and sell these securities?

6. **The capital market**
   a. What are the general characteristics of the securities issued and traded in the capital market?
   b. What are the major types of instruments in the capital market? For each type of instrument, give the issuer and the principal holders.
   c. Which capital market instruments have active trading, which have moderate trading, and which have no trading at all? What is the implication of trading frequency for the liquidity of these instruments?

7. **The money market**
   a. What are the general characteristics of the securities issued and traded in the money market?
   b. Who are the major participants in the money market?
   c. What securities are issued and traded in the money market? For each security give the issuer and the principal holders.
   d. What are federal funds, and what role do they play in the money market?

SELF-TESTS

Completion Questions

Complete each of the following statements by entering the missing words and/or choosing the best alternative proposed.

1. Financial markets are the transmission mechanism between _____ _____ and _____ _____.

2. It is through financial markets that the excess funds of _____ _____ are made available to _____ _____. This mechanism enables _____ _____ to spend more than their current income.

3. In order to raise funds via the financial markets, ultimate _____ _____ must issue *(primary/secondary)* securities which are purchased by either ultimate _____ or _____ _____. When the purchase is made by ultimate ___ _____, the process is called _____ finance. When the purchase is made by _____ _____, the process is called indirect _____.

4. Municipal bonds are not subject to _____.

5. Bonds that make no periodic interest payments are called _____ _____ bonds. Bonds that never mature are _____ bonds or _____. The former bonds are issued at a price which is always *(higher than/equal to/lower than)* the price at which they are reimbursed at maturity.

6. Coupon-bearing securities make periodic _____ payments. These payments are usually fixed, but they can also be _____ _____ or _____.

7. Common stocks represent *(creditorship/ownership)*, whereas debt instruments represent _____.

8. Common stocks make *(fixed/variable)* _____ payments. Contrary to debt instruments, common stocks do not have a _____ _____ date.

9. A packaging innovation in the mortgage business is _____ _____, also called _____ _____ securities.

10. Financial markets are usually broken down into two separate submarkets, the

_____ markets and the _____

markets. Instruments traded in the former include _____

and _____. Instru-

ments traded in the latter include _____

_____ and _____.

True and False Questions

For each of the following statements, circle the letter T if it is correct or the letter F if it is *partially* or totally incorrect.

T F   1. Savers are security-holders and borrowers are security-issuers.

T F   2. Ultimate lenders are always households, and ultimate borrowers are always business firms or the government.

T F   3. The process whereby ultimate lenders purchase primary securities directly from savers is called direct finance.

T F   4. Lack of adequate information about borrowers and lenders may enhance the flow of funds from savers to spenders.

T F   5. Direct finance refers to the use by corporations of internally generated funds for investment expenditures.

T F   6. The main function of financial markets is to bring together buyers and sellers of credit.

T F   7. Primary securities are those issued by corporations with the highest credit rating.

T F   8. If financial markets fail to channel the existing flow of saving into the hands of borrowers who stand ready to invest this amount, the result will probably be a reduced level of GDP and a reduced flow of saving.

T F   9. The capital market is the market for capital goods.

T F   10. U.S. government securities are liabilities of the Federal Reserve banks.

T F   11. Securities with no secondary markets have no liquidity.

T F   12. The money market is the market for the demand deposits of commercial banks, that is, the market for money.

T F   13. Short-term securities are generally more liquid than long-term securities.

T F   14. Individuals are some of the most important participants in the money market.

T F   15. Negotiable bank CDs are assets of commercial banks.

T F   16. Commercial paper is a liability of business firms.

T F   17. Federal funds are excess reserves that banks lend one another to cover temporary deficiencies.

T F   18. Mortgages are assets of homeowners.

T F   19. Bankers' acceptances are one of the most important money market instruments.

T F   20. Bonds issued by the City of New York and held by a resident of the city are exempt from federal, state, and city income taxes. If held by a resident of Chicago, however, they are exempt only from federal income taxes.

T F   21. A zero-coupon, perpetual bond would be worthless. No borrower would ever be able to issue that type of security.

T F   22. One can distinguish between two types of mortgages: unconventional mortgages, which are not insured, and conventional mortgages, which are insured by either the Federal Housing Authority (FHA) or the Veterans Administration (VA).

T F   23. Treasury bills are an example of a zero-coupon debt instrument.

T F   24. The return stockholders will receive on their investment will depend on future dividend payments and expected stock price appreciation. Their investment is risky, because future cash dividends are variable and capital gains are uncertain.

T F   25. Interest on municipal bonds is exempt from federal income taxation, but interest on federal government bonds is not exempt from state and local income taxation.

T F   26. All securities share a common characteristic in that they represent a claim to a future stream of payments, often called expected future cash flows.

T F   27. The price of a security is partly determined by its capacity to generate future cash.

T F 28. Common stockholders get a fixed dividend and they are entitled to it before preferred stockholders receive any dividend.

T F 29. Options and futures contracts derive their value from the underlying asset on which these contracts are written.

T F 30. Options and futures contracts are traded on organized securities exchanges such as the New York Stock Exchange.

T F 31. The buyer of a futures contract is called the short, whereas the seller is called the long.

T F 32. The buyer of a futures contract has the *right and obligation* to purchase the underlying asset at some future date at a predetermined price, whereas the buyer of an option contract has the *right but not the obligation* to purchase the underlying asset at a predetermined price over a specific time interval.

T F 33. Millions of stock market deals are sealed over the telephone every day.

Multiple-Choice Questions

Answer the following multiple-choice questions by circling the best alternative.

1. Which of the following is *not* a financial instrument?
   a. Treasury bills
   b. consols
   c. real estate
   d. mortgages
   e. none of the above
2. A borrower is
   a. a bondholder
   b. a bond issuer
   c. a stockholder
   d. a stock issuer
   e. both (b) and (d)
3. Which of the following stock market indexes is based on the smallest number of stocks?
   a. Standard and Poor's Composite Index
   b. The New York Stock Exchange Index
   c. The Dow Jones Industrial Average
   d. Standard and Poor's Industrial Average
4. Which of the following government agencies insures mortgages?
   a. The Federal Housing Authority
   b. The National Mortgage Association
   c. The Homeowner Insurance Administration
   d. The Federal Reserve
5. Mortgage pools are insured by the
   a. Federal Housing Authority
   b. Veterans Administration
   c. Government National Mortgage Association
   d. American Bankers Association
6. A put option gives the owner the right to
   a. sell the underlying asset at a fixed price
   b. buy the underlying asset at a fixed price
   c. convert the underlying asset at a fixed price
   d. take delivery of the underlying asset at a fixed price
7. Suppose that you expect the price of the underlying asset to rise rapidly in the near future. Then you should
   a. buy a futures contract on the underlying asset
   b. sell a futures contract on the underlying asset
   c. buy a call option on the underlying asset
   d. both (a) and (c) could be profitable
8. Suppose that you expect the price of the underlying asset to fall sharply in the near future. Then you should
   a. buy a futures contract on the underlying asset
   b. sell a futures contract on the underlying asset
   c. buy a put option on the underlying asset
   d. both (b) and (c) could be profitable
9. An investor who anticipates that bond prices will rise in the future should buy
   a. a variable-rate bond
   b. long on a Treasury bond futures contract
   c. preferred corporate stock
   d. a municipal bond
10. Which of the following instruments is in the top three in dollars outstanding in the capital market?
    a. residential mortgages
    b. municipal bonds
    c. corporate bonds
    d. commercial paper
11. An example of a money market instrument is
    a. a demand deposit at a commercial bank
    b. a negotiable certificate of deposit
    c. a corporate bond
    d. a mortgage
    e. a municipal bond
12. As holders of commercial paper, business firms are
    a. increasing their liabilities
    b. raising temporary cash in the money market
    c. acting as borrower-spenders

d. all of the above

e. none of the above

13. The federal funds market refers to the market where

  a. banks can borrow reserves from the Federal Reserve

  b. state and local governments can obtain funds from the federal government

  c. federal agencies such as the Federal Land Banks supply funds to farmers

  d. banks can borrow reserves from one another

14. Bankers' acceptances are money market instruments

  a. arising mostly in the course of international trade

  b. issued by prime business firms and finance companies

  c. of great importance in terms of their value outstanding

  d. none of the above

15. Money market instruments are characterized by their

  a. high degree of liquidity

  b. low risk

  c. near-moneyness

  d. short maturity

  e. all of the above

16. Commercial banks issue negotiable CDs

  a. in order to compete with the U.S. Treasury for the surplus funds of money market participants

  b. and have been doing so since around 1929

  c. in order to increase their portfolio of securities

  d. as an alternative to borrowing reserves from the Federal Reserve

  e. (a) and (b) above

17. Which of the following are *not* typical money market participants?

  a. commercial banks

  b. Federal Reserve banks

  c. individuals

  d. prime business firms

  e. finance companies

18. Which of the following are not stock market participants?

  a. commercial banks

  b. individuals

  c. pension funds

  d. mutual funds

  e. insurance companies

19. An example of a primary security is

  a. a U.S. Treasury bill

  b. a negotiable certificate of deposit

  c. a share of a mutual fund

  d. a money market certificate

  e. none of the above

20. Municipal bonds are securities issued by

  a. state governments

  b. the federal government

  c. local governments

  d. both (a) and (c)

  e. none of the above

chapter 4

Financial Institutions: Purposes and Profile

Central Themes and Major Points

The role of financial markets and instruments was examined in the previous chapter. It is through financial markets that the surplus funds held by saver-lenders are transferred to spender-borrowers, who then use these funds to undertake real investment, which will eventually contribute to economic growth.

It was pointed out in the previous chapter that most of savers' surplus funds are channeled to ultimate spender-borrowers through a large number of financial institutions collectively known as financial intermediaries. The process whereby ultimate savers make their funds available to financial intermediaries, which in turn lend these funds to ultimate borrowers, is called financial *intermediation* (or *indirect finance*). Financial *disintermediation* is the reverse process. In this case, ultimate savers take their funds out of financial intermediaries and lend them directly to ultimate borrowers, thus bypassing financial intermediaries.

The different types of financial intermediaries are described in this chapter. They include commercial banks, *thrift institutions* (savings and loan associations, mutual savings banks, and credit unions), life insurance companies, pension and retirement funds, property and casualty insurance companies, sales and consumer finance companies, and mutual funds. Commercial banks and thrift institutions are known as *depository institutions*. They are examined in detail in Chapters 7 and 8. The other intermediaries are referred to as *nondeposit financial institutions* (they do not offer checking-type accounts). They are examined in detail in Chapter 9.

The chapter also speculates on what the banking industry will look like in twenty years, in the light of current trends. Bank profits have been squeezed by intense competition and loss of their monopoly powers over checking accounts and business loans. A major consequence of these pressures is consolidation of the banking industry. By 2010, the industry is almost certain to have fewer but larger banks with nationwide bank branching. The emergence of large banks with nationwide operations is likely to lead to stricter regulation.

The chapter concludes with the observation that financial institutions are becoming increasingly similar. This trend is very evident for depository institutions. Two important pieces of legislation (The Banking Act of 1980 and the Garn-St. Germain Act of 1982) broadened the powers of thrift institutions to offer checking accounts and commercial loans. The net result of these changes is an erosion of the barriers that have distinguished different types of financial institutions since the 1930s.

New Terms

Define and/or explain the following terms introduced in this chapter:

Financial
  intermediaries
Financial
  intermediation
Financial
  disintermediation
Depository
  institutions:

Commercial banks
Thrift institutions
Thrift institutions:
  Savings and loan
  associations
  Mutual savings
  banks
  Credit unions

Life insurance
  companies
Insurance premiums
Annuities
Property and casualty
  insurance companies
Sales and consumer
  finance companies
Mutual funds
Money market mutual
  funds
Depository

Institutions
Deregulation and
Monetary Control
Act of 1980
(Banking Act of
1980)
Garn–St. Germain
Depository
Institutions Act of
1982
NOW accounts

Essay Questions and Problems

1. **Financial intermediation**
  *a. First distinguish between direct finance and indirect finance and then distinguish between financial intermediation and financial disintermediation. Explain the relationship, if any, between the two pairs.
  *b. Indicate if the following transactions taking place in the financial markets are examples of direct finance, indirect finance, financial intermediation, or financial disintermediation:
    (1) Ms. Lugo calls her broker and orders him to buy U.S. government bonds issued seven years ago with a remaining maturity of three years (the bonds had an original maturity of ten years). The broker executes the order.
    (2) IBM issues new common stock, some of which is purchased by Mr. Williams through his broker.
    (3) New York State issues bonds that are purchased by an insurance company.
    (4) Mr. Lawrence withdraws $10,000 from his passbook savings account and purchases a 91-day Treasury bill (maturing in 91 days).
    (5) A mutual fund buys some of the common stock IBM has just issued.
    (6) Mrs. Smith deposits $1,000 in a time deposit at her savings bank. The bank extends a mortgage loan to a home buyer.
  c. Under which circumstances do you expect financial disintermediation to take place? What could be done to reduce financial disintermediation?

2. **Financial intermediaries**
  a. What exactly are financial intermediaries, and what functions do they perform in financial markets?

  b. What are the effects of their presence on
    (1) the level of interest rates
    (2) economic growth
    (3) the efficiency of financial markets
    (4) the income velocity of money
  *c. Is the broker who executed Ms. Lugo's order to buy government bonds [see question 1b(1)] a financial intermediary? Explain.
  *d. Are the Federal Reserve banks financial intermediaries? Explain.

3. **The major financial institutions** Financial institutions intermediate between ultimate saver-lenders and ultimate borrower-spenders.
  a. Explain briefly how financial intermediation takes place.
  b. Compare commercial banks, savings and loan associations, mutual savings banks, life insurance companies, and pension and retirement funds with respect to
    (1) number of institutions in operation
    (2) size in terms of assets outstanding
    (3) degree of diversification of assets and liabilities
    (4) principal source of funds
    (5) principal use of funds
    (6) average maturity of portfolio assets and liabilities

4. **Trends in the banking industry** Describe the forces that have squeezed bank profits in recent years. How has the industry responded to these pressures? How is the banking industry of 2010 likely to differ from today's industry?

5. **Mutual funds** What advantages do mutual funds offer investors? In what markets are mutual funds active?

6. **Money market mutual funds**
  a. What are money market mutual funds?
  b. What service do they provide as intermediaries?
  c. Why are money market mutual funds popular in periods of high interest rates?
  *d. It is said that money market mutual funds tend to reduce the size of the money supply (M1). Explain how and why this would be the case.

7. **The increasing similarity of financial institutions** Developments during the 1980s blurred the traditional distinctions between commercial banks and thrift institutions. What were these developments and how did they make financial institutions more alike?

SELF-TESTS

Completion Questions

Complete each of the following statements by entering the missing words and/or choosing the best alternative proposed.

1. Financial _____ acquire funds from _____ _____ by issuing their own *(liabilities/ assets)* and then turn around and obtain *(liabilities/assets)* when they channel the funds to _____.

2. Financial _____ make a profit on the spread between the rate of interest they charge on the _____ they sell and the *(higher/lower)* interest rate they pay on the _____ they have *(lent/acquired)*.

3. *Thrift institutions* is a term that refers to

   a. _____

   b. _____

   c. _____

4. Commercial banks and thrift institutions are known as _____ institutions.

5. Savings and loan associations have a large proportion of their assets in _____ _____ and a large proportion of their liabilities in the form of _____ _____.

   Because of this structure, they are caught in a profit squeeze whenever *(short-term/long-term)* interest rates rise above *(short-term/long-term)* interest rates.

6. The _____ of 1980, formally known as the _____ _____ gave savings and loan associations the power to issue checking accounts called _____ _____ and to make _____ loans.

7. Nondeposit financial institutions include the following:

   a. _____

   b. _____

   c. _____

   d. _____

   e. _____

8. _____

_____ insure people against financial consequences of death, receiving their funds in the form of periodic payments called _____.

9. The Banking Act of 1980 and the Garn–St. Germain Act broadened the lending powers of savings banks so that they could make _____ __ and _____ loans.

10. General Motors Acceptance Corporation and Household Finance are financial intermediaries called _____

_____.

True and False Questions

For each of the following statements, circle the letter T if it is correct or the letter F if it is *partially* or totally incorrect.

T F 1. Intermediaries acquire funds by selling their own liabilities to ultimate saver-lenders.

T F 2. Intermediaries make a profit on the differential between the rate of interest they charge ultimate saver-lenders and the rate of interest they pay ultimate borrower-spenders.

T F 3. A financial intermediary is a go-between that brings ultimate lenders and ultimate borrowers together and leaves them to work out the terms on which the lending and borrowing between them will take place.

T F 4. Savings and loan associations, mutual savings banks, and credit unions are collectively known as nonbank depository institutions or thrift institutions.

T F 5. Some mutual funds specialize in mortgages.

T F 6. There are fewer mutual savings banks than savings and loan associations and they are concentrated mostly on the East Coast.

T F 7. Financial disintermediation is the reverse process of financial intermediation: savers withdraw their funds from intermediaries and hoard them either by holding currency or by increasing their demand deposits at commercial banks.

T F 8. Money market funds issue money market time certificates to raise funds which, in turn, they invest in money market instruments such as U.S. Treasury bills and bank CDs.

T F 9. The Garn–St. Germain Act of 1982 allowed depository institutions to offer NOW accounts, which combined unlimited checking facilities with market interest rates.

T F 10. Mutual savings banks and savings and loan associations are not allowed to make consumer loans. They specialize in making long-term mortgage loans.

T F 11. Life insurance companies have a high percentage of their assets in the form of long-term corporate bonds and mortgages.

T F 12. Pension and retirement funds are different from life insurance companies, since they are concerned mostly with liquidity, and life insurance companies are concerned mostly with long-term investments.

T F 13. Credit unions can offer checking accounts called credit union share drafts and they can also make long-term mortgage loans.

T F 14. The Banking Act of 1980 is formally known as the Depository Institutions Deregulation and Monetary Control Act of 1980. This piece of legislation gave savings banks the power to make consumer loans.

T F 15. Pension and retirement funds are very risky financial institutions because they are unable to predict how much they will have to pay out in pensions for many years into the future.

T F 16. Both life insurance companies and pension and retirement funds face substantial short-term uncertainties due to the nature of the business. As a result they must invest mostly in long-term assets.

T F 17. Buying a share in a mutual fund is more risky than opening a savings account at a savings and loan association.

T F 18. Mutual funds are usually stock market–related institutions.

T F 19. The spread of computer technology has been a factor reducing the competitiveness of small banks.

Multiple-Choice Questions

Answer the following multiple-choice questions by circling the best alternative.

1. Which of the following are the largest financial intermediaries in terms of assets?
   a. savings and loan associations
   b. commercial banks
   c. mutual savings banks
   d. life insurance companies
   e. pension funds

2. Which of the intermediaries in question 1 are identical in most respects?
   a. (a) and (c)
   b. (a) and (b)
   c. (b) and (d)
   d. (d) and (e)
   e. (b) and (c)

3. Which of the intermediaries in question 1 are not considered depository institutions?
   a. (a) and (c)
   b. (a) and (e)
   c. (d) and (e)
   d. (a) and (d)

4. By the year 2010, the commercial banking industry is likely to
   a. no longer exist
   b. consist of fifty banks, one in each state
   c. consist of fewer and larger banks compared with today's industry
   d. be run by the federal government

5. One of the problems that thrift institutions face is that
   a. they are unable to go to the discount window at the Federal Reserve to borrow short-term funds because they are not members of the Fed
   b. in periods of high short-term interest rates, they have to pay more to obtain new funds or retain existing funds than they get from their long-term mortgages
   c. they are holding short-term assets and long-term liabilities. This mismatching of maturities puts a squeeze on their profits when short-term interest rates are low
   d. they are unable to offer demand deposits at

low cost because they are not part of the Federal Reserve System
   e. both (b) and (d)

6. Which of the following services cannot be offered by savings banks?
   a. interest-bearing checking accounts
   b. consumer loans
   c. mortgage loans
   d. business loans
   e. none of the above

7. Which of the following institutions have their assets invested mainly in long-term securities?
   a. commercial banks
   b. property and casualty insurance companies
   c. life insurance companies
   d. pension funds
   e. both (c) and (d)
   f. both (b) and (d)

8. Which of the institutions listed in the previous question receive their funds in the form of *periodic* payments called premiums?
   a. (b) and (c)
   b. (b) and (d)
   c. (c)
   d. (b)
   e. (b), (c), and (d)

9. Other factors held constant, financial disintermediation will take place when
   a. the rate of differential between the yield on the assets of intermediaries and the rate they paid on their liabilities widens to over 3 percent
   b. interest rates are high—say, around 10 percent
   c. the spread between the yield on primary securities and the rate paid by thrift institutions on their liabilities is large (say, 3 to 6 percent)
   d. the economy is experiencing a recession
   e. the velocity of money is relatively low

10. Depository financial intermediaries are able to offer securities that are relatively liquid and safe because they
   a. can minimize their total risk through portfolio diversification
   b. can hire experts to evaluate the risk of various financial assets
   c. can always keep a portion of their total assets liquid to meet their customers' demand for cash
   d. all of the above
   e. only (a) and (b)

11. Sales and consumer finance companies
   a. specialize in lending money to individuals who want to buy consumer goods

b. specialize in lending money to business firms to finance their inventories
c. are often owned by a manufacturing firm that wants to lend money to those who buy the firm's products
d. get their funds by selling commercial paper
e. all of the above

12. Credit unions
a. are thrift institutions
b. are relatively small but their number is relatively large
c. are organized as cooperatives
d. are allowed to make long-term mortgage loans
e. all of the above

13. Mutual funds
a. are depository institutions
b. make short-term loans to the public
c. are financial intermediaries that provide diversified portfolios of financial assets to the general public
d. are organized as cooperatives
e. none of the above

14. Buying shares in a mutual fund is
a. less risky than buying a savings deposit or a money market instrument
b. less risky than buying a Treasury bill
c. less risky than buying stocks directly from the stock market
d. extremely difficult and very expensive
e. both (c) and (d)

15. Money market mutual funds
a. are a special type of mutual funds that purchase short-term money market instruments
b. have experienced phenomenal growth during the 1970s and early 1980s
c. have highly liquid investments
d. are financial intermediaries
e. all of the above

16. Commercial paper is often purchased by
a. life insurance companies
b. pension funds
c. money market mutual funds
d. mutual funds

17. Checking accounts can be offered by
a. thrift institutions
b. life insurance companies
c. consumer finance companies
d. pension funds

18. In recent years financial institutions
a. have changed considerably and are becoming increasingly different from one another
b. have become more alike because of increased financial regulation
c. have become more alike because of increased financial deregulation
d. have become increasingly different from one another because of financial regulation
e. have not changed very much

19. The primary motive of financial instituions is to maximize
a. the money supply
b. loans
c. total assets
d. profits

chapter 5

Calculating Interest Rates

Central Themes and Major Points

Individuals and institutions cannot make sound financial and investment decisions without understanding first why interest rates move and how they are calculated. The next chapter examines the forces that influence the movement of interest rates. This chapter looks at how they are calculated.

First the concept of *simple interest* is introduced and compared with the concept of *compound interest*. An initial sum of money grows faster with compound interest than with simple interest because compounded interest is earned on the amount of interest income accumulated during the previous year.

Second, the concept of *discounting* is introduced. It is shown to be the reverse of *compounding*. The concept of discounting is important because it allows you to calculate the price *(present value)* of a security if you know its future *cash flow stream*.

Third, the chapter goes back to the subject of bonds and shows how one can measure their yield or rate of return. There is no unique measure of a bond's rate of return. It depends on what the bondholder wants to measure. Several rates of return are presented. These are: (1) the *coupon rate,* (2) the *current yield,* (3) the *yield to maturity,* (4) the *holding period yield,* and (5) the *total return.* The special case of zero-coupon bonds is also examined in the chapter.

Finally, the chapter examines the relationship between the price of a bond and its yield. Two important results are demonstrated. First, bond prices and yields move in opposite directions. For example, an increase in the price of a bond reduces its yield and a decrease in the price of a bond raises its yield. Second, not all bonds respond in the same manner to a given change in interest rates (yields). Suppose, for example, that interest rates (yields on bonds) increase. As a result, the price of long-term bonds will drop more than the price of short-term bonds. In general, the price of long-term bonds fluctuates (increases or decreases) more than the price of short-term bonds in response to a given change in interest rates.

The chapter concludes with an explanation of the difference between *nominal* and *real* interest rates. Nominal interest rates do not account for the reduction in purchasing power caused by inflation (see Chapter 2). For example, if you are promised a yield of 10 percent per year (nominal yield) and the annual rate of inflation is 6 percent, you end up with a real rate of interest of only 4 percent.

New Terms

Define and/or explain the following terms introduced in this chapter:

Simple interest	bonds)
Compound interest	Face value (of
Compounding	bonds)
Discounting	Current yield (on
Principal	bonds)
Present value	Yield to maturity (of
Cash flow stream	bonds)
Coupon rate (on	Internal rate of return

Holding period yield
Out-of-pocket loss
Total return
Zero-coupon bonds
Nominal versus real
  interest rates†
Expected versus

realized rate of
  inflation
Expected versus
  realized interest rate
Ex ante = expected
Ex post = realized

†More on these terms in Chapters 6, 19, 23, and 24.

Essay Questions and Problems

*1. **Bond yields and bond prices**
   a. Suppose that you paid $980 for a $1,000-face-value, 4-percent–coupon bond that will mature in exactly one year.
      (1) What is the bond's coupon rate?
      (2) What is the annual coupon payment on this bond?
      (3) Before computing the bond's current yield, could you tell if it is lower than, equal to, or higher than 4 percent? Explain.
      (4) Compute the bond's current yield.
      (5) What does the bond's current yield measure? Is it an adequate measure of your total annual return on the bond?
      (6) Before computing the bond's yield to maturity, could you tell if it is lower than, equal to, or higher than 4 percent? Explain.
      (7) Compute the bond's yield to maturity.
      (8) What does the bond's yield to maturity measure? Why is it considered an adequate measure of your total annual return on the bond *only* if the bond is held to maturity?
      (9) Could you have computed the bond's yield to maturity if the term to maturity were, for example, five years instead of one year? If your answer is no, how then would you have obtained the bond's yield to maturity?
      (10) Assume that the bond is a three-year bond that you bought for $980 and sold at face value after two years. What is the bond's total return? What are the limitations of this measure?
      (11) Suppose that the rate of inflation for next year is expected to be 8 percent. What will the real rate of return be on the bond in this case?
   b. A $1,000-face-value, 9-percent–coupon bond that will mature in three years has a yield to maturity of 8 percent.
      (1) Without computing the price of the bond, could you tell if the price will be higher than, equal to, or lower than $1,000? Explain.
      (2) Based on the information below, compute the price of the bond.

$(1 + .08)^1 = 1.080; (1 + .08)^2 = 1.166; (1 + .08)^3 = 1.260$
$(1 + .09)^1 = 1.090; (1 + .09)^2 = 1.188; (1 + .09)^3 = 1.295$

   Note: Not *all* the information is required to compute the price of the bond.
      (3) If available, use a business calculator to determine the yield to maturity of the following asset: A $90-coupon bond, purchased for $950 with a face value of $1000 that will be paid at maturity in 8 years.

2. **Relationship between bond prices and yields** In the previous problem we have seen that bond prices and bond yields move in opposite directions. Higher prices mean lower yields to maturity and lower prices mean higher yields to maturity. This fundamental relationship can be further illustrated with a special type of bond called consols or perpetuities.
   a. *Consols or perpetuities*
      (1) A consol or perpetual bond or perpetuity is a bond that does not have a maturity date. It simply pays interest forever. Obviously, these bonds have the longest maturity possible (infinity). Their price is very simple to calculate. It is given by the formula

$$\text{Price of perpetuity} = \frac{\text{coupon payment}}{\text{market yield}}$$

   For example, a perpetual bond with a face value of $100 and a coupon rate of 5 percent has a coupon payment of $5. At a market yield of 8 percent, the price of this perpetual bond or consol will be

$$P = \frac{\$5}{.08} = \$62.50$$

      *(2) Suppose that a consol with a $1,000 face value has a coupon rate of 6 percent. What is the price of this consol if the rate of interest (or yield on the consol) is 4 percent? 6 percent? 8 percent? What can you now conclude?
   *b. *Long-term bonds compared with short-term bonds*
   Although the price of all bonds (short and long) will decrease when the interest rate rises, or increase when the interest rate drops, long-term bonds decrease in price or increase in price *more* than short-term

yield r	price of the consol (coupon = 6%)	price of the one-year bond (coupon = 6%)
4%	$_____	$_____
6%	$_____	$_____
8%	$_____	$_____

bonds in response to a change in interest rates.

(1) This important difference in the response of long-term and short-term bonds can be illustrated numerically using a consol (a long-term bond since its maturity is infinity) and a one-year bond (short-term bond compared with the consol). Suppose that both the consol and the one-year bond have a face value of $1,000 and a coupon rate of 6 percent. If the interest rate or yield r is alternatively 4 percent, 6 percent, or 8 percent (first column in the table above), enter in the second column the corresponding prices of the consol which you determined in question a above. Then compute the corresponding prices for the one-year bond and enter your results in the third column.

(2) When the interest rate r decreases from 6 percent to 4 percent, what is the magnitude of the price increase for the consol? for the one-year bond? What do you conclude?

(3) Answer the same questions when r increases from 6 percent to 8 percent.

(4) Using the above results, could you explain why the consol may be considered "riskier" than the one-year bond?

SELF-TESTS

Completion Questions

Complete each of the following statements by entering the missing words and/or choosing the best alternative proposed.

1. When one examines the yield on bonds, it is important to distinguish between four different yields or rates. These are the

   a. _____

   b. _____

   c. _____

   d. _____

2. When the price of a bond rises, its yield _____.

3. When the yield on a bond drops, its price _____.

4. An increase in the level of interest rates will cause the price of _____ -term bonds to _____ less than the price of _____ _____-term bonds.

5. The real rate of interest is equal to the difference between the _____ _____ and the _____ _____.

True and False Questions

For each of the following statements, circle the letter T if it is correct or the letter F if it is *partially* or totally incorrect.

T   F   1. A dollar today is worth more than a dollar tomorrow.

T   F   2. The discounted value of one dollar is smaller than its compounded value.

T   F   3. The compounded value of $100 at 10

percent for two years is equal to $121.

T   F   4. At a simple interest rate of 15 percent, the future value of $100 after two years will be $115.

T   F   5. The present value of $110 to be received at the end of one year is $90.

T   F   6. The compounded value of $100 at 20 percent for two years is the same as the value of $100 after two years at a simple interest rate of 22 percent.

T   F   7. The holder of a zero-coupon bond receives only the face value of the bond.

T   F   8. U.S. government bond prices and yields move in the same direction.

T   F   9. When interest rates rise, bondholders suffer out-of-pocket losses.

T   F   10. If a bond sells at its face value, then the bond yield to maturity is equal to both the bond current yield and the bond coupon rate.

T   F   11. Under most circumstances, total return is considered a superior measure to both yield to maturity and holding period yield.

T   F   12. Short-term bonds fluctuate in price more than long-term bonds in response to changes in interest rates.

T   F   13. When interest rates increase, the drop in the price of short-term bonds is less than the rise in the price of long-term bonds.

T   F   14. The nominal rate of interest can be negative if the rate of inflation exceeds the effective or real rate of interest.

Multiple-Choice Questions

Answer the following multiple-choice questions by circling the best alternative.

1. At a simple interest rate of 20 percent, one dollar will double in
   a. 4 years
   b. 5 years
   c. 20 years
   d. 2 years
   e. none of the above

2. If the compounded value of $100 is $144 after two years, then the interest rate must be
   a. 20 percent
   b. 44 percent
   c. 22 percent
   d. 24 percent
   e. none of the above

3. A bond with an annual coupon income of $8 and a face value of $1,000 has a coupon rate of
   a. 8 percent
   b. 8 dollars
   c. 80 dollars
   d. 80 percent
   e. none of the above

4. A bond with a face value of $1,000 and a coupon rate of 10 percent sells at $800. What is its current yield?
   a. 1.25 percent
   b. 12 percent
   c. 12.50 percent
   d. 10 percent
   e. none of the above

You paid $900 for a bond with a face value of $1,000 and a coupon rate of 6 percent. You sold it one year later for $930. Answer the following three questions.

5. The bond's yield to maturity
   a. exceeds 6 percent
   b. is equal to 6 percent
   c. is less than 6 percent
   d. cannot be computed
   e. both (a) and (d)

6. The bond's current yield
   a. exceeds 6 percent
   b. is equal to 6 percent
   c. is less than 6 percent
   d. cannot be computed
   e. none of the above

7. Your holding period yield is equal to
   a. 3.33 percent
   b. 10 percent
   c. 9 percent
   d. 6 percent
   e. none of the above

8. Assume that a $90-coupon bond is purchased for $900 and sold three years later for $950. The total return for this asset is
   a. 10 percent
   b. 35.6 percent
   c. 21.7 percent
   d. 18.4 percent

9. Which of the following is a characteristic of zero-coupon bonds?
   a. Their coupon rate is always equal to their yield to maturity.
   b. Their current yield is always equal to their yield to maturity.
   c. They are issued at a discount from their face value.
   d. They have low coupon rates.
   e. none of the above

10. If the yield to maturity is 10 percent, then the price of a zero-coupon bond with a $1,000 face value due in two years is
    a. $826.45
    b. $909.09
    c. $833.33
    d. $806.45
    e. none of the above

11. Which of the following is a characteristic of Treasury bills?
    a. They differ from zero-coupon bonds.
    b. Their price cannot exceed their face value.
    c. They are short-term debt obligations of local government agencies.
    d. Their yield exceeds their coupon rate.
    e. none of the above

12. If a bond's current yield is equal to its coupon rate, then all of the following are correct *except*
    a. the bond's yield to maturity equals its current yield
    b. the bond is undervalued
    c. the bond sells at its face value
    d. the bond's coupon rate equals its yield to maturity
    e. both (a) and (b)

13. What is the price of a $1,000-face-value, 7-percent–coupon bond due in one-year? The one-year rate of interest is currently 8 percent.
    a. $990.74
    b. $1,000.00
    c. $99.07
    d. $1,009.34
    e. none of the above

14. The yield to maturity on a zero-coupon bond with a one-year maturity, a face value of $500, and a purchase price of $400 is equal to
    a. 25 percent
    b. 20 percent
    c. 10 percent
    d. 5 percent

15. Which of the following statements is correct?
    a. Higher yields usually imply higher bond prices.
    b. Higher yields always imply higher bond prices.
    c. Higher yields usually imply lower bond prices.
    d. Higher yields always imply lower bond prices.

16. The shorter the maturity of a debt instrument,
    a. the larger the change in price resulting from a change in interest rates
    b. the smaller the change in price resulting from a change in interest rates
    c. the more risky it is
    d. both (a) and (c)
    e. both (b) and (c)

17. When interest rates increase,
    a. the price of short-term bonds increases less than the price of long-term bonds decreases
    b. the price of long-term bonds decreases more than the price of short-term bonds increases
    c. the price of short-term bonds decreases less than the price of long-term bonds decreases
    d. the price of long-term bonds increases more than the price of short-term bonds decreases
    e. none of the above

18. If the nominal rate of interest is equal to 9 percent and the expected inflation rate is 4 percent, then
    a. the realized real rate of interest is 5 percent
    b. the expected real rate of interest is 5 percent
    c. the ex post real rate of interest is 5 percent
    d. the ex ante real rate of interest is 5 percent
    e. both (b) and (d)

19. If the inflation rate is expected to be 6 percent and creditors will lend only if the real rate of interest is 3 percent, the nominal interest rate will be
    a. 2 percent
    b. 3 percent
    c. 6 percent
    d. 9 percent

chapter 6

The Level of Interest Rates

Central Themes and Major Points

This chapter explains how interest rates are determined and why they change. The level of interest rate is the price of *credit* or *loanable funds*. It is the price borrowers of funds are willing to pay lenders of funds. For example, if the interest-rate level is currently at 8 percent, then borrowers are willing to pay $8 to borrow $100 from lenders for one year. At the end of the year $100 is returned to lenders along with an additional $8 for lending out their funds. Note that the interest-rate level is defined *not* as the price of money but as the price of credit or loanable funds. The former is a stock (quantity of money or money supply), whereas the latter is a flow (a flow of $100 over a period of one year).

Since the interest-rate level is a price, it is simply determined by the interaction of the demand for and supply of loanable funds. The *equilibrium* interest rate level is found at the point where the demand and supply curves of loanable funds intersect. The equilibrium level will change whenever the demand and/or the supply curves shift in response to factors unrelated to the current level of interest rates. These factors are examined in the chapter. They include expectations about inflation as well as expectations about the *future* level of interest rates.

The chapter concludes with a look at the historical behavior of interest rates in the United States since the early 1950s. The level of interest rates is related to the business cycle. It rises during periods of expansion and falls during periods of recession. The level of interest rates generally rose between 1950 and 1981 but has trended down since then.

New Terms

Define and/or explain the following terms introduced in this chapter:

The equilibrium
 interest rate
Credit = loanable
 funds
The demand for
 loanable funds
 (credit)

The supply of loanable
 funds (credit)

Essay Questions and Problems

1. **The determination of interest rates**
   a. How are interest rates determined?
   b. What factors cause shifts in the demand curve for loanable funds?
   c. What factors cause shifts in the supply curve for loanable funds?
   d. How do expectations affect the level of interest rates?

2. **The behavior of interest rates over time**
   a. What has been the long-term interest rate trend since 1981?
   b. How can you explain this long-term trend in interest rates?
   c. How does the level of interest rates vary over the business cycle?
   d. How can you explain this cyclical behavior of interest rates?

*3. **Interest rate forecasting** Suppose that you wish to predict next year's level of interest rates (we assume a unique rate for the sake of simplicity). Your credit projections at current interest rates are a demand for credit equal to $300 billion and a potential supply of credit equal to $350 billion for the next year. The rate of interest is now at 10 percent. Answer the following questions.

a. From your credit projections, what can you conclude regarding the direction of change in the rate of interest from this year to the next?

b. Plot the two projected points in a graph, with interest rates on the vertical axis and credit on the horizontal axis. Could you predict from these two points what the value of the rate of interest will be next year? What additional information do you need to make a prediction of the future level of the interest rate?

c. Suppose that you have estimated the demand-for-credit curve and the supply-of-credit curve to be linear in the range of interest rates you are analyzing. Suppose, furthermore, that you have estimated the interest-sensitivity of these curves to be such that the supply curve rises by $50 billion for every two-percentage-point increase in the rate of interest and that the demand curve rises by $50 billion for every two-percentage-point decrease in the rate of interest. Using this information, what is your forecast of next year's interest rate?

SELF-TESTS

Completion Questions

Complete each of the following statements by entering the missing words and/or choosing the best alternative proposed.

1. The interest rate is the _____ that *(lenders/borrowers)* receive and *(lenders/borrowers)* have to pay to obtain loanable funds.

2. Since the interest rate is a _____ it must be determined by the interaction of the _____ of and _____ for _____ or _____.

3. _____ funds are funds that *(lenders/borrowers)* are willing to make available for *(lenders/borrowers)* to borrow.

4. The supply-of-funds curve is *(upward/downward)* sloping, reflecting the fact that *(lenders/borrowers)* are willing to extend *(more/less)* credit the *(higher/lower)* the rate of interest is.

5. The demand-for-funds curve is *(upward/downward)* sloping, reflecting the fact that *(lenders/borrowers)* are willing to get *(more/less)* credit the *(higher/lower)* the rate of interest is.

6. When analyzing fluctuations in the level of interest rates, it is important to distinguish between movements _____ a demand or supply curve and a _____ in the curve.

7. Most borrowing comes from

a. _____

b. _____

c. _____

d. _____

8. Business firms borrow to acquire *(securities/real assets)*.

9. The federal government borrows to finance federal _____ _____.

10. Anything that increases the eagerness to borrow shifts the *(demand/supply)* curve for loanable funds to the *(right/left)* and drives interest rates *(higher/lower)*.

11. Interest-rate forecasters start with the premise that interest rates are influenced by _____ factors in the short term and _____ _____ factors over the long term.

True and False Questions

For each of the following statements, circle the letter T if it is correct or the letter F if it is *partially* or totally incorrect.

T F 1. The level of interest rates refers to all rates taken as a group (rates on car loans, on home mortgages, on government securities, on corporate bonds, etc.).

T F 2. The level of interest rates is the price of money, the price one must pay to get one dollar for one year.

T F 3. Lenders are suppliers of loanable funds, whereas borrowers are demanders of loanable funds.

T F 4. The equilibrium interest rate is the rate that makes the demand for credit equal to the supply of credit.

T F 5. There is strong evidence that interest rates can be temporarily rigged by a few large financial institutions with substantial market power.

T F 6. When the amount of loanable funds demanded or supplied changes in response to a change in the interest rate, then we have a movement along a demand or supply curve.

T F 7. A shift in a supply/demand curve occurs when the amount of loanable funds demanded or supplied changes, at each interest rate, in response to some factor unrelated to the rate of interest.

T F 8. An increase in the amount of loanable funds demanded in response to a fall in the interest rate is an example of what we call "a shift of the demand curve."

T F 9. If many tenants suddenly decide that they want to become home-owners, then the interest rate will rise because of a movement down along the demand curve for loanable funds.

T F 10. Expectations play an important role in the determination of interest rates through their influence on the demand curve for loanable funds. Supply curves, however, are not affected by expectations.

T F 11. Expectations that interest rates will rise in the near future will cause today's interest rates to rise. This phenomenon creates what we call a self-fulfilling prophecy.

T F 12. The level of interest rates tends to fall during periods of business cycle expansion and rise during periods of cyclical recession.

T F 13. Business firms borrow to acquire inventories and buy capital equipment, whereas households borrow to buy securities.

T F 14. When the demand for loanable funds increases, the supply of securities issued by borrowers declines.

T F 15. When the supply of loanable funds increases, the demand for securities by lenders also increases.

T F 16. During economic expansions the Federal Reserve typically eases credit, which increases the supply of loanable funds and lowers interest rates.

T F 17. Since 1981, the level of interest rates has been on an upward long-term trend.

T F 18. Large federal government deficits caused interest rates to rise sharply in the 1980s.

T F 19. During recessions the Federal Reserve typically eases credit, which reduces the supply of loanable funds and lowers interest rates.

T　F　20. Business cycles are responsible for changes in interest rates, but they do not affect the level of interest rates.

Multiple-Choice Questions

Answer the following multiple-choice questions by circling the best alternative.

1. The interest rate is the price of
   a. money
   b. credit
   c. loanable funds
   d. securities
   e. both (b) and (c)
2. Along the demand curve for loanable funds
   a. the behavior of borrowers is insensitive to changes in the level of interest rates
   b. prospects for business activity are held constant
   c. prospects for business activity are allowed to vary
   c. both (a) and (b)
   d. both (a) and (c)
3. Along the supply curve for loanable funds
   a. the behavior of lenders is insensitive to changes in the level of interest rates
   b. borrowers' creditworthiness is held constant
   c. borrowers' creditworthiness is allowed to vary
   d. both (a) and (b)
   e. both (a) and (c)
4. The equilibrium rate of interest
   a. is at the intersection point of the supply and demand curves
   b. is that rate for which the quantity of funds lenders are willing to lend equals the quantity of funds borrowers want to borrow
   c. has no tendency to change given stable supply and demand curves
   d. all of the above
   e. only (a) and (b)
5. One reason the interest rate cannot be at a level that differs from the equilibrium rate of interest is that
   a. insiders have substantial market power
   b. financial markets are competitive
   c. there are fewer lenders than borrowers
   d. there are fewer borrowers than lenders
   e. all of the above
6. Assume that the current interest rate is 8 percent. At this rate you expect that next year the demand for loanable funds will exceed the supply of loanable funds. As a result, next year's interest rate should

   a. rise above 8 percent
   b. remain at 8 percent
   c. fall below 8 percent
   d. one cannot tell where the rate will go
   e. none of the above
7. Assume that the current interest rate is 6 percent. At this rate you expect that next year the supply of loanable funds will exceed the demand for loanable funds. As a result, next year's interest rate should
   a. rise above 6 percent
   b. remain at 6 percent
   c. fall below 6 percent
   d. one cannot tell where the rate will go
   e. none of the above
8. Everything else being the same, the anticipation of stronger business activity should result in
   a. a shift of the supply curve for loanable funds to the right
   b. a shift of the supply curve for loanable funds to the left
   c. a shift of the demand curve for loanable funds to the right
   d. a shift of the demand curve for loanable funds to the left
   e. none of the above
9. As a result of the shift in the curve in the preceding question,
   a. interest rates will fall
   b. interest rates will rise
   c. interest rates will fluctuate
   d. interest rates will remain the same
   e. none of the above
10. Everything else being the same, the anticipation of a weakening of business activity should result in
    a. a shift of the supply curve for loanable funds to the right
    b. a shift of the supply curve for loanable funds to the left
    c. a shift of the demand curve for loanable funds to the right
    d. a shift of the demand curve for loanable funds to the left
    e. none of the above
11. As a result of the shift in the curve in the preceding question,
    a. interest rates will fall
    b. interest rates will rise
    c. interest rates will fluctuate
    d. interest rates will remain the same
    e. none of the above
12. Everything else being the same, the anticipation of a deterioration of borrowers' creditworthiness should result in

a. a shift of the supply curve for loanable funds to the right

b. a shift of the supply curve for loanable funds to the left

c. a shift of the demand curve for loanable funds to the right

d. a shift of the demand curve for loanable funds to the left

e. none of the above

13. As a result of the shift in the curve in the preceding question,
    a. interest rates will fall
    b. interest rates will rise
    c. interest rates will fluctuate
    d. interest rates will remain the same
    e. none of the above

14. Everything else being the same, the anticipation of an improvement in borrowers' credit-worthiness should result in
    a. a shift of the supply curve for loanable funds to the right
    b. a shift of the supply curve for loanable funds to the left
    c. a shift of the demand curve for loanable funds to the right
    d. a shift of the demand curve for loanable funds to the left
    e. none of the above

15. As a result of the shift in the curve in the preceding question,
    a. interest rates will fall
    b. interest rates will rise
    c. interest rates will fluctuate
    d. interest rates will remain the same
    e. none of the above

16. Which of the following factors should shift the demand curve for loanable funds to the right?
    a. expectations of lower incomes on the part of consumers
    b. anticipated weaker profits on the part of business firms
    c. a buildup in military outlays, producing larger than expected budget deficits
    d. a reduction in services provided by state and local governments
    e. all of the above

17. Which of the following factors should shift the supply curve for loanable funds to the left?
    a. a restriction on the ability of banks to extend loans
    b. expectations of lower incomes on the part of consumers
    c. anticipated weaker profits on the part of business firms
    d. a reduction in services provided by state and local governments
    e. all of the above

18. Expectations of an increase in inflation should
    a. increase the demand for loanable funds
    b. decrease the supply of loanable funds
    c. raise the nominal interest rate
    d. affect the equilibrium rate of interest
    e. all of the above

19. Expectations of an increase in interest rates next month should
    a. affect today's interest rates
    b. not have any influence on today's interest rates
    c. accelerate the rate of inflation
    d. reduce the rate of inflation
    e. only (a) and (b)

20. In periods of recession interest rates fall because
    a. business firms cut down their use of credit
    b. consumers rein in their borrowing
    c. the Federal Reserve eases credit
    d. the banking system is flush with reserves
    e. all of the above

part II

Intermediaries and Banks

chapter 7

The Regulation and Structure of Depository Institutions

Central Themes and Major Points

This chapter looks at the regulation and structure of the commercial banking system, thrift institutions (savings and loan associations, mutual savings banks, and credit unions), and money market mutual funds.

Because banks play a crucial role in the economic life of the nation, particularly as creators of money, they are strictly controlled by governmental authorities. The other depository institutions are also strictly supervised, with the exception of money market mutual funds.

The U.S. banking system has two special features: banks can obtain either a *federal* charter or a *state* charter *(dual banking system)*, and most banks are small.

The regulation and supervision of the banking system are shared by various authorities. At the federal level there are the Federal Reserve, the Federal Deposit Insurance Corporation (FDIC), and the *Comptroller of the Currency* (within the U.S. Treasury). At the state level there are *state banking authorities*. The implications of multiple federal regulation as well as the function and operation of the FDIC are discussed in this chapter.

Insolvencies in the banking industry have severely stretched the FDIC in recent years. An important reform is to adjust bank premium payments for degree of risk, requiring banks that make more risky loans to pay more for insurance. The FDIC actually ran out of money in the early 1990s, but the key to the stability of the banking system is the government's commitment to stand behind the FDIC.

The structure and performance of the banking industry are examined: the number and the relative size of banks, the relationship between bank size and bank *profitability,* and the degree of competition within the banking industry. Although there are a large number of small banks, the top 3 percent of banks account for 70 percent of industry assets. This fact indicates that banking is not as competitive as it may first appear.

In recent years a large number of savings and loan associations have become insolvent. The chapter examines the causes and consequences of this industry crisis. A new set of regulatory institutions has been created to replace the earlier structure. It is important to consider the changes and determine if they are sufficient to clean up the financial mess and prevent further damage. The potential cost of the crisis is enormous, with estimates running as high as $400 to $500 billion.

At least some of the problems encountered by the savings and loan industry are seen as resulting from deregulation. This point raises the question of how much regulation is best for the system. While there is no clear-cut answer, it appears that some regulation is necessary for the stability of the system.

One important factor that used to influence the behavior of depository institutions is the now-defunct *Regulation Q,* the maximum interest rate that depository institutions were allowed to pay on savings and time deposits. The chapter examines various aspects of Regulation Q—when and why it was introduced, what its effects on the behavior of depository institutions and financial market participants were, and why it was finally abolished.

New Terms

Define and/or explain the following terms introduced in this chapter:

Dual banking system:
  National banks
  State banks
National Currency Act
  of 1863
National Bank Act of
  1864
Comptroller of the
  Currency
Federal Deposit
  Insurance
  Corporation (FDIC):
  The payoff method
  The assumption
  method
Federal Savings and
  Loan Insurance
  Corporation
  (FSLIC)
National Credit Union
  Share Insurance
  Fund
Federal Home Loan
  Bank Board
National Credit Union
  Administration
Banking Act of 1933
McFadden Act of 1927
Zaibatsus

One-bank holding
  companies
Securities and
  Exchange
  Commission
Resolution Trust
  Corporation
Resolution Funding
  Corporation
Bank Insurance Fund
Savings Association
  Insurance Fund
Office of Thrift
  Supervision
Federal Housing
  Finance Board
Regulation Q
Federal National
  Mortgage
  Association (Fannie
  Mae)
Govenment National
  Mortgage
  Association (Ginnie
  Mae)
Federal Home Loan
  Mortgage
  Corporation
  (Freddie Mac)

Essay Questions and Problems

1. **The dual banking system**
   a. Why is the American banking system known as a dual banking system?
   b. What historical developments led to that structure?
   c. How is the structure justified today?

2. **Bank regulation** The banking system may possibly be one of the most tightly supervised and regulated sectors of the U.S. economy.
   a. How would you justify the need for strict control of the banking system?
   b. Who are the supervisors and the regulators, and what are their respective functions?

3. **The regulated and the regulators** A unique feature of the U.S. banking system is that the regulated can choose their regulators. What does this statement mean? Illustrate your answer with specific examples.

4. **Multiple federal regulation of banks** Summarize the arguments advanced by the proponents and the opponents of multiple federal regulation of the commercial banking system. What is your opinion on this issue?

5. **The Federal Deposit Insurance Corporation**
   a. What events led to the establishment of the FDIC?
   b. What type of coverage does the FDIC provide? Which financial institutions have deposits insured by the FDIC? Which corporations or agencies provide deposit insurance coverage to depository financial institutions not covered by the FDIC?
   c. Where did the original capital of the FDIC come from? Where does the current capital of the FDIC come from? Is this capital sufficient to pay off all insured deposits?
   d. If the capital of the FDIC is not sufficient to pay off all insured deposits, what then is the premise upon which the FDIC is based?
   *e. What are the two procedures employed by the FDIC in taking over failed banks? Compare and contrast these two procedures. Which would be preferred by large depositors?
   f. The FDIC recently shifted to a risk-adjusted insurance premium system. Explain how this works. What was the reason behind the shift?

6. **The modern version of a "run on the bank"** It is said that today a "run on the bank" can take place without any line at all forming in front of the tellers' windows. How could this occur? Illustrate your answer with a specific example.

7. **Branching** The National Bank Act of 1864 totally prohibited national banks from branching, either within a state or across state lines.
   a. What amendment to the National Bank Act of 1864 was introduced by the McFadden Act of 1927 and the Banking Act of 1933 regarding branching regulations of national banks?
   b. What branching regulations apply to state banks?
   c. What exactly is a branch? Is an automated

teller machine that accepts and dispenses cash around the clock a branch?

d. Developments in the 1980s indicate that the McFadden Act's prohibition against interstate branching may be on its last legs. Give some examples of these developments.

8. **The competitive structure of the banking industry** Discuss the various factors that inhibit competition in the banking industry despite the existence of over 12,000 commercial banks in operation in the United States.

9. **One-bank holding companies**
   a. What is a one-bank holding company?
   b. Why did large commercial banks convert to this new corporate structure?
   c. Are Japan's *zaibatsus* similar to U.S. one-bank holding companies? What is the major difference between these two types of corporations?

10. **Savings and loan crisis**
    a. What is the savings and loan crisis and what caused it?
    b. Could the crisis have been prevented? If so, how?

11. **New savings and loan regulatory structure**
    a. Describe the new institutions which were established in response to the savings and loan crisis.
    b. What impact do these changes have on the Federal Deposit Insurance Corporation and the U.S. Treasury Department?

SELF-TESTS

Completion Questions

Complete each of the following statements by entering the missing words and/or choosing the best alternative proposed.

1. In a _____ banking system we have _____ _____ chartered banks and _____ chartered banks.

2. The three federal banking authorities are the _____ _____, the _____ _____, and the office of the _____ _____.

3. The Federal Deposit _____ provides deposit insurance for _____ banks, ____ _____ banks, and _____ _____ associations, up to an amount of _____ per _____ per _____.

4. The _____ _____ provides deposit insurance to federally chartered credit _____.

5. The Federal Deposit Insurance Corporation's funds are divided into the _____ _____ and the _____.

6. In the United States there are a few *(small/large)* banks and a large number of *(small/large)* banks.

7. The _____ Act of 1927 and the _____

Act of 1933 permit *(state/national)* banks to branch within a _____

to whatever extent _____

banks can branch in that state.

8. As a result of the savings and loan association crisis, the _____

_____ was abolished and its

chartering, regulating, examining, and supervising responsibilities transferred

to the _____

_____.

9. Ginnie Mae guarantees the payment of interest and principal on mortgage pools

that are insured by the _____

_____ and _____

_____.

10. In the 1970s and early 1980s financial disintermediation was caused by _____

_____.

True and False Questions

For each of the following statements, circle the letter T if it is correct or the letter F if it is *partially* or totally incorrect.

T F   1. The concept of a dual banking system refers to the fact that some commercial banks are members of the Federal Reserve System and others are not.

T F   2. State-chartered banks are for the most part larger institutions, but federally chartered banks are more numerous.

T F   3. Because of the existence of several bank regulators, individual banks are subject to multiple examinations.

T F   4. A bank with $50 billion in assets would make the list of the ten largest banks in the United States (1992).

T F   5. The consolidation of bank regulators at the federal level would eliminate the dual banking system.

T F   6. Less than 1 percent of the largest banks in the United States hold approximately one-third of all bank assets.

T F   7. In recent years, the number of bank failures has fallen sharply.

T F   8. Most observers think nationwide bank branching will be common by the end of the century.

T F   9. Negotiable CDs with minimum denomination are not fully insured by the FDIC.

T F   10. Under the so-called "payoff" method, the FDIC may allow a bank to go into receivership.

T F   11. All of the following statements are correct: all member banks are insured banks; all national banks are member banks; all noninsured banks are state banks.

T F   12. The FDIC insures about 99 percent of the volume of all bank deposits.

T F   13. Gresham's Law of bank supervision says that good regulations drive out bad regulators.

T F   14. The insurance fund of the FDIC is sustained by annual premiums paid by insured institutions.

T F   15. The dual banking system means that in the United States a commercial bank can operate with a federal and a state charter.

T F   16. The FDIC has recently shifted to a flat insurance premium system to fund operations.

T F   17. The Office of Thrift Supervision is a division of the U.S. Treasury.

T F   18. A large depositor in a failed insured bank will probably be better off if the FDIC uses the so-called "payoff" method rather than the "assumption" method in handling that bank.

T F   19. One of the factors banking authorities evaluate before chartering a new bank is the general character of its management.

T F 20. Although the United States is much larger than England, the fact that our market is covered by over 12,000 banks and the English market is covered essentially by 5 (the Big Five) in and of itself is sufficient evidence to warrant the conclusion that there is more competition among banks here than there.

T F 21. In 1991, the Bank Insurance Fund segment of the FDIC ran out of money.

T F 22. The one-bank holding company was a device turned to during the late 1960s to permit the management and owners of commercial banks to engage in kinds of business activities that commercial banks as such were not permitted to engage in.

T F 23. The Federal Savings and Loan Insurance Corporation (FSLIC) has been abolished.

T F 24. Fraud and mismanagement played an important role in the savings and loan crisis.

T F 25. Credit unions have become increasingly active in mortgage lending.

T F 26. Congressional legislation enacted late in 1970 regulating one-bank holding companies has eliminated the possibility of *zaibatsus* appearing in the United States.

T F 27. Congress has recently imposed heavy import duties on Japan's *zaibatsus*.

T F 28. Savings and loan associations and mutual savings banks are not under the supervision of the Federal Reserve and therefore they are not required to hold reserves against their deposits. Furthermore they do not have access to temporary borrowing from the Federal Reserve. If the need to borrow occurs, they should go to the Federal Home Loan Bank Board.

T F 29. Credit unions are supervised by the FDIC.

T F 30. Regulation Q was designed to prevent excessive interest-rate competition among banks.

Multiple-Choice Questions

Answer the following multiple-choice questions by circling the best alternative.

1. The American banking system is known as a dual banking system because there are
   a. many small banks and a few large ones
   b. commercial banks and consumer banks
   c. state-chartered and nationally chartered banks
   d. unit banks and multibranch banks

2. The dual banking system in existence in the United States
   a. refers to the fact that some commercial banks are members of the Federal Reserve and others are not
   b. refers to the fact that both commercial banks and thrift institutions accept deposits from the public
   c. refers to the fact that banks are regulated by both the Federal Reserve and the FDIC
   d. none of the above

3. Federally chartered banks
   a. are required to be insured by the FDIC
   b. are members of the Federal Reserve System
   c. are under the supervision of the Comptroller of the Currency
   d. all of the above
   e. only (b) and (c) are correct

4. The Federal Deposit Insurance Corporation
   a. was established in 1934 as a result of the Banking Act of 1933
   b. insures deposits at commercial banks and mutual savings banks up to $100,00 per depositor per bank
   c. examines state-chartered member banks
   d. all of the above
   e. only (a) and (b) are correct

5. Which of the following institutions provides deposit insurance?
   a. The Federal Reserve
   b. The Federal Home Loan Bank Board
   c. The National Credit Union Share Insurance Fund
   d. The Federal Savings and Loan Insurance Corporation

6. The number of commercial banks operating in the United States is approximately
   a. 12,000
   b. 8,000
   c. 1,500
   d. 6,000

7. The approximate percentage of all commercial banks that are members of the Federal Reserve System is
   a. 70 percent
   b. 40 percent
   c. 90 percent
   d. 60 percent

8. The opponents of multiple federal banking authorities
   a. advocate the abolition of all federal bank-

ing authorities now in existence and the transfer of bank supervision to the executive branch

b. favor the elimination of the existing federal banking authorities and the transfer of bank supervision to state banking authorities

c. recommend the unification of all federal banking authorities but generally disagree on how this unification should be achieved

d. would like the Comptroller of the Currency to take over all banking supervision and regulation at the federal level

9. Which of the following best describes the current structure of the U.S. banking industry?

a. There are a few giants and a preponderance of very small banks.

b. Eighteen giant banks make up the banking industry, much as the three giant car makers make up the automobile industry.

c. There are a large number of banks of roughly the same size.

d. It is extremely competitive because of the large number of banks vying for the public's funds.

10. Federal regulations require that

a. national banks comply with the branching laws of the state in which they are headquartered

b. national banks be members of the Federal Reserve System

c. national banks be insured by the FDIC

d. all of the above

e. only (b) and (c) are correct

11. The approximate percentage of commercial banks that are state-chartered is

a. 30 percent

b. 70 percent

c. 50 percent

d. 40 percent

12. In 1984, the FDIC in effect nationalized

a. the saving and loan association industry

b. Continental Illinois National Bank

c. Bank of America

d. all credit unions

13. National banks

a. are federally chartered banks

b. are examined by the office of the Comptroller of the Currency

c. make up approximately one-third of all commercial banks

d. were first established in order to drive state banks out of business

e. all of the above

f. only (a) and (b) are correct

14. The FDIC gets the funds it uses to pay off depositors of failed banks from

a. the Federal Reserve

b. premiums paid by insured banks

c. the stock market

d. securities it sells in financial markets

15. The National Credit Union Share Insurance Fund

a. is to all credit unions what the FDIC is to commercial banks

b. is to federally chartered credit unions what the FDIC is to commercial banks and mutual savings banks

c. is to federally chartered credit unions what the Comptroller of the Currency is to national banks

d. none of the above

16. The largest U.S. commercial bank in terms of assets is

a. Citibank (New York)

b. Bank of America (San Francisco)

c. First National (Chicago)

d. Continental Illinois (Chicago)

17. The so-called "assumption" method refers to

a. the fact that the FDIC assumes the responsibility of insuring bank deposits

b. the nationalization of a failed bank

c. FDIC attempts to save failing banks by merging them with healthy ones

d. the regulation that prohibits the FDIC from assuming that a bank will fail just because of poor management

18. Before granting a charter to a new bank, both federal and state banking authorities evaluate all of the following *except*

a. the adequacy of the bank's capital structure

b. the bank's intention to join the Federal Reserve System and the FDIC

c. the bank's future earnings prospects

d. the convenience and the needs of the community it proposes to serve

19. In the late 1960s and early 1970s large commercial banks reorganized their corporate structures into one-bank holding companies in order to

a. acquire out-of-state banks

b. diversify their financial activities

c. take over industrial companies

d. all of the above

e. only (a) and (b)

20. Fannie Mae finances its activities by

a. borrowing from the U.S. Treasury

b. charging commercial banks

c. issuing bonds to the public

d. collecting taxes on home owners

21. Japan's *zaibatsus* are
    a. similar to U.S. one-bank holding companies
    b. financial-industrial conglomerates
    c. what we call commercial banks in the United States
    d. none of the above
22. The most numerous of the thrift institutions is
    a. credit unions
    b. commercial banks
    c. savings and loan associations
    d. mutual savings banks
23. Which of the following agencies has some regulatory power over money market mutual funds?
    a. the Federal Reserve Board
    b. the Securities and Exchange Commission
    c. the U.S. Treasury
    d. the Comptroller of the Currency
    e. none of the above
24. According to the Garn–St. Germain Act of 1982, a thrift institution is allowed to
    a. offer the public money market mutual funds
    b. convert its charter to that of a commercial bank
    c. receive short-term loans from the Federal Reserve whenever in trouble
    d. all of the above
    e. none of the above
25. The Federal Home Loan Bank Board
    a. monitors the savings and loan industry
    b. monitors credit unions
    c. monitors all thrift institutions
    d. has recently been abolished
26. Estimates of the costs associated with the savings and loan crisis are
    a. $10–$20 million
    b. $5–$10 billion
    c. $400–$500 billion
    d. negligible
27. The closing and merging of insolvent savings and loan associations is the responsibility of the
    a. Federal Savings and Loan Insurance Corporation
    b. Bank Insurance Fund
    c. Comptroller of the Currency
    d. Resolution Trust Corporation
28. Among the negative effects of Regulation Q was (were) that
    a. it discriminated against the small saver
    b. it caused financial disintermediation
    c. it prevented aggressive, well-managed banks from offering depositors more attractive interest rates than the bank next door
    d. all of the above
    e. only (b) and (c)
29. Regulation Q was eliminated on April 1, 1986, by
    a. the Banking Act of 1980
    b. the Congress of the United States
    c. the Depository Institutions Deregulation Committee
    d. the Federal Reserve Board
    e. none of the above
30. Some of the regulatory changes introduced in the 1970s in order to soften the disintermediation-inducing effects of Regulation Q are
    a. the elimination of the rate ceilings on large-size negotiable CDs with a maturity of more than ninety days
    b. the permission given to depository institutions to issue six-month money market time certificates with rates tied to the yield on Treasury bills
    c. the increase in the rate ceiling imposed on passbook savings deposits from about 5 percent in the late 1970s to approximately 8 percent
    d. all of the above
    e. only (a) and (b)

chapter 8

Commercial Bank Asset and Liability Management

Central Themes and Major Points

Commercial banks are financial intermediaries: they attract funds by selling liabilities against themselves and then turn around and acquire assets by making loans and buying securities with the funds they have attracted.

The liabilities created by commercial banks in the form of deposits are the banks' *source* of funds. The acquired assets in the form of loans and securities are the banks' *uses* of funds.

The first part of this chapter surveys the asset and liability sides of banks' balance sheets. The asset side of banks' balance sheets indicates the various uses to which bank funds are applied. The trend analysis of the composition of banks' assets since 1970 indicates a relative decline in cash assets and the holding of securities and an upsurge in bank loans as a use of funds. The liability side of banks' balance sheets shows the various sources of funds available to banks. A trend analysis of the changes in the composition of banks' liabilities since 1970 shows a relative decline of demand deposits as a source of funds and the emergence of *negotiable certificates of deposit* (CDs) as a new source of bank funds.

The second part of this chapter is devoted to the examination of the liquidity and profitability of commercial banks since 1970. As a business firm a bank seeks to maximize its profits and should therefore be holding high-yield assets, which are usually not very liquid. However, as a depository institution a bank must be liquid in order to meet cash withdrawals. A bank is constantly confronted with a trade-off between *profitability* and *liquidity,* and

the art of sound bank management consists in part of striking the right balance between these two factors.

After a survey of the profitability of commercial banks since 1970, the chapter moves to the examination of the issue of how a single bank should best provide for its liquidity needs. According to the approach called liability management, a bank should draw its liquidity from the liability side of its balance sheet in order to meet a target asset growth.

Today the central focus of bank management is a modified version of liability management best described as "discretionary funds management." According to this approach a bank would first project expected net outflows or net inflows of nondiscretionary funds (funds beyond the bank's immediate control) and then use its liabilities and its assets to raise funds in the case of a net outflow or dispose of them in the case of any inflow.

To conclude, it is pointed out that exclusive reliance on a single route to liquidity is hazardous. Prudent banking practice requires that potential needs for liquidity be provided from diverse sources.

The Appendix shows how banks go about the job of meeting their reserve requirements on a day-to-day basis.

New Terms

Define and/or explain the following terms introduced in this chapter:

45

Uses of bank funds
Sources of bank funds
Time deposits
Repurchase
  agreements (RPs)†
Overnight RPs
Federal funds
Secondary reserves
Capital adequacy
Risk assets
Collateral
Securitization
Redlining
Equal Credit
  Opportunity Act
Home Mortgage
  Disclosure Act

Community
  Reinvestment Act
Fair Housing Act
Equity capital
Retained earnings
Stock flotations
Bank liquidity and
  profitability
Interest-rate risk
  borne by banks
Floating (or variable)
  rates
Liability management
Discretionary funds
  management
Nondiscretionary
  funds

The following terms are from the Appendix to this chapter.

A bank's money
  position
Money desk manager
Demand balances due
  from domestic banks

Net demand deposits
Correspondent bank
Contemporaneous
  reserves
Lagged reserves

†More on this term in Chapter 15.

Essay Questions and Problems

1. **Uses of bank funds**
   a. Discuss the evolution of the composition of bank portfolio assets since 1970.
   b. What factors account for the changes that have taken place?
   c. Why do holdings of U.S. government securities by banks usually show a countercyclical pattern over the business cycle? Why do loans generally move in harmony with the business cycle?

2. **Sources of bank funds** Since 1970, the composition of banks' liabilities has changed.
   a. Which sources of funds have declined in relative importance and which have expanded or emerged?
   b. What factors account for these relative changes?

3. **Negotiable certificates of deposit (CDs)**
   a. What exactly are negotiable certificates of deposit?
   b. When and for what purpose were they first issued?

*4. **Bank capital adequacy** Consider the following items, *some* of which are entries in a

bank's balance sheet. Numerical values are in millions of dollars.

Certificates of		Loans	400
deposit	90	Equity capital	40
Common stocks	30	Commercial	
Time deposits	200	paper	30
Cash	110	Government	
Demand		securities	130
deposits	310		

Answer the following questions:
   a. Draw the bank's balance sheet (ignore missing items, if any).
   b. What is the value of this bank's risk assets?
   c. Determine this bank's ratio of equity capital to risk assets. Does this bank have adequate capital when compared with the average for the whole banking system?

5. **Repurchase agreements**
   a. What exactly are repurchase agreements?
   *b. The purpose of this question is to illustrate how a bank that is loaned up can obtain excess reserves by selling securities, under agreement to repurchase, to corporate customers.

   Suppose the First National Bank is loaned up and the reserve requirement against demand deposits is 15 percent. The bank sells under agreement to repurchase $10 million worth of government securities to a large corporation, which is one of its customers. Enter in the T-account below the changes in the balance sheet that reflect the transaction just described.

FIRST NATIONAL BANK

The bank's balance sheet will show a rise in its borrowing entered as "securities sold under agreement to repurchase" and a corresponding drop in its demand deposits.
   (1) What is the change in the bank's required reserves?
   (2) What is the change in the bank's total reserves?
   (3) What is the change in the bank's excess reserves or deficiency in reserves? What do you conclude?
   (4) By how much will First National be able to expand its portfolio of loans (assuming that it can sell securities under

agreement to repurchase on a continual basis)?
  (5) What is the implication of the above T-account for the measurement of the money supply?

6. **The trade-off between liquidity and profitability** Sound bank management requires striking the correct balance between liquidity and profitability. Explain the nature of this trade-off confronting bank managers.

7. **Liability management**
  a. What does liability management mean, how is it implemented, and how does it differ from other approaches to bank management (for example, asset management)?
  b. Which particular money market instrument has contributed to the development of liability management since the early 1960s? Why?
  c. Apart from the money market instrument mentioned in your answer to (b), what other sources of funds are relied upon under liability management?
  d. What are the limitations of liability management as a provider of bank liquidity?

*8. **Liability management** Assume the banking system has a $100 million reserve deficiency and banks wish to eliminate this deficiency by issuing certificates of deposit (CDs) to their depositors, that is, by borrowing from their depositors.
  a. Is it possible for the banking system to eliminate its $100 million reserve deficiency by issuing CDs? Explain.
  b. If your answer to the previous question is yes, what dollar amount of CDs should be issued? To answer this question you need the following information: the reserve requirement against demand deposits is 15 percent, and the reserve requirement against time deposits (including CDs) is 5 percent.

9. **Interest-rate risk and floating-rate loans** It is said that banks generally borrow short and lend long.
  a. What does this sentence mean?
  b. Describe the type of risk faced by banks when they follow a borrowing-short, lending-long strategy?
  c. How can banks protect themselves against the type of risk described in your answer to the previous question?

10. **Discretionary funds management**
  a. What does discretionary funds management mean, and how is this approach to bank management implemented?
  b. Compare this approach to bank management with the other approaches discussed in this chapter. Why is discretionary funds management a sounder and more reliable method of bank management than the others?

11. **Basic factors underlying bank liquidity** Fundamental to the state of bank liquidity are three basic factors that are often overlooked.
  a. What are these three factors?
  b. Explain carefully why each of these factors is fundamental to the state of bank liquidity.

12. **Redlining** What is meant by redlining? What are the causes of the practice? What has the federal government done to try to prevent redlining?

The following questions are based on the Appendix to this chapter.

13. **Net demand deposits**
  a. What exactly are a bank's net demand deposits?
  b. Explain why reserves are held against these net demand deposits rather than against the total demand deposits.
  c. Which of the two measures should be used when measuring the money supply?

14. **Managing a bank's reserve position**
  a. Explain why a lower or higher than target volume of reserves will penalize a bank.
  b. A money desk manager wants to increase a bank's reserves. What action should be taken?
  c. A money desk manager wants to decrease a bank's reserves. What action should be taken?
  *d. Suppose that Treasury bills are currently yielding 11 percent and that the federal funds rate is at 13 percent. If the money desk manager wishes to increase reserves, which alternative would be preferred? If the money desk manager wishes to decrease reserves, which alternative would be preferred? Why?

*15. **Computation of required reserves** Consider the case of the First National Bank (FNB). You are given below its daily closing figures for business time deposits, net demand deposits, vault cash, and deposits with the

Week Number		Time Deposits	Vault Cash	Week Number		Demand Deposits	Deposits with Fed
Week 1:	Tues	100	1.5	Week 5:	Tues	80	9.0
	Wed	120	2.0		Wed	70	8.5
	Thur	130	2.0		Thur	90	9.5
	Fri	110	1.5		Fri	80	9.0
Week 2:	Mon	100	1.5	Week 6:	Mon	70	8.5
	Tues	120	2.0		Tues	75	8.5
	Wed	120	2.0		Wed	85	9.5
	Thur	120	1.5		Thur	90	9.0
	Fri	110	1.0		Fri	80	9.0
Week 3:	Mon	140	1.0	Week 7:	Mon	80	9.0

Federal Reserve for a selected number of days over a period of seven weeks. All figures are in millions of dollars. Answer the following questions:

a. How much required reserves does FNB have to hold against business time deposits? Recall that Friday's closing figure counts three times (since it counts for Saturday and Sunday as well). Assume that reserve requirements against business time deposits are zero on the first $2 million and 3 percent on the rest.

b. How much required reserves does FNB have to hold against net demand deposits? Recall that Friday's closing figure counts three times (since it counts for Saturday and Sunday as well). Assume that reserve requirements against net demand deposits are 3 percent for the first $25 million and 12 percent for the rest.

c. What is the total amount of required reserves FNB must hold?

d. Required reserves must be held in the form of vault cash and/or deposits with the Federal Reserve. A bank's vault cash is used to satisfy reserve requirements during the same two weeks as its business time deposits. What is FNB's average daily vault cash over the two-week period starting Tuesday of Week 1 and ending Monday of Week 3?

e. Given FNB's total amount of required reserves (see your answer to question c) and its average daily vault cash (see your answer to question d), what amount of required reserves must FNB hold in the form of deposits with the Federal Reserve in order to meet its reserve requirements?

f. The final reserve holding period over which FNB (or any other bank) must comply with the reserve requirements imposed by the Federal Reserve is a two-week period starting on Thursday and ending on Wednesday two weeks later (including Saturdays and Sundays). Note that the two-week reserve *holding* period starts on a Thursday, whereas the two-week reserve *computation* period starts on a Tuesday (that is, two days earlier). FNB's money desk manager knows exactly the amount of required reserves in the form of average daily deposits FNB must hold with the Federal Reserve. It is the number you found in your answer to question e. Is this amount sufficient to meet FNB's reserve requirements? If not, what is the amount of required reserves FNB must hold with the Federal Reserve on Tuesday and Wednesday of Week 7 in order to satisfy its reserve requirements?

SELF-TESTS

Completion Questions

Complete each of the following statements by entering the missing words and/or choosing the best alternative proposed.

1. Commercial banks are financial _____. They attract

funds in the form of _____ against themselves and use

these funds to acquire _____ in the form of

_____ to business, consumers, and so on, and in the form of

_____ of the U.S. government, its agencies, and _____

_____ and _____ governments.

2. The following items are considered sources of bank funds: _____

   _____ , _____

   _____ , and _____

   _____ .

3. Bank loans in descending order of importance are: _____

   loans, _____ loans, and _____

   loans.

4. Bank liabilities in descending order of importance are: _____

   _____ deposits, _____ deposits, _____

   _____ deposits, and _____

   _____ .

5. List the three major groups of bank assets in descending order of relative

   liquidity: _____ , _____

   _____ , and _____ .

6. Risk assets are determined by subtracting _____

   _____ and _____

   _____ from _____

   _____ .

7. The ratio of a bank's _____

   to _____ is a mea-

   sure of the adequacy of a bank's capital.

8. Commercial banks are prohibited from holding corporate _____ _____

   and _____ . They can, however, buy and sell

   them for the _____ , _____ , and

   _____ that they man-

   age for others. Such _____

   ____ holdings are not included among a bank's own *(liabilities/assets)*.

9. The nature of a bank's *(assets/liabilities)* dictates its need to hold *(liquid/risky)*

   assets.

10. Bank management is a constant attempt to maintain the right balance between

    _____ and _____ .

11. An increase in liquidity means that banks are becoming *(riskier/safer)* but *(less/more)* profitable.

12. The sources of bank income are: _____

    _____ , _____

    _____ , _____

    _____ ,

    and _____

    _____ .

13. The major costs incurred by banks are: _____

    _____ , _____

    _____ , and

    _____

    _____ .

14. When practicing liability _____ , a bank increases its

    _____ by *(buying/selling)* money.

15. _____

    _____ is a modified version of liability management according to which

    banks first project their *(discretionary/nondiscretionary)* net _____

    _____ or _____ of funds. An expected net *(out-flow/inflow)* means funds must be raised to fill the gap: an expected net _____

    _____ means there are *(deficit/surplus)* funds to dispose of.

    The second step is to use *(discretionary/nondiscretionary)* *(assets/liabilities/assets and liabilities)* to raise funds in the case of a net _____

    and to dispose of them in the case of a net _____ .

16. Three basic factors fundamental to the state of bank liquidity are: _____

    _____ ,

    _____

    _____ , and _____

    _____ .

True and False Questions

For each of the following statements, circle the letter T if it is correct or the letter F if it is *partially* or totally incorrect.

T F   1. Twenty years ago the fraction of total commercial bank liabilities made up of demand deposits was much smaller than it is today, and the fraction made up of time deposits was much larger than it is today.

T F   2. Commercial bank holdings of govern-ment securities tend to vary with the business cycle, increasing in the cyclical upswing as loan demand rises and decreasing during the cyclical downswing as loan demand falls.

T F   3. Passbook saving deposits are approximately the same proportion of bank liabilities as they were twenty years ago.

T F   4. Short-term U.S. Treasury bills are considered a cash asset because of their high liquidity.

T F 5. Federal funds sold are a use of bank funds in the form of overnight loans to other banks.

T F 6. Commercial banks are financial intermediaries that issue debt claims that circulate as money.

T F 7. A bank's equity capital is typically less than 10 percent of its assets.

T F 8. Redlining refers to bank efforts to fix deposit rates at low levels while inflating interest rates charged to consumers.

T F 9. The Community Reinvestment Act was designed to discourage redlining.

T F 10. The sharp decrease in the percentage of bank assets held in the form of cash assets (non-interest-producing) since 1970 is primarily explained by the rise in interest rates that made liquidity of this kind unaffordable to banks.

T F 11. Equity capital should not be considered a source of bank funds. It is only one way for banks to be liquid.

T F 12. Deposits of banks with the Federal Reserve Banks are part of their cash assets.

T F 13. Federal funds purchased are a use of bank funds in the form of overnight borrowing from other banks.

T F 14. A kind of commercial bank deposit liability that did not exist before the 1960s is the large-size negotiable CD.

T F 15. Although commercial banks' equity capital, as a percentage of total assets, has remained fairly stable since 1970, the cushion against adversity and protection to depositors provided by equity capital has lessened because the percentage of total assets composed of risk assets has increased.

T F 16. Government securities are not as desirable as loans when loans can be extended, but they are preferable to cash when loans cannot be made.

T F 17. Since 1970 there has been a steady improvement in the ratio of bank equity capital to risk assets.

T F 18. Sales of securities and loans that banks have agreed to buy back at a later date at a predetermined price are called repurchase agreements.

T F 19. Bank holdings of short-term U.S. Treasury bills are frequently called "secondary" reserves because they are highly liquid.

T F 20. For banks, equity is typically more expensive than deposits or other short-term borrowed funds.

T F 21. At the present time, the largest expense incurred by banks is the payment of interest on the deposits of their customers.

T F 22. Over the last twenty years the liquidity of banks has improved substantially.

T F 23. For the banking system as a whole the ultimate source of liquidity is the Federal Reserve.

T F 24. Modern bank liquidity management calls for nearly all liquidity needs to be met on the asset side of the balance sheet.

T F 25. Commercial banks earn, on average, a higher yield on their portfolio of loans than on their portfolio of securities.

T F 26. Interest on securities is a bank expense.

T F 27. Interest on deposits is bank income.

T F 28. Securitization is a technique that allows banks to raise funds by transforming their loans into securities that are sold to investors.

T F 29. Liability management has been practiced by banks since World War II.

T F 30. All the banks in the banking system can simultaneously rely on their holdings of money market securities as a source of liquidity only if the Federal Reserve stands ready to buy such securities in appropriate amounts.

T F 31. Obtaining liquidity through liability management refers to the practice of banks selling securities out of their portfolios as a means of raising cash.

T F 32. Individual commercial banks that seek additional reserves in order to make more loans will obtain those reserves in the federal funds market rather than at the Federal Reserve discount window only if the rate in the federal funds market is below that charged at the discount window.

T F 33. The central focus of bank management today is a modified form of liability management best described as discretionary funds management.

T F 34. Discretionary funds management starts with a projection of the expected movements in nondiscretionary funds. The second step is to use discretionary liabilities and assets either to raise funds or to dispose of them, as the case may be.

The following questions are based on the Appendix to this chapter.

T F 35. A bank's money position refers to the volume of reserves it is holding at any point in time.

T F 36. A bank holds reserves against its total demand deposits and its total savings and time deposits.

T F 37. A bank's *net* demand deposits are equal to its total demand deposits *minus* cash items in the process of collection *plus* demand balances due from domestic banks.

T F 38. Foreign branches of U.S. commercial banks are called correspondent banks.

T F 39. Cash items in the process of collection are bank assets.

T F 40. Demand balances due from domestic banks are bank liabilities.

Multiple-Choice Questions

Answer the following multiple-choice questions by circling the best alternative.

1. Demand deposits at commercial banks
   a. are a source of bank funds
   b. have declined in volume since 1970
   c. have been overtaken by large-size negotiable CDs as the single most important source of bank funds
   d. all of the above
   e. only (a) and (b)

2. Large-size negotiable certificates of deposit
   a. are issued in denominations of $100,000 or more
   b. are subject to Regulation Q
   c. have been in existence since the end of World War II
   d. are held mostly by wealthy individuals
   e. all of the above

3. Which of the following is *not* a source of bank funds?
   a. borrowing from the Federal Reserve
   b. federal funds sold
   c. large-size negotiable CDs
   d. equity capital
   e. time deposits

4. The largest asset of commercial banks is
   a. their portfolio of securities
   b. their portfolio of loans
   c. their cash holdings
   d. their buildings and other real assets

5. The function of bank equity capital
   a. is to serve as a cushion against adversity
   b. is to provide funds to banks on short notice
   c. is primarily to increase the liquidity of banks
   d. all of the above

6. A bank's risk assets are determined by
   a. subtracting cash assets from total assets
   b. subtracting demand deposits from total assets
   c. subtracting cash assets and U.S. government securities from total assets
   d. subtracting U.S. government securities from total assets

7. Since 1970 the ratio of bank equity capital to risk assets
   a. has increased as a result of additional sales of common stocks by banks
   b. has decreased because risk assets have grown faster than equity capital
   c. has decreased because equity capital has not changed while the size of risk assets has increased
   d. has decreased because equity capital has dropped while the size of risk assets has not changed

8. Which of the following is true regarding changes in the assets of commercial banks over the past ten years?
   a. Consumer loans have surpassed U.S. securities as the largest asset.
   b. Mortgage loans have surpassed business loans as the largest asset.
   c. Cash assets have surpassed consumer loans as the largest asset.
   d. Business loans have surpassed U.S. government securities as the largest asset.

9. Of the following types of securities, which is the one held most often by commercial banks?
   a. U.S. government securities
   b. securities of government agencies
   c. (a) and (b) combined
   d. state and local government securities
   e. large-size negotiable certificates of deposit

10. A repurchase agreement is a transaction in which
    a. a lender agrees to buy back securities at a specified future date at a predetermined price
    b. a borrower agrees to buy back securities at a specified future date at a predetermined price
    c. a borrower agrees to sell back securities at

a specified future date at a predetermined price

d. none of the above

11. By purchasing government securities commercial banks are
    a. making a "loan" to the government
    b. acquiring earning assets
    c. putting their funds to use
    d. all of the above
    e. only (b) and (c)

12. Which of the following is *not* an asset to commercial banks?
    a. U.S. government bonds
    b. municipal bonds
    c. business loans
    d. corporate bonds
    e. real estate loans

13. A bank with $100 million in assets has $15 million worth of cash assets and $25 million worth of securities. If its equity capital equals $6 million, then this bank's ratio of equity capital to risk assets is equal to
    a. 10
    b. 0.4
    c. 0.1
    d. 0.6
    e. none of the above

14. Your answer to question 13 indicates that this bank has a ratio of equity capital to risk assets
    a. comparable to the average for the whole banking industry in 1990
    b. much larger than the average for the whole banking industry in 1990
    c. much smaller than the average for the whole banking industry in 1990
    d. that cannot be compared with that of the banking industry as a whole

15. Which of the following bank operating expenses has proportionately decreased relative to total expenses since 1970?
    a. salaries and wages
    b. interest on deposits
    c. interest on borrowed funds
    d. none of the above

16. The largest source of a bank's income is
    a. its portfolio of securities
    b. service charges and fees
    c. interest on deposits
    d. its portfolio of loans

17. A traditional rule-of-thumb measure of a bank's liquidity is
    a. the ratio of total non-cash assets to total deposits
    b. the ratio of total loans to equity capital
    c. the ratio of total loans to total deposits
    d. the ratio of total non-cash assets to equity capital

18. A bank may enhance its profitability by
    a. reducing its liquidity
    b. cutting back on its holding of securities and enlarging its portfolio of loans
    c. making riskier loans
    d. all of the above
    e. none of the above

19. The most liquid asset of commercial banks is
    a. their holdings of U.S. Treasury bills
    b. vault cash
    c. short-term business loans
    d. (a) and (b) are equally liquid

20. The major factor restricting the *ability* of banks to hold riskier assets than those they currently hold is
    a. the recent deterioration of their liquidity
    b. the reduction in the ratio of equity capital to risk assets
    c. governmental regulations of banking operations
    d. prudent bank management

21. Liability management relies on which of the following as a source of liquidity?
    a. an increase in indebtedness
    b. a reduction in indebtedness
    c. an increase in net worth
    d. a decrease in net worth
    e. an increase in assets

22. Which of the following money market instruments played an important role in the early development of liability management?
    a. U.S. Treasury bills
    b. commercial paper
    c. negotiable certificates of deposit
    d. bankers' acceptances
    e. none of the above

23. The daily federal funds rate is rarely below the discount rate because
    a. borrowing from the Federal Reserve cannot be used as a permanent source of liquidity to support the growth of bankers' assets
    b. large money market banks rely on the federal funds market on a continuous basis in order to expand their lending activities and thus tend to bid up the price of federal funds
    c. the Federal Reserve is considered by banks as a lender of last resort
    d. all of the above
    e. only (a) and (c)

24. Under discretionary funds management a bank would use
    a. the asset side of its balance sheet to raise funds actively and the liability side to dispose of them

b. the liability side of its balance sheet to raise funds actively and the asset side to dispose of them

c. the bank's net worth and capital position to raise funds actively and both the asset and liability sides of its balance sheet to dispose of them

d. both the asset and the liability sides of its balance sheet to raise funds or dispose of them, as the case might be

25. Which of the following is *not* used by banks to raise funds under discretionary funds management?
   a. a purchase of federal funds
   b. a sale of U.S. Treasury bills
   c. a sale of securities under repurchase agreements
   d. a purchase of negotiable CDs
   e. borrowing from its Federal Reserve district bank

The following questions are based on the Appendix to this chapter.

26. A bank's net demand deposits are equal to
   a. its total demand deposits less cash items in process of collection
   b. its total demand deposits less demand balances due from domestic and foreign banks less cash items in process of collection
   c. its total demand deposits less cash items in process of collection less demand balances due from domestic banks
   d. none of the above

27. A bank with a reserve deficiency
   a. will have to pay the Federal Reserve a penalty on the deficiency equal to a rate of interest of 2 percent
   b. answer (a) is correct only if the deficiency has been carried over more than one week
   c. may borrow reserves from its Federal Reserve district bank
   d. both (b) and (c)

28. A correspondent bank usually holds deposits with another bank
   a. to increase its liquidity
   b. as a collateral against borrowing
   c. to facilitate check clearing
   d. as an emergency source of funds

29. A bank with $200 million in demand deposits outstanding and no time deposits has $4 million in vault cash, $15 million in deposits at the Federal Reserve, and $2 million in demand deposits at another bank. Given a reserve requirement ratio of 10 percent, it follows that this bank has

a. a reserve deficiency of $1 million
b. a reserve deficiency of $.8 million
c. excess reserves of $1 million
d. a reserve deficiency of $1.2 million

30. Bank A, with a reserve requirement ratio of 12.5 percent, holds all of its reserves in the form of demand deposits at bank B, whose reserve requirement ratio is 20 percent. In this case the value of the deposit multiplier for bank A based on bank B reserves would be equal to
   a. 8
   b. 5
   c. 40
   d. none of the above

31. The system of reserve requirements currently enforced by the Federal Reserve is known as
   a. a contemporaneous reserves system
   b. a leading reserves system
   c. a lagged reserves system
   d. a simultaneous reserves system

32. Prior to 1984, the system of reserve requirements enforced by the Federal Reserve was known as
   a. a contemporaneous reserves system
   b. a leading reserves system
   c. a lagged reserves system
   d. a simultaneous reserves system

33. Under the current system of reserve requirements, depository institutions hold
   a. contemporaneous reserves against demand deposits
   b. lagged reserves against demand deposits
   c. contemporaneous reserves against time deposits
   d. lagged reserves against time deposits
   e. both (a) and (d)
   f. both (a) and (c)

34. One reason the Federal Reserve moved to a system of contemporaneous reserves is that
   a. the lagged reserves system was difficult to implement
   b. the contemporaneous reserves system may strengthen the Federal Reserve's control over the money supply
   c. lower reserve requirement ratios could be imposed under a system of contemporaneous reserves
   d. a system of contemporaneous reserves gives the Federal Reserve better control over the portion of reserves held by depository institutions in the form of vault cash

35. Under the current system of reserve requirements
   a. a bank's required reserves are computed

against the bank's average daily deposits over a two-week period

b. Friday's closing figure on deposits counts three times since it also counts for Saturday and Sunday

c. the two-week "reserve" period over which average daily deposits are computed starts

on a Tuesday and ends on a Monday two weeks later

d. the computation period for figuring reserves against demand deposits starts two weeks after the computation period for time deposits ends

e. all of the above

chapter 9

Nondeposit Financial Institutions

Central Themes and Major Points

Chapter 7 dealt with the structure and regulation of depository institutions—commercial banks and thrift institutions (savings and loan associations, mutual savings banks, and credit unions). This chapter looks at the structure and regulation of nondepository financial institutions. Some of these were briefly introduced in Chapter 4. This chapter surveys the following: life insurance companies, pension funds, property and casualty insurance companies, securities brokers and dealers, mutual funds, and investment bankers.

The major point made in this chapter is that, until recently, financial institutions specialized in particular types of financial services such as commercial banking, insurance, brokerage, and so on. Today, things are changing. Financial institutions are now invading each other's territory. For example, insurance companies are getting into the brokerage business and brokerage houses are making inroads into the banking business. One important legal barrier still remains. According to the Glass-Steagall Act of 1933, commercial banks are prohibited from engaging in *investment banking;* that is, they are not allowed to issue, sell, or distribute new stock and bond offerings of corporations. However, the impact of the law has been substantially eroded through a series of Supreme Court and Federal Reserve decisions. In recent years, commercial banks have been granted limited authority to underwrite and deal in commercial paper, mortgage-backed securities, municipal revenue bonds, and securities backed by mortgage debt.

New Terms

Define and/or explain the following terms introduced in this chapter:

Life insurance
  companies:†
  premium rates
  reserves
  whole life policies
  term policies
  actuaries
Pension funds:†
  vesting
  funding
Employee Retirement
  Income Security Act
  (ERISA)
Pension Benefit
  Guaranty
  Corporation
Individual Retirement
  Account (IRA)
Keogh Plans

Property and casualty
  insurance
  companies†
Securities brokers and
  dealers‡
Mutual funds
  open-end funds
  closed-end funds
  load funds
  no-load funds
  net asset value
Securities and
  Exchange Acts of
  1933 and 1934
Investment Company
  Act of 1940
Investment bankers‡
Glass-Steagall Act
Nonbank bank

†These terms were first introduced in Chapter 4.
‡More on these terms in Chapter 29.

Essay Questions and Problems

1. **Life insurance companies** Life insurance companies are the largest of the nondepository financial intermediaries based on the size of the assets they hold.
   a. How are they organized?

b. Who is responsible for their supervision and regulation?

c. What are the two major types of insurance that these institutions sell to individuals? Compare their features.

d. What changes have recently occurred in the investment policy of insurance companies, and why have these changes taken place?

2. **Pension funds** Pension funds are the second largest of the nondepository financial intermediaries based on the size of the assets they hold.

a. What purpose do they serve?

b. How are they organized?

c. What does it mean that an employee's pension benefits are vested? In what case are they said not to be vested?

d. When is a pension fully funded and when is it partly funded?

e. What legislation governs the activities of pension funds?

f. What alternatives to employer-sponsored pension plans are available to individuals?

3. **Property and casualty insurance companies** Property and casualty insurance companies are the third largest of the nondepository financial intermediaries based on the size of the assets they hold.

a. What are property and casualty insurance companies, and how do they differ from life insurance companies?

b. What are some of the unusual forms of property and casualty insurance sold recently by these companies?

c. Who is responsible for their regulation and supervision?

4. **Insurance premiums** Why do gender differences exist in the premiums for life insurance? auto insurance? and health insurance?

5. **Securities brokers and dealers and investment bankers**

*a. Are securities dealers and investment bankers financial intermediaries as defined in Chapter 4—that is, do they purchase the liabilities of ultimate borrowers with funds obtained by selling their own liabilities to ultimate savers?

b. Distinguish between a securities broker and a securities dealer.

c. Distinguish between a securities dealer and an investment banker.

d. What was the purpose of the Glass-Steagall Act and why was it enacted?

e. Why do commercial banks believe they are being discriminated against by the provisions of the Glass-Steagall Act?

f. Describe how regulatory decisions in recent years have diminished the impact of the Glass-Steagall Act on commercial bank activities.

SELF-TESTS

Completion Questions

Complete each of the following statements by entering the missing words and/or choosing the best alternative proposed.

1. Life insurance companies are organized either as _____ _____ or as _____ _____.

2. Life insurance companies and _____ _____ are supervised and regulated almost entirely by the _____ in which they operate.

3. The two major types of life insurance are known as _____ _____ policies and _____ policies.

4. _____ are statisticians who specialize in mortality probabilities.

5. All pension plans involve the twin problems of _____ and _____ of future benefits.

6. Because of abuses and mismanagement in many private pension plans, Congress enacted in 1974 the _____ _____ and created the _____ _____.

7. Individuals are given tax incentives to establish their own pension plans through _____ and _____.

8. _____ mutual funds offer redeemable shares for sale to the public, while _____ ____ mutual funds offer only limited shares which are not available to the public.

9. _____ operate in *(primary/secondary)* markets, selling and distributing new stocks and bonds directly from the issuing corporations to their original purchasers.

10. _____ act as pure middlemen, whereas _____ trade securities for their own accounts.

11. The _____ Act of 1933 divorced _____ banking from _____ banking.

12. In a significant departure from the Glass-Steagall Act, the Federal Reserve granted a large commercial bank permission to _____ and _____ in corporate _____.

True and False Questions

For each of the following statements, circle the letter T if it is correct or the letter F if it is *partially* or totally incorrect.

T F 1. One can say that the differences between depository institutions are quickly fading. However, sharp differences still exist between depository and nondepository financial institutions, neither of them seeking to invade the other's territory.

T F 2. As in the case of commercial banks and thrift institutions, life insurance companies are regulated by either a federal authority or by the states in which they operate.

T F 3. The large life insurance companies tend to be mutuals.

T F 4. The largest life insurance companies are structured as stock companies in which the business is owned and controlled by regular stockholders, whereas the vast majority of life insurance companies are organized as mutual associations, where ownership and control technically rest with the policyholders.

T F 5. Whole life insurance policies have a constant premium throughout the entire life of the policy, whereas term life insurance policies have relatively low premiums at first followed by rising premiums as people grow older.

T F 6. Unlike whole life insurance policies, term policies are pure insurance and do not involve a reserve or savings element.

T F 7. In recent years, life insurance companies have acquired firms with expertise in money market funds.

T F 8. Life insurance companies have recently altered their investment policies, moving away from their traditional heavy holdings of long-term corporate bonds and commercial mortgages toward common stocks and real estate.

T F 9. The Employee Retirement Income Security Act of 1974 stipulates that an employee's pension benefits must be fully vested.

T F 10. A pension fund wishing to fully fund a pension of $2,160 due in one year must set aside today $2,000 if the fund is expected to earn a 7 percent annual return on its investments.

T F 11. The pension described in the preceding question is partly funded.

T F 12. Because of the power of compound interest over time, a higher level of funding does not necessarily imply a safer pension.

T F 13. The Employee Retirement Income Security Act (ERISA) allows individuals to establish their own pension plans through Individual Retirement Accounts (IRAs) with interest and dividends tax-deferred until retirement.

T F 14. Contrary to life insurance companies, property and casualty insurance companies cannot predict accurately the amount of funds they will have to pay out every year in the future. Consequently their investment policy differs from that of life insurance companies, who invest a substantial amount of their funds in long-term assets.

T F 15. The Supreme Court recently ruled that auto insurance companies could not practice price discrimination based on gender.

T F 16. If the stocks that make up a mutual fund portfolio decline in value, the net asset value of the fund will rise.

T F 17. Securities brokers trade principally in secondary markets, whereas securities dealers, including investment bankers, trade principally in primary markets.

T F 18. The Banking Act of 1933—often called the Glass-Steagall Act—completely divorced commercial from investment banking.

T F 19. Investment banking refers to the trust department activity of commercial banks, which consists of managing the stock and bond portfolios of trusts, estates, and pension funds.

T F 20. The Glass-Steagall Act carries less and less weight among regulators.

Multiple-Choice Questions

Answer the following multiple-choice questions by circling the best alternative.

1. Life insurance companies are structured as
   a. thrift institutions
   b. either mutual associations or stock companies
   c. stock companies, exclusively
   d. mutual associations, exclusively

2. Which of the following authorities regulates life insurance companies?
   a. the Federal Reserve Board
   b. the Insurance Benefit Guaranty Corporation
   c. the state insurance commissioner
   d. the state banking commissioner
   e. either (c) or (d)

3. Suppose that an individual has purchased an insurance policy with a constant premium (the annual payment made to the insurance company) throughout the entire life of the policy. This individual has purchased
   a. a whole life policy
   b. a term policy
   c. an actuarial policy
   d. a pure insurance policy
   e. none of the above

4. Term life insurance policies give the holder
   a. pure insurance with no reserves or savings attached
   b. the same amount of protection as whole life policies at a generally lower premium
   c. rates of return that are commensurate with open market yields
   d. the option to combine life insurance with investment in a money market fund or a mutual fund
   e. both (a) and (b)
   f. both (c) and (d)

5. Regulators of life insurance companies look at these companies'
   a. sales practices
   b. premium rates
   c. calculation of reserves
   d. investment policies
   e. all of the above

6. Which of the following assets has traditionally been held by life insurance companies?
   a. long-term corporate bonds

b. real estate
c. residential mortgages
d. both (a) and (c)
e. both (a) and (b)

7. Compared with the average man, the average woman pays
    a. less for life insurance but more for health insurance
    b. less for health insurance but more for life insurance
    c. more for life and health insurance
    d. less for life and health insurance

8. How does a partly funded pension plan meet its pension commitments when they come due?
    a. with additional employees' contributions
    b. out of current earnings
    c. through funds borrowed from the Pension Benefit Guaranty Corporation
    d. with higher social security taxes
    e. none of the above

9. Individuals can establish their own pension plans through
    a. Individual Retirement Accounts (IRAs)
    b. Keogh Plans
    c. shares in a mutual fund with interest and dividends tax-deferred until retirement
    d. all of the above
    e. only (a) and (b)

10. The most important insurance in dollar terms offered by property and casualty insurance companies is
    a. automobile liability insurance
    b. fire insurance
    c. theft insurance
    d. medical insurance
    e. life insurance

11. Most mutual fund companies are
    a. close-ended
    b. open-ended
    c. fully vested
    d. fully funded

12. Assume that a no-load, open-end mutual fund owns securities with an aggregate market value of $3 million, has no liability, and has 500,000 shares outstanding. The net asset value per share of this fund is equal to
    a. $3
    b. $6
    c. $1.5 billion
    d. $3 million

13. A mutual fund is
    a. a financial intermediary
    b. an investment company
    c. an institution that sells shares in a diversified portfolio

d. all of the above
e. only (b) and (c)

14. An open-end mutual fund
    a. offers redeemable shares in the fund for sale to the general public
    b. never sells its shares directly to the public
    c. is also known as a no-load fund
    d. always charges a sales commission
    e. never charges a sales commission

15. A fund's net asset value per share
    a. varies inversely with the value of the securities that make up the fund's portfolio
    b. varies directly with the value of the securities that make up the fund's portfolio
    c. is not related to the value of the securities that make up the fund's portfolio
    d. is based on the accounting value of the securities that make up the fund's portfolio
    e. both (b) and (d)

16. A closed-end investment company
    a. is also known as a load fund
    b. has a variable number of shares outstanding
    c. has a fixed net asset value
    d. has unredeemable shares
    e. is not regulated by the Securities and Exchange Commission

17. A 1988 U.S. Supreme Court decision granted commercial banks limited authority to
    a. purchase corporate stock
    b. branch across state lines
    c. underwrite commercial paper
    d. underwrite U.S. Treasury bonds

18. Secondary securities markets refer to markets in which
    a. securities brokers are involved
    b. outstanding securities are traded
    c. originally issued securities are traded for the first time
    d. investment bankers perform most of their activities
    e. none of the above

19. Investment bankers are
    a. dealers operating in secondary markets
    b. brokers operating in primary markets
    c. dealers operating in primary markets
    d. brokers operating in secondary markets
    e. broker-dealers operating in both the primary and secondary markets

20. Investment banking consists of
    a. managing trusts, estates, and pension funds for others
    b. organizing and operating mutual funds
    c. managing large pools of investments in stocks and bonds
    d. underwriting new securities issues
    e. none of the above

21. Which of the following divorced commercial from investment banking?
    a. the National Currency Act of 1863
    b. the National Bank Act of 1864
    c. the Glass-Steagall Act of 1933
    d. the McFadden Act
    e. none of the above
22. Which of the following securities are commercial banks permitted to underwrite under the Glass-Steagall Act?

a. government bonds
b. corporate bonds
c. municipal revenue bonds
d. money market mutual fund shares

23. Which of the following services can a nonbank bank offer?
    a. accepting deposits from the public
    b. making consumer loans
    c. either (a) or (b)
    d. both (a) and (b)

chapter 10

International Banking

Central Themes and Major Points

The chapter presents a general introduction to international banking. This includes the banking activities—that is, deposit-taking and loan-making—of American banks, which are conducted abroad through their foreign branches and subsidiaries, such as the London branch of the Bank of America. It also covers the banking activities of foreign banks, which are conducted in the United States through their branches and subsidiaries. For example, the Union Bank of Los Angeles is British-owned. Finally, international banking also refers to those activities of American banks conducted in the United States and involving international finance. These international operations are carried out through so-called *Edge Act corporations* and, more recently, through what are known as *International Banking Facilities*.

The chapter also introduces the *Eurodollar* and *Eurobond* markets. Although these markets get their names from Europe, where they originated, they now have much broader meaning. A Eurodollar is created when an account is held anywhere outside the United States but is still denominated in dollars. Eurobonds are bonds sold outside the borrowing company's country but still denominated in the home country's currency for interest and principal payments. These markets have played an important role in the globalization of money and capital markets.

The chapter concludes with a discussion of two recent issues. The first is the debt crisis that revolved around loans to developing countries in the 1980s. Although the worst of the crisis appears to have passed, largely because of the work of the International Monetary Fund, it will have an impact on bank behavior for many years to come. The second issue is economic union in Western Europe. Western Europe has set a course toward establishing a single currency and a single central bank. The result of this process is still evolving, but the implications for world trade are very significant.

New Terms

Define and/or explain the following terms introduced in this chapter:

International banking	Facilities (IBFs)
Edge Act corporations	International Banking
branch	Act of 1978
subsidiary	Recycling of
representative office	petrodollars
agency	International
Eurodollars	Monetary Fund†
Eurobonds	European Currency
"Shell" branches	Unit (ECU)
International Banking	

†More on this term in Chapter 34.

Essay Questions and Problems

1. What are the major reasons behind the rapid growth in the number of American banks with

branches and subsidiaries abroad over the last twenty-five years?

2. Describe the organizational options available to a foreign bank contemplating doing business in the United States. Which of the options would be the most cautious? Which would be the most bold?

3. **Eurodollars** This chapter introduced the term Eurodollars. Answer the following questions.
   a. What are Eurodollars?
   b. How are Eurodollars created?
   c. Why did Regulation Q and tax considerations have a great deal to do with the growth of Eurodollars?
   d. Why would anyone want to hold Eurodollars?
   e. It is said that Eurodollars have become an integral and accepted part of overall global bank asset and liability management. Explain.
   f. How can Eurodollars partially offset a restrictive Federal Reserve monetary policy?

4. **Eurobonds** Who are the major borrowers in the Eurobond market? Why are American companies attracted to this market?

5. **International Banking Facilities (IBFs)** This chapter introduced the term IBFs in the context of international banking and finance. Answer the following questions.
   a. What are IBFs?
   b. When and why were they created?
   c. Explain their phenomenal early growth.
   d. Under what terms are banks allowed to open IBFs?
   e. Compare IBFs to Edge Act corporations as a means to conduct international banking operations.

6. **International Banking Act of 1978** The activities of foreign banks in the United States are governed by the International Banking Act of 1978. Under what conditions were foreign banks allowed to operate in the United States prior to this Act and what changes did the Act introduce?

7. **International debt problem** What is the origin of the current international debt problem? What role did American banks play after the increase in the price of oil in 1973–74 and again in 1979–80? How did U.S. banks respond to their growing risk exposure?

SELF-TESTS

Completion Questions

Complete each of the following statements by entering the missing words and/or choosing the best alternative proposed.

1. Domestic _____ of U.S. banks which engage strictly in

   international activities are known as _____

   _____.

2. *(McFadden Act/Edge Act)* corporations are located *(abroad/in the United States)*

   and are exempt from the *(McFadden Act's/Edge Act's)* prohibition against inter-

   state *(banking/branching)*.

3. _____ deposits are deposits denominated in U.S. dollars

   and held in banks located _____.

4. Eurodollars are created when a *(dollar/foreign currency)* deposit is transferred

   from _____ to _____

   _____ and is kept there in _____

   _____.

5. So-called _____ branches are primarily bookkeeping

operations, with fund-raising and lending decisions made in the banks' head

offices in _____.

6. A bond sold in France by a U.S. corporation with interest and principal paid in

dollars is an example of a _____.

7. Foreign banks operate in the United States through four main organizational

forms. These are _____, _____,

_____, and _____

_____.

8. The operations of foreign banks (*in the United States/abroad*) are governed by the

_____

_____ of 1978.

9. The nations of Western Europe are developing plans to move toward a single

_____, with a single _____

used for payments and a single _____

_____ to conduct monetary policy.

True and False Questions

For each of the following statements, circle the letter T if it is correct or the letter F if it is *partially* or totally incorrect.

T F   1. According to the McFadden Act, American banks can participate in international financing through the so-called McFadden Act corporations. These are subsidiaries of U.S. banks that can engage in international banking operations anywhere in the United States.

T F   2. Financing trade with foreign countries would be considered an international banking operation, and a bank that wishes to engage in this activity would be allowed to do so anywhere in the United States, according to the International Banking Act of 1978.

T F   3. Contrary to the thriving activities of American banks abroad, foreign banks do not play a significant role in the United States.

T F   4. Some of the largest banks in the United States are foreign-owned.

T F   5. Foreign banks do business in the United States exclusively through branches or representative offices.

T F   6. Until 1978, foreign banks operating in the United States were largely unregulated. Since then their activities have been governed by the International Banking Act of 1978.

T F   7. The International Banking Act of 1978 has brought foreign banks under essentially the same federal regulations that apply to domestic banks.

T F   8. The Eurodollar market has been a major force behind the movement toward the international integration of domestic banking systems and financial markets.

T F   9. A Eurodollar is a dollar issued by the European branch of a Federal Reserve bank.

T F   10. Eurodollars are created when individuals with dollars deposited in American banks transfer some or all of these dollars to a foreign bank.

T F   11. Today, Eurodollars are considered an integral and accepted part of a bank's asset and liability management.

T F   12. The preeminence of London as the heart of the Eurodollar market is best explained by the fact that it is a tax haven with almost zero taxation and practically no regulations.

T F   13. A so-called shell branch is a subsidiary of an American bank established abroad for the purpose of conducting covert operations.

T F   14. Only private borrowers and lenders participate in the Eurobond market.

T F   15. International Banking Facilities are

essentially bookkeeping operations of American banks that are treated by the Federal Reserve as though they were foreign branches of American banks.

T F 16. The services offered by International Banking Facilities are not available to domestic residents.

T F 17. Although IBFs were created in response to an urgent need for such facilities by American banks, they have been slow to take off. However, they are expected to be quite successful in the near future.

T F 18. The International Monetary Fund has played only a minor role in managing the international debt problem of less developed countries.

T F 19. A number of U.S. banks responded to the international debt problem by adding reserves and shoring up capital.

T F 20. The European Currency Unit currently exists only in the abstract.

T F 21. The financial press lists a daily value quotation for the European Currency Unit.

Multiple-Choice Questions

Answer the following multiple-choice questions by circling the best alternative.

1. In 1960 the number of American banks with branches abroad was only eight. By 1992 this number had risen to approximately
   a. 2,000
   b. 100
   c. 20
   d. none of the above

2. The expansion of American banks into foreign countries can be explained by
   a. the rapid growth of international trade over the last twenty-five years
   b. the increase in the number of American multinational corporations over the last two decades
   c. the ability of American banks to serve American business abroad better than foreign banks
   d. the imposition of Regulation Q interest rate ceilings on large-size CDs in the 1960s
   e. all of the above

3. An Edge Act corporation is
   a. a subsidiary of a foreign bank located in the United States that is allowed to compete with American banks in domestic banking operations.
   b. a subsidiary of an American bank located abroad to help U.S. multinational corporations conduct their foreign business
   c. a subsidiary of an American bank engaged in international banking operations and located in the United Staes
   d. none of the above

4. Which of the following banks is foreign-owned?
   a. The Bank of America
   b. The Union Bank of Los Angeles
   c. Citibank
   d. Continental Bank
   e. Chase Manhattan

5. Foreign banks do business in the United States through
   a. branches of the parent bank
   b. subsidiaries of the parent bank
   c. agencies of the parent bank
   d. representative offices
   e. all of the above

6. The difference between an agency and a representative office of a foreign bank is that
   a. the former cannot accept deposits but the latter can
   b. the former cannot make loans but the latter can
   c. the former can accept deposits but the latter cannot
   d. the former can make loans but the latter cannot
   e. the former can make loans and accept deposits but the latter cannot

7. According to the International Banking Act of 1978, foreign banks
   a. do not have to hold reserves but must comply with all other laws and regulations to which domestic banks are subject
   b. must comply with essentially the same laws and regulations that apply to domestic banks
   c. with the exception of being able to branch across state lines, must comply with the same laws and regulations that apply to domestic banks.

8. In the 1960s, European banks were able to offer more attractive yields than American banks on deposits denominated in U.S. dollars because these banks
   a. did not have to comply with regulations setting ceilings on interest rates
   b. were more competitive and better managed than American banks
   c. did not have to hold as much required reserves against deposits as did American banks

d. were able to lend funds in the international money markets at higher rates than American banks.

e. both (a) and (c)

9. Which of the following would be considered a Eurodollar?

   a. a U.S. dollar in a bank outside the United States

   b. a U.S. dollar held as an international reserve asset by a foreign central bank

   c. a Federal Reserve note (a dollar bill) in the pocket of a tourist visiting Europe

   d. a unit of new currency worth one dollar which will soon be used by all the European countries that are members of the Common Market

   e. none of the above

10. Which of the following factors have contributed to the growth of Eurodollars?

    a. the establishment of Edge Act corporations

    b. the opening of International Banking Facilities

    c. interest-rate ceiling on deposits in U.S. banks (Regulation Q)

    d. increased international capital movements

    e. both (a) and (c)

11. Favored locations for the establishment of shell branches by American banks include

    a. the Bahamas and the Cayman Islands

    b. Paris and Tokyo

    c. Cuba and Jamaica

    d. Aruba and Martinique

    e. none of the above

12. The so-called shell branches of American banks are

    a. subsidiaries of these banks established in some Caribbean islands

    b. branches of these banks established under the Edge Act to allow them to conduct international banking operations

    c. primarily bookkeeping operations established in countries with almost zero taxation and practically no regulation

    d. established abroad to conduct legal but covert operations

    e. both (a) and (b)

13. The Eurobond market is often preferred by American corporations because

    a. interest rates are higher

    b. they can avoid Regulation Q

    c. it is a risk-free market

    d. it has few regulations

14. An International Banking Facility is

    a. a foreign branch of an American bank

    b. an Edge Act corporation

    c. a branch of an American bank that operates as a shell branch but is located in the United States

    d. a bank involved in Eurodollars—making loans and taking deposits that are denominated in U.S. dollars but booked outside the United States

    e. none of the above

15. Offshore transactions of American banks are transactions that

    a. are free from domestic regulations

    b. are not subject to reserve requirements

    c. do not necessitate deposit insurance assessments

    d. are exempt from interest rate ceilings

    e. all of the above

16. Which of the following *cannot* use the services offered by International Banking Facilities?

    a. domestic residents

    b. foreign subsidiaries of American multinationals

    c. foreign-based customers

    d. central banks of foreign countries

    e. both (a) and (d)

17. After the rise in the price of oil in 1973–74 and again in 1979–80, American banks

    a. recycled petrodollars

    b. behaved as intermediaries between OPEC countries and deficit nations

    c. lent funds to third world countries

    d. all of the above

18. Debt restructuring and rescheduling refer to

    a. a change in the terms and conditions of a loan including the lengthening of the period of time over which the loan will be repaid

    b. a modification of banks' capital structure

    c. the recycling of petrodollars

    d. both (a) and (b)

19. Which of the following currencies are included in the ECU?

    a. the Swiss franc

    b. the U.S. dollar

    c. the Italian lira

    d. all of the above.

20. ECUs are currently used for

    a. transactions between Western European governments

    b. transactions in the Eurobond market

    c. retail purchases throughout western Europe

    d. all of the above

chapter 11

Financial Innovation

Central Themes and Major Points

Chapter 3 provided a survey of the many financial instruments now available in the financial markets. Several of these did not exist a few years ago. We have also seen in Chapters 4 and 9 that many traditional financial institutions have changed and are still in the process of changing.

What are the causes of all these innovations that have swept through the financial system over the recent past? And why did they happen at this particular moment in the history of the financial system? This chapter provides answers to these questions. Several factors that can explain financial innovation are identified and discussed. Among these are (1) excessive regulation, (2) high inflation rates, (3) wide interest rate fluctuations, (4) a favorable legislative and political climate, (5) technological progress, and (6) a demand from the public for innovative institutions, products, and markets.

New Terms

Define and/or explain the following terms introduced in this chapter:

Financial innovations	Floating-rate loans
Financial-services industry	Individual Retirement Accounts (IRAs)
Fixed-rate loans	Keogh Accounts

Essay Questions and Problems

1. **The process of financial innovation** Over the past fifteen years, innovations have been introduced in the financial system at an increasing pace.
   a. What factors explain the birth of innovative products, markets, and institutions?
   b. Why are these innovations occurring at this particular moment in the history of the U.S. financial system and not earlier?
   c. What are the benefits brought about by these innovations? Do innovations have negative side effects?

*2. **Zero-coupon bonds and interest-rate risk**
   Suppose the government issued today two bonds that will mature exactly two years from now. Both bonds (Bond A and Bond B) are issued at $1,000. Bond A is a zero-coupon bond. It can be purchased today for $1,000. Two years from now it will mature and the holders of this bond will get back $1,210. No coupon payments are made on this bond. Bond B is a coupon security with a coupon rate of 10 percent and a face value (or principal) of $1,000. It can be purchased today for $1,000 (the same price as Bond A). A year from now it will pay its first coupon of $100 (10 percent of $1,000). Two years from now it will pay its second and last coupon

of $100, and holders will get back the $1,000 face value. Answer the following questions.

a. What is the return on the zero-coupon bond (Bond A) if held to maturity? (That is, what will an investor earn if he or she purchases this bond for $1,000, holds it for two years, and receives $1,210 at the end of the second year?) Note that $(1 + 10\%)^2 = 1.21$.

b. What is the return on the 10 percent coupon bond (Bond B) if held to maturity, *assuming that a 10 percent interest rate will prevail over the second year?* (In other words, the first coupon payment of $100 received at the end of the first year can be reinvested over the second year at 10 percent.)

c. What is the return on the zero-coupon bond (Bond A) if held to maturity, *assuming that the interest rate will drop to 6 percent in year two?* Is it different from the return you found in your answer to question a?

d. What is the return on the 10 percent coupon bond (Bond B) if held to maturity, assuming that the interest rate will drop to 6 percent in year two? Is it different from the return you found in your answer to question b? (In other words, the first coupon payment of $100 received at the end of the first year can be reinvested over the second year at 6 percent.)

e. Compare your answer to question c with your answer to question d. What can you conclude regarding the risk of these two bonds?

f. Answer questions c, d, and e assuming that the interest rate will rise to 15 percent in year two.

3. **Regulatory Philosophy**

a. Describe the trade-offs confronted by regulators attempting to achieve both safety and flexibility in the financial system.

b. In which direction has regulatory philosophy moved in recent years?

c. What have been the costs and benefits of moving in this direction?

4. What groups in society have not been affected by innovations in the financial system? Are there those who have been adversely affected?

SELF-TEST

Completion Questions

Complete each of the following statements by entering the missing words and/or choosing the best alternative proposed.

1. Financial innovation has spawned new financial institutions such as _____
   _____.

2. Financial innovation has given rise to new financial markets such as the financial _____ market and the financial _____ market.

3. Financial innovation has given birth to new financial products such as _____
   _____
   _____ accounts.

4. Financial innovation is often a response to excessively constricting _____
   _____. For example, money market _____ would probably never have come into existence if it hadn't been for _____.

5. The _____
   _____ pass-through program was inaugurated by the _____
   _____.

This program successfully increased the _____

of mortgages.

6. _____ and _____

_____ are *(compulsory/voluntary)* retirement funds available to

individuals.

7. Under specific conditions, contributions to the funds mentioned in the question

immediately above are _____ from taxable income and

the income received from these funds is *(exempt/deferred)* from _____

_____ until the owner actually retires.

8. In the field of finance there has always been a special conflict between _____

_____ and _____.

9. Recently, many stock market firms have acquired *(large/small)* banks and then

converted them into _____.

10. Technological progress has given birth to many innovations in the field of

finance such as _____

machines and _____ cards.

True and False Questions

For each of the following statements, circle the letter T if it is correct or the letter F if it is *partially* or *totally* incorrect.

T   F   1. Financial innovation refers to the process that gives birth to new financial institutions, markets, and products.

T   F   2. Rapid financial innovation has been a characteristic of the U.S. financial system since the end of World War II.

T   F   3. Recent government regulations enforced by the Board of Governors of the Federal Reserve as well as several government agencies such as the Securities and Exchange Commission have slowed down significantly the rapid pace of financial innovation in the United States.

T   F   4. Floating-rate mortgages shift interest-rate risk from borrowers to lenders.

T   F   5. There exist today new financial instruments that allow investors to buy or sell the entire market rather than just individual securities. These are financial futures and options written against stock market indexes.

T   F   6. Spurred by the trend toward financial innovation that now characterizes the U.S. financial system, some large banks and insurance companies merged to create a new and highly sophisticated financial-services industry.

T   F   7. Ginnie Mae was established to purchase the mortgages of failed savings and loan associations.

T   F   8. In financial regulation there has always been a conflict between safety and flexibility.

T   F   9. Historically, U.S. financial regulators have erred on the side of flexibility.

T   F   10. Technological progress has had a major impact in the field of finance. Without it, fast and inexpensive transfers of funds would have been impossible.

T   F   11. Innovations in the payments system have had little impact on some groups in society.

Multiple-Choice Questions

Answer the following multiple-choice questions by circling the best alternative.

1. In the 1970s small savers were unable to earn open market interest rates on their money because
   a. the Federal Reserve imposed a minimum rate of interest on bank deposits

b. of high minimum denominations on most negotiable money market instruments

c. the U.S. Treasury raised the maximum denomination of its bills

d. all of the above

2. Which of the following financial products is *not* an instrument that allows banks to raise funds in order to satisfy profitable loan opportunities?

a. negotiable certificates of deposit

b. Eurodollar deposits

c. money market deposit accounts

d. money market mutual fund shares

3. Which of the following items is *not* considered to be a significant factor underlying financial innovation?

a. wide fluctuations in the level of interest rates

b. the country's saving rate (defined as the difference between disposable income and consumption divided by GDP)

c. uncertainty about the future rate of inflation

d. constricting regulation of the financial system

4. During the 1980s, a large number of savings banks have found themselves on the brink of bankruptcy because

a. the average rate of return on their portfolio of mortgages exceeded the average rate they were paying to retain deposits

b. of the deceleration in the rate of inflation, which raised interest rate uncertainty

c. long-term rates exceeded, on average, rates on short-term deposits, thus creating a dangerous interest-rate gap for savings institutions

d. none of the above

5. To protect themselves against fluctuating interest rates, financial institutions began to make loans with

a. variable rates of interest

b. longer maturity

c. higher rates of interest

d. all of the above

6. Which of the following financial instruments help reduce (or eliminate) interest-rate risk?

a. zero-coupon bonds

b. financial futures contracts

c. floating-rate notes

d. all of the above

e. only (a) and (b)

7. Zero-coupon bonds can be used to eliminate the risk resulting from wide fluctuations in interest rates because

a. they do not make periodic interest payments

b. they have very long maturities

c. their yield rises with the rate of inflation

d. their yield fluctuates in parallel with the market conditions

e. none of the above

8. Financial instruments that were created in response to constricting governmental regulation include

a. Individual Retirement Accounts (IRAs)

b. Keogh Accounts

c. mortgage-backed pass-through securities

d. both (a) and (b)

e. none of the above

9. In recent years regulators of the U.S. banking system have shifted emphasis toward greater

a. safety

b. equity

b. government control

c. flexibility

10. Supporters of further financial deregulation argue that the private sector is

a. the best provider of services to low-income groups

b. less risky than the public sector

c. better able to cope with economic change

d. risk-free

11. The major cost to the financial system of excessive regulation is

a. increased risk

b. high inflation

c. high interest rates

d. reduced flexibility

12. An example of the potential costs of financial deregulation can be seen in the

a. development of zero-coupon bonds

b. falling overall saving rate

c. reduced flexibility of bank managers

d. savings and loan crisis

13. Groups who frequently do not use checks or deal with banks are:

a. recent immigrants

b. inner city minorities

c. the poor elderly

d. all of the above

chapter 12

The Payments System

Central Themes and Major Points

This chapter begins with a brief report on the modern evolution of money (the medium of exchange) from gold coins to demand deposits transferred by means of checks. This evolution has yet to reach its final stage. Demand deposits transferred by checks are not the ultimate payments system. Various electronic funds transfer systems are surveyed.

The authors speculate on what tomorrow's payment mechanisms may be and discuss the implications for the performance of financial markets and the conduct of economic policy.

New Terms

Define and/or explain the following terms introduced in this chapter:

Payments system
Clearing house
Correspondent balances
Credit cards

Automated teller machines (ATMs)
Fed wire transfer system

Automated clearing houses (ACHs)
Magnetic Ink Character Recognition (MICR)
Clearing House Interbank Payment System (CHIPS)
Society for Worldwide

Interbank Financial Transactions (SWIFT)
Electronic funds transfer systems (EFTs)
Point of sale terminals (POS)

Essay Questions and Problems

1. How are checks cleared in a modern financial system? What role does the Federal Reserve play in the process?
2. What currently available payment mechanisms are making checks obsolete?
3. How would a system based on a "National Ledger" coupled with credit/debit cards work? What are the advantages and disadvantages (dangers?) of such a system?
4. How are the financial markets of tomorrow expected to operate?

SELF-TESTS

Completion Questions

Complete each of the following statements by entering the missing words and/or choosing the best alternative proposed.

1. Monetary exchange is superior to a _____ system.

2. A check is an order to a _____ to _____
_____ funds from one person's account to someone else's.

3. In order to process out-of-town checks, banks maintain checking accounts with each other. These are called _____.

4. _____ is a telecommunications system operated by the Federal Reserve.

5. The _____ network is operated by banks associated with the New York Clearing House, which specializes in _____ _____ transactions.

6. Withdrawal of currency with the use of bank _____ _____ is done through _____ _____ machines.

7. _____ _____ that are connected on-line with banks' computers will allow direct payments for goods and services at *(tellers' windows/checkout counters)*.

True and False Questions

For each of the following statements, circle the letter T if it is correct or the letter F if it is *partially* or totally incorrect.

T F 1. Checks have been the dominant means of payment for the last two centuries.

T F 2. One advantage of using a medium of exchange to consummate transactions is that it cuts down the time needed for exchange.

T F 3. Checks came into use to overcome the costs of consummating a transaction by means of coins and paper currency.

T F 4. Interbank settlement of claims is the major complication in the current check-based payments system.

T F 5. Many of the institutional wrinkles in the current payments system arose in connection with interbank settlement of claims.

T F 6. The oldest institution used to settle interbank claims is the local clearinghouse.

T F 7. Only 10 percent of one's checks are currently collected through the network of correspondent balances.

T F 8. The so-called Bank Wire consists of the Fed wire transfer system and an Interbank communications system. Together they permit corporations and individuals to make "payments by wire" rather than by checks.

T F 9. Both the CHIPS and SWIFT electronic payment systems specialize in international transactions.

T F 10. In 1990, the Fed Wire accounted for less than 0.1 percent of the total value of all payments in the U.S. financial system.

T F 11. One can say that the payments system of today is a mixture of paper, electronics, and plastic.

T F 12. Point of sale terminals are an example of an electronic funds transfer system.

Multiple-Choice Questions

Answer the following multiple-choice questions by circling the best alternative.

1. Monetary exchange is superior to a barter-based system because
   a. it cuts down on the time needed to exchange
   b. it facilitates trade among strangers who can readily identify the medium of exchange
   c. it does not necessitate the existence of a "double" coincidence of needs
   d. all of the above

2. Which of the following *never* served as money in the United States?
   a. gold coins
   b. bank notes

c. paper currency
d. demand deposits
e. none of the above
3. A bank is
a. a medium of exchange
b. money
c. a means to transfer funds among depositors
d. all of the above
e. only (a) and (b)
4. Processing checks drawn against out-of-town banks is facilitated by
a. correspondent balances
b. clearinghouses
c. automated teller machines
d. the Fed wire transfer system
e. none of the above
5. Which of the following would *not* be considered part of an electronic funds transfer system?
a. automated teller machines
b. credit cards
c. point of sale terminals
d. automated clearinghouses
e. the Fed wire transfer system
6. Which of the following electronic systems specializes in international transfers of funds?
a. Bank Wire
b. the CHIPS network
c. the SWIFT network
d. both (b) and (c)
7. Which of the following systems enables checks to be sorted and processed rapidly by machines?
a. the MICR system

b. the CHIPS network
c. the SWIFT network
d. none of the above
8. In terms of total transactions, the Fed Wire and CHIPS account for
a. less than 0.1 percent of the total
b. about 25 percent of the total
c. about 50 percent of the total
d. about 80 percent of the total
9. Direct electronic link-ups between retail stores and customer bank accounts are known as
a. SWIFT systems
b. point of sale terminals
c. CHIPS systems
d. National Ledgers
10. In order to transfer preauthorized regular payments, the Federal Reserve operates
a. the Fed Wire
b. the CHIPS system
c. point of sales terminals
d. automated clearinghouses
11. Which of the following payments is likely to be transferred to the recipient through an ACH?
a. stock dividend payment
b. royalty payment
c. social security payment
d. tax refund
12. Checks are likely to be eliminated by
a. the Fed Wire
b. the SWIFT network
c. the CHIPS network
d. the National Ledger

part III

The Art of Central Banking

chapter 13

Who's in Charge Here?

Central Themes and Major Points

This chapter provides a detailed picture of the Federal Reserve System, an institution created by Congress in 1913 to act as the central bank of the United States. The Federal Reserve System has unique features not found in the central banks of other countries. These features are examined in this chapter.

First, the Federal Reserve's formal structure and functions are fully described, from the *chairman of the Board of Governors* down to member commercial banks.

The fact that the Federal Reserve System is a decentralized institution blending public and private authorities should not be interpreted to mean that no one person or group affiliated with the Federal Reserve has enough power to formulate and direct monetary policy. This chapter tells us where the real power resides within the Federal Reserve and how monetary policy is actually formulated and implemented.

Finally, the chapter raises the issue of how independent the Federal Reserve should be from Congress and the president. The pros and cons of Federal Reserve independence are examined. There is also a discussion of central banks in other countries and how their degree of independence compares with that of the Federal Reserve.

New Terms

Define and/or explain the following terms introduced in this chapter:

Board of Governors
Chairman of the
   Board of Governors
Regional Federal
   Reserve banks
Federal Reserve bank
   presidents

Federal Advisory
   Council
Federal Open Market
   Committee (FOMC)
Bank of England
Swiss National Bank
Deutsche Bundesbank

Essay Questions and Problems

1. Why is the Federal Reserve System often described as a unique institution that blends public and private authorities? Describe the formal structure of the Federal Reserve System and indicate which elements are public and which are private.

2. Compare the role and functions performed by the Federal Reserve when it was initially established in 1913 with its current role and functions.

3. The formal structure of the Federal Reserve System as described in your answer to question 1 does not tell us where the real power lies within the Federal Reserve. Briefly indicate the dominant figures and describe the relative importance of the different bodies that make up the Federal Reserve System.

4. The issue of the Federal Reserve's independence hinges on the relationship between the Federal Reserve and Congress and the relationship between the Federal Reserve and the president. Discuss the nature of the controversies sur-

rounding these two relationships and examine the major arguments in favor of and against Federal Reserve independence.

5. How does the independence of the Federal Reserve compare with that of central banks in other industrial countries?

SELF-TESTS

Completion Questions

Complete each of the following statements by entering the missing words.

1. The central bank of the United States is called the _____

   _____ .

2. The principal spokesman for the central bank is _____

   _____

   _____ .

3. The Federal Reserve is responsible to the _____ and

   was established by it in _____ .

4. The Federal Reserve System consists of the _____

   _____ in Washington, D.C., twelve _____

   _____ , and

   over 5,000 _____ .

5. Open market operations are directed by a body known as the _____

   _____ .

6. Members of the _____

   of the Federal Reserve System are appointed by the _____

   and confirmed by the _____ .

7. The president of a Federal Reserve _____ is appointed

   by the nine _____ .

8. A _____ of a Federal Reserve _____

   can either be elected by _____

   or appointed by _____ .

9. The _____ of

   the _____

   sets (within limits) _____ ,

   reviews and determines the _____ ,

   and directs _____ .

10. Although the Federal Reserve has a _____

    status within the Federal government, its chairman is appointed by the _____

_____ and it is ultimately the creation of _____

_____.

11. Looking at the central banks of other countries, one generally finds that the

more _____ the central bank is from the rest of the

government, the (lower/higher) is the inflation rate.

True and False Questions

For each of the following statements, circle the letter T if it is correct or the letter F if it is *partially* or totally incorrect.

T F 1. The Board of Governors of the Federal Reserve System is made up of five members, one of whom is appointed chairman by Congress.

T F 2. A member of the Board of Governors can serve a fourteen-year term and the chairman serves a four-year term.

T F 3. The president of a regional Federal Reserve Bank is chosen by the member banks operating in that district.

T F 4. No two board members may come from the same Federal Reserve district.

T F 5. Two-thirds of the directors of the Federal Reserve banks are elected by member banks, and the remaining third are appointed by the Board of Governors.

T F 6. Unlike the presidents of the other regional Federal Reserve banks, the president of the Federal Reserve Bank of New York is a permanent member of the Federal Open Market Committee.

T F 7. The term of the chairman of the board of the Federal Reserve System is concurrent with that of the president of the United States.

T F 8. Commercial banks can freely join or leave the Federal Reserve System.

T F 9. The Board of Governors has the final say on reserve requirements and the discount rate.

T F 10. There are twenty-four Federal Reserve banks geographically dispersed throughout the nation.

T F 11. Each Federal Reserve bank has seven directors, and the Board of Governors has nine members.

T F 12. The chairman of the Federal Open Market Committee is always the President of the Federal Reserve Bank of New York.

T F 13. The annual salary of the chairman of the Board of Governors of the Federal Reserve System is larger than the annual salary of any president of a regional Federal Reserve Bank.

T F 14. Coordination between the different bodies responsible for economic policy is achieved through regular meetings held by the president with the chairman of the Board of Governors, the secretary of the Treasury, and the chairman of the Council of Economic Advisors.

T F 15. The Federal Reserve is responsible mainly to member commercial banks.

T F 16. No woman has ever been a member of the Board of Governors of the Federal Reserve System.

T F 17. Federal Reserve banks are owned by private citizens.

T F 18. The directors of each Federal Reserve bank select one person to serve on the Federal Advisory Council, which makes recommendations regarding the conduct of monetary policy.

T F 19. The Board of Governors of the Federal Reserve System is responsible to the president, while the Federal Open Market Committee is responsible to Congress.

T F 20. Both the ownership and control of the twelve Federal Reserve banks are in the hands of the member banks of the Federal Reserve System.

T F 21. Decisions with respect to the major tools of monetary control—open market operations, reserve requirements, and the discount rate—are all made exclusively by the Federal Reserve Board.

T F 22. The case for an "independent central bank" is supported by the need for coordination of monetary and fiscal policies.

T F 23. A glaring weakness in the present structure of the Federal Reserve System is that commercial banks become subject to Federal Reserve regulation as members of the system, but they own the Federal Reserve banks that do the regulating.

T F 24. The sole purpose of an *independent* monetary authority is to forestall the asserted natural propensity of governments to resort to inflation.

T F 25. If the Federal Reserve is to continue to exercise a high degree of independence in its conduct of monetary policy, it must continue to be free of standard government audits and free of congressional appropriations to finance itself.

T F 26. A good answer to the question of who determines monetary policy in the Federal Reserve System is that the Board of Governors and the twelve Federal Reserve banks have approximately equal voices in this area.

T F 27. Compared with the central bank in most other countries, the Federal Reserve is not very independent from the rest of government.

T F 28. The Bank of Japan is the best example of a highly independent central bank.

Multiple-Choice Questions

Answer the following multiple-choice questions by circling the best alternative.

1. Members of the Board of Governors of the Federal Reserve System are
   a. elected by the people
   b. appointed by the president of the United States
   c. appointed by the Congress of the United States
   d. chosen by the presidents of the twelve district Federal Reserve banks
2. The funds required to finance the operation of the Board of Governors of the Federal Reserve System come from
   a. the earnings of the twelve regional Federal Reserve banks
   b. the federal government
   c. the General Accounting Office
   d. contributions from the public
3. Federal Reserve banks are owned by
   a. the U.S. government
   b. the Board of Governors of the Federal Reserve System
   c. member commercial banks
   d. wealthy private citizens

4. The function of the Federal Advisory Council is to
   a. direct open market operations
   b. conduct monetary policy
   c. make recommendations regarding which commercial banks should become members of the Federal Reserve System
   d. none of the above
   e. both (a) and (b)
5. The implementation of monetary policy is under the authority of
   a. the Board of Governors of the Federal Reserve System
   b. the Federal Advisory Council
   c. the Federal Open Market Committee
   d. all of the above
   e. only (a) and (c)
6. Which of the following cities does not have a district Federal Reserve Bank?
   a. New York
   b. Washington
   c. Chicago
   d. San Francisco
7. The Federal Open Market Committee is composed of
   a. the members of the Board of Governors of the Federal Reserve System
   b. some of the presidents of the twelve Federal Reserve banks
   c. the Comptroller of the Currency
   d. all of the above
   e. only (a) and (b)
8. The chairman of the Board of Governors of the Federal Reserve System plays many roles, *except*
   a. implementing open market operations
   b. negotiating with Congress
   c. advising the president of the United States
   d. chairing the FOMC
9. Which of the following statements about the Federal Reserve System is *incorrect?*
   a. It is the central bank of the United States.
   b. It was created by an Act of Congress in 1913.
   c. It is a complex structure headed by a Board of Governors in Washington.
   d. It is supervised by the secretary of the Treasury.
10. The Federal Reserve has the authority to
    a. change the reserve requirement ratio within limits set by Congress
    b. change the discount rate
    c. set the legal maximum interest rate a bank can pay its depositors
    d. all of the above
    e. only (a) and (b)

11. The most powerful individual within the Federal Reserve System is
    a. the president of the Federal Reserve Bank of New York
    b. the chairman of the Board of Governors
    c. the account manager at the Federal Reserve Bank of New York
    d. (a) and (b) are equally powerful
12. Some of the members of the Federal Open Market Committee have been originally appointed or elected by
    a. the president of the United States
    b. the directors of the district Federal Reserve banks
    c. the Congress of the United States
    d. all of the above
    e. only (a) and (b)
13. Which of the following bodies has *no* direct responsibility in the formulation of economic policy?
    a. the Board of Governors of the Federal Reserve System
    b. the secretary of the Treasury
    c. the Board of Directors of the Federal Reserve banks
    d. the chairman of the Council of Economic Advisors
14. Monetary authority should be dissociated from the Treasury because
    a. the Treasury has fiscal authority and should not be burdened with an additional responsibility
    b. monetary stability may be sacrificed to the government's revenue needs
    c. the Treasury would receive most of the income earned by the district Federal Reserve banks
    d. a division of authority is a more efficient way of conducting economic policy
15. The Board of Governors of the Federal Reserve System is located in

    a. New York
    b. Washington
    c. Chicago
    d. none of the above
16. Which of the following Federal Reserve bodies has the final say in the setting of the discount rate?
    a. the Federal Open Market Committee
    b. the Board of Governors
    c. the Federal Reserve banks
    d. (b) and (c) have an equal say in this matter
17. The U.S. Congress has given the Federal Reserve
    a. a broad mandate to conduct monetary policy
    b. a tight budget to carry out its many functions
    c. the power to bypass banking laws when conditions warrant
    d. strict guidelines for money supply growth
18. The most important reason for maintaining Federal Reserve independence from the executive branch is to
    a. restrain inflationary pressures
    b. keep taxes down
    c. keep interest rates down
    d. reduce bank failures
19. Two of the most independent central banks in the world can be found in Germany and
    a. Switzerland
    b. Italy
    c. Great Britain
    d. Japan
20. In most democracies, the public appears to be most concerned about
    a. inflation
    b. unemployment
    c. budget deficits
    d. foreign exchange rates

chapter 14

Bank Reserves and the Money Supply

Central Themes and Major Points

This chapter shows how banks in conjunction with and under the supervision of the Federal Reserve can create money in the form of demand deposits when they either extend loans to or buy bonds from the public. The business of banking is illustrated with an example describing the various steps required to set up a bank. Changes in the bank's *balance sheet (T-accounts)* are used to keep track of the transactions undertaken by the bank.

The link between banks and the Federal Reserve is provided by *bank reserves,* which consist of currency in bank *vaults* and deposits made by banks in their Federal Reserve bank. These reserves perform various functions, including providing the banking system with a means of clearing checks between banks. Reserves perform another important function: they are nothing less than the stuff out of which banks create money in the form of demand deposits.

First, the process of *deposit expansion* is examined from the point of view of a single bank and then from the point of view of the whole banking system. It is shown that there is a fundamental difference between the two. Finally, the process of *deposit contraction* is investigated. Deposits will shrink—money will vanish—when loans previously extended by banks are repaid or when banks sell bonds to the public.

Three major points are made in this chapter:

1. *Check collection and clearing* between banks does not affect the total volume of reserves within the banking system.
2. A single bank cannot safely lend or buy securities in an amount greater than its *excess reserves.*
3. The banking system can create deposits up to a *multiple* of the system's excess reserves. In the absence of savings and time deposits and assuming no cash deposits or withdrawals by the public, the demand deposit *multiplier* is equal to the reciprocal of the *reserve requirement ratio* against demand deposits.

This is an important and somewhat difficult chapter. Make sure you solve all the numerical problems correctly before proceeding to the Self-Tests section.

The Appendix is devoted to a reexamination of the connection between reserves and the money supply. In the chapter it is shown that the value of the deposit multiplier is simply the reciprocal of the reserve requirement ratio against demand deposits. This is correct only if we ignore three possible "real-world" complications. These are: (1) the public may withdraw part of the additional demand deposits created by banks to hold in the form of currency; (2) the public may transfer part of the additional demand deposits created by banks into savings and time deposits at banks; and (3) the banks may not use the full amount of their available excess reserves to expand their loans and/or buy securities.

It is shown that any one of these three complications will reduce the value of the deposit multiplier.

New Terms

Define and/or explain the following terms introduced in this chapter:

Balance sheets:	Inter-District
Assets	Settlement Fund
Liabilities	Excess reserves
Net worth	Check collection
T-accounts	Bank loans
Legal reserves	Earning assets
Vault cash	Deposit expansion
Cash items in process	Deposit multiplier
of collection	A loaned up banking
Reserve requirement	system
ratio	Deficiency in reserves
Required reserves	Deposit contraction

The following terms are from the Appendix to this chapter:

Time and savings	Currency/demand
deposits/demand	deposits ratio
deposits ratio	Monetary base
Idle excess reserves	

Essay Questions and Problems

Note: In the problems that follow, in this and all other chapters, we will say that the banking system is *loaned up* or *in equilibrium* if total reserves held are equal to required reserves. That is, no excess reserves or deficiencies exist. In this case the banking system cannot extend further loans or purchase additional securities without acquiring additional reserves. It is said to be loaned up or in equilibrium.

1. **The process of check collection**   Explain how checks are collected between two member banks in different cities but within the same Federal Reserve district. What would happen if the two member banks were in different Federal Reserve districts? What if one of the two banks were not a member of the Federal Reserve System?

2. **The single bank versus the banking system**   There are many differences between a single bank and the banking system as a whole. The following questions are related to this issue.

   a. Why can't an individual bank safely lend or buy bonds in an amount exceeding its available excess reserves? Why can the banking system as a whole do so?

   b. The premise upon which our banking system is based is that all depositors will not withdraw all their money from banks at the same time. Explain this statement in light of the fact that the banking system can lend an amount equal to the multiple of its reserves.

   *c. An individual bank experiences a reserve deficiency. What are the various alternatives available to the bank to eliminate its reserve deficiency? If, instead, we consider the banking system as a whole experiencing a deficiency, are all the alternatives available to the single bank also available to the banking system?

*3. **Bank reserves**   What are the functions performed by bank reserves held in the form of deposits at the Federal Reserve? What is the function of bank reserves held in the form of vault cash?

*4. **Excess reserves and reserve deficiencies**   Why does a reserve deficiency in the banking system automatically lead to a deposit contraction, whereas the existence of excess reserves does not guarantee an expansion of deposits? Discuss the implication of this asymmetrical behavior for the implication of monetary policy.

*5. **Cash items in process of collection**   Explain why "cash items in process of collection" should be subtracted from total demand deposits outstanding when one is measuring the money supply.

*6. **Deposit contraction versus deposit expansion**   The mechanics of deposit contraction are the opposite of those of deposit expansion. There are, however, two important differences between the two mechanisms. What are they?

*7. **Changes in a bank's balance sheet**   Indicate how the transactions listed below affect the balance sheets of the Federal Reserve, the commercial banking system, and the nonbank public. For example, the effect of a cash withdrawal of $10 from the banking system would be shown as:

Federal Reserve

assets	liabilities
0 (no change)	0 (no change)

Banking System

assets	liabilities
Reserves −10	Deposits −10

Nonbank Public

assets	liabilities
Cash +10 Deposits −10	0 (no change)

a. The banking system buys $10 million of bonds from an insurance company.

b. The banking system borrows $1 million from the Federal Reserve.

c. Mr. Williams deposits $100 at his commercial bank.

d. Mrs. Vega borrows $1,000 from her commercial bank.

e. The banking system pays back a $1 million loan to the Federal Reserve.

f. Mr. Chin writes a $20 check to Mr. Williams as a loan.

g. The Federal Reserve credits the account of Bank A by $1 million and simultaneously debits the account of Bank B by $1 million as a result of a $1 million loan extended by Bank B to Bank A.

h. An individual withdraws $100 in currency from his passbook savings account at his mutual savings bank.

i. A corporation writes a $20 million check to buy stocks issued by a newly founded bank.

j. A bank buys a $2 million building from a savings and loan association.

*8. **Money creation by banks** The purpose of this problem is to acquaint you with the manner in which banks create money.

a. *Check clearance*

In the following table you are given par-

tially complete balance sheets for three banks in the Federal Reserve System.

Federal Reserve Bank of New York

Upstate Bank	$200,000
City Bank	250,000

City Bank		**Upstate Bank**	
F.R. Reserves $250,000	A. Jones $100	F.R. Reserves $200,000	B. Jones

You are A. Jones, a student at the City University, and you have an account at City Bank. Your father, B. Jones, who banks at the Upstate Bank, sent you a check for $100, which you deposit to your account.

(1) By means of arrows, show the actual path of the check from the time you make the deposit.

(2) Show on the balance sheets the changes which occur in the items of each bank. Note the items that would change, by how much they would change, and whether they would be decreases (−) or increases (+).

(3) How would your answer to (2) have differed if you had cashed the check at the bank instead of depositing it?

Although the technical aspects are somewhat different if the checks are cleared through local clearinghouses, or if they are cleared between the two Federal Reserve districts, the results properly obtained above are substantially the same.

b. *Bank lending: The case of the individual bank*

Below you are given a simplified balance sheet for a commercial bank. Assume that the reserve requirement for this bank is 20 percent.

Local National Bank

F.R. Reserves	$ 200,000	Demand Deposits	$3,060,000
Gov't Securities	1,100,000	Capital Stock	
Other Securities	300,000	and Surplus	440,000
Loans	1,300,000		
	$3,500,000		$3,500,000

Answer the following questions:

(1) The amount of the required reserves is $ _____

(2) The amount of excess reserves is $ _____

(3) Suppose the Local National Bank now made a business loan of $75,000. (The normal way for such a loan to be made is for the bank to open a checking account for the borrower.) What would the *immediate* effect of this loan be on the balance sheet items shown above? Note the *items* which would change, by how much they would change, and whether they would be decreases (−) or increases (+).

(4) The borrower now uses the full amount of his loan to pay Smith, who deposits it in the Jackson State Bank. What is the effect of check clearance on the Local National Bank's national sheet items?

(5) Draw a *new* balance sheet for the Local National Bank, incorporating the changes caused by the transactions in questions 3 and 4 above.

Local National Bank

---

(6) Returning to the initial figures given above, suppose the bank has expanded its loans by $940,000. This would have increased demand deposits to $4,000,000, so that its reserves would have been just 20 percent of demand deposits, the minimum set by the Fed. This would be a very foolish banking policy. Explain why.

(7) In the initial situation, as the balance sheet originally appeared above, the maximum amount the bank could safely expand its loans is $_____ _____.

(8) If you have done your work carefully and correctly, you have just figured out the "why" of a very important banking principle: *No one bank can expand its demand deposits through increasing its lending by more than the amount of its excess reserves.* Explain in words how you reached this conclusion.

c. *Bank lending: The case of multiple expansion through a banking system*
   Shown below are balance sheets for a very simple system composed of Banks A, B, C, and D.

Bank A	(1)	Bank B	(1)	Bank C	(1)	Bank D	(1)
	(2)		(2)		(2)		(2)
	(3)		(3)		(3)		(3)

Follow these instructions carefully and answer all questions.

(1) Assume Bank A is initially loaned up. It sells $200,000 of its holdings of government securities to the Federal Reserve Bank and receives deposit credit in exchange. Show the changes and their sign in Bank A's balance sheet (1). Bank A's excess reserves are now $ _____.

(2) Bank A sold its government bonds to get reserves with which to increase its loans. Bank A now makes the largest loan consistent with safety to Mr. Jones [see 8b(8)], assuming a 20 percent reserve requirement. Enter the proper balance sheet changes in balance sheet (2). Enter under the column "Increase in Demand Deposits" any change you have shown in demand deposits (that is, the amount of created money) for Bank A.

(3) Mr. Jones writes a check for the full amount of his loan and gives it to Mr. Smith, who deposits it in Bank B. The check is cleared through the Federal Reserve bank. Show the appropriate changes in Bank A's balance sheet (3) and in Bank B's balance sheet (1). Notice what the *net effect* has been for Bank A.

(4) Assume Bank B was loaned up before. It now has excess reserves of _____ _____.

(5) Bank B now makes the largest loan consistent with safety to a Mr. Adams, and then so does Bank C, D, and so on. Repeat for Banks B, C, and D the steps you have performed in two and three above, substituting different borrowers and the proper bank letters.

(6) For the "Increase in Demand Deposits," compute the remaining figures for Banks E–J. The total should approximate $892,625, and if you included enough banks it would equal $1,000,000.

Increase in Demand Deposits

Bank A _____

B _____

C _____

D _____

E _____

F _____

G _____

H _____

I _____

J _____

_____

Total _____

_____

_____

_____

Answer the following questions.

(7) You discovered in part b that one bank could safely increase its demand deposits by no more than the amount of its excess reserves. Here you have seen how *several banks in a system can expand demand deposits by some multiple of the excess reserves.* Explain why this can happen.

(8) What is the relationship between the reserve requirement, the original amount of excess reserves, and the final amount ($1,000,000) of increased money (demand deposits)? Put your answer in words and in an equation.

(9) How would the results have varied in the problem if the reserve requirements had been 25 percent instead of 20 percent? 10 percent instead of 20 percent?

(10) Why do we consider demand deposits "money"? By what process does the banking system manufacture or create money?

(11) This was a very simple example. Suppose that instead of only Bank A gaining excess reserves, each bank had gained excess reserves by the sale of bonds to the Federal Reserve banks as follows: Bank A, $60,000; Bank B, $20,000; Bank C, $80,000; and Bank D, $40,000. How would your final conclusion have varied? Why?

*9. **The banking system's balance sheet, reserves, and deposit expansion** The banking system is initially loaned up (in equilibrium) with $100 billion in demand deposits, $20 billion in reserves, and $80 billion in loans and securities; answer the following questions:

a. Draw the balance sheet of the banking system. Ignore real assets and net worth.

b. What is the volume of required reserves that banks must hold?

c. Determine the reserve requirement ratio against demand deposits as well as the deposit multiplier.

d. The public deposits $1 billion in currency into the banking system.

(1) What is the initial effect of this currency deposit on the money supply (M1)?

(2) What is the effect on banks' total reserves and required reserves?

(3) What is the theoretical maximum expansion in demand deposits the banking system can achieve, and what is the corresponding amount of additional loans the banking system can extend?

(4) What is the theoretical maximum amount of bonds the banking system can purchase from the public, and what is the corresponding expansion in demand deposits?

(5) What is the effect of either (3) or (4) on the money supply?

(6) Draw the balance sheet of the banking system after either (3) or (4) has taken place.

*10. **Currency withdrawal from the banking system** The banking system (BS) is initially loaned up (in equilibrium) with $1,000 billion of demand deposits outstanding. Total reserves held by the BS equal $250 billion. The public withdraws $1 billion in currency from the BS.

a. What is the immediate and direct effect of the cash withdrawal on M1?

b. What is the volume of reserve deficiency created by the cash withdrawal?

c. What contraction in the volume of loans will bring the BS to a position where it is again loaned up (in equilibrium)? Draw the balance sheet of the BS in this case.

d. What is the final effect of the cash withdrawal on M1?

*11. Changes in bank deposits   The banking system is made up of two groups of banks initially in equilibrium (loaned up). Group A has deposits of $100 billion and a reserve requirement of 25 percent. Group B has deposits of $200 billion and a reserve requirement of 15 percent. Assume that the two groups merge and that a uniform reserve requirement of 20 percent is imposed on all banks.

a. What is the volume of total reserves held by banks in groups A and B before the merger? What is the total volume of loans and securities outstanding for each group before the merger?

b. Will the merger affect the money supply? If yes, by how much?

*12. Deposit contraction   The banking system has $19 billion in reserves and $200 billion in demand deposits outstanding. The reserve requirement is 10 percent. Answer the following questions:

a. Is the banking system in equilibrium?

b. How much borrowing from the Federal Reserve will enable the banking system to be in equilibrium? What are the effects of this transaction on deposits outstanding and the size of the money supply?

c. Alternatively, the banking system can return to a position in which it is in equilibrium by selling bonds to the public. What amount of bonds should the banking system sell to achieve this objective? What is the effect on the money supply?

*13. The deposit multiplier revisited

a. What would happen to the value of the deposit multiplier if the public wanted to hold part of any increase in demand deposits in the form of currency and/or if the public transferred part of any increase in demand deposits into time and savings accounts?

b. What are the implications for the Fed's control over the money supply?

*14. Idle excess reserves   Why would an individual bank hold idle excess reserves that do not earn any interest rather than buy securities or extend loans, both of which are earning assets?

*15. The monetary base

a. What is the monetary base?

b. Suppose that the public withdraws or deposits currency from or into the commercial banking system. Will these transactions affect the size of the monetary base?

c. Suppose that the public withdraws or deposits currency from or into thrift institutions. Will these transactions affect the size of the monetary base?

d. Why is it often more convenient to examine the process whereby the Fed absorbs or supplies reserves to the banking system in terms of the monetary base rather than of bank reserves?

*16. The general deposit multiplier   The commercial banking system is initially loaned up. The reserve requirement ratio is 14 percent against demand deposits and 4 percent against savings deposits. The ratio of currency to demand deposits is 30 percent, and the ratio of time deposits to demand deposits is 150 percent. The banking system sells securities to the public in order to pay back a loan of $200 million to the Federal Reserve. Answer the following questions.

a. What is the size of the reserve deficiency created by the loan repayment?

b. What is the value of the deposit multiplier?

c. What contraction in demand deposits will bring the banking system back to a loaned up position?

d. What is the size of the currency inflow into the banking system resulting from the demand deposit contraction?

e. What is the effect of (c) and (d) on the money supply?

f. What is the contraction in time deposits resulting from the demand deposit contraction?

g. What amount of securities does the banking system have to sell the public in order to return to a loaned up position?

h. Draw the balance sheet of the banking system after the deposits have contracted.

17. Assume that reserve requirements equal 0.1 on demand deposits and .05 on time deposits. Further assume that the ratio of currency to demand deposits is equal to 0.2, the ratio of time deposits to demand deposits is 4, and banks hold no excess reserves. What is the demand deposit multiplier? What is the M1 multiplier?

SELF-TESTS

Completion Questions

Complete each of the following statements by entering the missing words and/or choosing the best alternative proposed.

1. Demand deposits are *(assets/liabilities)* of _____ _____ and *(assets/liabilities)* of _____ _____.

2. Reserves are *(assets/liabilities)* of the _____ _____ and *(assets/liabilities)* of _____.

3. Banks can hold their *(reserves/cash)* either in the form of _____ _____ or in the form of _____ _____.

4. When a bank receives a check drawn on another bank, it *(gains/loses)* _____ _____ equal to the _____. The bank on which the check was drawn *(gains/loses)* _____ equal to the _____ _____.

5. Excess reserves are equal to the difference between _____ _____ and _____ _____.

6. Control over bank _____ gives the _____ _____ considerable power over the _____ _____ supply.

7. The banking system can create _____ deposits up to a _____ of an original injection of _____.

8. The simple deposit multiplier is equal to _____ _____.

9. Check _____ and _____ do not affect the total volume of reserves within the banking system.

10. A single bank can safely lend up to _____ _____.

    The following questions are based on the Appendix to this chapter:

11. The monetary _____ is defined as the sum of _____ _____ and _____ _____.

12. Complications such as _____

_____ , _____

_____ , and _____

_____ will

(decrease/increase) the value of the _____

_____ multiplier ($1/r_{dd}$).

True and False Questions

For each of the following statements, circle the letter T if it is correct or the letter F if it is *partially* or totally incorrect.

T   F   1. Demand deposits are the major asset of banks.

T   F   2. Only member banks are permitted to have deposits with the Federal Reserve Banks.

T   F   3. The value of the reserve requirement ratio is imposed by the Board of Governors of the Federal Reserve.

T   F   4. A bank's earning assets consist of its loans outstanding and its portfolio of securities.

T   F   5. Cash in the vault of thrift institutions is part of their total reserves.

T   F   6. Cash items in process of collection are assets to banks.

T   F   7. The Federal Reserve can control the reserve position of each individual bank in the system.

T   F   8. The total volume of reserves available to the banking system is under the complete control of the Federal Reserve.

T   F   9. When banks borrow from the Federal Reserve banks, their total reserves increase by the amount of the borrowing.

T   F   10. Reserves are liabilities of the Federal Reserve banks and assets of banks.

T   F   11. A cash outflow from banks decreases their reserves.

T   F   12. When a bank receives a check drawn on another bank, it loses reserves equal to the amount of the check.

T   F   13. A single bank can lend up to a multiple of its excess reserves and no more.

T   F   14. The simple deposit expansion multiplier is equal to the reciprocal of the reserve requirement ratio.

T   F   15. When the banking system experiences a reserve deficiency, the maximum contraction in demand deposits can conceivably occur in a single bank.

T   F   16. Reserves held by banks consist of cash items in process of collection and deposits with the Federal Reserve banks.

T   F   17. Nonmember banks are required to hold deposits with the Federal Reserve banks only to help check collection.

T   F   18. The reserve requirement ratio equals demand deposits outstanding divided by required reserves.

T   F   19. The banking system can create demand deposits up to a multiple of an original injection of excess reserves.

T   F   20. Member banks in different Federal Reserve Districts have their reserve positions settled up through the Inter-District Settlement Fund in Washington, D.C.

T   F   21. Required reserves can be changed within limits by the Federal Reserve without getting the approval of Congress.

T   F   22. The maximum expansion of bank deposits as a result of an injection of excess reserves can occur in a single bank.

T   F   23. Banks create money as a by-product of their lending activities.

T   F   24. When total reserves are equal to required reserves, the banking system cannot extend loans anymore.

T   F   25. Required reserves are obtained by multiplying total reserves by the reserve requirement.

T   F   26. The most important asset of banks is their portfolio of loans and securities.

T   F   27. Banks hold reserves in the form of vault cash only because they must comply with Federal Reserve regulations.

T   F   28. If Bank A receives from its depositors $1 million in checks drawn on other banks, there is an increase of $1 million in reserves for both Bank A and for all banks combined.

T F 29. In the check collection process, $5 million in Bank A's balance sheet item "cash items in process of collection" becomes $5 million of demand deposits in Bank A's balance sheet once those $5 million in checks are collected by Bank A.

T F 30. All depository institutions must hold in reserve an amount equal to the same percentage of their deposits.

T F 31. With a legal reserve requirement of 20 percent, a $1,000 deposit of currency in a checking account will not expand the amount of loans and securities held by the receiving bank if that bank chooses to carry an extra $200 of excess reserves.

T F 32. In some instances, an increase in the reserve requirement ratio will increase the deposit expansion multiplier.

T F 33. A single bank in a multibank system can lose reserves to other banks through the flow of checks among banks; therefore, the single bank follows the conservative rule of lending and creating demand deposits equal to only half its excess reserves.

T F 34. When a bank makes a loan, it must transfer part of its reserves to its demand deposit accounts.

T F 35. When a loan is made by one bank but the proceeds of the loan are deposited in another bank, the supply of money is not affected.

T F 36. The Federal Reserve needs control over the dollar amount of reserves and over nothing else to control the money supply effectively.

T F 37. If banks as a group have a reserve deficiency of $100 million, they will find it necessary to reduce their loans and investments by $500 million to remove the deficiency, assuming a 20 percent reserve requirement against demand deposits.

T F 38. If there were no reserve requirements imposed on banks by government, the banks would not include among their assets non-interest-bearing currency and coin.

T F 39. If there are no excess reserves in the banking system and $200 million of currency flows into the banks, excess reserves of the banks increase by $200 million.

The following questions are based on the Appendix to this chapter:

T F 40. If the public wants to hold part of any increase in the money supply in the form of currency, the value of the deposit multiplier will drop.

T F 41. The monetary base is synonymous with bank reserves.

T F 42. The power of the deposit multiplier is magnified if the public wants to transfer into savings and time deposits at commercial banks any increase in the money supply.

T F 43. The value of the deposit multiplier is reduced if banks hold unused excess reserves.

T F 44. In the 1930s idle excess reserves were plentiful. However, in the past two decades most banks have been close to being fully loaned up.

T F 45. An increase in the reserve requirement ratio against demand deposits will increase the level of required reserves.

T F 46. An increase in the reserve requirement ratio against demand deposits will increase total bank reserves.

T F 47. Assuming that there are no time and savings deposits, that banks choose to hold zero excess reserves, that all banks are subject to a 20 percent reserve requirement, and that the public chooses to hold $1 in currency for every $5 of demand deposits, then $100 million of excess reserves will result in a $200 million increase in demand deposits.

T F 48. On the same assumption as the preceding question, $100 million of excess reserves will result in a $300 million increase in the money supply (M1).

T F 49. The larger the ratio of savings and time deposits to demand deposits, the smaller the increase in M1 that follows from an increase in the monetary base.

T F 50. The value of the demand deposit multiplier will be affected by banks' distribution of earning assets between loans and securities.

Multiple-Choice Questions

Answer the following multiple-choice questions by circling the best alternative.

1. The balance sheet identity can be stated as
   a. total assets equal total liabilities
   b. total assets minus total liabilities equal net worth
   c. total assets minus total liabilities equal zero
   d. total assets plus total liabilities minus net worth equal zero
   e. none of the above

2. Which one of the following items is *not* an asset of banks?
   a. vault cash
   b. cash items in process of collection
   c. borrowing from the Federal Reserve banks
   d. bonds
   e. both (c) and (d)

3. Bank reserves consist of
   a. deposits with the Federal Reserve banks
   b. currency inside banks
   c. cash items in process of collection
   d. the sum of (a) and (b)
   e. the sum of (b) and (c)

4. Before making a loan an individual bank will specifically examine its
   a. demand deposits outstanding
   b. excess reserves
   c. total reserves
   d. vault cash
   e. none of the above

5. A decrease in the reserve requirement ratio
   a. increases total reserves
   b. increases required reserves
   c. necessarily creates excess reserves
   d. reduces the value of the deposit multiplier
   e. none of the above

6. The *maximum* volume of demand deposits the banking system may have outstanding depends on
   a. the banking system's ability to make loans
   b. the value of the reserve requirement ratio and the volume of the banking system's total reserves
   c. the banking system's ability to obtain excess reserves from Federal Reserve banks
   d. all of the above
   e. only (a) and (b)

7. A withdrawal from a demand deposit account at an individual bank will
   a. decrease both its total reserves and its required reserves
   b. reduce its reserve requirement ratio
   c. necessarily create a reserve deficiency
   d. all of the above
   e. none of the above

8. If the reserve requirement ratio were equal to 100 percent, then
   a. the deposit multiplier would be equal to one
   b. total reserves would be equal to required reserves
   c. the banking system would not be able to create money
   d. all of the above
   e. only (a) and (b)

9. The largest component of the money supply is
   a. a liability of the banking system
   b. a liability of the Federal Reserve System
   c. a liability of the U.S. Treasury
   d. none of the above
   e. (a) and (b) are equally important

10. The reserve requirement ratio
    a. cannot be changed without the approval of Congress
    b. is imposed by the U.S. Treasury
    c. is changed once a month
    d. none of the above

11. A bank has excess reserves of $2 million. The reserve requirement ratio is 10 percent. The bank can extend loans by an amount equal to
    a. $20 million
    b. $10 million
    c. $2 million
    d. $200 million
    e. $8 million

12. If the reserve requirement ratio were equal to zero, then
    a. the deposit multiplier would be infinitely large
    b. required reserves would be equal to zero
    c. the banking system would theoretically be able to create an infinitely large amount of demand deposits
    d. all of the above
    e. only (a) and (b)

13. Reserves held by banks perform the following function:
    a. they are a source of immediate liquidity to banks
    b. they serve as a device for check collection
    c. they are a tool of monetary control which the Federal Reserve can use to implement its monetary policy
    d. all of the above
    e. only (b) and (c)

14. If an individual bank anticipates a currency withdrawal in excess of its vault cash,
    a. it can obtain currency from its Federal Reserve Bank

b. it will necessarily experience a reserve deficiency
c. it will have to sell bonds to the public to raise cash
d. it will be unable to extend loans
e. all of the above

15. Total currency issued by the Federal Reserve and the U.S. Treasury is equal to $110 billion. Total reserves held by banks is $40 billion, three-quarters of which are deposited with Federal Reserve banks. The reserve requirement ratio is 20 percent. The maximum value of the money supply will be
a. $200 billion
b. $310 billion
c. $300 billion
d. $210 billion
e. $330 billion

16. The banking system is initially loaned up (in equilibrium). Total reserves are $20 billion, and $200 billion of demand deposits are outstanding. Depositors withdraw $1 billion in currency. This withdrawal creates a reserve deficiency of
a. $1 billion
b. $0.1 billion
c. $0.9 billion
d. $0.8 billion
e. none of the above

The banking system has $39 billion of legal reserves, demand deposits of $200 billion, and the reserve requirement ratio is 20 percent. Answer the following *three* questions (17–19):

17. The banking system
a. is not in equilibrium, since required reserves exceed total reserves
b. is in equilibrium, since required reserves exceed total reserves
c. is not in equilibrium, since total reserves exceed legal reserves
d. is in equilibrium, since excess reserves are zero
e. none of the above

18. In order to attain a position in which it is in equilibrium, the banking system can borrow from the Federal Reserve banks an amount equal to
a. $39 billion
b. $1 billion
c. $0.2 billion
d. $7.8 billion
e. none of the above

19. Alternatively, to attain a position in which it is in equilibrium the banking system can
a. sell $5 billion worth of bonds to the public
b. sell $1 billion worth of bonds to the public

c. sell $39 billion worth of bonds to the public
d. buy $1 billion worth of bonds from the public

20. An individual bank has a $1 million reserve deficiency, and all other banks in the system are loaned up. The reserve requirement ratio is 20 percent. Which of the following alternatives will *not* eliminate the bank's deficiency?
a. calling in $5 million in loans
b. selling $1 million in bonds to its own depositors
c. selling $1 million in bonds to depositors of other banks
d. borrowing $1 million from the Federal Reserve
e. none of the above

The following questions are based on the Appendix to this chapter:

21. If the public wants to hold part of the additional money created by banks in the form of currency and to transfer another part of it into savings accounts, then
a. the value of the deposit multiplier will drop
b. the increase in the banking system's portfolio of earning assets will be greater than the increase in the demand deposits component of the money supply
c. the money supply (M1) will decrease
d. all of the above
e. only (a) and (c)

22. The banking system is in equilibrium (loaned up) with total reserves worth $60 billion. Demand deposits are worth $200 billion, and time and savings deposits twice as much. If the reserve requirement ratio against demand deposits is equal to 20 percent, the reserve requirement against time deposits
a. is equal to 10 percent
b. is equal to 15 percent
c. is equal to 5 percent
d. is equal to 7.5 percent

23. The currency/demand deposits ratio is 30 percent, the time deposits/demand deposits ratio is 150 percent, the reserve requirement against demand deposits is 15 percent and against time deposits is 5 percent. The value of the deposit multiplier is therefore equal to
a. 0.525
b. 1.905
c. 1.833
d. 1.111

24. A cash drain from banks
a. reduces the monetary base
b. reduces the currency component of the money supply

c. increases bank reserves

d. reduces the money supply

e. none of the above

25. Total currency issued by the Federal Reserve and the U.S. Treasury is equal to $120 billion. Demand deposits outstanding are $300 billion, and the banking system is in equilibrium (loaned up), with a reserve requirement ratio equal to 20 percent. If the money supply is $400 billion, then

a. bank deposits in the Federal Reserve are worth $40 billion

b. the monetary base is equal to $160 billion

c. vault cash is $40 billion

d. all of the above

e. only (a) and (b)

The banking system is initially in equilibrium (loaned up). The reserve requirement ratio against demand deposits is 14 percent, the reserve requirement ratio against time deposits is 3 percent, the currency/demand deposit ratio is equal to 30 percent, and the time deposits/demand deposit ratio is equal to 200 percent. The Federal Reserve purchases $100 million worth of bonds from banks. Answer the following eight questions (26–32).

26. The banking system has excess reserves equal to

a. $86 million

b. $100 million

c. $200 million

d. $114 million

27. The deposit multiplier is

a. 7.14

b. 2.20

c. 2.00

d. 5.00

28. In order to return to a position where it would again be in equilibrium (loaned up), the banking system should expand demand deposits by an amount equal to

a. $200 million

b. $172 million

c. $228 million

d. $400 million

29. The cash the public will withdraw as a result of the expansion in demand deposits is equal to

a. $120 million

b. $60 million

c. $68.4 million

d. $51.6 million

30. After the banking system has expanded deposits, the money supply (M1) will increase by

a. $200 million

b. $260 million

c. $172 million

d. $223.6 million

31. The volume of demand deposits that the public will convert into time deposits is equal to

a. $100 billion

b. $400 billion

c. $344 billion

d. $456 billion

32. In order to expand the volume of demand deposits by the amount of the answer to question 28, the banking system should make loans equal to

a. $200 million

b. $567.6 million

c. $660 million

d. $600 million

chapter 15

The Instruments of Central Banking

Central Themes and Major Points

The three main instruments used by the Federal Reserve to implement its monetary policy are: (1) the Fed's authority to change the value of the reserve requirement ratios against demand deposits and business-owned time and savings deposits; (2) the Fed's power to change the *discount rate,* which is the rate of interest that is charged to any depository institution borrowing reserves from Federal Reserve banks; and (3) the Fed's ability to buy and sell government securities in the open market (open market operations).

The Banking Act of 1980 and the Garn-St. Germain Depository Institutions Act of 1982 require that all depository institutions be subject to reserve requirements. These acts also stipulate that all depository institutions have access to borrowing from the Federal Reserve. Hence, the three instruments of central banking are directed to all depository institutions. Prior to the Banking Act of 1980, the Federal Reserve had the authority to set the reserve requirement ratios of member banks only, and borrowing from the Fed was available only to member banks.

Suppose the Federal Reserve wants to supply depository institutions with excess reserves. In principle, it can achieve this objective by (1) lowering the reserve requirement ratios, (2) decreasing the discount rate, or (3) purchasing government securities in the open market either *outright* or under *agreement to repurchase* at a later date. If the Fed wants to absorb reserves from depository institu-

tions it can, in principle, make changes in the opposite direction of those listed above. This chapter describes how the Federal Reserve goes about applying the instruments of central banking. The chapter also examines the relative merit and efficiency of each of the three instruments. The conclusion is that open market operations are the best tool under most circumstances. However, during times of financial crisis such as the stock market crash of 1987, the Federal Reserve must stand ready as a lender of last resort (through the discount window) to prevent a breakdown of the financial system.

New Terms

Define and/or explain the following terms introduced in this chapter:

Reserve requirements against:	Open market sale
	Account Manager
business-owned deposits	Tax and loan accounts
personal deposits	Repurchase agreements (repos)†
Discount mechanism	Reverse repurchase
Discount rate	agreements‡
Lender of last resort	Outright
Announcement effect	purchases/sales
Open market purchase	

†This term was first introduced in Chapter 8.
‡More on this term in Chapter 16.

Essay Questions and Problems

1. **The function of reserve requirements**
   a. What is the primary function of bank reserve requirement ratios today?
   b. What was this function thought to be many years ago?

2. **The effects of an elimination of reserve requirements**
   a. If the legal reserve requirement ratios were abolished, would banks still hold reserve assets in the form of vault cash and/or deposits with the Fed?
   b. Could the Federal Reserve implement its monetary policy in this case?

3. **Reserve requirements as instruments of monetary policy**   Changes in the reserve requirement ratios are so effective in altering the required reserve position of banks that we might conclude that they constitute the ideal instrument of monetary control.
   a. Explain why this is not the case in practice.
   b. How does the Federal Reserve usually lessen the impact on banks of a change in the reserve requirement ratio?

4. **Discounting policy**   Modern discounting is considered by the Federal Reserve to be a privilege rather than a right. What does this mean? How can the Federal Reserve enforce a discounting mechanism based on privilege? Use an example to illustrate how difficult it is for the Federal Reserve to enforce such a policy.

5. **The announcement effect**   How does the announcement effect of a change in the discount rate operate? What types of discount rate policies would eliminate this effect?

6. **Use of the discount window**   Describe how the Fed used the discount window in response to the stock market crash of 1987. What were the potential effects if the Fed had failed to respond?

7. **Open market operations as a tool of monetary control**
   a. What are open market operations?
   b. Why do they constitute the best method available to the Federal Reserve to control bank reserves?
   *c. Could open market operations take place
      (1) in a country without financial markets?
      (2) with securities other than government bonds?
      (3) any time the Fed is ready to buy or sell securities?

*8. **Problem on open market operations**   The commercial banking system has $100 million of excess reserves. The reserve requirement ratio against demand deposits is 20 percent. The Federal Reserve sells a total of $500 million of government securities in the open market, $100 million to commercial banks and $400 million to insurance companies. Answer the following questions:
   a. What is the direct and immediate effect of this open market sale on the money supply?
   b. What are the effects on total bank reserves and required reserves?
   c. What amount of borrowing from the Federal Reserve banks, if any, will allow the commercial banking system to be in equilibrium?
   d. Suppose the Fed does not extend any loans to banks. What is the change in the banks' portfolio of loans that will bring the banking system to a position in which it is in equilibrium?
   e. What is the effect of (d) on the money supply?
   f. What is the total effect on the money supply, that is, the effect of (d) and the direct and immediate effect discussed in (a)?
   g. Draw the balance sheet of the banking system after it has reduced its portfolio of loans.

*9. Answer the same questions as in problem 8, assuming that the commercial banking system is initially in equilibrium.

*10. Answer the same questions as in problem 8, assuming that the commercial banking system is initially in equilibrium and that the Federal Reserve *buys* the $500 million of government securities in the open market, $200 million from commercial banks and $300 million from insurance companies.

*11. **Bank reserve deficiency**   An individual bank has a $10 million reserve deficiency, and all other banks in the system are in equilibrium. The reserve requirement against demand deposits is 20 percent.
   a. What are the alternatives available to this bank that will allow it to eliminate its reserve deficiency? In your answer give the dollar amount involved in any action taken by the bank to remove the deficiency.

b. What are the other possible sources of reserves that this bank could have used to eliminate its deficiency but cannot use in this case?

12. **The execution of monetary policy through open market operations** Open market operations are the major instrument of monetary control.
   a. What are open market operations, and who is responsible for the execution of these operations?
   b. Which Federal Reserve Bank is in charge of the execution of money market operations? Why?
   c. Before undertaking an open market operation, the Account Manager is said to get the "feel of the market." Explain.

*d. Which type of security is used to execute the Fed's open market operations? Would the effect of open market operations on bank reserves be different if open market operations were executed with securities other than those used by the Federal Reserve?
e. To whom does the Account Manager actually sell or buy securities when carrying out an open market operation?
*f. Suppose that the Account Manager is planning a $50 million sale in the open market. Could the Account Manager be unable to execute the sale because of a lack of buyers?
g. What are repurchase agreements and reverse repurchase agreements? To what types of open market operations are they particularly well suited?

SELF-TESTS

Completion Questions

Complete each of the following statements by entering the missing words and/or choosing the best alternative proposed.

1. The three methods employed by the Federal Reserve to control bank reserves are:

   a. _____

   b. _____

   c. _____

2. The _____ mechanism refers to the process through which the _____ may alter the _____ of banks by *(lending/borrowing)* reserves, temporarily, to _____. The _____ charges an interest rate called the _____ _____ on such loans.

3. A major weakness of the _____ mechanism is that the _____ rests with the borrowing institution rather than with the _____.

4. _____ operations refer to the _____ and _____ of government securities by the _____

_____ in order to _____

_____ .

5. The primary function of bank _____

_____ is to serve as an instrument of _____

_____ .

6. Currently, reserves against business-owned timed deposits are set at _____

_____ .

7. According to the _____

of 1980 and the _____

_____ of 1982, *(commercial banks/thrift institutions/all depository institutions)* must hold reserves against their _____ deposits.

8. As the ultimate supplier of bank liquidity, the Federal Reserve is often referred to as the _____ of _____

_____ .

9. The discount facilities established in 1913 by the Federal Reserve Act were intended to prevent the occurrence of _____

_____ .

10. One possible way that changes in the discount rate might directly affect market interest rates is through the _____

_____ .

11. Changes in the discount rate tend to *(follow/lead)* rather than *(follow/lead)* changes in short-term market interest rates.

12. The _____ is an administered rate set by commercial banks on loans to their most creditworthy business customers.

13. The job of the _____ is to carry out _____ operations for the purpose of implementing the *(monetary policy/open market operations)* directive issued at the last meeting of the _____

_____ held in *(New York/Washington)*.

14. _____ operations are performed from the _____ room of the Federal Reserve Bank of _____ .

15. Before executing an _____

operation, the _____ Manager will usually have a conferencewithamemberofthe*(Board of Governors/Congress)* and one of the presidents.

16. The earliest available indicator of bank reserve conditions is _____

_____ .

17. The _____ rate is the most volatile and variable rate in the money market.

18. _____ are particularly well designed for the execution of *(a temporary/an outright)* open market purchase of government securities by the Federal Reserve, whereas _____

_____

are well suited for the execution of *(a temporary/an outright)* open market *(purchase/sale)*.

19. Reverse repurchase agreements are also known as _____

_____ .

True and False Questions

For each of the following statements, circle the letter T if it is correct or the letter F if it is *partially* or totally incorrect.

T F   1. The Federal Reserve alters bank reserves by physically removing currency from, or adding currency to, the vault of banks.

T F   2. Excess reserves held by banks may change if either the reserve requirement ratios are changed or the amount of reserves held by banks is changed.

T F   3. The Federal Reserve frequently uses its authority to change reserve requirement ratios, because the effects of the change are very powerful.

T F   4. Changes in the value of the reserve requirement ratio against demand deposits are inversely related to changes in the value of the deposit expansion multiplier.

T F   5. The Federal Reserve must set the reserve requirement ratio against demand deposits between 3 and 10 percent as specified by Congress.

T F   6. The fact that some banks are not members of the Federal Reserve System may weaken the Fed's control over the money supply.

T F   7. The reserve requirement ratios may vary between Federal Reserve Districts by no more than one-half of a percentage point.

T F   8. The reserve requirement ratios of nonmember banks differ from those of member banks.

T F   9. The reserve requirement ratios against savings and time deposits are usually smaller than the reserve requirement ratios against demand deposits.

T F   10. The limits within which the reserve requirement ratios can be changed are determined by the Board of Governors of the Federal Reserve System and approved by Congress.

T F   11. The reserve requirement ratio against demand deposits is changed once a month on average. Changes have not been more frequent because they are very powerful.

T F   12. Whenever the reserve requirement ratio against demand deposits is changed by the Federal Reserve, the magnitude of the change rarely exceeds one-half of a percentage point.

T F   13. If the reserve requirement ratio against demand deposits increases up to a maximum of 12 percent as the size of *additional* deposits rises, then the average reserve requirement ratio on a bank deposit will be lower than 12 percent.

T F   14. Thrift institutions are required to

hold reserves against their savings and time deposits according to reserve requirement ratios equal to those imposed by the Federal Reserve on banks.

T F 15. The primary reason for reserve requirements remains that of contributing to the liquidity of banks.

T F 16. The discount rate is the rate member banks charge nonmember banks for the borrowing of excess reserves.

T F 17. In order to expand its portfolio of loans and securities, a bank may borrow excess reserves from its Federal Reserve Bank.

T F 18. The Federal Reserve controls bank borrowing solely by varying the discount rate, standing ready to lend without restriction any amount at the designated discount rate.

T F 19. When you borrow from a bank, the reserves of the banks as a group are unchanged, but when a bank borrows from the Federal Reserve Bank, the reserves of the banks as a group are increased.

T F 20. When a bank repays a loan to its Federal Reserve Bank, there is a decrease in that bank's demand deposit liabilities and in its reserves.

T F 21. Changes in bank reserve requirements, in the amount of loans outstanding at the Federal Reserve banks, and in the amount of securities held by Federal Reserve banks, all occur at the initiative of the Federal Reserve authorities.

T F 22. The discount rate is the rate of interest charged by banks to their most creditworthy business customers.

T F 23. The Federal Reserve was established in 1933, following a wave of bank failures caused by the Great Depression.

T F 24. When the Federal Reserve Act was passed in 1913, bank reserve requirements were fixed by Congress and could not be changed by the Federal Reserve.

T F 25. In periods of financial panic the banking system cannot meet depositor withdrawals by calling in loans or selling securities.

T F 26. The Fed's response to the stock market crash of 1987 is an excellent example of using the discount window as a "lender of last resort."

T F 27. The Federal Reserve Act of 1913 provided that the central bank could and should lend as much as possible to commercial banks in times of financial emergency.

T F 28. The Federal Reserve will suspend the borrowing privilege of any bank that borrows excessive amounts of funds.

T F 29. Bank discounting is encouraged when the discount rate is higher than short-term interest rates.

T F 30. When the discount rate is above short-term interest rates, then it can be viewed as a "penalty rate."

T F 31. The doctrine of the central bank as the "lender of last resort" refers to the Federal Reserve's open market operations.

T F 32. In recent years changes in the discount rate have usually come after basic changes in the money market rates have already occurred.

T F 33. The most important way the Federal Reserve alters the actual amount of reserves the banks hold is through open market operations.

T F 34. An open market purchase of securities by the Federal Reserve decreases the reserves held by banks.

T F 35. In its open market operations the Federal Reserve deals exclusively with commercial banks.

T F 36. An open market sale of securities by the Federal Reserve will eventually lead to an increase in the money supply.

T F 37. A Federal Reserve open market purchase of securities from banks raises bank reserves by an amount equal to the value of the securities purchased.

T F 38. One difference between the purchase by the Federal Reserve Bank of New York of $1 million of government securities from Citibank in New York and from General Motors Corporation is that, other things being equal, in the former case there is an increase in excess reserves of $1 million and in the latter case there is an increase in excess reserves of less than $1 million, assuming banks are initially in equilibrium.

T F 39. If the Federal Reserve were to conduct open market operations in terms of corporate stocks and bonds, its purchases and sales would not affect bank reserves in the same basic way that its purchases of government securities do.

T F 40. The Federal Reserve's ability to reduce bank reserves is at times restricted by its inability to find purchasers for the government securities it seeks to sell.

T F 41. An expansion or contraction of the money supply by the Federal Reserve through open market operations respectively adds to the public's wealth or subtracts from the public's wealth.

T F 42. The federal funds rate is an example of an administered rate.

T F 43. Federal Reserve open market purchases affect nonmember banks more than they affect member banks.

T F 44. The Chairman of the Board of Governors of the Federal Reserve System is also the manager of the System Open Market Account.

T F 45. Open market operations are conducted every thirty days.

T F 46. Other factors held constant, an open market purchase by the Federal Reserve will reduce the federal funds rate.

T F 47. Between meetings of the Federal Open Market Committee, the Account Manager is in constant contact with the Board of Governors.

T F 48. If one finds that the Federal Reserve has been a net seller of U.S. government securities over the past month, one can reliably conclude that the Federal Reserve is undertaking a restrictive monetary policy.

T F 49. In a given week the decision of the Account Manager to buy or sell U.S. government securities is based on the current market price of these securities relative to the price paid by the Federal Reserve when those securities were purchased.

T F 50. Competition among the various dealers in government securities ensures that the Federal Reserve will get the highest possible price when it sells and the lowest possible price when it buys.

T F 51. The Federal Reserve does not engage in open market operations in order to make a profit.

T F 52. When the Federal Reserve enters into a repurchase agreement with a dealer

in government securities, it withdraws reserves temporarily from the banking system.

Multiple-Choice Questions

Answer the following multiple-choice questions by circling the best alternative.

1. Given that the reserve requirement against demand deposits is larger than the reserve requirement against savings deposits, the transfer of $10 from demand deposits into savings deposits at commercial banks will
   a. reduce the money supply (M1) at the time the transfer takes place
   b. not affect the total volume of reserves held by banks
   c. increase excess reserves, assuming the banking system was initially loaned up (in equilibrium)
   d. decrease the amount of required reserves
   e. all of the above

2. By varying the bank reserve requirement ratio, the Federal Reserve can alter the level of
   a. bank reserves
   b. bank required reserves
   c. bank excess reserves
   d. all of the above
   e. only (a) and (b)
   f. only (b) and (c)

3. An increase in the bank reserve requirement ratio
   a. will increase the value of the deposit multiplier
   b. should result in an expansion of bank deposits
   c. should result in an expansion of bank loans and holdings of securities
   d. all of the above
   e. none of the above

4. Because the effect of a change in the reserve requirement ratio is so powerful
   a. it is often used by the Federal Reserve to conduct monetary policy
   b. it is rarely employed as a tool of monetary control
   c. it is ineffective and cannot be trusted as an instrument of monetary policy
   d. member banks have been withdrawing from the Federal Reserve System
   e. both (b) and (d)

5. The value of the reserve requirement ratio against demand deposits may depend on
   a. whether it is a national bank or a state bank
   b. the size of its deposits

c. its geographical location
d. all of the above
e. only (a) and (b)

6. If the central bank sets the reserve requirement ratio against demand deposits at 10 percent for the first $400 million and 15 percent for deposits above $400 million, then the effective reserve requirement for a bank with $500 million in deposits is equal to
   a. 15 percent
   b. 11 percent
   c. 10 percent
   d. 9 percent
   e. none of the above

7. If the reserve requirement ratio is set equal to 100 percent against all deposits (which are the only liabilities of banks), then
   a. the deposit multiplier will be equal to unity
   b. banks would be unable to expand deposits
   c. excess reserves will be zero
   d. all of the above
   e. only (a) and (b)

8. With the reserve requirement ratios currently imposed by the Federal Reserve, the transfer of one dollar from a savings deposit to a demand deposit at the same bank will
   a. increase the bank's total reserves
   b. increase the bank's required reserves
   c. create excess reserves if the bank is initially in equilibrium (loaned up)
   d. all of the above
   e. only (a) and (c)

9. A bank with $200 million in demand deposits and $400 million in savings and time deposits holds reserves worth $52 million. The uniform reserve requirement ratio is 15 percent against demand deposits and 5 percent against savings and time deposits. The Federal Reserve raises the reserve requirement ratio against demand deposits to 16 percent. As a result of this action the bank
   a. has a reserve deficiency of $2 million
   b. is unable to extend further loans
   c. has $2 million of excess reserves
   d. both (a) and (b)

10. A bank in equilibrium (loaned up) with $90 million of reserves has $400 million of demand deposits and $600 million in savings and time deposits. If the reserve requirement against demand deposits equals 15 percent, then the average value of reserve requirement ratios against savings and time deposits is equal to
    a. 10 percent
    b. 3 percent
    c. 5 percent
    d. none of the above

11. Banks hold twice as much in time deposits as in demand deposits and are in equilibrium (loaned up). The reserve requirement ratio against demand deposits is lowered by one percentage point. What change in the average reserve requirement ratio against time deposits will prevent banks from having excess reserves?
    a. the change cannot be determined
    b. an increase of one-half of a percentage point
    c. an increase of two percentage points
    d. none of the above

12. The discount rate is
    a. set by Congress within specific limits
    b. set by the Federal Reserve banks
    c. set by the Board of Governors in Washington, D.C.
    d. determined by the relative strength of the demand for borrowed reserves by banks
    e. both (b) and (c)

13. As a tool of monetary control, the discount rate may affect
    a. the volume of borrowed reserves
    b. the volume of excess reserves
    c. the volume of total reserves
    d. all of the above
    e. only (a) and (c)

14. As a lender of last resort, the function of a central bank is to
    a. increase the supply of currency by printing as many notes as the public desires in a period of financial panic
    b. provide additional reserves to the banking system through the discount mechanism in periods of liquidity shortages
    c. lend funds to any commercial bank unable to obtain liquidity to make a loan
    d. lend funds to the federal government in periods of budgetary deficits

15. Open market operations were not used to implement monetary control in the early years of the Federal Reserve because
    a. they were mistakenly thought to be ineffective
    b. the Federal Reserve Act of 1913 prohibited Federal Reserve banks from owning U.S. government securities
    c. their potential as a possible tool of central banking was unknown
    d. the public did not trade in U.S. government securities

16. The only instrument of monetary policy contained in the original Federal Reserve Act was
    a. the power to alter reserve requirement ratios
    b. the ability to conduct open market operations

c. the power to set maximum interest rates banks may pay to depositors

d. the power to impose margin requirements on borrowings to finance the purchase of common stocks and bonds

e. none of the above

17. Which of the following actions, if taken by a bank, would be considered improper by the Federal Reserve?

a. borrowing from the Federal Reserve to cover a short-run, temporary deficiency in reserves

b. borrowing from the Federal Reserve to cover recurring reserve needs arising from seasonal variations in loans or deposits

c. borrowing from the Federal Reserve at a discount rate of 10 percent and selling these funds in the federal funds market at 11 percent, thereby making a profit of 1 percent

d. both (b) and (c)

18. To prevent abuse of the discount facility, the Federal Reserve can

a. increase the discount rate

b. introduce tighter surveillance procedures

c. check on banks that borrow too much or too frequently

d. all of the above

e. only (b) and (c)

19. The announcement effect refers to

a. the fact that the Federal Reserve usually announces a new discount rate a few days before it becomes effective

b. the fact that changes in the discount rate generate expectations regarding future interest rates

c. the fact that bond prices fall when the discount rate rises

d. the fact that the Federal Reserve uses changes in the discount rate to signal any forthcoming open market operation of substantial size

20. Which of the following actions would eliminate the uncertain announcement effects associated with the Federal Reserve's discount policy?

a. frequent changes in the discount rate in smaller steps

b. linking the discount rate to the yield on U.S. Treasury bills

c. setting a fixed discount rate that will never change

d. all of the above

e. only (a) and (b)

21. In recent years movements in the discount rate have

a. paralleled the movements of short-term money market rates

b. preceded the movements of short-term money market rates

c. followed the movements of short-term money market rates

d. not behaved in any consistent pattern in relation to the movements of short-term money market rates

22. Which of the following interest rates would typically be the highest at a given point in time?

a. the discount rate

b. the three-month Treasury bill rate

c. the commercial paper rate

d. the federal funds rate

23. Which of the following interest rates is market-determined?

a. prime rate

b. discount rate

c. federal funds rate

d. all of the above

24. Open market operations are carried out by

a. the Federal Open Market Committee

b. the President of the Federal Reserve Bank of New York

c. the manager of the System Open Market Account

d. the Board of Governors

25. The most sensitive indicator of pressure in the market for reserves is

a. the discount rate

b. the federal funds rate

c. required reserves

d. bank borrowing from the Federal Reserve

e. the three-month Treasury bill rate

26. A good indicator of the direction of monetary policy is

a. the amount of securities the Federal Reserve bought or sold during the week

b. borrowing of banks from their Federal Reserve Bank

c. required reserves

d. none of the above

27. The federal funds rate will tend to move upward if

a. a few banks have reserve deficiencies and the rest have ample excess reserves

b. a few have excess reserves and the rest have a significant deficiency in reserves

c. the Federal Reserve is buying government securities in the open market

d. the Federal Reserve raises the discount rate

28. Before carrying out open market operations, the Account Manager will examine all of the following *except*

a. the discount rate

b. movements in the U.S. Treasury deposits at

commercial banks and at the Federal Reserve banks

c. the reserve position of the banking system

d. deposits in foreign accounts at Federal Reserve banks

29. Open market operations are conducted
    a. once every month
    b. on a daily basis
    c. right after each meeting of the Federal Open Market Committee
    d. only when the Account Manager receives a go-ahead instruction from the Federal Open Market Committee

30. The actual purchase or sale of securities by the Federal Reserve is made
    a. through a limited number of government securities dealers
    b. by direct contact with any potential seller or buyer of government securities
    c. through brokers who specialize in bringing together buyers and sellers of government securities
    d. Any of the above can be used. The least costly alternative is usually selected by the Account Manager.

31. When the Federal Reserve buys bonds in the open market, the reserves of banks increase by
    a. an amount equal to the value of the bonds only if they are purchased from banks
    b. an amount equal to the value of the bonds regardless of the nature of the seller
    c. an amount smaller than the value of the bonds if they are purchased from nonbank institutions or individuals
    d. an amount larger or smaller than the value of the bonds purchased
    e. one cannot tell

32. The effect of a Federal Reserve open market sale of bonds to banks is
    a. an immediate decrease in bank reserves by the amount of the sale
    b. no immediate change in the money supply
    c. an immediate increase in banks' required reserves if they were initially loaned up
    d. an eventual decrease in the money supply if banks were initially loaned up
    e. all of the above
    f. all *but* (c)

33. The effect of a Federal Reserve open market sale of bonds to nonbank institutions
    a. creates no immediate change in the money supply
    b. creates a decrease in bank reserves by the amount of the sale
    c. creates no change in banks' required re-

serves if they were initially loaned up (in equilibrium)

    d. all of the above
    e. only (b) and (c)

The Federal Reserve sells $300 million of securities, $200 million to banks and $100 million to insurance companies. Answer the following three questions (34–36):

34. The effect of the above sale on the total reserves of the banking system is a decrease of
    a. $300 million
    b. $200 million
    c. $100 million
    d. $500 million
    e. none of the above

35. The immediate and direct effect of the open market sale on the money supply is a decrease of
    a. $200 million
    b. $300 million
    c. $500 million
    d. $400 million
    e. none of the above

36. If the reserve requirement against demand deposits is 10 percent, the banking system could return to a position where it would be in equilibrium (assume the banking system was initially in equilibrium) by
    a. borrowing $300 million from the Federal Reserve
    b. borrowing $200 million from the Federal Reserve
    c. borrowing $290 million from the Federal Reserve
    d. borrowing $180 million from the Federal Reserve
    e. none of the above

37. When the Federal Reserve enters into a reverse repurchase agreement with a dealer in government securities, it
    a. withdraws reserves from the banking system temporarily
    b. sells securities to the dealer
    c. carries out an open market sale
    d. all of the above

In executing open market operations the Account Manager trades government securities with a limited number of U.S. government securities dealers, some of whom are banks. Suppose that the Account Manager has decided to sell $300 million of securities in the open market, $100 million to bank dealers and the balance to nonbank dealers. Answer the following three questions (38–40):

38. The above open market sale will reduce bank reserves by

a. $100 million
b. $300 million
c. $200 million
d. none of the above

39. The direct and immediate effect of the above open market sale is to reduce the money supply by
    a. $400 million
    b. $100 million
    c. $300 million
    d. none of the above

40. Assuming the banking system was initially in equilibrium (loaned up) with a reserve requirement of 15 percent, the above open market sale will create a reserve deficiency of
    a. $300 million
    b. $255 million
    c. $270 million
    d. $285 million

41. Which of the following is an accurate statement of the expected result of a Federal Reserve open market operation?
    a. A sale of securities would lower interest rates.
    b. A sale of securities would raise interest rates.
    c. A purchase of securities would raise interest rates.
    d. both (a) and (c)

42. Which of the following Federal Reserve actions would temporarily remove reserves from the banking system?
    a. an increase in the discount rate
    b. a decrease in the discount rate
    c. a reverse repo
    d. a repo

chapter 16

Understanding Movements in Bank Reserves

Central Themes and Major Points

The preceding chapter examined each one of the three instruments of monetary control available to the Federal Reserve. It was shown how discount policy and open market operations affect the level of total reserves available to the banking system and how changes in reserve requirement ratios affect the level of required reserves available but not the level of total reserves.

There are other factors that affect the level of total bank reserves. We know, for example, that if the public withdraws currency from banks, bank reserves will decrease. Also, if the U.S. Treasury transfers funds from its tax and loan accounts at banks to its deposits at the Fed, bank reserves will decrease.

There exist, then, a set of factors that can either decrease or increase the level of bank reserves. Some are under the direct control of the Fed (loans to banks and open market operations); others are not under the control of the Fed (currency held by the public, Treasury operations).

This chapter presents a general framework allowing us to determine *all* the factors that increase or decrease the level of bank reserves. It is summarized in the *"bank reserve equation"* expressed as:

Bank reserves = (Factors supplying reserves) −
(Factors absorbing reserves)

This equation simply says that bank reserves *must increase* if either a factor supplying reserves *increases* or a factor absorbing reserves *decreases*. Also, bank reserves *must decrease* if either a factor supplying reserves *decreases* or a factor absorbing reserves *increases*. (This assumes that all other factors are held constant.)

The list of factors supplying and absorbing reserves are presented and discussed in this chapter.

The chapter concludes with a reexamination of open market operations. A distinction is made between two types of open market operations. These are (1) *defensive* open market operations aimed at offsetting undesired changes in bank reserves and (2) *dynamic* open market operations aimed at altering the overall level of reserves.

New Terms

Define and/or explain the following terms introduced in this chapter:

Bank reserve equation
Largest Federal
    Reserve assets:
    U.S. gov't. and
    agency securities
    Gold certificates
    Loans to banks
Largest Federal
    Reserve liabilities:
    Federal Reserve
    notes outstanding
    Bank deposits
    U.S. Treasury
    deposits
Cash (as a Federal
    Reserve asset)

Float (equal to cash
    items in process of
    collection minus
    deferred availability
    cash items)
Treasury currency
    outstanding
Treasury cash
    holdings
Currency in
    circulation
Federal Reserve credit
Special Drawing
    Rights (SDRs)
Defensive open market
    operations

Dynamic open market operations

Monetary base (equals member bank reserves plus currency in circulation)

Essay Questions and Problems

*1. **The Federal Reserve balance sheet** The items that appear on the consolidated balance sheet of all Federal Reserve Banks are listed below in alphabetical order, with their corresponding values in billions of dollars as of the end of the year 19XX. Note that the value of the item "bank deposits" is not given.

1. Capital account	5
2. Cash	1
3. Cash items in process of collection	20
4. Deferred availability cash items	10
5. Federal Reserve notes outstanding	120
6. Foreign deposits	5
7. Gold certificates	20
8. Loans to banks	4
9. Bank deposits	?
10. Treasury deposits	10
11. U.S. government and agency securities	155

Answer the following questions:

a. Define each one of the items above and indicate if it is an asset or a liability of the Federal Reserve banks.

b. According to the balance sheet identity, the sum of all assets must be equal to the sum of all liabilities plus capital accounts. Using this identity, determine the value of bank deposits.

c. Enter the relevant items in the Fed's consolidated balance sheet.

Fed Consolidated Balance Sheet at Year End 19XX

Assets	Liabilities
1.	1.
2.	2.
3.	3.
4.	4.
5.	5.
6.	6.
Total assets	Total liabilities & capital accts.

d. What is the value of the gold stock held by the U.S. Treasury at the end of the year 19XX? Explain.

e. What is the Federal Reserve float? Determine the value of the float at the end of the year 19XX.

f. Which three items on the Fed's balance sheet constitute the Federal Reserve credit? Explain why these three items are lumped together apart from the other Federal Reserve Assets and Liabilities. Determine the value of the Federal Reserve credit at the end of 19XX.

g. Can you determine bank reserves from the Fed's consolidated balance sheet? If not, why not?

*2. **The bank reserve equation** The bank reserve equation is obtained by integrating the items on the Fed's consolidated balance sheet with some of the items appearing on the U.S. Treasury balance sheet. In order to determine the bank reserve equation, you will need the following items in addition to those given in question 1:

Currency in circulation	127
Currency in bank vaults	?
Treasury cash	2
Treasury currency outstanding	20

All items are in billions of dollars as of the end of year 19XX. This is the year for which the Fed's consolidated balance sheet in question 1 has been drawn. Note that the value of the item "currency in bank vaults" is not given. Answer the following questions:

a. Define each of the items above.

b. The bank reserve equation gives the value of bank reserves as the difference between those factors which supply reserves to banks and those which absorb reserves from banks. Using this equation, determine the value of the item "currency in bank vaults."

c. Enter the relevant items in the bank reserve equation (enter the Federal Reserve credit as one item):

The Bank Reserve Equation at End of Year 19XX

Factors supplying reserves:
1.
2.
3.

Minus factors absorbing reserves:
1.
2.
3.
4.

Equals bank reserves:
1.
2.

d. Check that all the items on the Fed's consolidated balance sheet in question 5 as well as the items given in this problem are accounted for in the bank reserve equation. What has happened to the items "cash" and "Federal Reserve notes outstanding," which appear on the Fed's consolidated balance sheet but not on the bank reserve equation?

e. What is the usefulness of the bank reserve equation?

f. In question (b) the item "currency in bank vaults" was determined using the bank reserve equation. It is possible, however, to determine "currency in bank vaults" directly from the three items given in this problem and the items "Federal Reserve notes outstanding" (120) and "cash" (1). Set up an equality between these six items and determine the value of the item "currency in bank vaults" from the other five.

g. *The monetary base*
What is the definition of the monetary base, and what is its value as of the end of 19XX? It is said that "an open market operation of $1 billion can be more closely associated with a change in the monetary base than with a change in reserves." Explain.

*3. **The effects of a gold sale by the U.S. Treasury** Suppose that the U.S. Treasury sells $50 million worth of gold to the U.S. public (excluding banks), who pay with checks drawn on their demand deposits at banks. What is the net effect of this sale on

a. the Treasury balance sheet?

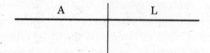

b. the Federal Reserve balance sheet?

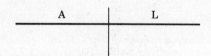

c. the banks' balance sheet?

d. the U.S. public's balance sheet?

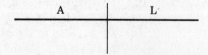

e. the money supply, assuming that the banking system does not change its portfolio of loans and investment? (That is, what is the direct effect of the sale on the money supply?)

f. the money supply, after the banking system has changed its portfolio of loans and investments to return to a position where it is again in equilibrium (loaned up)? The banking system was initially in equilibrium (loaned up) and the reserve requirement against demand deposits was 20 percent.

g. Answer the preceding questions for the case where the $50 million worth of gold is purchased by a foreign central bank with funds on deposit at the Federal Reserve Bank of New York.

*4. **Federal Reserve notes and Treasury coins**
Banks return to the Federal Reserve $20 million in Federal Reserve notes and $5 million in Treasury coins.

a. What happens to the Federal Reserve notes and the Treasury coins when they are received by the Federal Reserve?

b. What changes occur in the balance sheet of the Federal Reserve Banks as a result of this transaction? Use T-accounts in your explanation.

c. What has happened to bank reserves as a result of this transaction?

*5. **More on U.S. Treasury coins** When the U.S. Treasury produces another $100 million of coins to meet the needs of the public, how do these coins get into the hands of the public? Use T-accounts in your explanation.

*6. **Federal Reserve float** The purpose of this exercise is to show how Federal Reserve float expands, how it contracts, and what the implications are of this phenomenon. Consider the following set of events.

(1) Alana writes a $100 check to Marci as a birthday present.
(2) Marci deposits the check at her bank.
(3) Marci's bank sends the check to the Fed for collection.
(4) The Fed sends the check to Alana's bank.
(5) Two days have passed since the Fed sent the check and the Fed has not yet heard from Alana's bank.
(6) Alana's bank acknowledges receipt of the check three days after it was sent by the Fed.

Answer the following questions:

a. Draw a T-account for the Fed, Alana, Marci, Alana's bank (Bank A), and Marci's bank (Bank B), and indicate on each T-account the effect of each of the six events described above. Assume that when Marci deposits the check at her bank, Bank B credits Marci's account for $100 and increases the bank's assets called "Cash Item in Process of Collection" by the same amount.

b. Do the first and fourth events affect any of the five balance sheets?

c. When exactly is the float created and when is it destroyed in the above case? What is the length of time this float is in existence, and what is its size (in dollars)? Is it possible for the float to be negative?

d. What is the effect of the float on bank reserves?

e. Under what circumstances would there be no float in the case described above?

f. Why doesn't the Fed get rid of the float by simply reducing the reserve account of the bank against which the check is drawn (Bank A) at the same time that it is increasing the reserve account of the bank in which the check is deposited (Bank B)?

g. Which specific developments outside the control of the Federal Reserve may cause an unexpected increase in the size of the float? An unexpected increase in the size of the float may create an undesired rise in bank reserves. How can the Federal Reserve prevent bank reserves from rising as a result of an increase in the float?

*7. **Factors affecting bank reserves** What will be the effect of each of the following combinations of changes on bank reserves, other things being equal?

a. Foreign deposits at Federal Reserve banks increase by $100 million; capital accounts of the Federal Reserve banks increase by $25 million; and Federal Reserve float decreases by $200 million.

b. Federal Reserve credit increases by $300 million; Treasury currency outstanding increases by $50 million; and Treasury cash holdings increase by $100 million.

c. Currency held by the nonbank public decreases by $150 million; Treasury deposits at Federal Reserve banks decrease by $100 million; and gold stock decreases by $50 million.

8. **Types of open market operations** A distinction is usually made between two types of open market operations carried out by the Federal Reserve: defensive versus dynamic open market operations.

a. What is the difference between these two types of open market operations?

b. Give some examples of events that may lead the Federal Reserve to carry out a defensive open market operation.

c. Which type of open market operation is most frequently conducted by the Federal Reserve?

d. *Repurchase Agreements*
Repurchase agreements (also called "repos") and reverse repurchase agreements (also called "reverse repos") are two techniques used by the Federal Reserve to carry out defensive open market operations. What are "repos" and "reverse repos"? Why are they convenient techniques for the execution of defensive open market operations?

e. If one has available the record of sales and purchases of U.S. government securities made by the manager of the Federal Reserve System Open Market Account, would it be possible to tell which trading was carried out for defensive purposes and which for dynamic purposes? Explain.

SELF-TESTS

Completion Questions

Complete each of the following statements by entering the missing words and/or choosing the best alternative proposed.

1. The largest and the second largest assets of Federal Reserve Banks are, respectively, _____

_____, and _____

_____.

2. The largest and the second largest liabilities of the Federal Reserve Banks are, respectively, _____

_____, and _____

_____.

3. Federal Reserve float is defined as the difference between the Fed's *(asset/ liability)* called _____

_____ and the Fed's *(asset/liability)* called _____

_____.

4. Bank reserves equal total *(assets/liabilities)* of the Federal Reserve Banks minus all Federal Reserve Bank *(assets/liabilities)* and _____

_____ other than those _____

that comprise bank reserves plus _____

_____ held in vaults of banks.

5. The _____ base is equal to the sum of _____

_____

and _____

6. Federal Reserve credit outstanding is equal to the sum of _____

_____, _____,

and _____. Two of these items are *(assets/liabilities)* of the

_____

_____ and the other is the difference between the Fed's _____

and the Fed's _____.

7. Other things being equal, the net effect on the Federal Reserve's balance sheet of a gold purchase by the U.S. Treasury is *(a decrease/an increase)* in a Fed asset called _____ and an equal *(decrease/increase)* in a Fed liability called _____

_____. The net effect of the same transaction on the U.S. Treasury's balance sheet is an increase in *(an asset/a liability)* called _____

_____ and an equal *(increase/decrease)* in *(an asset/a liability)* called ____

_____.

8. In the *(Fed's balance sheet/bank reserve equation)* the largest factor supplying reserves is _____

_____ and the largest factor absorbing reserves is _____

_____.

9. There are two types of Federal Reserve open market operations. The _____ _____ type are aimed at _____

_____

_____, whereas the _____ type are aimed at _____

_____

_____.

10. _____ and reverse _____ _____ are two techniques

usually used by the Federal Reserve to undertake _____

open market operations.

11. U.S. government securities owned by Federal Reserve Banks are either held

_____ or held under _____

_____.

True and False Questions

For each of the following statements, circle the letter T if it is correct or the letter F if it is *partially* or totally incorrect.

T F 1. All of the assets that qualify as bank reserves appear among the liabilities of the Federal Reserve banks.

T F 2. By the nature of the balance sheet, anything that increases the assets of Federal Reserve Banks without increasing their capital accounts or increasing their liabilities other than bank reserves will increase bank reserves by that amount.

T F 3. Other things being equal, if the Treasury sells $100 million of its gold stock to U.S. buyers, the final results in the balance sheet of the Federal Reserve Banks will typically be a $100 million decrease in holdings of gold certificates and a $100 million decrease in deposits of commercial banks at Federal Reserve Banks.

T F 4. The item "cash" on the assets side of the balance sheet of Federal Reserve Banks includes Federal Reserve notes outstanding, U.S. notes ("greenbacks"), and coin.

T F 5. Federal Reserve float is the excess of cash items in process of collection over deferred availability cash items.

T F 6. Federal Reserve float is often negative.

T F 7. If commercial banks call on Federal Reserve Banks to send them $10 million in coin and $50 million in Federal Reserve notes, the changes in the balance sheet of the Federal Reserve Banks will be a $60 million decrease in the liability item "bank deposits" and an offsetting increase of $60 million in other liability items.

T F 8. When worn-out Federal Reserve notes are sent back to the Federal Reserve Banks by banks, they are destroyed, and the balance sheet of the Federal Reserve Banks is adjusted to show a decrease in Federal Reserve notes outstanding and an equal increase in bank deposits.

T F 9. Other things being equal, when the Treasury transfers funds from its "tax and loan accounts" at banks to its accounts at the Federal Reserve Banks, bank deposits drop by an equal amount.

T F 10. A large proportion of our currency is issued on a regular basis by the U.S. Treasury.

T F 11. Other things being equal, if the Treasury draws down its deposit balance at the Federal Reserve Banks, bank reserves increase by an equal amount.

T F 12. Bank reserves are equal to total Treasury currency and coin outstanding plus total Federal Reserve Bank assets minus all Federal Reserve Bank capital accounts and liabilities other than those liabilities that comprise bank reserves.

T F 13. All of the following are factors supplying member bank reserves: Federal Reserve credit, gold stock, and Treasury cash holdings.

T F 14. If during a week the Federal Reserve buys $500 million of U.S. government securities but during that week currency outside banks increases by $200 million and float decreases by $300 million, other things being equal, bank reserves will remain unchanged.

T F 15. If the Federal Reserve buys government securities to offset an increase in Treasury deposits with the Federal Reserve Banks, that open market operation is described as *dynamic*.

T F 16. During some time periods when the Federal Reserve authorities seek to increase bank reserves by a particular amount, they may find it necessary to *sell* government securities in the open market to achieve this particular goal.

T F 17. The Federal Reserve is likely to respond to rising inflation concerns with dynamic open market operations.

T F 18. By the structure of the system, it is impossible for bank reserves to be a larger total than the total deposits at the Federal Reserve Banks.

T F 19. One can determine the precise amount of change in bank reserves from the last day of one month to the last day of the next month from the information given in the balance sheet of the Federal Reserve Banks for each of those two dates.

T F 20. If the Treasury draws down its deposit balance at the Federal Reserve Banks by $1 billion by issuing checks in that amount to the public, bank reserves increase by $1 billion as these checks are deposited in the commercial banks by the public, other things being equal.

T F 21. If the Treasury were to deposit into its accounts in the Federal Reserve Banks all of the checks received from taxpayers in the days preceding the April 15th tax payment deadline, it is likely that the Federal Reserve would find it necessary to buy U.S. government securities in the open market to avoid undesired consequences.

T F 22. One can easily identify whether the Fed's open market operations in any period are defensive or dynamic by observing what happens to total bank reserves, an increase indicating that the operations are dynamic and a decrease indicating that they are defensive.

T F 23. Repurchase agreements are usually used by the Federal Reserve when it seeks to temporarily absorb reserves from the banking system and reverse repurchase agreements are usually used to temporarily supply reserves to the banking system.

Multiple-Choice Questions

Answer the following multiple-choice questions by circling the best alternative.

1. Federal Reserve liabilities including capital accounts must always equal
   a. Federal Reserve assets
   b. Federal Reserve notes
   c. the money supply
   d. bank reserves

Questions 2–9 are based on the items listed below:
   I. Gold stock
   II. Treasury deposits with Federal Reserve Banks
   III. Bank deposits with Federal Reserve Banks
   IV. Government securities
   V. Loans to business firms
   VI. Federal Reserve notes outstanding
   VII. Federal Reserve float

2. Which items are assets of the U.S. Treasury?
   a. I, II, and IV
   b. I and II
   c. II and IV
   d. II, IV, and VI
   e. I, II, and VI

3. Which items are assets of commercial banks?
   a. III, IV, V, and VI
   b. III, IV, and V
   c. III, IV, and VI

d. III, V, and VI

e. IV, V, and VI

4. Which items are part of Federal Reserve credit?

a. III, IV, and VI

b. III, V, and VI

c. IV and VII

d. IV, V, and VII

e. III, VI, and VII

5. Which items are assets of commercial banks *and* liabilities of the Federal Reserve banks?

a. III only

b. III and VI

c. VI only

d. III and VII

e. III and IV

6. Which item is the largest Federal Reserve asset?

a. Item I

b. Item VI

c. Item IV

d. Item VII

e. Item V

7. Which item is the largest Federal Reserve liability?

a. Item III

b. Item II

c. Item V

d. Item VI

e. Item I

8. Which item will appear on the balance sheet of the U.S. Treasury, the Federal Reserve Banks, and banks?

a. Item I

b. Item IV

c. Item VI

d. Item VII

e. Item II

9. Which items are part of the monetary base?

a. III and VI

b. III only

c. VI only

d. III, VI, and VII

e. II, III, and VI

10. Which of the following *cannot* cause a decrease in bank deposits with the Federal Reserve banks?

a. a decrease in the float

b. a decrease in government securities held by Federal Reserve banks

c. an increase in the reserve requirement ratios

d. a decrease in loans to member banks

e. an increase in currency in circulation

11. Float is created by

a. the difference between "cash items in pro-cess of collection" and "deferred availability cash items"

b. fluctuations in the federal funds rate

c. Federal Reserve open market operations

d. conditions affecting the clearing and collection of checks

e. Treasury operations

12. Which of the following will tend to reduce bank reserves?

a. an increase in loans to banks

b. a decrease in currency in circulation

c. an increase in the float

d. a decrease in Treasury currency outstanding

e. an increase in Federal Reserve credit outstanding

13. Suppose that over a given period the monetary gold stock (including SDRs) decreases by $10 million; Federal Reserve credit outstanding increases by $20 million; Treasury currency outstanding decreases by $5 million; and nonbank deposits with Federal Reserve Banks decrease by $10 million. The net effect of all these changes on the monetary base (over the same period of time) is

a. nil, it remains the same

b. to increase it by $15 million

c. to decrease it by $5 million

d. to increase it by $5 million

e. impossible to compute from the information given

14. The U.S. Treasury sells $10 million worth of gold to the nonbank public. If the reserve requirement ratio against demand deposits is 20 percent, the direct effect of the gold sale is

a. to increase both the money supply and bank reserves by $10 million

b. to increase the money supply by $10 million and bank reserves by $8 million

c. to reduce both the money supply and bank reserves by $10 million

d. to reduce the money supply by $10 million and bank reserves by $8 million

15. Which of the following factors may *decrease* the size of the float?

a. bad weather conditions

b. a breakdown of the Federal Reserve's computers

c. a mail strike

d. all banks in the country moving to New York City

16. Banks return $10 million in dollar bills and $1 million in coins to the Federal Reserve banks. As a result of this transaction all of the following will take place except

a. member bank reserves with the Federal Reserve will increase by $11 million
b. member bank deposits with the Federal Reserve will increase by $11 million
c. Federal Reserve notes outstanding will decrease by $10 million
d. cash will increase by $1 million

17. Repurchase agreements are
    a. used by the Federal Reserve to undertake only defensive open market operations
    b. issued by the Federal Reserve to absorb reserves from the banking system temporarily
    c. contractual obligations to buy securities with an agreement that the seller will repurchase them at a predetermined price on a specific date in the future
    d. all of the above

18. The Federal Reserve may conduct defensive open market purchases to offset the effect of
    a. a decrease in reserve requirements
    b. an increase in currency in circulation
    c. a decrease in the Treasury deposit at the Fed
    d. a decrease in foreign deposits at the Fed
    e. an increase in Treasury currency outstanding

19. The Federal Reserve will conduct defensive open market sales to offset the effect of
    a. a sale of gold to the public
    b. a reduction in the size of the float
    c. a decrease in the Federal Reserve credit outstanding
    d. a decrease in the monetary base
    e. none of the above

20. Defensive open market operations are carried out for the purpose of
    a. creating repurchase agreements and reverse repurchase agreements
    b. offsetting the effects of earlier open market purchases that have supplied reserves to the banking system
    c. offsetting undesired and unexpected changes in member bank reserves
    d. influencing the federal funds rate
    e. implementing the Fed's countercyclical monetary policy

21. Open market operations undertaken to attain a desired monetary policy are called
    a. defensive
    b. offensive
    c. aggressive
    d. dynamic
    e. none of the above

22. Which of the following is likely to lead the Fed to sell reverse repurchase agreements?
    a. an increase in float
    b. a seasonal increase in currency held by the public
    c. a recession
    d. rising inflation

23. Which of the following is likely to cause the Fed to step up outright purchases of government securities?
    a. a recession
    b. an increase in currency holding associated with the Christmas shopping season
    c. an increase in inflation
    d. a rise in float

chapter 17

Hitting the Monetary Targets

Central Themes and Major Points

The *ultimate* objective of monetary policy is to influence economic activity. This objective, however, cannot be achieved by the Federal Reserve directly, because the Fed has no direct control over variables such as production, employment, and GDP. The purpose of this chapter is to show how the Fed attempts to achieve its ultimate objective.

The Federal Reserve attempts to achieve its ultimate objective by controlling a set of variables called *operating targets* (bank reserves or the federal funds rate), which in turn should affect the Fed's *intermediate target* (the money supply) and eventually influence economic activity. Until October 1979 the Federal Reserve used the federal funds rate as its operating target. Reserve aggregates were the dominant operating target from October 1979 until mid-1982. At that time the Fed started again to pay attention to the federal funds rate as an operating target. Following the 1981–82 recession, the Federal Reserve paid roughly equal attention to the money supply and the federal funds rate for a number of years. In 1986, specific growth targets for M1 were dropped. In 1992, the Fed appears to have moved full circle back to a policy that focuses on the federal funds rate more than the monetary aggregates.

It is important to realize that a multitude of variables separate an open market operation from the economy's GDP, the Fed's ultimate goal. This makes the execution of monetary policy an extremely difficult exercise for the Federal Reserve. The chapter concludes with an examination of the Fed's track record. The evidence suggests that over the recent past the Federal Reserve has stayed more or less within the target range for M2, although there have been substantial deviations from the midpoint targets.

New Terms

Define and/or explain the following terms introduced in this chapter:

The Federal Open
  Market Committee
  (FOMC) directive
Fed's operating
  targets
Fed's intermediate
  targets

Fed's ultimate
  objectives
Reserve aggregate
Monetary aggregates
Nonborrowed reserves
Gurley-Shaw argument

Essay Questions and Problems

1. **The Federal Open Market Committee (FOMC) directive** The primary thrust of monetary policy is summarized in the FOMC directive.
   a. What is the FOMC directive? How is it formulated and to whom is it directed?
   b. What types of instructions are contained in the FOMC directive? How often is it issued? Does the FOMC directive necessarily change after every meeting of the FOMC?

2. **Federal Reserve strategy** The Federal Reserve has no way of directly achieving its ulti-

mate objective. The Fed's game plan is to use its instruments to hit selected operating targets and through these to attain intermediate targets that in turn may help it achieve the ultimate objective.

a. What is the ultimate goal of monetary policy? Why is the Fed unable to exert direct control over its ultimate objective?

b. What is the Fed's intermediate objective or target, and how is it specified?

c. What is the Fed's operating target, and how is it specified?

d. Why does the Federal Reserve have difficulty in hitting a target figure for bank reserves, and why does it have even more difficulty in hitting a target figure for the money supply?

*3. **The choice of operating targets** Consider the federal funds rate and bank reserves as two alternative operating targets that the Federal Reserve can use to implement its monetary policy. Explain why the Federal Reserve would lose its control over the federal funds rate if the volume of bank reserves were chosen as the sole operating target and why the Federal Reserve would lose its control over the volume of bank reserves if the federal funds rate were chosen as the sole operating target. You should conclude that the Federal Reserve cannot control both the volume of bank reserves and the federal funds rate simultaneously.

4. **Selecting the appropriate money supply** Discuss the advantages and potential problems associated with using the different money supply measures (M1, M2, M3) as an intermediate target. Which measure has the Fed tended to use in recent years?

5. **The Federal Reserve track record** What does recent experience indicate regarding the Fed's ability to control the money supply (M2 and M3)? Why has the Fed abandoned setting a target for M1? In 1992, the Fed appeared to shift attention to the federal funds rate. Is this a step backward? Explain.

SELF-TESTS

Completion Questions

Complete each of the following statements by entering the missing words and/or choosing the best alternative proposed.

1. The primary thrust of *(monetary/fiscal)* policy is summarized in the _____ _____.

2. The _____ directive generally presents long-term target ranges for monetary *(policy/aggregates)*, which are usually expressed in *(an annual/a quarterly)* growth rate from one *(month/quarter)* to the same *(month/quarter)* of the following *(year/semester)*.

3. The _____ rate is the most volatile and variable rate in the money market.

4. The Federal Reserve's ultimate objective is to influence economic variables such as _____, _____, _____, and _____. The Federal Reserve, however, has no _____ over this set of variables.

5. In conducting _____ policy, the Federal Reserve employs its _____ to hit certain _____ targets, which in turn should influence the Fed's _____

targets and eventually achieve the Fed's _____ objective.

6. Targets over which the Federal Reserve has some direct control are called ___ _____ targets. Examples of these are _____ _____ and _____ _____.

7. *(Monetary aggregates/Reserve aggregates)* are considered *(intermediate/ultimate)* targets of the Federal Reserve.

8. In October 1979 the Federal Reserve switched its _____ target from a _____ target to a _____ target.

9. Reserve targets and federal funds rate targets will be compatible when the Federal Reserve wants to *(contract/expand)* reserves and simultaneously *(lower/ raise)* the federal funds rate.

10. Reserve targets and federal funds rate targets will be incompatible when the Federal Reserve wants to *(contract/expand)* reserves and *(lower/raise)* the federal funds rate at the same time.

True and False Questions

For each of the following statements, circle the letter T if it is correct or the letter F if it is *partially* or totally incorrect.

T F 1. Long-run target ranges for monetary aggregates presented in the directive of the Federal Open Market Committee are usually broad rather than narrow.

T F 2. An example of a monetary aggregate in a directive of the Federal Open Market Committee is the money supply narrowly defined.

T F 3. A directive of the Federal Open Market Committee contains substantial information about the current state of the economy.

T F 4. The target growth ranges for nonborrowed reserves and other measures of bank reserves can be found clearly stated in the Federal Open Market Committee's directive.

T F 5. The federal funds rate is the rate of interest charged on immediately available funds that are loaned overnight between banks.

T F 6. To achieve ultimate goals (full employment, price stability, and growth in GDP), the Federal Reserve employs its instruments to hit certain operating targets, hoping that in so doing it will indirectly contribute to the achievement of its ultimate goals.

T F 7. To serve as an intermediate target, a variable need not be completely under the control of the Federal Reserve but it must be one that can be strongly influenced by the Federal Reserve policy.

T F 8. The Federal Reserve exercises approximately the same degree of control over M2 and GDP.

T F 9. In establishing its plan, the Federal Reserve first decides on the rate of growth in bank reserves and then sets a target range for the growth in the monetary aggregates that is most consistent with the desired growth rate in bank reserves.

T F 10. In the Federal Reserve game plan, long-term rates of interest would qualify as operating targets, whereas short-term rates of interest would fall into the intermediate targets category.

T F 11. There is a consistency between reserve targeting and federal-funds-rate targeting. An increase in the former will generally produce higher federal

T F 12. The greater the stability and predictability of the velocity of a particular measure of the money supply, the better is that monetary aggregate as an intermediate target.

T F 13. The Gurley-Shaw argument would favor a narrowly defined money supply as the Federal Reserve's intermediate target.

T F 14. There is strong disagreement within the Federal Reserve System over whether monetary aggregates or long-term interest rates are the superior intermediate target.

T F 15. Monetary policy in the early 1990s was reminiscent of policy in the early 1970s.

T F 16. The Fed appeared to target the federal funds rate as the primary lever of monetary policy in the early 1990s.

T F 17. Setting a federal funds target would insulate the economy from shifts in the investment function.

T F 18. The Federal Reserve has been more successful in hitting its targeted growth rate for the money supply defined as M1 than for the money supply defined as M2.

T F 19. In mid-1982 the Federal Reserve switched from a federal funds target to a reserve aggregate target.

T F 20. In 1986, the Federal Reserve stopped setting growth targets for M1.

T F 21. In recent years there have been substantial deviations of M2 from the midpoint targets set by the FOMC.

Multiple-Choice Questions

Answer the following multiple-choice questions by circling the best alternative.

1. The Federal Reserve's ultimate objective is to
   a. influence the money supply
   b. influence money market rates
   c. influence total spending
   d. both (a) and (b)

2. Which of the following is *not* a part of the Federal Reserve's game plan?
   a. ultimate objectives such as the growth rate in GDP
   b. an intermediate target such as the money supply
   c. a change in the income tax rate that would

be consistent with a given growth rate in the monetary aggregates
   d. the tools of central banking
   e. both (c) and (d)

3. Clues as to the Fed's desired monetary policy can be found in
   a. the directive of the Federal Open Market Committee
   b. the Federal Reserve Bulletin
   c. the Federal Reserve weekly statement
   d. all of the above

4. The Federal Open Market Committee meets approximately
   a. once a week in Washington, D.C.
   b. once a month in New York City
   c. once a month in Washington, D.C.
   d. once a week in New York City

5. The formal general statement of Federal Reserve policies is known as the
   a. discount rate announcement
   b. Federal Open Market Committee directive
   c. money supply target
   d. Economic Report of the President

6. The directive of the Federal Open Market Committee (FOMC)
   a. always changes from one meeting to the next
   b. is made public one year after the meeting of the FOMC
   c. usually contains ten paragraphs with the last one stating in great detail how the Account Manager should implement open market operations on a daily basis
   d. all of the above
   e. none of the above

7. Which of the following items is considered a monetary aggregate?
   a. the monetary base
   b. total bank reserves
   c. total spending
   d. none of the above

8. Nonborrowed reserves are defined as
   a. total reserves minus bank borrowing from the Fed
   b. excess reserves minus bank borrowing from the Fed
   c. required reserves minus bank borrowing from the Fed
   d. the monetary base minus bank borrowing from the Fed

9. Which of the following is an operating target of the Federal Reserve?
   a. long-term interest rates
   b. the three-month Treasury Bill rate
   c. total reserves
   d. M2

10. The federal funds rate is an example of a Federal Reserve
    a. tool
    b. intermediate target
    c. operating target
    d. goal

11. The most sensitive indicator of pressure in the market for bank reserves is
    a. the discount rate
    b. the federal funds rate
    c. free reserves
    d. bank borrowing from the Federal Reserve
    e. the three-month Treasury bill rate

12. The federal funds rate will tend to move upward if
    a. a few banks have reserve deficiencies and the rest have ample excess reserves
    b. a few have excess reserves and the rest have a significant deficiency in reserves
    c. the Federal Reserve is buying government securities in the open market
    d. the Federal Reserve lowers the discount rate

13. A good intermediate target must meet certain requirements, such as
    a. it can be controlled by the Federal Reserve
    b. it is closely related to the Federal Reserve's ultimate goals (unemployment, inflation, and growth rate in GDP)
    c. it must be unique—that is, no alternative intermediate target must be available
    d. all of the above
    e. only (a) and (b)

14. The Federal Reserve's game plan includes an intermediate target because
    a. the Fed may miss its operating target
    b. the Fed's operating target is usually unreliable
    c. it usually takes too long to wait for a signal from the ultimate target (overall economic activity)
    d. ultimate targets (overall economic activity) can only be reached via an intermediary target

15. Which of the following economists would favor M1 over M2 as the Federal Reserve's intermediate target?
    a. Allan Meltzer
    b. Milton Friedman
    c. Edward Shaw
    d. John Gurley
    e. both (c) and (d)

16. In the early 1990s, as in the early 1970s, the Fed's policies appeared geared toward
    a. M1
    b. M2
    c. the monetary base
    d. the federal funds rate

17. The main advantage of targeting the monetary aggregates over interest rates as an intermediate target is that it helps to insulate the economy from unanticipated shifts in
    a. velocity
    d. the price level
    c. investment spending
    d. money demand

18. The Federal Reserve's recent track record regarding the growth rate in M2 and M3 shows an
    a. inability to stay within wide target ranges
    b. ability to stay within wide target ranges
    c. ability to stay within narrow target ranges
    d. ability to hit very precise targets

19. Before October 1979, the Federal Reserve favored the following operating target
    a. the federal funds rate
    b. reserve aggregates
    c. the money supply
    d. borrowed reserves
    e. none of the above

20. Throughout most of the 1980s, the Fed adopted an operating target stategy
    a. that focused on bank reserves
    b. that focused on the federal funds rate
    c. that focused on GDP
    d. that alternated between bank reserves and the federal funds rate

chapter 18

Budget Deficits and the Money Supply

Central Themes and Major Points

Fiscal policy—like monetary policy—is undertaken for the purpose of controlling and stabilizing economic activity. This chapter takes a closer look at fiscal policy (budget deficits) and its relationship to monetary policy (money supply).

The execution of fiscal policy is a two-step operation. First the government must raise a certain amount of funds to finance its expenditures. Then, the government spends these funds on goods and services. This fiscal process raises two questions of interest to us: (1) How does the government finance its expenditures? In other words, where does the money come from? It may come from any one of five sources: taxation, borrowing from the nonbank public, borrowing from banks, borrowing from the Federal Reserve, or printing money. (2) After the funds are raised and spent, has the quantity of money in circulation changed? In other words, what is the net effect of fiscal policy on the money supply? The answer depends on which method of *financing* the government has used. Some methods leave the money supply unaffected (taxation and borrowing from the nonbank public or from banks with zero excess reserves), while others change the money supply (borrowing from banks with excess reserves, or from the Fed, or printing money).

It is clear from the preceding paragraph that fiscal policy and monetary policy are not always independent. Fiscal policy may have monetary implications.

The second part of this chapter examines the connection between budget deficits and inflation. Do budget deficits produce excessive growth in the money supply, which in turn causes inflation? There is no definitive answer to this question. Deficits can at times be responsible for inducing faster growth in the money supply, but there is little evidence that this has indeed been the case in the United States in recent years. Nonetheless large deficits impose significant costs on the economy by reducing private investment and slowing economic growth.

New Terms

Define and/or explain the following terms introduced in this chapter:

Financing of government spending	Deficit spending
Taxation	Monetization of the public debt
Tax and loan accounts	Pegging the price of bonds

Essay Questions and Problems

*1. Financing government spending by taxation or by borrowing from the nonbank public are the same in terms of their effects on bank reserves and the money supply. These two financing methods, however, may differ from borrowing from commercial banks.

a. Explain why taxation and borrowing from the nonbank public are similar. What differences, if any, are there between the two methods of finance?

b. When will these two methods differ from borrowing from commercial banks and when will they be similar?

c. Suppose the public pays part of its taxes with funds borrowed from commercial banks. What, in this case, is the effect on bank reserves and the money supply? Illustrate your answer with T-accounts.

*2. What are the similarities and/or differences, if any, between the borrowing operations undertaken by the U.S. Treasury and the open market operations undertaken by the Federal Reserve? Are these two types of financial operations related in any manner?

*3. Suppose the U.S. Treasury has a budget surplus and decides to use these excess funds to *retire* a portion of its outstanding securities, that is, pay back a part of the national debt that is coming due.

a. How can the Treasury end up with a budget surplus?

b. What are the effects on bank reserves and the money supply of the Treasury's debt retirement operations?

*4. In terms of the effects on bank reserves and the money supply, financing government spending by Treasury borrowing from the Federal Reserve Banks or Treasury printing of currency are the same. Explain. What differences, if any, are there between the two methods of finance?

5. Explain why the sale of securities by the Treasury may end up as new money creation when the Federal Reserve is committed to a policy of holding down interest rates.

6. During and immediately after World War II, the Federal Reserve agreed to peg the price of U.S. Treasury bonds. How would the Fed implement this strategy? What were the economic consequences of this strategy?

7. The large deficits of the 1980s and 1990s have not caused significant inflation. Does this mean that deficits are not a problem? Why or why not?

SELF-TESTS

Completion Questions

Complete each of the following statements by entering the missing words and/or choosing the best alternative proposed.

1. The federal government can _____ its expenditures in any one of five alternative ways. It can raise the funds it needs by:

a. _____

b. _____

c. _____

d. _____

e. _____

2. When financing of government expenditures is undertaken through borrowing, the U.S. Treasury *(sells/buys)* bonds. This is called _____ spending.

3. Financing of government expenditures by taxing, borrowing from _____ _____, and borrowing from _____ _____ with zero excess reserves leaves the _____ _____ and _____ _____ unaltered. Borrowing from commercial banks with _____ raises the _____

_____ by the amount of the

_____, but leaves _____

_____ unchanged after the government spends. The net effect

of borrowing from the _____

_____ or _____ raises the

_____ and _____

_____ by the amount of the deficit.

4. The way _____ policy is financed has _____

_____ implications.

5. The _____

_____ Accord means that the Fed no longer has to _____

_____ the price of government securities.

6. When the Fed is forced to buy government securities, it inflates the volume of

bank _____ and turns the national debt into _____

_____. This process is referred to as the _____

_____.

True and False Questions

For each of the following statements, circle the letter T if it is correct or the letter F if it is *partially* or totally incorrect.

T F   1. The U.S. Treasury cannot borrow from banks if the banking system is loaned up, since no excess reserves will be available to banks to purchase securities.

T F   2. Shifts of funds from the "tax and loan" accounts at banks to the deposit of the U.S. Treasury at the Federal Reserve do not affect the money supply, because government demand deposits at banks are not counted in the money supply.

T F   3. Shifts of funds from the "tax and loan" accounts at banks to the deposit of the U.S. Treasury at the Federal Reserve do not affect bank reserves, because banks do not have to hold required reserves against government deposits.

T F   4. The only difference between the financing of government expenditures through taxation and through borrowing from the nonbank public is that in the case of borrowing the public becomes wealthier, since it winds up owning more government bonds than before.

T F   5. The difference between financing government spending by taxation and by borrowing from the nonbank public is that in the former (taxation) the nonbank public ends up with tax receipts, and in the latter (borrowing) the nonbank public ends up with interest-bearing government obligations.

T F   6. Assuming that banks have excess reserves, financing a federal deficit by Treasury sales of securities to banks increases the money supply when the Treasury spends the funds so obtained, but it does not increase total bank reserves.

T F   7. If the Treasury first increases its tax collections and subsequently increases its spending by an equal amount, there will be a temporary but not a lasting decrease in the money supply, other things being equal.

T F   8. If the Treasury finances government spending by selling bonds to banks, bank reserves are not affected even if the banks have excess reserves.

T F   9. If it is the growth in the money supply that causes inflation, then it may be said that increased government spending financed by borrowing from the nonbank public is no more inflationary than if that increase in spending were financed by taxation.

T F 10. A sale of $1 billion of newly issued U.S. government securities by the Treasury to Federal Reserve banks or to commercial banks in and of itself has no effect on total bank reserves or on the money supply.

T F 11. The inflationary pressures that result are the same whether the Treasury finances a $1 billion deficit by selling $1 billion of new Treasury currency to the Federal Reserve banks or by selling $1 billion of Treasury securities to the Federal Reserve banks.

T F 12. In general, the most inflationary method of financing a deficit is for the Treasury to obtain funds from Federal Reserve Banks.

T F 13. If the Treasury obtained additions to its checking accounts at Federal Reserve Banks by selling them Treasury currency instead of interest-bearing obligations, there could be a reduction in taxes, because the public would not have to pay the taxes needed to finance Treasury interest payments to Federal Reserve Banks on their holdings of these interest-bearing obligations.

T F 14. Financing an increase in government spending by "printing money" will produce a larger increase in GDP than will financing by borrowing from the nonbank public, because the latter will tend to lead to somewhat higher interest rates.

T F 15. When the Federal Reserve pegged the price of bonds, it lost control over the money supply, because it had to buy government securities whenever any holder wanted to sell, thereby supplying reserves to the banking system.

T F 16. Under the Treasury–Federal Reserve Accord the Fed agreed to maintain orderly conditions in the government securities market.

T F 17. Although the printing of money by the Treasury and the purchase of bonds by the Federal Reserve have the same effect on the money supply, they are not equivalent, because the Federal Reserve has the option of not buying the Treasury bonds.

T F 18. The U.S. Treasury has the constitutional authority to issue currency.

T F 19. Everything else being the same, a bond sale by the Treasury will raise interest rates. In order to prevent interest rates from rising, the Federal Reserve has to buy bonds. The result is a monetization of the public debt.

T F 20. Large government deficits in the 1980s were a major cause of inflation.

T F 21. Although deficits are not necessarily associated with high money supply growth, they do drive up interest rates.

Multiple-Choice Questions

Answer the following multiple-choice questions by circling the best alternative.

1. The government can finance its expenditures by raising funds through all of the following *except*
   a. taxing the public
   b. an open market sale undertaken by the Federal Reserve
   c. a borrowing from the public
   d. a bond sale to the Federal Reserve
2. Which of the following actions by the U.S. Treasury will leave the money supply unchanged after it has raised taxes to finance its expenditures?
   a. The U.S. Treasury deposits collected taxes in its accounts at the Federal Reserve Banks.
   b. The U.S. Treasury leaves collected taxes in its "tax and loan" accounts at commercial banks.
   c. The U.S. Treasury pays its suppliers.
   d. both (a) and (b)
3. When the Treasury borrows from the nonbank public and makes an expenditure of an equal amount, bank reserves
   a. are unaffected
   b. fall by an amount equal to the expenditure
   c. rise by an amount equal to the expenditure
   d. rise by an amount greater than the expenditure
4. The U.S. Treasury decides to build up its deposits at Federal Reserve Banks by shifting $100 million to the Fed from its "tax and loan accounts" at banks. The reserve requirement against demand deposits is 15 percent. This transfer will
   a. reduce bank reserves and the money supply by $100 million

b. reduce bank reserves by $100 million and leave the money supply unchanged

c. reduce bank reserves by $100 million and the money supply by $85 million

d. reduce bank reserves and the money supply by $85 million

5. The immediate and direct effect of a government expenditure of funds on deposit at the Federal Reserve banks is an

a. increase in bank reserves and the money supply by an amount equal to government spending

b. increase in bank reserves with no change in the money supply

c. increase in the money supply with no change in bank reserves

d. increase in bank reserves and the money supply by a smaller amount than government spending

6. An increase in government expenditures financed by borrowing from banks will

a. increase the money supply by an amount equal to the borrowing

b. not affect the money supply

c. increase the money supply by a multiple of the amount of the borrowing

d. either (a) or (b)

7. An increase in government expenditures financed by printing money will have the same effect on the economy as if the Treasury had

a. borrowed an equal amount from commercial banks

b. borrowed an equal amount from the non-bank public

c. borrowed an equal amount from the Federal Reserve

d. raised a lump-sum tax by an equal amount

e. none of the above

8. If the U.S. Treasury borrows from the public and uses the proceeds to pay off previously issued bonds that have reached their term to maturity, then

a. the money supply increases by an amount equal to the borrowing

b. the government debt outstanding increases by an amount equal to the borrowing

c. the economy's GDP increases by an amount equal to the borrowing

d. none of the above

9. Which of the following methods of financing government expenditures will have the largest net effect on the money supply?

a. taxing the public

b. borrowing from banks that have excess reserves

c. borrowing from banks that are loaned up

d. borrowing from the nonbank public

10. The reserve requirement against demand deposits is 20 percent. The government finances its expenditures by selling $100 million worth of bonds to the Federal Reserve. The effect of this action is a potential expansion in the money supply of

a. $100 million

b. $500 million

c. $400 million

d. none of the above

11. When comparing the Treasury's printing of money with the Treasury sale of bonds to the Federal Reserve, one should note that

a. T-accounts for these two methods of financing are almost the same

b. with the former financing method the Treasury gives the Fed a non-interest-bearing debt, but with the latter the Fed acquires an interest-bearing debt

c. the former financing method creates new money, whereas the latter creates money only if the Federal Reserve decides to purchase the newly issued Treasury securities

d. all of the above

12. The monetization of the public debt refers to

a. the Federal Reserve purchase of newly issued Treasury securities

b. the creation of money by commercial banks through the deposit multiplier

c. the printing of money by the Treasury in order to finance a budget deficit

d. the Treasury–Federal Reserve Accord of 1951, which resulted in the Fed purchasing all newly issued government bonds for a period of one year

e. none of the above

13. The reason Congress created the Federal Reserve was to

a. establish a means of financing a budget deficit that would not directly involve the Treasury

b. keep the printing presses away from the Treasury

c. have an agency that would regulate interest rates in the financial markets

d. ease the pain of deficit financing

e. all of the above

14. If the Federal Reserve decides to peg the price of government securities, then

a. the price of government securities will not fluctuate

b. the level of interest rates will not fluctuate

c. the amount of bonds the Fed buys and sells cannot be controlled

d. bank reserves and the money supply cannot be controlled

e. all of the above

15. The key element of the Treasury–Federal Reserve Accord of 1951 was an agreement that the Federal Reserve would
    a. not allow banks to borrow through the discount window
    b. not print currency
    c. minimize monetization of the debt
    d. guarantee the federal debt

16. Assume that the inflation rate is running at relatively high levels but the unemployment rate is low. If the government is running a deficit, good stabilization policy would suggest that the Treasury should finance the deficit by
    a. borrowing from the nonbank public
    b. borrowing from the Federal Reserve
    c. reducing taxes
    d. printing currency

17. If the unemployment rate is high but the inflation rate is low, sound stabilization policy would suggest that the Treasury finance a deficit by
    a. borrowing from the Federal Reserve
    b. taxation
    c. borrowing from the nonbank public
    d. borrowing from foreign investors

18. The evidence regarding the connection between budget deficits and the growth in the money supply in the United States in recent years indicates that
    a. the two are directly related
    b. the two are inversely related
    c. there is practically no long-run relationship between budget deficits and the growth in the money supply
    d. there is a weak but definite relationship between budget deficits and the growth in the money supply
    e. none of the above

19. The decision to monetize the federal debt is made by the
    a. Treasury
    b. Federal Reserve
    c. Congress
    d. President

20. When the Treasury sells bonds to the public, bond prices
    a. fall
    b. rise
    c. are unaffected
    d. rise or fall depending on whether deposit or nondeposit institutions purchase them

part IV

Monetary Theory

chapter 19

The Foundations of Monetarism

Central Themes and Major Points

This is the first of a series of chapters dealing with the issue of how changes in the money supply affect economic activity. It was pointed out as early as the first chapter that this fundamental question does not have a simple and standard answer. Different schools of economic thought have differing views on how money affects the course of the economy.

The dominant view from the eighteenth century until the mid-1930s was that of the *Classical school.* Its downfall came in 1936, the year John Maynard Keynes's *The General Theory of Employment, Interest and Money* was published. In his book Keynes presented revolutionary views on how the economic system works and how it is affected by money. Since the early 1960s a modified version of the Classical model, called *Monetarism,* has been challenging the *Keynesian* view. In the 1980s, rational expectations emerged, with even greater similarities to the Classical system. The implications of rational expectations are presented in Chapter 24.

This chapter examines the Classical economic system and shows how it is modified by the modern Monetarists. The following chapters deal with the Keynesian economic system and the dialogue between the Monetarists and the Keynesians.

The Classical economic system is built on two fundamental principles: (1) *Say's Law,* according to which market forces will ensure that the economy is always producing *the full employment level of output,* and (2) *The Quantity Theory of Money,* according to which a change in the money supply produces a proportionate change in the level of prices. Thus the Classical economic system is characterized by a full employment level of output, with changes in the quantity of money affecting only prices and nominal wages but not real output, employment, or real wages. The market mechanisms that will ensure this state of affairs are investigated in the chapter. In this respect, the *Classical theory of interest rate determination* plays an important role.

Keynes rejected the Classical view of the economic system. In particular, he showed that the economy can settle at less than full employment and that money may affect the level of production and employment. These and other aspects of the Keynesian revolution are developed in the next two chapters.

The chapter concludes with three additional topics. The first is a presentation of the quantity theory of money within an aggregate demand–aggregate supply framework. It is shown that an increase in the money supply will raise aggregate demand. If aggregate supply is fixed at full employment then the effect of an increase in the money supply is to raise prices. The second topic is a discussion on the differences between real and nominal rates of interest. The closing section examines how the Classical economic system has been modified by modern Monetarists, who treat the quantity theory more flexibly and allow for short-term unemployment.

New Terms

Define and/or explain the following terms introduced in this chapter:

Classical economics
Keynesian economics
Monetarism
Say's Law
Principle of
   laissez-faire
Equation of exchange:
   Transactions
   version
   Income version
   Cambridge version
Investment schedule
Aggregate demand
   schedule
Aggregate supply
   schedule
Transactions velocity
   of money
Income velocity of
   money

Cambridge k
Cash balances
Transactions demand
   for money
Quantity theory of
   money
Real versus nominal
   income
Real versus nominal
   wage rates†
Real versus nominal
   money supply
Real versus nominal
   interest rates†
Full employment level
   of output
Inflation premium
Rational expectations†

†More on these terms in Chapters 23 and 24.

Essay Questions and Problems

1. **Say's Law** State Say's Law and carefully explain its meaning. Define full employment and describe the market mechanisms that will ensure full employment in a Classical world.

2. **Malthus's criticism of Say's Law** What is the argument used by Thomas Malthus to criticize Say's Law? What is the response made by Classical economists to this criticism?

3. **The investment schedule** Explain why the investment schedule is inversely related to the level of interest rates. Is there disagreement between Keynesians and Classical economists on this matter?

4. **The Classical interest theory** How is the level of interest rates determined in the Classical economic system? Explain the process through which the interest rate adjusts to a new equilibrium level following a shift in the saving or investment curve.

5. **The principle of laissez-faire** Discuss the importance for the Classical economic system of the principle of laissez-faire, that is, noninterference in the interplay of market forces.

6. **The equation of exchange** Identify the three versions of the equation of exchange, and distinguish between the income velocity of money, the transactions velocity of money, and the factor k in the Cambridge equation of exchange.

7. What is the difference between the level of real income in the income version of the equation of exchange and the level of total transactions in the transactions version of the equation of exchange? Which of the two is larger?

8. Distinguish between the equation of exchange and the quantity theory of money. What assumptions are required to get from the equation of exchange to the quantity theory of money? What is the major conclusion reached by the quantity theory of money?

9. **The transmission process of a change in the money supply** Explain the transmission process whereby a change in the money supply affects other variables in the system, using the cash-balance version of the quantity theory of money.

10. **Monetarism** Show how the Classical quantity theory of money was modified by the modern Monetarists, and discuss the implications for monetary policy.

*11. **The equation of exchange** Suppose that the money supply (M) is equal to \$400 billion, the income velocity of money (V) is equal to 5, and the price level (P) is equal to 2. Answer the following questions.
   a. What is the value of the nominal money supply?
   b. What is the level of real output (Y)?
   c. What is the value of the economy's GDP?
   d. What is the value of the real money supply?
   e. What is the value of the fraction (k) of GDP that the public has command over in the form of money balances, according to the Cambridge version of the equation of exchange?
   f. Suppose that the transactions velocity (V_t) of money is equal to 50. What is the total level of real transactions in the economy? Why is it larger than the real output?

*12. **The quantity theory of money** Use the same information as in problem 11. Suppose that the money supply increases by \$40 billion. Answer the following questions.
   a. What is the corresponding increase in the price level according to the quantity theory of money?
   b. Has the price level increased by an amount equal to the increase in the money supply

or by an amount proportionate to the increase in the money supply? What is the proportionality factor?

c. What assumptions about the income velocity (V) and the real output (Y) did Classical economists make in order to answer question b?

d. What is the *percentage* change in the money supply?

e. What is the corresponding *percentage* change in the level of prices, according to the quantity theory of money? What can you conclude?

f. What is the real money supply, according to the quantity theory of money? What can you conclude?

*13. **Monetarism** Assume that the money supply (M) is equal to $500 billion, the price level (P) is equal to 2, and the real output (Y) is equal to $1,500 billion. According to the modern Monetarists, the economy may not be at the full employment level of output in the short run. Suppose that the full employment real output (Y_{FE}) is equal to $1,650 billion. Answer the following questions.

a. What is the economy's current GDP?

b. What is the full employment GDP at the current price level?

c. Monetarists claim that in a situation of underemployment an increase in the money supply will produce an increase in both the price level and the real output. Suppose that in the short run the income velocity and the price level are fixed. By how much should the money supply be increased in order to bring the economy to the full employment level of output?

d. Question c ignores the price response of an increase in the money supply. It assumes that the additional money raises real output only. Suppose that an increase in the money supply raises both real output and the price level. If the income velocity of money remains constant and the price level increases by 5 percent, by how much should the money supply be increased in order to bring the economy to the full employment level of output? Assume that all changes occur over the same time period.

SELF-TESTS

Completion Questions

Complete each of the following statements by entering the missing words and/or choosing the best alternative proposed.

1. Say's Law can be succinctly stated as follows: _____
_____.

2. The dominant force in macroeconomics from the eighteenth century until 1936 is referred to as the _____ school. It was replaced by the _____ school named after its founder, the British economist _____.

3. In the 1960s and 1970s economists known as the _____ reconstructed the _____ school and mounted a determined challenge to _____ economics.

4. The two pillars that supported the structure of the Classical school were _____ _____ and the _____
_____.

5. According to the Classical school the level of interest rates is determined by the interplay of _____ and
_____.

6. In the Classical economic system the equilibrium level of output is the _____ _____ level of output. If the economy is not at the _____ level of output, there are market mechanisms that will bring it back to the _____ level. These are _____ _____, _____, and _____ _____.

7. The three versions of the *(equation of exchange/quantity theory of money)* are the _____ version, the _____ version, and the _____ or _____ version.

8. According to the income version of the *(quantity theory of money/equation of exchange)*, the product of the _____ and the _____ must be identical to the product of the _____ and the level of output.

9. According to the transactions version of the _____ _____, the product of the _____ and the _____ must be identical to the product of the _____ and by the total level of _____.

10. According to the Classical *(equation of exchange/quantity theory of money)* a change in the *(price level/money supply)* produces *(an equal/a proportionate)* change in the *(money supply/price level)*.

11. According to the _____ perspective, government efforts at fine-tuning the economy will be unsuccessful, because increases in the _____ simultaneously generate expectations of higher prices.

True and False Questions

For each of the following statements, circle the letter T if it is correct or the letter F if it is *partially* or totally incorrect.

T F   1. Classical and Keynesian economists have somewhat related views on how money affects economic activity. The difference between the two schools is that the Classical economists believe that money plays a minor role, whereas the Keynesians contend that money plays a major role in determining the level of income.

T F   2. Monetarists and Classical economists

have diametrically opposed views on the impact of money on economic activity.

T F 3. The quantity theory of money and Say's Law constitute the foundation upon which Keynesian economics was built.

T F 4. According to the French economist J. B. Say, the actual level of production would always be at the full employment level.

T F 5. Thomas Malthus launched a vigorous attack on the teaching of the Classical school.

T F 6. The two pillars that supported the structure of the Classical school were "Say's Law" and "The Saving Theory."

T F 7. According to Say's Law demand creates its own supply, meaning that the business sector will always produce enough goods to satisfy the public's demand.

T F 8. Keynesian economics can be viewed as an adaptation of Classical economic theory to the realities of modern economies.

T F 9. Some of the arguments advanced by Thomas Malthus in the early nineteenth century were later refined and formalized by Keynes.

T F 10. A necessary condition for the validity of the Classical interest theory is that saving must be an increasing function of the level of interest rates.

T F 11. In the Classical economic system money does not influence the rate of interest.

T F 12. According to the Classical economists, an increase in the money supply will increase the economy's real output.

T F 13. The Classical theory of interest rate determination is nothing more than an elaboration of one of the market mechanisms underlying Say's Law.

T F 14. In the Classical model, changes in the rate of interest are brought about by shifts in the saving curve and not from shifts in the investment curve.

T F 15. According to Classical interest theory, the rate of interest is a real phenomenon and not a monetary phenomenon.

T F 16. The Classical model shows that the interest rate will decline as a result of

either an increase in the thriftiness of the public or an increase in the money supply.

T F 17. The equation of exchange and the quantity theory of money are alternative names used to describe the role played by money within the Classical economic system.

T F 18. An increase in the fraction of the economy's GDP held by the public in the form of money will increase the income velocity of money.

T F 19. All versions of the equation of exchange are identities that must be true by definition.

T F 20. If one wants to look at money as something demanded by the public as opposed to money as something that is turned over in exchange for goods, then the $M = kPY$ version of the equation of exchange should be used rather than the $MV = PY$ version.

T F 21. According to the Classical quantity theory of money, an increase in the money supply by one dollar will increase prices by one dollar, assuming that the velocity of money remains constant.

T F 22. The cash-balance version of the quantity theory of money emphasizes that the public is concerned with its nominal money balances rather than its real money balances.

T F 23. The cash-balance version of the quantity theory makes it clear that a doubling of the money supply leads to a doubling of real GDP.

T F 24. According to quantity theory reasoning, an initial equilibrium upset by a change in the total money supply is replaced by a new equilibrium as a result of actions by the public that restore the total money supply to its original amount.

T F 25. In the equation of exchange, MV may be equal to, less than, or greater than PY.

T F 26. The assumptions of the Classical economic system led to the conclusion that a change in the nominal money supply affects prices and money wage rates but not real output, employment, or real wage rates.

T F 27. According to the Classicists, inflation is a monetary phenomenon.

T F 28. According to Irving Fisher, the difference between the nominal and the real rate of interest reflects an inflation premium.

T F 29. If the *current* rate of inflation is 6 percent and the real rate of interest is 4 percent, then, according to Irving Fisher, the nominal rate of interest should be equal to 10 percent.

T F 30. Inflationary expectations, according to Irving Fisher, should raise the real and the nominal rates of interest.

T F 31. A vertical aggregate supply schedule reflects the Classical assumption that the economy is at the level of full employment.

T F 32. An increase in the price level will shift the aggregate supply curve to the right.

T F 33. In the Classical system, shifts in the aggregate demand curve in response to changes in the money supply are graphic representations of the quantity theory of money.

T F 34. Though allowing for short-term unemployment, modern Monetarists view the economy as highly stable.

T F 35. Rational expectations is based on the theory that people use all available information to determine their expectations about the future inflation rate.

Multiple-Choice Questions

Answer the following multiple-choice questions by circling the best alternative.

1. Which of the following economists would *not* be considered a member of the Classical school?
   a. Jean Baptiste Say
   b. Thomas Malthus
   c. Adam Smith
   d. Irving Fisher
   e. both (b) and (c)
2. According to Classical economists, saving is
   a. inversely related to the level of interest rates
   b. directly related to the level of income
   c. directly related to the level of interest rates
   d. inversely related to the level of income
   e. none of the above
3. In the Classical economic system, the economy's real GDP is determined by
   a. the supply of capital, the labor force, and

existing technology
   b. the level of interest rates
   c. the thriftiness of the public and the productivity of capital
   d. the quantity of money in circulation
4. According to Classical economists, a change in the money supply should affect
   a. the economy's GDP
   b. the price of goods and services
   c. the level of real output
   d. all of the above
   e. only (a) and (b)
5. The transactions velocity of money
   a. is larger than the income velocity of money
   b. is smaller than the income velocity of money
   c. is about equal to the income velocity of money
   d. cannot be compared with the income velocity of money without additional information on prices and the volume of transactions
6. Which of the following is an assumption of the Classical economic system?
   a. Prices, wages, and the level of interest rates are perfectly flexible.
   b. The level of prices changes proportionately to a change in the money supply.
   c. The velocity of money is constant.
   d. all of the above
   e. only (a) and (c)
7. Using the cash-balance version of the quantity theory with $k = 0.2$ and GDP equal to $500 billion, cash balances must be equal to
   a. $2500 billion
   b. $100 billion
   c. $20 billion
   d. $500 billion
8. The Cambridge version of the equation of exchange is also referred to as
   a. the cash-balance approach to the equation of exchange
   b. the transactions approach to the equation of exchange
   c. the Fisherian approach to the equation of exchange
   d. none of the above
9. The Cambridge version of the equation of exchange can be interpreted as
   a. a supply-of-money equation
   b. a demand-for-money equation
   c. a theory-of-interest-rate determination
   d. both (a) and (b)
10. If the money supply and the price level double but the velocity of money remains the same, then one can say that
    a. the nominal amount of money held by the public has increased

b. the real amount of money held by the public has not changed

c. the economy's GDP has increased

d. all of the above

e. only (a) and (b)

11. If the fraction of the economy's GDP held by the public in the form of money is equal to 20 percent, then the income velocity of money should be equal to
    a. 2
    b. 4
    c. 5
    d. 0.5
    e. none of the above

12. In the Classical model aggregate demand determines the
    a. money supply
    b. price level
    c. level of output
    d. interest rate

13. In the Classical economic system the level of interest rates is determined by
    a. savings and investment
    b. thrift and productivity
    c. the demand for capital goods by entrepreneurs
    d. all of the above
    e. only (a) and (b)

14. The money supply originally at 400 units is increased by 20 additional units by the Central Bank. If the price level was originally 10 units, then the quantity theory of money predicts that the price level should increase to a new level equal to
    a. 10.5
    b. 30
    c. 15
    d. cannot be determined without additional information

15. In the absence of inflationary expectations we should expect
    a. the real and nominal rates of interest to be equal
    b. the real rate to exceed the nominal rate of interest
    c. the nominal rate to exceed the real rate of interest
    d. none of the above

16. Which of the following economists would best represent the Monetarist approach?
    a. Milton Friedman
    b. Paul Samuelson
    c. Irving Fisher
    d. William Ritter

17. The quantity theory of money can be summarized by the following expression

a. $MV = PY$

b. $MV = PT$

c. $M = kPY$

d. any of the above

e. none of the above

18. According to the quantity theory of money
    a. a change in the nominal money supply will produce an equal change in the price level
    b. a percentage change in the nominal money supply will produce an equal percentage change in the price level
    c. a change in the real money supply will produce a proportionate change in the price level
    d. a change in the nominal money supply will produce a proportionate change in the price level
    e. both (b) and (d)

19. If the nominal money supply is equal to $200 million and the price level is equal to 2, the real money supply is equal to
    a. $100 billion
    b. $400 billion
    c. $50 billion
    d. none of the above

20. If the nominal money supply increases at a faster rate than inflation, then the real money supply
    a. will drop
    b. will rise
    c. will remain the same
    d. cannot be determined

21. Suppose that the nominal money supply is equal to $300 billion, the income velocity of money is equal to 6, and the price level is equal to 3. Then real output should be equal to
    a. 1,800
    b. 600
    c. 900
    d. 1,200

22. According to the previous question, the economy's GDP is equal to
    a. 1,800
    b. 600
    c. 900
    d. 1,200

23. In the Classical economic system the velocity of money is determined by
    a. the basic payment habits of the community
    b. the level of interest rates

c. the real value of the money supply
d. dividing GDP by the nominal money supply

24. Assuming a fixed downward sloping investment schedule, an increase in saving will, in the Classical model,
    a. reduce the level of interest rates
    b. not affect the level of interest rates
    c. increase the level of interest rates
    d. increase real output
    e. both (a) and (b)

25. According to the Monetarists, an increase in the money supply may
    a. raise the price level
    b. increase real output
    c. increase the economy's GDP
    d. all of the above
    e. only (a) and (c)

26. When one moves down along the aggregate demand schedule,
    a. the money supply drops and the income velocity of money rises
    b. the money supply remains the same but the income velocity of money rises
    c. the money supply and the income velocity of money remain the same
    d. the money supply drops and the income velocity of money decreases

27. The reason why the aggregate demand schedule is inversely related to the general price level is that
    a. a given stock of money buys more goods and services at a lower price level
    b. the income velocity of money rises as the economy approaches full employment
    c. lower prices generate more demand, since consumers substitute cheaper goods for other goods (substitution effect)
    d. lower prices generate higher real income, which in turn increases demand (income effect)
    e. both (c) and (d)

28. An increase in the money supply will
    a. shift the aggregate demand schedule to the right
    b. shift the aggregate demand schedule to the left
    c. leave the aggregate demand schedule unaffected
    d. reduce the general level of prices
    e. both (b) and (d)

29. Modern monetarists argue that the velocity of money is
    a. constant
    b. immeasurable
    c. unstable
    d. predictable

30. Monetarists have maintained the Classical tradition by emphasizing the
    a. inherent stability of the economy
    b. importance of government fiscal policy
    c. instability of money demand
    d. inflationary impact of government spending

GDP Definitions and Relationships

Central Themes and Major Points

The performance of the economy is the result of the interrelationships between the various participants in the daily economic life of the nation. These basic interrelationships are examined in this appendix with the help of what is called the *circular flow* of spending, income, and output. The participants in economic activity are divided into three groups: (1) *households,* (2) *business firms,* and (3) *the government.*

First, the simplest circular flow is analyzed. In this case there is no leakage in the form of household saving, no business investment, and no government sector. Firms produce goods and services (output) for sale, and households buy these goods and services and consume them. This basic circular flow is then modified to take into account the existence of saving, investment, and *government expenditure.*

The economy's GDP, which is equal to the sum of *consumption* expenditure by households (C), investment expenditure by firms (I), and government expenditure (G), is said to be in *equilibrium* when there is no tendency for output to change—that is, the level of production is maintained. This will occur whenever the *desired* level of savings by households plus taxes collected by the government ($S + T$) is equal to the *desired* level of investment spending by firms plus government expenditure ($I + G$).

It is important that you distinguish between desired *(ex ante)* saving and investment, which refer to what households and business firms *want* to do, and *actual (ex post)* savings and investment, which are mere accounting data. Ignoring the government sector, the former may *differ* whereas the latter are *always* equal.

Finally, it should be recognized that GDP can be looked at as the sum of households, firms, and government expenditures (GDP = $C + I + G$) as well as the product of the money supply and the velocity of money (GDP = $M \times V$), since $M \times V$ is nothing more than the total spending by all economic participants to buy the year's GDP.

New Terms

Define and/or explain the following terms introduced in this appendix:

Circular flow diagram	Actual (ex post)
Real flows	saving
Money flows	Desired (ex ante)
Households	investment
Business firms	Actual (ex post)
National income (Y)	investment
Consumer expenditure	Equilibrium output
Desired (ex ante)	Government
saving	expenditure (G)

Essay Questions and Problems

1. **The circular flow diagram**
   a. What is a circular flow diagram?
   b. What are the various elements required to draw a circular flow diagram?
   c. Why is the circular flow diagram a useful tool to describe economic activity?
   d. What is the role of financial markets in the circular flow of spending, income, and output?

2. **Two ways of measuring the economy's GDP** Explain why annual GDP can be measured either by adding up the value of all final goods and services produced by the economy in the course of one year or by adding up the annual income of every individual in the economy.

3. **Real versus financial investment**
   a. What is the difference between a consumption good and an investment good?
   b. Distinguish between financial investment and real investment undertaken by business firms.

4. **Desired saving and investment versus actual saving and investment**
   a. What is the difference between desired (ex ante) saving and investment and actual (ex post) saving and investment?
   b. Explain why the level of production is maintained whenever desired saving equals desired investment (ignore the government sector).
   c. Why is actual saving always equal to actual investment regardless of what is happening to the level of production?
   Note: Ex ante means *before* all is said and done, and ex post means *after* all is said and done.

5. **Equilibrium output**
   a. What is meant by "the economy is in equilibrium"?
   b. Show that in the presence of a government sector a situation of equilibrium implies that $S + T = I + G$.

6. **The relationship between the economy's GDP and the money supply** The economy's GDP equals total spending on goods and services and can be expressed either as $Y = C + I + G$ or as $Y = M \times V$.
   a. How does each expression view total spending?
   *b. Would it be possible in *practice* to measure the economy's actual GDP using either one of these two expressions?
   c. Under which circumstances would you emphasize one expression over the other?
   *d. Suppose that for a given year consumer expenditure is 1,000, investment spending is 200, government spending is 300, and the money supply is 300. What is the value of the velocity of money?

SELF-TESTS

Completion Questions

Complete each of the following statements by entering the missing words and/or choosing the best alternative proposed.

1. The total value of goods and services produced by resources located in the United States over a given period of time is called _____ _____ or simply _____.

2. Households supply firms with _____, _____ _____, _____, and _____, which are the factor services required for production. In exchange, households receive a total income in the form of _____, _____ _____, _____, and _____ _____.

3. The _____ diagram is used to depict the interrelationships between groups of economic participants. It consists of _____ flows and _____ flows linking the _____ sector, the _____ _____ sector, and the _____ sector.

4. The three components of GDP are _____ expenditure, _____ expenditure, and _____ expenditure.

5. *(Desired/Actual)* saving and _____ may differ, but _____ saving and _____ are _____ .

6. If *(desired/actual)* _____ plus _____ _____ equals *(desired/actual)* _____ plus _____ _____ , then the level of production will be maintained.

7. GDP can be viewed as total spending made by _____ , _____ , and the _____ . Alternatively, it can be viewed as total spending measured by the _____ _____ times the _____ _____ .

True and False Questions

For each of the following statements, circle the letter T if it is correct or the letter F if it is *partially* or *totally incorrect*.

T F   1. The circular flow is a convenient representation of the interrelationships between economic participants.

T F   2. Saving is the part of current production that is not consumed.

T F   3. When the economy is in equilibrium, saving plus government spending equals investment plus taxes.

T F   4. Investment refers to the purchase of financial assets by business firms.

T F   5. Investment goods are used in the production of consumption goods.

T F   6. Assuming no government sector, if business firms underinvest, then their saving must exceed business investment.

T F   7. Desired saving must always equal desired investment. It's an accounting identity, always true by definition.

T F   8. It is through financial markets that household saving is channeled to business firms.

T F   9. If government expenditure equals taxes, then desired saving equals desired investment.

T F   10. The circular flow diagram shows a flow of goods and services from households to firms and a flow of factor services from firms to households.

T F   11. In the simple circular flow diagram, the money flow in the form of income payments is equal in value to the real flow in the form of factor services.

T F   12. If all income payments made to households were used by households to purchase consumer goods and services, the role of financial markets in the economy would be far less important than it actually is.

T F   13. As GDP is equal to $C + I + G$ (for a closed economy, that is, no imports or exports) and is equal to $M \times V$, there is no difference in terms of economic content or meaning between writing GDP = $C + I + G$ and writing GDP = $M \times V$.

T F 14. A financial transaction, by itself, need not imply any real expenditure.

Multiple-Choice Questions

Answer the following multiple-choice questions by circling the best alternative.

1. Saving represents
   a. a leakage in the circular flow
   b. consumption expenditure in excess of total income
   c. the portion of income deposited in savings accounts
   d. all of the above
   e. only (a) and (b)
2. When economic activity is in a state of equilibrium,
   a. desired saving is equal to desired investment
   b. national income remains unchanged
   c. the level of production is the same
   d. all of the above
   e. only (a) and (c)
3. Which of the following is *not* an investment expenditure?
   a. the purchase of a new car
   b. the construction of an office building
   c. the purchase by a firm of a new machine tool
   d. a buildup in a firm's inventory
   e. none of the above
4. If investment expenditure is 200, government spending is 400, the money supply is 400, and the velocity of money is 4, then consumption expenditure is
   a. 800
   b. 1,000
   c. 400
   d. 600
   e. cannot be determined with the information given
5. If consumption expenditure is 900, saving is 250, and taxes are 450, then national income
   a. cannot be determined since no information

is given on either investment or government expenditure
   b. is 1,350
   c. is 1,250
   d. is 1,000
   e. is 1,600
6. The largest component of GDP is
   a. consumer expenditure
   b. investment expenditure
   c. government expenditure
   d. none has consistently been the largest over the last twenty years
   e. (a) and (c) are of equal magnitude
7. Which of the following is *not* a form of income received by households?
   a. wages
   b. rent
   c. capital
   d. interest
   e. profits
8. The economy's GDP is
   a. the market value of all new goods and services produced by the economy in the course of one year
   b. the market value of all final goods and services produced by the economy in the course of one year
   c. the total dollar volume of all expenditures undertaken in the economy in the course of one year
   d. defined as either (a) or (b)
   e. none of the above
9. If consumer expenditure is 470, investment is 160, government spending is 170, and the money supply is 200, then the velocity of money is equal to
   a. 5
   b. 3
   c. 4
   d. 2
   e. 6
10. Which of the following is a leakage in the circular flow?
   a. investment
   b. government spending
   c. taxes
   d. consumption
   e. none of the above

chapter 20

The Keynesian Framework

Central Themes and Major Points

The previous chapter described the Classical economic system and the foundations of Monetarism. The major weakness of the Classical model was its inability to explain extended periods of unemployment. According to the Classics, unemployment could not persist over too long a period of time, because market forces are always at work to bring the economy back to full employment. To the Classics, full employment was the *equilibrium* level of output.

Then came Keynes. He built a new economic system capable of explaining why the economy could settle at a level of equilibrium output that differed from the full employment level. The Keynesian economic system is examined in this chapter.

According to Keynes the level of output is determined by the level of total desired expenditure of consumers, firms (investment), and the government. If desired total expenditures are below the level that will ensure full employment, then the government should intervene to restore full employment. The economy has no built-in mechanisms that will move it toward full employment by itself.

What did Keynes have to say about the rate of interest and the effect of money on economic activity? First recall the position of the Classics on these matters: the rate of interest is determined by the interaction of the investment and the savings decisions of the public, and money affects prices only. Keynes took a radical position: the rate of interest is determined by the interaction

of the supply of money made available by the monetary authority and the demand for money of the public. Money may affect the level of economic activity via the interest rate. A change in the money supply will change the interest rate, which in turn will alter investment spending and the economy's real GDP.

Keynesians' monetary theory is built around the public's demand for money and liquidity preference. According to Keynes the public demands money for two major purposes: to carry out day-to-day transactions—the transactions demand for money—and to purchase interest-bearing financial assets (bonds)—the speculative demand for money. The former is directly related to the level of income, and the latter is inversely related to the rate of interest. The second part of the chapter examines the Keynesian liquidity preference function in detail and discusses its implications for monetary policy. The chapter concludes with an aggregate demand and supply analysis of the Keynesian system and introduces the notion of supply-side economics.

New Terms

Define and/or explain the following terms introduced in this chapter:

Economic models
Desired expenditures
Consumption function
Marginal propensity
  to save

Induced changes in
  spending
Autonomous changes
  in spending
Multiplier

Disposable income
Liquidity preference
Total demand for
 money
Speculative demand
 for money
Transactions demand
 for money
Marginal propensity
 to consume
Saving function
Flow variables
Keynesian "normal"
 interest rate

Liquidity trap†
Anticipation of
 monetary policy
Investment function
Interest sensitivity of:
 the demand for
 money
 the investment
 function
Exogenous variables
Hoarding
Supply-side economics

†More on this term in Chapter 21

Notes: 1. Other important terms directly related to this chapter were introduced in the Appendix to Chapter 19. Those terms should be reviewed before proceeding with this chapter.
2. The terms *income, GDP,* and *output* are used interchangeably and are represented by the capital letter *Y*.

Essay Questions and Problems

1. If, contrary to the Classical school of thought, the interest rate does not fall to eliminate an excess of saving over investment and if prices and wages do not fall as unsold goods pile up, how does the economy adjust to correct for this disequilibrium, according to Keynes?

2. Contrast the effects of a shift in the investment curve with the saving and investment diagram of the Classical school's theory, and with the saving and investment diagram of Keynes's theory.

3. Explain the concept of the multiplier. Explain the relationship between the size of the multiplier and the size of the marginal propensity to consume or the size of the marginal propensity to save.

4. Distinguish carefully between autonomous changes in spending and induced changes in spending, and then discuss the implications of this distinction for the Keynesian economic system.

*5. Consider a simple economy in which investment is constant and equal to $50 billion. There are no government or foreign sectors, and the price level is constant. Assume that consumption behavior can be described as *C* = $40 billion + 0.8 *Y*.

a. What is the value of the marginal propensity to consume?
b. What would be the value of consumption if *Y* = $500 billion?
c. What is the equilibrium value of GDP in this model? Verify by showing that saving equals investment in equilibrium.
d. What is the value of the multiplier in this model? What determines the size of the multiplier?
e. Suppose that desired investment were to fall to $40 billion. What would happen to equilibrium income?

*6. **Problem on the determination of the equilibrium level of output** The purpose of this problem is to illustrate (1) how the equilibrium output (GDP) is determined in the simple Keynesian framework, and (2) how changes in government expenditure and taxation affect the equilibrium output. Consider an economy in which desired investment spending is autonomous and equal to $175 billion (*I* = 175) and government spending is equal to $25 billion (*G* = 25). The consumption schedule is:

Income *(Y)*	0	400	800	1,200
Consumption *(C)*	50	350	650	950

This means that consumption expenditure equals $50 billion when income is zero, $350 billion when income is $400 billion, and so on. Answer the following questions:

a. *Determination of the consumption function* Based on the consumption schedule above, draw the *consumption function* in Figure 20.1. We also wish to derive the *equation* that represents this consumption function. We know that it can be expressed as:

C = (Autonomous consumption) + (MPC) × *Y*

where MPC stands for the marginal propensity to consume.
(1) From the consumption schedule get the autonomous consumption. Recall that this is the level of consumption at zero income.
(2) The MPC is equal to the ratio of a change in consumption to the corresponding change in income. Using the consumption schedule, get the MPC and write the equation of the consumption function.
(3) *Derivation of the saving function from the consumption function*

Derive the equation of the saving function from that of the consumption function. Recall that saving (S) is equal to ($Y - C$). Show that the equation of the saving function is expressed as:

$$S = - \text{(Autonomous consumption)} + \text{(MPS)} \times Y$$

where MPS stands for the marginal propensity to save. Fill in the values of saving in the saving schedule below and draw the saving function in Figure 20.2.

Income (Y)	0	400	800	1,200
Saving (S)				

b. *Determination of the equilibrium output*
Draw on Figure 20.1 the 45 degree line that starts at the origin.
(1) What do points along the 45 degree line indicate?
(2) Draw the total expenditure line. Recall that total expenditures equal $C + I + G$. You have to add ($I + G$) to the consumption function.
(3) What is the level of equilibrium output in Figure 20.1?
(4) *Algebraic determination of equilibrium output*
We also wish to determine the equilibrium output algebraically, without using the graphs in Figure 20.1. This can be done by solving the equation:

Total Expenditures = Equilibrium Output

$$C + I + G = Y_{eq}$$

where C is the consumption function. Using the above equation determine Y_{eq}.
(5) *Determination of equilibrium output using the Saving-Investment Approach*
You can use the Saving-Investment diagram in Figure 20.2 to determine equilibrium output geometrically. Equilibrium output is found at the intersection point of the saving function and total investment. Recall that total investment consists of a firm's investment ($I = 175$) plus government spending ($G = 25$). Draw in Figure 20.2 the horizontal line ($I + G = 200$), which represents total investment. It is horizontal because total investment is independent of income.

c. *Disequilibrium*
Suppose that output is equal to $1,200 billion instead of the equilibrium output obtained above.
(1) Show that in this case output exceeds total expenditures.
(2) In this case desired saving must be different from desired investment. What is the value of *undesired* investment?
(3) What will happen to next period's output: will it remain the same, will it rise, or will it decline? What will be the magnitude of the change in output?
d. *Change in government spending without taxation*
Suppose that the full employment level of output is equal to $1,200 billion and that actual output is at the level determined in question b above.
(1) What is the value of the *output gap*? According to Keynes, is there a tendency for the economy to bridge this gap automatically?
(2) Keynes argued that the government should intervene to bridge the output gap. By how much should government expenditure (unaccompanied by taxation) rise in order to accomplish this objective? Recall that a change in government expenditure will change output by a multiple k_y of the change in government expenditure where k_y is the *income multiplier* derived from the consumption function.
e. *Change in government spending with lump-sum taxes*
Suppose that the government collects a $50 billion lump-sum tax in order to finance its expenditure.
(1) What is the equation that represents the consumption function when the $50 billion tax is taken into account? Recall that consumption expenditure is a function of *disposable* income, that is, after-tax income.
(2) What is the value of autonomous consumption in the after-tax consumption function? What is the change in autonomous consumption (the difference between autonomous consumption without taxes and with taxes)?
(3) The imposition of the tax will reduce consumption and lower output by a multiple k_y of the change in autonomous consumption spending. By how much

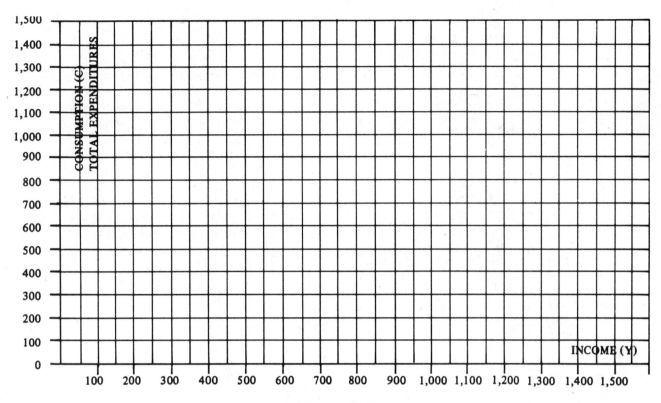

Figure 20.1
The Cross Diagram

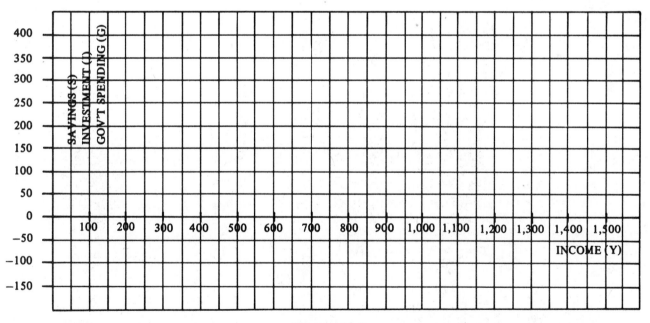

Figure 20.2
The Saving-Investment Diagram

will output decline as the result of the tax collection? Recall that the simple income multiplier k_y applies in this case, since this multiplier gives the change in output (or income) in response to a change in any autonomous spending (government, investment, or consumption).

(4) What is the net effect on output if the government spends $50 billion financed by a lump-sum tax of $50 billion?

*7. **Determination of the equilibrium level of interest rates**   The purpose of this exercise is to illustrate (1) how the equilibrium rate of interest is determined in the Keynesian framework, and (2) how monetary policy operates and under which conditions it is more effective in influencing the economy's GDP.

a. *The liquidity preference function*
   According to Keynes the public's liquidity preference or demand for money has two components: (1) the transactions demand for money, which is determined primarily by income Y, and (2) the speculative demand for money, which is determined primarily by the interest rate r. The schedules in Table 20.1 give the transactions and speculative demands for money. Note that the transactions demand is fixed at $100 billion as the interest rate ($r\%$) changes.
   (1) Fill in the last row in the table. This is the public's liquidity preference. It can be viewed as the sum of the transactions and speculative demands for money. All numbers are in billions of dollars.
   (2) Draw the liquidity preference curve on Figure 20.3 and label it LP_1. Explain why it is downward sloping.
   (3) At which rate of interest is the economy in a liquidity trap?

b. *Determination of the equilibrium interest rate*
   The money supply is assumed to be autonomous (exogenous). This means that the money supply is determined by the Federal Reserve and not by the interest rate or any other variable. Suppose the money supply is set by the Federal Reserve at $275 billion. What is the equilibrium interest rate in this case? Recall that in the Keynesian framework the equilibrium interest rate is that rate which equates the supply and the demand for money.

c. *Disequilibrium*
   Suppose that the rate of interest is not the equilibrium rate but is equal to 9 percent.
   (1) At 9 percent how much money is demanded by the public? How much money does the public have? Describe the mechanism that will restore equilibrium between the demand for money (what the public wants) and the supply of money (what the public has) and bring the interest rate back to its equilibrium level.
   (2) Answer the same questions as in (1) above, assuming that the interest rate is not the equilibrium rate but is equal to 7 percent.

d. *Monetary policy*
   Suppose that the Federal Reserve increases the money supply by $100 billion and that the liquidity preference curve is not affected by this change.
   (1) What is the new equilibrium rate of interest?
   (2) You have just shown that an increase in the money supply initially reduces the level of the interest rate. How will this lower rate affect the level of output in the Keynesian framework?

e. *Interest sensitivity of the liquidity preference curve*
   As the interest rate drops, the demand for money increases, since the liquidity preference is downward sloping (movement along an LP curve).
   (1) By how much will the demand for money increase in response to a drop in the interest rate by one percentage point from 8 percent to 7 percent?
   (2) Different liquidity preference curves have different interest sensitivities. In order to determine the conditions under which a given liquidity preference is

Table 20.1

The Liquidity Preference Schedule LP

Interest Rate (r %)	13%	11%	9%	7%	5%	3%	1%
Demand for Money:							
Transactions demand	100	100	100	100	100	100	100
Speculative demand	50	100	150	200	250	300	350 +
Total Demand (Liquidity preference)							

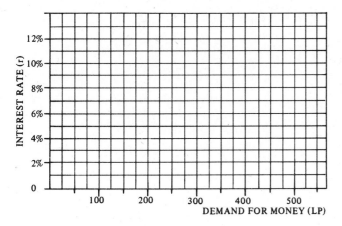

Figure 20.3
Liquidity Preference

more interest-sensitive than another, draw this new liquidity preference curve in Figure 20.3 according to the data in Table 20.2 and label it LP_2. The new liquidity preference curve (LP_2) is clearly flatter than the original one (LP_1) or, in other words, the original liquidity preference curve (LP_1) is steeper than the new one (LP_2).

(3) By how much will the demand for money increase in response to a drop in the interest rate by one percentage point from 8 percent to 7 percent when the liquidity preference curve is LP_2? Compare your result with that obtained when the liquidity preference curve is LP_1. What can you conclude? Are steep liquidity preference curves more or less interest-sensitive than flat liquidity preference curves?

f. *Effectiveness of monetary policy*
In question d the money supply was increased by the Federal Reserve by $100 billion resulting in a drop in the rate of interest.
(1) By how much does the rate of interest

drop in the case of liquidity preference curve LP_2?
(2) Compare your answer to f(1) with your answer to d(1). What can you conclude? Is monetary policy more effective when the liquidity preference is flatter or when it is steeper?
(3) Would monetary policy be effective if the economy were in a liquidity trap?
(4) Given a liquidity preference curve that is not flat, the effectiveness of monetary policy will depend on the interest-sensitivity of the investment function. Will monetary policy be more effective if the investment function is more or less interest-sensitive?

g. *Shifts in the liquidity preference curve*
Suppose that the transactions demand for money increases by $50 billion.
(1) Which factors may account for this shift?
(2) Draw in Figure 20.3 the original liquidity preference curve (LP_1) after adjustment for the *higher* transactions demand for money and label it LP'_1. The money supply is still at $275 billion. What happens to the rate of interest?
(3) The transactions demand for money has increased, but the money supply is still the same. What happened to the speculative demand for money in this case?

*8. **Factors affecting the fraction k in the transactions demand for money** For a given level of income, the transactions demand for money is determined by the fraction k of total income that the public wants to hold in the form of cash balances. For example, if $k = 0.1$ and the current level of income is $500 billion, the transactions demand for money is $50 billion. The value of the fraction k is affected by many factors. Changes in some of these factors are listed below. Indicate if these changes

Table 20.2

The Liquidity Preference Schedule LP_2

Interest Rate	11%	9%	7%	5%	3%
Demand for Money:					
Transactions demand	100	100	100	100	100
Speculative demand	25	125	225	325	425 +
Total Demand (Liquidity preference)					

will increase k, decrease k, or leave k unchanged. Explain.

a. A rise in the current price level (inflation).
b. An expansion in the availability of credit (loans in general and credit cards in particular can be obtained easily).
c. A rise in the frequency of payments to the factors of production (labor is paid weekly instead of yearly or dividends are distributed to shareholders monthly instead of yearly, and so on).
d. A lengthening of the time separating receipts from expenditures (firms receive monthly instead of weekly payments from their customers but have to make weekly payments to their suppliers).
e. A decline in the *current* level of income.
f. An increase in the level of interest rates offered by financial intermediaries on savings and time deposits.
g. Expectations of a decline in the *future* level of income.
h. Expectations of a decline in the *future* rate of inflation.

SELF-TESTS

Completion Questions

Complete each of the following statements by entering the missing words and/or choosing the best alternative proposed.

1. According to Keynes the economy's GDP will be at an _____ _____ level when the *(ex post or realized/ex ante or desired)* total _____ _____ of households is equal to the _____ _____ total _____ of firms. *(Ex post or realized/Ex ante or desired)* total _____ ____ is, however, always equal to *(ex post or realized/ex ante or desired)* total _____.

2. Keynes was primarily concerned with the *(long/short)*-run determination of the level of _____ _____.

3. Realized or actual investment is equal to the sum of _____ investment and _____ _____.

4. According to Keynes, entrepreneurs will react to unwanted accumulated ____ _____ by _____ _____.

5. The change in consumption for each unit change in income is called the ____ _____.

6. Income is at equilibrium when _____ equals production.

7. Total expenditures are equal to the sum of _____, _____, and _____ _____.

8. Desired saving is the difference between ———————————————— and

   ————————————————————————————.

9. Income will change by a ———————————————— of a change in investment or government expenditure because of *(autonomous/induced)* changes in
   ———————————————— spending.

10. The ———————————————— is equal to the reciprocal of the marginal
    propensity to ————————————————.

11. Keynes argued that ———————————————— spending was largely *(au-
    tonomous/induced)*, while ———————————————— was largely ————
    ————————————————. Consequently, ———————————————— spending
    is the primary source of instability in the economy's ————————————————.

12. An increase in income will *(shift the consumption function upward/increase con-
    sumption)* whereas an increase in the market value of the public's portfolio of
    assets will ————————————————————————————————

    ————————————————————————————.

13. Income minus taxes is defined as ————————————————————————

    ————————————.

14. Keynes called the demand for money ————————————————————————
    ————————————————. It is directly related to the ————————————————
    ———————————————— and inversely related to the ————————————
    ————————————————————————————. The demand for money that is
    motivated by the first variable is called the ————————————————————
    ———————————————————————————— whereas the de-
    mand for money which is motivated by the second variable is called the ————
    ————————————————————————————.

15. An increase in the money supply with a fixed demand for money will, according
    to Keynes, lower the ————————————————————————————————
    ————————————————, raise the price of ————————————————,
    stimulate ————————————————————————————————,
    and increase ———————————————————————————— by
    a *(multiple/proportion)* of the increase in ————————————————.

16. If the economy is in a ————————————————————————————————,
    a change in the ————————————————————————————
    will not affect ———————————————————————— because any increase in the
    ———————————————————————————— will be ————
    ———————————————— by the public. In this case ————————————————

_____ is completely ineffective in influencing the

course of _____.

17. The *(flatter/steeper)* the _____

_____, the less effective is _____

_____ in changing interest rates.

18. The transactions demand for money is affected by factors such as _____

_____,

_____

_____, and _____

_____.

19. According to Keynes, the level of interest rates is determined by the interaction

of the _____ and

the _____

_____.

20. If the current rate of interest is below its "normal" level, then, according to

Keynes, the public will expect the interest rate to *(rise/fall)* in the future. If it is

above its "normal" level, expectations are that the rate will _____

in the future.

True and False Questions

For each of the following statements, circle the letter T if it is correct or the letter F if it is *partially* or *totally* incorrect.

T   F   1. According to Keynes, entrepreneurs will react to a disequilibrium between desired saving and desired investment by adjusting the *level* of output, whereas the Classics claim that they will react by adjusting the *price* of output.

T   F   2. When desired saving exceeds desired investment, the economy is not in equilibrium and output will rise, since firms will attempt to get rid of their accumulated inventories.

T   F   3. In the Keynesian model, when the economy is in a position of equilibrium the next period's GDP will be the same as the current GDP. This points out that Keynes was essentially concerned with the short-run behavior of income rather than the long-run growth in the economy's GDP.

T   F   4. Keynes sought to show that the economy could be in a position of equilibrium that differs from the full employ-

ment level of income. The Classics, however, maintained that the economy can be in equilibrium only at the full employment level of income.

T   F   5. In the Keynesian model, ex post or realized investment is always equal to ex post or realized saving, but in the Classical model these two may be unequal.

T   F   6. The consumption function, $C = a + bY$, will shift upward if there is an increase in income.

T   F   7. If the marginal propensity to consume happened to be zero, a decrease in investment would result in a decrease in income equal to the decrease in investment.

T   F   8. Keynes argued that the level of income tends to show wide swings because the consumption function is quite unstable.

T   F   9. The multiplier is another name for the marginal propensity to consume.

T   F   10. As Keynes saw the operation of the economy, equilibrium at full employment could not occur in the absence of government intervention to produce that result.

T F 11. A decline in desired investment of $5 billion in the simple Keynesian model, will result in a decline in income of $25 billion if the marginal propensity to consume equals 0.8.

T F 12. Keynes accepted the Classical position that investment varies inversely with the rate of interest—that is, that the investment curve slopes downward to the right when plotted on the usual axes.

T F 13. Other things being equal, changes in the level of income result in changes in the interest rate in the opposite direction.

T F 14. The sum of the marginal propensity to consume and the marginal propensity to save is equal to one.

T F 15. If the simple multiplier is equal to 5, then the marginal propensity to consume must be equal to 0.75.

T F 16. The simple Keynesian model for the determination of the equilibrium level of real income or output (Y) and the simple Classical model for the determination of the rate of interest are constructed entirely of variables described as flows.

T F 17. Since any person who holds liquid assets other than money can at any time increase the amount of money he or she holds by selling such assets, the public as a whole can in the same way, at any time, increase the amount of money it holds.

T F 18. As Keynes explained the interest rate, people receive interest not because they save but because they are willing to sacrifice liquidity, or hold their savings in a less than perfectly liquid form.

T F 19. If there were no uncertainty as to what the rate of interest or the price of bonds would be at a future date, there would be no such thing as what Keynes called the speculative demand for liquidity or speculative demand for money.

T F 20. It would appear that there is some rate of interest sufficiently high to result in the speculative demand for money becoming zero.

T F 21. One can hold bonds without incurring what Keynes referred to as the speculative risk of holding bonds by holding only U.S. government bonds, on which there is no risk whatsoever that payment will not be made as promised.

T F 22. If the rate of interest is above the equilibrium rate, the quantity of bonds supplied by owners of bonds in the bond market will exceed the quantity of bonds demanded in that market.

T F 23. The simple Keynesian model of interest rate determination shows that a disequilibrium in which the amount of money demanded exceeds the amount supplied is corrected as market forces increase the amount supplied until it equals the amount demanded.

T F 24. According to the transactions demand for money, the amount of money demanded varies directly with the rate of interest, but according to the speculative demand for money, the amount of money demanded varies inversely with the rate of interest.

T F 25. If a person could earn only 1 percent instead of the current $5\frac{1}{2}$ percent on a passbook savings account, the average person would maintain a larger money balance for transactions purchases than he now does with the $5\frac{1}{2}$ percent interest rate.

T F 26. Liquidity preference is synonymous with the demand for money.

T F 27. An anticipated monetary policy may change the interest rates before that policy is implemented.

T F 28. The transactions demand for money is directly related to both the level of income and the level of interest rates.

T F 29. At full employment, the aggregate supply curve is vertical.

T F 30. The aggregate demand schedule is negatively sloped, because people spend less at lower income levels.

T F 31. According to supply side economists, the main effect of reducing tax rates is increased production incentives.

Multiple-Choice Questions

Answer the following multiple-choice questions by circling the best alternative.

Suppose that firms are currently producing an output (GDP) of $2,000 billion at full employment. They expect to sell $1,600 billion to consumers and want to use the remaining $400 billion for investment in the next period. Answer the following questions (1–6).

1. The behavior of firms indicates that their
   a. desired investment spending is $400 billion
   b. realized investment spending is $400 billion
   c. desired investment spending exceeds $400 billion
   d. desired investment spending is less than $400 billion
2. If consumers plan to buy $1,600 billion in consumer goods and services, then
   a. realized saving is $400 billion
   b. desired saving is $400 billion
   c. desired saving exceeds $400 billion
   d. desired saving is less than $400 billion
3. It follows from the answers to questions 1 and 2 that the next period's output
   a. will be more than the $2,000 billion current output, implying that output should rise. This is so because desired investment exceeds desired saving.
   b. will be less than the $2,000 billion current output, implying that output should fall. This is so because desired saving exceeds desired investment.
   c. will be equal to the $2,000 billion current output, implying that output remains the same and the economy is in equilibrium
   d. cannot be determined by comparing desired investment and desired saving
4. If consumers decide they want to spend only $1,400 billion on consumer goods and services, then
   a. realized saving exceeds actual investment
   b. desired saving exceeds desired investment
   c. desired investment exceeds desired saving
   d. realized investment exceeds actual saving
5. According to the Classics, the effect(s) of the disequilibrium (saving differing from investment) you have indicated in your answer to question 4 is
   a. a drop in the price of output, which should eliminate unsold inventories and restore equilibrium
   b. a drop in the wage rate, which should prevent underemployment
   c. a drop in the interest rate, which should raise investment and restore equilibrium
   d. all of the above
   e. only (a) and (b)
6. According to Keynes the effect(s) of the disequilibrium (saving differing from investment) you have indicated in your answer to question 4 is (are)
   a. a drop in the level of output, since firms will reduce the next period's production in order to get rid of their undesired accumulated inventories of unsold goods
   b. a rise in the level of output, since firms will increase the next period's production in order to replenish their depleted inventories
   c. a change in the level of output, the direction of which cannot be predicted at this point
   d. a drop in the interest rate, which should raise investment and restore equilibrium
   e. both (c) and (d)
7. In the Keynesian model the economy is at equilibrium when
   a. desired saving equals desired investment
   b. desired expenditure equals total production
   c. undesired investment is zero
   d. all of the above
   e. only (a) and (b)
8. In the Keynesian cross diagram, a point above the line drawn from the origin at an angle of 45 degrees indicates that
   a. the economy is not in equilibrium
   b. expenditure exceeds production
   c. production exceeds expenditure
   d. both (a) and (c)
   e. both (a) and (b)

A hypothetical consumption function is given by $C = \$50$ billion $+ 0.8Y$ where C is consumption expenditure and Y is the level of income. Answer the following eight questions (9–16).

9. Autonomous consumption
   a. is equal to zero
   b. is equal to $50 billion
   c. is equal to 80 percent of income
   d. cannot be determined without additional information
10. The marginal propensity to consume is equal to
    a. 0.8
    b. 5
    c. 0.2
    d. none of the above
11. Desired consumption expenditure at a level of income of $100 billion is equal to
    a. $80 billion
    b. $50 billion
    c. $130 billion
    d. $70 billion
12. If income rises by $10 billion, desired consumption expenditure will increase by
    a. $58 billion
    b. $8 billion
    c. $60 billion
    d. $10 billion
13. The marginal propensity to save is equal to
    a. 0.8
    b. 5
    c. 0.2
    d. none of the above
14. The saving function can be written

a. $S = \$50$ billion $+ 0.2Y$
b. $S = -\$50$ billion $+ 0.2Y$
c. $S = \$50$ billion $- 0.2Y$
d. $S = -\$50$ billion $- 0.8Y$

15. Suppose that investment is autonomous and equals $50 billion. In this case the equilibrium level of income equals
    a. $90 billion
    b. $500 billion
    c. $125 billion
    d. $250 billion

16. At the equilibrium level of income, desired consumption expenditure is equal to
    a. $122 billion
    b. $450 billion
    c. $150 billion
    d. $250 billion

A hypothetical consumption function is given by $C = \$60$ billion $+ 0.75Y$. Answer the following three questions (17–19).

17. The simple multiplier is equal to
    a. 0.75
    b. 0.25
    c. 4
    d. 5

18. Suppose that there is an autonomous increase in consumption of $10 billion. The consumption function becomes
    a. $C = \$60$ billion $+ 0.75(Y + 10)$
    b. $C = \$70$ billion $+ 0.75Y$
    c. $C = \$67.5$ billion $+ 0.75Y$
    d. $C = \$50$ billion $+ 0.75Y$

19. As a result of the autonomous shift in consumption, the level of income will increase by
    a. $10 billion
    b. $7.5 billion
    c. $50 billion
    d. $40 billion

20. In his analysis of consumption and investment spending, Keynes argued that
    a. consumption spending is largely autonomous, while investment spending is largely induced
    b. consumption spending is largely induced, while investment spending is largely autonomous
    c. both types of spending are largely autonomous
    d. both types of spending are largely induced

21. Suppose that both consumption spending and investment spending are autonomous. If investment increases by $10 billion, then
    a. income will rise by a multiple of $10 billion because of the multiplier effect
    b. income will rise by $10 billion
    c. income will not change because the $10 bil-

lion rise in investment will be offset by a $10 billion drop in consumption
    d. one cannot tell what will happen to income since the consumption function is not given

22. The simple Keynesian model developed in this chapter shows that the level of income is primarily determined by
    a. the level of desired total expenditure in the economy
    b. the output of goods and services
    c. productivity gains
    d. growth in the labor force

23. The simple Keynesian multiplier will be larger
    a. the smaller the marginal propensity to consume
    b. the larger the marginal propensity to save
    c. the larger the marginal propensity to consume
    d. both (a) and (b)

24. If the simple multiplier is equal to ten, then the marginal propensity to consume must be equal to
    a. 0.9
    b. 0.1
    c. 1
    d. none of the above

25. If the marginal propensity to consume is zero, then
    a. the marginal propensity to save is 1
    b. the simple multiplier is equal to 1
    c. consumption spending is autonomous
    d. all of the above
    e. only (a) and (b)

26. The marginal propensity to consume is 0.75, the equilibrium level of income is $2,000, and the full employment level of income is $2,100 billion. In order to bring the economy to its full employment level of income, government expenditures should be increased by
    a. $100 billion
    b. $20 billion
    c. $25 billion
    d. $40 billion

27. The marginal propensity to save is 0.25. A $10 billion increase in the (lump-sum) tax collected by the government will reduce consumption expenditures by
    a. $10 billion
    b. $2.5 billion
    c. $7.5 billion
    d. one cannot tell

28. The government increases its spending by $10 billion and raises the funds by collecting a $10 billion lump-sum tax from the public. The net effect of this action is
    a. to leave the economy's GDP the same, since

the increase in taxes exactly offsets the increase in government spending

b. to increase the economy's GDP

c. to reduce the economy's GDP

d. one cannot tell without knowing the value of the multiplier

29. Which of the following is *not* a flow variable?

a. income

b. saving

c. business inventories

d. consumption

e. investment

30. In the Keynesian model the interest rate is determined by

a. the decision of households regarding savings

b. the decision of the public regarding the composition of its portfolio of financial assets

c. the decision of firms regarding investment spending

d. both (a) and (c)

31. The risk of the public's portfolio of financial assets (money and bonds)

a. rises as the proportion of wealth invested in bonds is increased

b. rises as the proportion of wealth invested in money is increased

c. drops as the proportion of wealth invested in bonds is increased

d. drops as the proportion of wealth invested in money is decreased

32. For a given demand for money, a decrease in the money supply will

a. raise the level of interest rates

b. lower the price of bonds

c. reduce investment spending

d. decrease the economy's GDP

e. all of the above

33. Monetary policy will not affect the equilibrium level of income if

a. the economy is in a liquidity trap

b. any increase in the money supply is hoarded by the public

c. the demand for money has a zero interest-sensitivity

d. both (a) and (b)

e. both (a) and (c)

34. Monetary policy is *more* effective when

a. the demand for money is highly interest-sensitive

b. the investment function is highly interest-sensitive

c. the marginal propensity to save is high

d. all of the above

e. only (a) and (b)

35. Which of the following would shift the demand for money function to the left (reduce the demand for money at every interest rate)?

a. an increase in the economy's GDP

b. a greater use of credit cards

c. the public's expectation of a decrease in the money supply

d. all of the above

36. The transactions demand for money emphasizes the function of money as

a. a store of value

b. a standard of deferred payment

c. a medium of exchange

d. a unit of account

37. A rising interest rate is associated with all of the following *except*

a. a decrease in the level of income

b. a reduction in real investment

c. falling bond prices

d. a decrease in money held for speculative purposes

38. The transactions demand for money

a. is the demand of the public for money as a medium of exchange

b. depends on the level of the economy's GDP

c. depends on the timing of receipts and expenditures

d. is not affected by the level of interest rates

e. all of the above

39. The speculative demand for money emphasizes the function of money as

a. a store of value

b. a standard of deferred payment

c. a medium of exchange

d. a unit of account

40. Monetary policy is *less* effective when

a. interest rates are high

b. the demand for money is relatively insensitive to changes in the interest rate

c. the investment function is relatively insensitive to changes in the interest rate

d. both (a) and (c)

e. none of the above

41. According to Keynes shifts in aggregate demand beyond full employment capacity will result in

a. price increases accompanied by a higher real output

b. price increases accompanied by a lower real output

c. price increases without any change in real output

d. price decreases accompanied by a higher real output

e. price decreases without any change in real output

42. The aggregate demand curve is negatively sloped because a
    a. lower price level raises the real money supply
    b. higher price level raises the real money supply
    c. lower price level reduces income
    d. higher price level reduces income
43. In terms of the aggregate supply and aggregate demand framework, a decrease in the money supply will shift the aggregate
    a. demand curve to the left
    b. demand curve to the right
    c. supply curve to the right
    d. supply curve to the left
44. According to supply-side economics
    a. in a full employment setting, the only way to increase real output is to expand productive capacity
    b. tax policies influence the willingness of households and business firms to supply labor and invest in capital
    c. the impact of tax reduction on aggregate supply will be more important than its impact on aggregate demand
    d. a tax reduction near full employment need not cause prices to rise
    e. all of the above

chapter 21

The *ISLM* World

Central Themes and Major Points

The previous chapter examined separately how the level of equilibrium income is determined in the *goods market* and how the equilibrium rate of interest is determined in the *money market*. These two Keynesian mechanisms are not independent of each other. Changes in the rate of interest influence the level of income, and changes in the level of output influence the rate of interest. Thus the equilibrium interest rate and the equilibrium level of income are actually determined simultaneously through the interactions between the goods markets and the money markets of the economy.

This chapter presents a *general equilibrium model* of the economy that integrates the goods markets and the money markets of the economy and shows how the equilibrium level of income and the equilibrium rate of interest are determined simultaneously.

The goods market is represented by an *IS function*, which consists of all the combinations of interest rates and income that will ensure equilibrium in the real sector. The money market is represented by an *LM function*, which consists of all the combinations of interest rates and income that will ensure equilibrium in the monetary sector. The *IS* and *LM* curves are then drawn in a diagram that indicates the rate of interest on the vertical axis and the level of income on the horizontal axis. The *IS* curve is downward sloping and the

LM curve is upward sloping. They intersect at the general equilibrium point that gives the only combination of interest rate and income that will ensure equilibrium simultaneously in both markets.

This chapter shows how to derive the *IS* and the *LM* curves and indicates which factors determine the slopes of these curves and the shifts in their respective positions.

The *ISLM* model is then used to examine the relative effectiveness of monetary and fiscal policy and to integrate the Classical and Keynesian economic systems into one conceptual framework. This framework is employed to demonstrate the fundamental features distinguishing the Classical system from the Keynesian system. Finally, the *ISLM* framework is used to derive the aggregate demand curve. Although some economists have criticized the *ISLM* analysis, it remains an integral part of macroeconomic theory.

New Terms

Define and/or explain the following terms introduced in this chapter:

Money market
  (equilibrium in)
LM curve
Slope of the *LM* curve
Shifts in the *LM*
  curve

Income-sensitivity of
  the demand for
  money
Goods market
  (equilibrium in)
IS curve

Investment demand
curve
Slope of the *IS* curve
Shifts in the *IS* curve
ISLM model
General equilibrium

Stable equilibrium
Wealth effect (of
interest rates)
Crowding-out effect
Deflation

Essay Questions and Problems

*1. **The *ISLM* model using a geometric analysis** In the previous chapter, questions 5 and 6 explained how the level of equilibrium income (or output or GDP) is determined in the goods market, and question 7 explained how the level of interest rate is determined in the money market. The general equilibrium analysis of the economy can be illustrated with the use of the *ISLM* model. The purpose of this problem is to show you how the *IS* and *LM* curves are derived and to illustrate how monetary and fiscal policy interact.

  a. *Derivation of the LM curve*

The money market is in equilibrium when the public's liquidity preference (demand for money) is equal to the money supply (*M*) made available by the Federal Reserve— that is, when *LP* = *M*. This equilibrium condition can be represented in Figure 21.1 with the help of an *LM* curve. Recall that an

LM curve is the locus of all combinations of income (*Y*) and interest rate (*r*) for which the money market is in equilibrium (*LP* = *M*). Thus to draw an *LM* curve in Figure 21.1 we must find various combinations of *Y* and *r* that are consistent with equilibrium in the money market. Our starting point is the *LP* (liquidity preference) curve given in question 6a in the previous chapter and drawn in Figure 20.3 (the steeper curve) with a transactions demand for $100 billion. We know that transactions demand is a fraction *k* of the level of income such as:

$$\text{Transactions Demand} = k \times Y \quad (21.1)$$

Assume that the fraction *k* is equal 0.1. This means that the public wants to hold one-tenth (10 percent) of the level of income for transactions purposes. In our case the level of income must be $1,000 billion, since one-tenth of $1,000 billion is equal to $100 billion (the transactions demand). It follows that the *LP* curve drawn in Figure 21.2 (the same as the one in Figure 20.3) is the prevailing *LP* when income *Y* is $1,000 billion. Assume that the money supply (*M*) is equal to $300 billion, then the money market is in equilibrium (*LP* = *M*) when the interest rate *r* is equal to 7 percent and

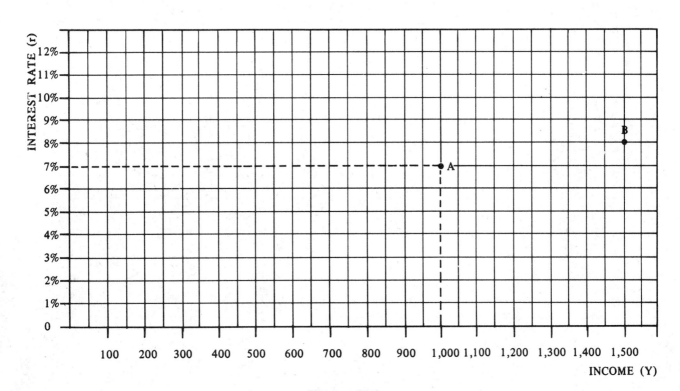

Figure 21.1
LM Curves

the income Y is equal to $1,000 billion. This is our first point (point A) on the LM curve, as shown in Figure 21.1.

(1) You are asked to find more points on the LM curve. This can be done by (1) taking different hypothetical levels of income, (2) deriving the corresponding level of transactions demand using equation (21.1) with $k = 0.1$, (3) drawing the corresponding LP curve, and (4) finding the equilibrium interest rate at the intersection point between the LP curve and the $300 billion money supply. Start with steps (1) and (2) and fill in Table 21.1 below.

For each of the derived transactions demands you can obtain the corresponding LP schedule by simply adding the transactions demand of Table 21.1 to the speculative demand of Table 20.1 (see problem 6, Chapter 20). Enter these values in Table 21.2 below.

Table 21.3 is the LM schedule. Using this information draw the LM curve in Figure 21.1 and label it LM_1.

(2) Explain why the LM curve is upward sloping.

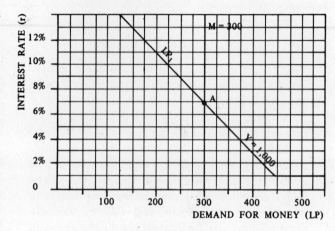

Figure 21.2
Liquidity Preference Curves (LP$_1$)

Table 21.1

The Transactions Demand for Money

Hypothetical Income (Y)	×	Fraction (k)	=	Corresponding Transactions Demand for Money
$250 billion	×	0.1	=	
$500 billion	×	0.1	=	
$750 billion	×	0.1	=	
$1,000 billion	×	0.1	=	
$1,250 billion	×	0.1	=	
$1,500 billion	×	0.1	=	

Table 21.2

Liquidity Preference (LP$_1$) for Various Levels of Income (in billions of dollars)

Interest Rate r	Liquidity Preference (LP$_1$) When:					
	Y = 250	Y = 500	Y = 700	Y = 1,000	Y = 1,250	Y = 1,500
13%				150		
11%				200		
9%				250		
7%				300		
5%				350		
3%				400		
1%				450 +		

Draw in Figure 21.2 the LP curves corresponding to each level of income. Determine the corresponding equilibrium interest rate. Enter these values in Table 21.3.

(3) How does the velocity of money behave as one moves up along an upward sloping LM curve? Fill in Table 21.4 to illustrate your answer.

Table 21.3

The LM_1 Schedule Corresponding to LP_1 Curves (Y in billions of dollars)

Y	250	500	1,000	1,250	1,500
r			.07		

Table 21.4

The Income Velocity of Money Along LM_1

Income (Y)	500	750	1,000	1,250	1,500
Velocity (V)					

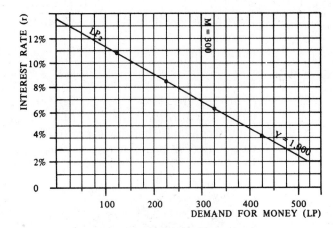

Figure 21.3
Liquidity Preference Curves (LP_2)

(4) *Disequilibrium*
Consider point B in Figure 21.1. This is a disequilibrium point. Is the demand for money higher or lower than the money supply at this point?

b. *Factors affecting the slope of the LM curve*
The two factors that affect the slope of the LM curve are the interest-sensitivity of the liquidity preference curve and the income-sensitivity of the liquidity preference curve, which is nothing more than the fraction k in equation (21.1).

(1) Consider first the *interest-sensitivity of the LP curve.* We have shown in problem 7e in the previous chapter that the flatter the LP curve the more interest-sensitive it is. The question we now wish to answer is, how will the slope of the LM curve vary when the LP curve becomes flatter? To find out, start with the flatter LP_2 curve drawn in Figure 21.3 according to the data in Table 20.2 (return to problem 6e(3), Chapter 20)

and go through the four steps described in that question and draw in Figure 21.1 the new LM curve that corresponds to the flatter LP_2 curves. Label this new LM curve LM_2. You should conclude that *the flatter the LP curve, the flatter the corresponding LM curve.* In other words, *the more interest-sensitive the demand for money (LP curve), the flatter the corresponding LM curve.* You should fill in Tables 21.5 and 21.6 provided below as you go through the various steps required to derive the new LM curve.

(2) Explain intuitively why we should expect the LM curve to be flatter the more interest-sensitive the LP curve is. Use the LM curves in Figure 21.1 to illustrate your answer.

Table 21.5

Liquidity Preference (LP_2) for Various Levels of Income (in billions of dollars)

Interest Rate r	Liquidity Preference (LP_1) When:					
	Y = 250	Y = 500	Y = 750	Y = 1,000	Y = 1,250	Y = 1,500
11%				125		
9%				225		
7%				325		
5%				425		
3%				525 +		

Table 21.6

The LM_2 Schedule Corresponding to Flatter LP_2 Curves (income in billions of dollars)

Y	250	500	750	1,000	1,250	1,500
r						

(3) The *income-sensitivity of the LP curve* is given by the fraction k. The larger the fraction k, the more income-sensitive the LP curve. How does the slope of the LM curve vary when the fraction k increases? To find out, you start with a

fraction k equal to 0.2 instead of the original $k = 0.1$. Go through all the steps summarized in Table 21.1, Table 21.2, and Table 21.3 after substituting $k = 0.2$ for $k = 0.1$. Construct new tables, fill them in, and draw the modified *LM* curve in Figure 21.1. Label it LM^*_1. You should conclude that the larger the fraction k, that is, *the more income-sensitive the demand for money, the steeper the corresponding* LM *curve*. Also note that the *LM* curve shifts leftward (rightward) when the transactions demand increases (decreases), that is, when the fraction k increases (decreases).

(4) Explain intuitively why we should expect the *LM* curve to be steeper the more income-sensitive the *LP* curve is. Use the *LM* curves in Figure 21.1 to illustrate your answer.

c. *Shifts in the position of the LM curve*
Refer to Figure 21.2. Suppose that the money supply is increased from \$300 billion to \$350 billion.

(1) Derive the new LM_1 curve that corresponds to a larger money supply and draw it in Figure 21.1. Label this new *LM* curve LM'_1. What can you conclude regarding the effects of a change in the money supply on the position of the *LM* curve?

(2) On Figure 21.1 the horizontal distance separating the LM_1 curve at a \$300 billion money supply from the LM'_1 curve at a \$350 billion money supply should be equal to \$500 billion. How could the size of the horizontal shift be determined without reference to Figure 21.1?

d. *The investment function*
This function indicates the amount of investment that firms will undertake at every interest rate. The investment schedule is given in Table 21.7 below.

Table 21.7

The Investment Schedule I_1 (in billions of dollars)

Interest Rate (r)	5%	7%	9%
Investment (I_1)	300	175	50

(1) Draw the investment function in Figure 21.4 and label it I_1. Explain why the level of investment is inversely related to the level of interest rates.

(2) What is the role played by the investment function in the transmission process of monetary policy?

(3) Suppose that the investment schedule indicates that the level of investment is \$175 billion at every level of interest rate. Draw this investment function in Figure 21.4. What does it imply for the effectiveness of the transmission process of monetary policy?

(4) Consider the new investment schedule I_2 given in Table 21.8 below.

Table 21.8

The Investment Schedule I_2 (in billions of dollars)

Interest Rate (r)	3%	7%	11%
Investment (I_2)	300	175	50

Draw the investment function (I_2) in Figure 21.4. It is steeper than I_1. Which of the two investment functions is more interest-sensitive? You should conclude that the flatter the investment function the more interest-sensitive it is.

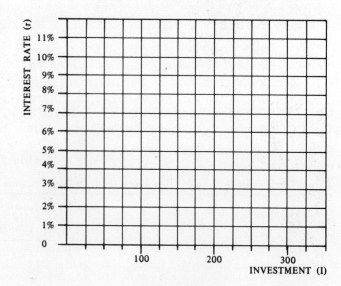

Figure 21.4
Investment Curve

e. *Derivation of the IS curve*
The goods market is in equilibrium when total expenditures are equal to output or when saving equals total investment (firm's investment plus government spending). This equilibrium condition can be represented in Figure 21.5 with the help of an *IS* curve. Recall that an *IS* curve is the locus of

all combinations of income (Y) and interest rate (r) for which the goods market is in equilibrium. Thus to draw an *IS* curve in Figure 21.5 we must find various combinations of Y and r that are consistent with equilibrium in the real sector.

Our starting point is the Saving-Investment diagram related to question 5b(5) in the previous chapter and drawn in Figure 20.2. At an interest rate of 7 percent the level of a firm's investment is $175 billion, total investment is $200 billion ($I + G$), and the corresponding level of equilibrium income is $1,000 billion. This gives us one combination of interest rate (7 percent) and income ($1,000 billion) that is consistent with equilibrium in the goods market. This is our first point (point A on the *IS* curve as shown in Figure 21.5).

(1) You are asked to find more points on the *IS* curve. This can be done as follows. Consider the investment schedule I_1 in Table 21.7. At a 9 percent interest rate the level of a firm's investment is $50 billion. The corresponding level of equilibrium income is determined by drawing the new total investment line (with $I_1 = 50$ instead of 175) in Figure 20.2. (See Figure 20.2 in the Solutions section for problem 5 in the previous chapter.)

Its intersection point with the saving function will yield the desired equilibrium income. Apply the same procedure for $r = 5$ percent and fill in Table 21.9 below. It gives three points on the *IS* curve. *Note:* You can also use the cross diagram in Figure 20.1 to get additional points for the *IS*. The Saving-Investment diagram is, however, much simpler to use.

Table 21.9

The IS_1 Schedule Corresponding to I_1 (in billions of dollars)

r	5%	7%	9%
Y		1,000	

(You can also determine the equilibrium level of income by using the algebraic method presented in question 5b(4) in the previous chapter.) Draw the *IS* curve in Figure 21.5 according to the information in Table 21.9 and label it IS_1.

(2) Explain why the *IS* curve is downward sloping.

f. *Factors affecting the slope of the IS curve*
The two factors that affect the slope of the *IS* curve are the interest-sensitivity of the

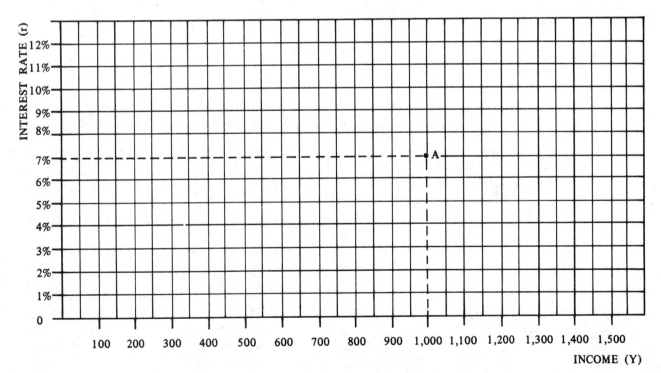

Figure 21.5
IS Curves

investment function and the income-sensitivity of the saving function, which is nothing more than the marginal propensity to save.

(1) Derive the new *IS* schedule based on the investment schedule I_2 given in Table 21.8. Fill in Table 21.10 below.

Table 21.10

The IS_2 Schedule Corresponding to I_2
(in billions of dollars)

r	3%	7%	11%
Y		1,000	

(2) Draw the new *IS* curve in Figure 21.5 and label it IS_2. Which *IS* curve is flatter? You should conclude that *the more interest-sensitive the investment function, the flatter the corresponding IS curve.*

(3) Explain intuitively why we should expect the *IS* curve to be flatter the more interest-sensitive the investment function. Use the *IS* curves in Figure 21.5 to illustrate your answer.

(4) Consider now the *effect of a change in the marginal propensity to save* (MPS). Suppose that the investment function is I_1 given in Table 21.9 and that the MPS is equal to 0.5 (it was originally equal to 0.25, see question 5a, Chapter 20). Show that in this case the *IS* curve is given by Table 21.11 below:

Table 21.11

The IS^*_1 Schedule Corresponding to I_1 and
MPS = .50 (income in billions of dollars)

r	3%	5%	7%	9%
Y	1,000	750	500	250

Draw the new *IS* curve in Figure 21.5 and label it IS^*_1. Which *IS* curve is flatter? (Compare the *IS* curve based on I_1 and MPS = 0.25 to the *IS* curve based on I_2 and MPS = 0.5.) You should conclude that *the higher the MPS (more income-sensitive saving function) the steeper the corresponding IS curve.*

(5) Explain intuitively why we should expect the *IS* curve to be steeper the higher the MPS. Use the *IS* curves in Figure 21.5 to illustrate your answer.

g. *Shifts in the position of the IS curve*

Any change in autonomous spending (consumption, investment, or government) will shift the position of the *IS* curve. Suppose that government spending increases from $25 billion (see question 6, Chapter 20) to $150 billion. Derive the new *IS* curve that corresponds to the increased government expenditure. Draw it in Figure 21.5 and label it IS'_1. Recall that the original *IS* curve is IS_1 given in Table 21.9. *Hint:* What is the size of the horizontal shift in the *IS* curve, given that the multiplier is equal to four and that the increase in government spending is equal to $125 billion? (You can also use a geometrical derivation based on the Saving-Investment diagram in Figure 20.2, Chapter 20.) What can you conclude regarding the effect of a change in any autonomous expenditure on the position of the *IS* curve?

h. *General equilibrium*

We can now put all the pieces together to determine the economy's general equilibrium. This is the point at which the *LM* curve and the *IS* curve intersect. It is the only point where the goods market and the money market are simultaneously in equilibrium.

(1) Draw the original LM_1 and IS_1 curves in Figure 21.6. These are the *LM* curve given in Table 21.3 and the *IS* curve given in Table 21.9. What is the equilibrium interest rate in the money market and the corresponding equilibrium level of income in the goods market for which the economy is in general equilibrium?

(2) Explain why no other point in Figure 21.6 qualifies as a general equilibrium point.

i. *Monetary policy in the ISLM model*

Suppose that the money supply increases from $300 billion to $350 billion as a result of an expansionary monetary policy conducted by the Federal Reserve.

(1) Draw the new *LM* curve in Figure 21.6 and label it LM'_1. (See question c and Figure 21.1.)

(2) What are the new equilibrium interest rate and level of income? What would have been the new equilibrium interest rate and level of income if monetary policy were contractionary (a reduction of $50 billion in the money supply)? What could you conclude from the analysis regarding the effects of monetary policy?

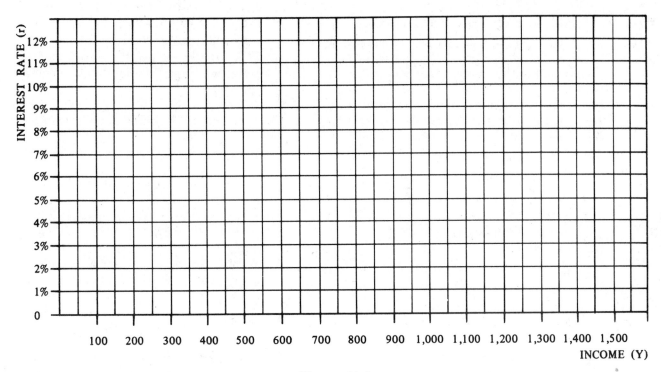

Figure 21.6
General Equilibrium: Monetary and Fiscal Policies

j. *Fiscal policy in the ISLM model*
Suppose that government expenditures increase from $25 billion to $150 billion as a result of an expansionary fiscal policy conducted by the Treasury.
(1) Draw the new *IS* curve in Figure 21.6 and label it IS'_1 (see question g and Figure 21.5). The original *IS* curve is the one in Table 21.9.
(2) What are the new equilibrium interest rate and level of income (assume the money supply remains at $300 billion)? What would have been the new equilibrium interest rate and level of income if fiscal policy were contractionary (a reduction in government expenditures by $125 million)? What can you conclude from this analysis regarding the effects of fiscal policy?
(3) What is the reduction in the level of income due to the crowding out effect of a higher interest rate under an expansionary fiscal policy?

*2. **The ISLM model using an algebraic analysis (Appendix)** The purpose of this problem is to show you how the general equilibrium rate of interest and level of income can be determined using an algebraic analysis. The solu-

tions are the same as in problem 1. The only difference is that in this problem the solutions are found by solving a set of equations that describe the state of the goods and money markets of the economy. In problem 1 the solution was found at the intersection point of two curves that represented the goods and money markets. The Appendix to Chapter 21 presents the algebraic analysis of income determination. It is not necessary to go through this presentation in order to solve this problem.
a. *Derivation of the LM function*
The *LM* function is the set of points for which the public's liquidity preference (*LP*) equals the money supply (*M*). We have (all data are in billions of dollars):

L = Transactions demand for money
$\quad = 0.1Y$ (1)

L^* = Speculative demand for money
$\quad = 375 - 2{,}500r$ (2)

M = Money Supply = 300   (3)

where r is the rate of interest and Y is the level of income.
(1) Verify that L^* corresponds to the speculative demand for money schedule given in Table 20.1 (question 7a, Chapter 20).
(2) Derive the equation of the *LM* function

using equations (1) to (3). *Hint:* The equilibrium condition $L + L^* = M$ should be solved and income (Y) expressed as a function of the interest rate (r).

b. *Derivation of the IS function*

The *IS* function is the set of points for which the total expenditures (E) equals the level of income (Y). We have (all data in billions of dollars):

$$E = \text{total expenditure} = C + I + G \quad (4)$$

$$C = \text{consumption function}$$
$$= 50 + 0.75\,Y \quad (5)$$

$$L = \text{investment function}$$
$$= 612.5 - 6{,}250r \quad (6)$$

$$G = 25 \quad (7)$$

(1) Verify that C corresponds to the consumption schedule given in question 6a in Chapter 20 and that I corresponds to the investment schedule given in Table 21.7 (question 1d, Chapter 21).

(2) Derive the equation of the *IS* function using equations (4) to (7). *Hint:* The equilibrium conditions $E = Y$ should be solved and income (Y) expressed as a function of the interest rate (r).

c. *General equilibrium*

The general equilibrium solution is found by solving simultaneously the equation for the *LM* curve found in question a(2) and the equation for the *IS* curve found in question b(2). The solution to this system will give the equilibrium interest rate (r_{eq}) and the equilibrium income (Y_{eq}).

d. *Monetary policy*

The money supply expands to $350 billion.

(1) Derive the equation of the new LM_1 function.

(2) Determine the new equilibrium interest rate and income.

(3) What are the changes in income and interest rate brought about by this monetary action?

e. *Fiscal policy*

Government expenditures increase to $150 billion.

(1) Derive the equation of the new IS_1 function.

(2) Determine the new equilibrium interest rate and income.

(3) What are the changes in income and interest rate brought about by this fiscal action?

(4) What is the reduction in income due to the crowding out effect of the rise in the interest rate?

3. If the *IS* and *LM* curves intersect at an income level below the full employment level, automatic forces within the economy (falling wage rates and prices) would be able to move the income level to its full employment position, according to the arguments of the Classical school. Explain.

4. Keynes maintained that under certain circumstances price deflation would be unable to move the economy to its full employment income level. These circumstances were the existence of a liquidity trap or the existence of investment demand insensitive to the rate of interest. Explain why under either of these circumstances deflation would not move the economy to full employment.

5. Show how the *ISLM* model can be used to derive the aggregate demand curve.

SELF-TESTS

Completion Questions

Complete each of the following statements by entering the missing words and/or choosing the best alternative proposed.

1. The *LM* curve indicates all those combinations of _____

_____ and _____

_____ at which the _____

_____ is equal to the _____.

2. The *LM* curve is the set of points for which there is *(equilibrium/disequilibrium)*

in the _____.

3. The *IS* curve indicates all those combinations of _____
_____ and _____
_____ at which _____ is equal to ____
_____ or _____
_____ is equal to _____.

4. The *IS* curve is the set of points for which there is *(equilibrium/disequilibrium)*
in the _____ of the
economy.

5. The position of the *LM* curve will shift as a result of a change in _____
_____.

6. The two factors that determine the slope of the *LM* curve are _____
_____
_____ and _____
_____.

7. The position of the *IS* curve will shift as the result of any change in _____
_____.

8. The two factors that determine the slope of the *IS* curve are _____
_____
and _____.

9. General equilibrium is found at the intersection point of the _____
_____ and the _____, since this is the only
point at which _____ equals _____
and _____ equals
_____. In this case the
_____ market and the _____
market are simultaneously in _____.

10. The Classical price mechanism that should automatically restore the economy's
equilibrium to its full employment level will break down under any one of the
following three cases:

   a. _____
   b. _____
   c. _____

11. Occurs _____
_____ when a rise in the rate of interest cuts off an amount of
private investment.

12. The *ISLM* model can be used to derive aggregate demand by finding different
combinations of _____ and _____

_____ in which equilibrium occurs in both the goods and

money markets.

True and False Questions

For each of the following statements, circle the letter T if it is correct or the letter F if it is *partially* or totally incorrect.

T F 1. The *LM* curve must slope upward to the right because, other things being equal, a higher level of income means a larger demand for money, and there must accordingly be a higher interest rate to produce an offsetting lower demand for money and thus keep the demand for money equal to the given supply of money.

T F 2. The greater the income-sensitivity of the demand for money, the flatter the *LM* curve will be, other things being equal.

T F 3. It is correct to say that the *LM* curve shows the extent to which a change in the money supply results in a change in the interest rate and a change in income.

T F 4. The nature of the *LM* curve is such that it will shift rightward by $15 billion at each possible interest rate if there is an increase in the money supply of $5 billion and if k (as in money demanded = $k[PY]$) is equal to ⅓.

T F 5. Changes in the supply of money shift both the *LM* and *IS* curves, but they shift the *LM* curve more than the *IS* curve.

T F 6. The *LM* curve may slope upward to the right or downward to the right.

T F 7. The *LM* curve shifts as a result of a change in either the interest rate or the income level.

T F 8. The *IS* curve shows combinations of a relatively low level of income and a relatively high interest rate and a relatively high level of income and a relatively low interest rate, because from one viewpoint, a relatively low interest rate will mean a relatively high level of investment and there must be a relatively high level of income to produce a relatively high level of saving to match the relatively high level of investment.

T F 9. The position of the *IS* curve depends on the sensitivity of saving to a change in the interest rate and the sensitivity of investment to a change in income.

T F 10. The slope of the *IS* curve depends on the sensitivity of saving to a change in the interest rate and the sensitivity of investment to a change in income.

T F 11. If the actual interest rate is below the interest rate at which the *IS* and *LM* curves intersect, and if the actual income level is above the income level at which the *IS* and *LM* curves intersect, the adjustment process will result in a fall in the interest rate and a rise in the income level.

T F 12. The point where the *IS* and *LM* curves intersect determines the full employment income level and the equilibrium interest rate.

T F 13. Given *IS* and *LM* curves and a combination of income level and interest rate at which there is equilibrium in the goods market but disequilibrium in the money market, there must be a rise in the interest rate in the adjustment process that results.

T F 14. The structure of the *ISLM* model is such that there may be disequilibrium in the goods market or disequilibrium in the money market but there may not be disequilibrium in both markets at the same time.

T F 15. Given an upward sloping *LM* curve and a downward sloping *IS* curve, we find that both expansionary monetary policy (increase in the money supply) and expansionary fiscal policy (increase in government spending) will raise the income level, but the former by itself will lower the interest rate and the latter by itself will raise the interest rate.

T F 16. In terms of the *ISLM* model, fiscal policy will be more effective the steeper the *LM* curve.

T F 17. In terms of the *ISLM* model, monetary policy will be more effective the flatter the *IS* curve.

T F 18. The multiplier effect of an increase in government expenditures is found to be less in the *ISLM* model than in the simple Keynesian model, because in the *ISLM* model the effect on income of the increase in government expenditures is offset in part by the effect on income of a decrease in investment spending that results from the rise in the interest rate caused by the increase in government expenditures.

T F 19. If the demand for money were totally insensitive to the rate of interest, the *LM* curve would be perfectly flat (horizontal).

T F 20. Given an upward sloping *LM* curve, each rightward shift in the *IS* curve along the *LM* curve means a fall in the velocity of money.

T F 21. When cast in the *ISLM* framework, the Classical theory yields an *LM* curve that has zero interest-sensitivity (vertical), in which case shifts in the *IS* curve have no effect on the income level.

T F 22. According to Classical theory, if the intersection yielded by the *ISLM* curves is at a level of income below full employment, a falling price level will automatically bring about a rightward shift in the *LM* curve that will lift income to the full employment level.

The following questions are based on the Appendix to this chapter.

T F 23. One of the criticisms leveled at the *ISLM* framework is that prices are either fixed or flexible with no allowance for degrees of flexibility.

T F 24. For a liquidity preference function of the form $L = f - h(R) + k(Y)$, fiscal policy is ineffective when $h = \infty$.

T F 25. Assume a liquidity preference function of the form $L = f - h(R) + k(Y)$. The impact of monetary policy on income rises as the value of h gets smaller.

Multiple-Choice Questions

Answer the following multiple-choice questions by circling the best alternative.

1. Which of the following is not a feature of the *ISLM* framework?
   a. It integrates in a single diagram the goods market and the money market.
   b. It shows how fiscal and monetary policies interact.
   c. It provides a short-run as well as a long-run analysis of economic activity for the Classical and Keynesian systems.
   d. It demonstrates the fundamental features that distinguish the Classical and Keynesian outlooks.

2. The *LM* curve can take any one of the following positions *except*
   a. upward sloping to the right
   b. horizontal
   c. downward sloping to the left
   d. vertical

3. If the demand for money were totally insensitive to the level of interest rates, then
   a. the *LM* curve would be vertical
   b. the economy's GDP would not be affected by changes in autonomous spending
   c. the velocity of money would be a constant
   d. all of the above
   e. only (a) and (b)

4. As one moves up along an upward sloping *LM* curve, all of the following hold *except*
   a. the demand for money equals the supply of money
   b. the velocity of money drops
   c. the money market is in equilibrium
   d. all of the above

5. As one moves up along a downward sloping *IS* curve, all of the following hold *except*
   a. the level of government expenditures is constant
   b. total expenditures equal output
   c. the goods market is in equilibrium
   d. none of the above

6. The slope of the *LM* curve depends on
   a. the interest-sensitivity of the liquidity preference curve
   b. the income-sensitivity of the liquidity preference curve
   c. the interest-sensitivity of the investment function
   d. all of the above
   e. only (a) and (b)

7. The slope for the *IS* curve depends on
   a. the interest-sensitivity of the liquidity preference curve
   b. the income-sensitivity of the liquidity preference curve
   c. the marginal propensity to save
   d. all of the above
   e. only (a) and (c)

8. A point to the right of the *IS* curve and below the *LM* curve indicates that
   a. the demand for money exceeds the supply of money
   b. investment spending exceeds saving

c. the money supply exceeds the demand for money

d. both (a) and (b)

9. If as a result of a $10 billion increase in the money supply the *LM* curve shifts to the right by $40 billion (at every interest rate), then the fraction of income that the public holds for transactions purposes must be equal to

a. 0.2

b. 0.25

c. 0.4

d. none of the above

10. Along an upward sloping *LM* curve all of the following are fixed *except*

a. the velocity of money

b. the money supply

c. the fraction of income that the public holds for transactions purposes

d. the interest-sensitivity of the liquidity preference curve

e. both (a) and (c)

11. The velocity of money will be equal to the reciprocal of the fraction of income the public holds for transactions purposes if

a. the demand for money has a zero interest-sensitivity

b. the *LM* curve is vertical

c. the *LM* curve is horizontal

d. both (a) and (b)

e. none of the above

12. An increase in income will

a. shift the *LM* curve and the *IS* curve to the right

b. shift the *LM* curve to the right and the *IS* curve to the left

c. shift the *LM* curve and the *IS* curve to the left

d. shift the *LM* curve to the left and the *IS* curve to the right

e. none of the above

13. According to the *ISLM* model, monetary policy will

a. change the level of income and the level of interest rates in the same direction as fiscal policy

b. change the level of income in the same direction as fiscal policy and change the level of interest rates in the direction opposite to that of fiscal policy

c. change the level of income and the level of interest rates in a direction opposite to that of fiscal policy

d. change the level of income in a direction opposite to that of fiscal policy and change the level of interest rates in the same direction as fiscal policy

14. In the *ISLM* curve, a change in government spending will not alter the equilibrium level of GDP if

a. the velocity of money is a constant

b. the velocity of money rises with the interest rate

c. the velocity of money falls with the interest rate

d. both (b) and (c)

15. Suppose that the marginal propensity to consume is equal to 0.8, then a reduction in taxes by $10 billion will

a. shift the *IS* curve to the left (at every interest rate) by an amount equal to $40 billion

b. shift the *IS* curve to the right (at every interest rate) by an amount equal to $50 billion

c. shift the *IS* curve to the right (at every interest rate) by an amount equal to $40 billion

d. shift the *IS* curve to the left (at every interest rate) by an amount equal to $50 billion

16. As one moves up along an *LM* curve, the income velocity of money

a. increases

b. decreases

c. remains the same

d. depends on the slope of the *LM* curve, and hence either (a) or (c) could be correct

17. An autonomous increase in investment spending will

a. shift the *IS* curve to the left and the *LM* curve to the right

b. shift the *IS* curve to the right and leave the *LM* curve unaffected

c. shift the *LM* curve to the right and leave the *IS* curve unaffected

d. shift the *IS* curve and the *LM* curve to the right

18. In the *ISLM* model general equilibrium means that

a. investment equals saving

b. liquidity preference equals money supply

c. the money market is in equilibrium

d. the goods market is in equilibrium

e. all of the above

19. The "crowding out" effect of fiscal policy will disappear if

a. the investment function is completely insensitive to changes in the interest rate

b. the demand for money is completely insensitive to changes in the interest rate

c. the economy is in a liquidity trap

d. both (a) and (c)

20. The steeper the *IS* curve

a. the more effective fiscal policy is and the less effective monetary policy is

b. the more effective monetary policy is and the less effective fiscal policy is

c. the more effective are both fiscal and monetary policies

d. the less effective are both fiscal and monetary policies

21. An increase in the proportion of income the public wants to hold for transactions purposes will

    a. raise the level of interest rates and the level of income

    b. raise the level of interest rates and lower the level of income

    c. lower the level of interest rates and the level of income

    d. lower the level of interest rates and raise the level of income

22. A decrease in the proportion of income the public wants to hold for transactions purposes will

    a. raise the levels of interest rates and income

    b. raise the level of interest rates and lower the level of income

    c. lower the levels of interest rates and income

    d. lower the level of interest rates and raise the level of income

23. Which of the following will prevent the economy from returning to its full employment level of income?

    a. Prices and wages are inflexible downward.

    b. The *LM* curve is horizontal.

    c. Investment is highly insensitive to the rate of interest.

    d. all of the above

24. Classical analysis within the *ISLM* model indicates that if there is a recession, then price deflation will restore GDP to its full employment level as a result of a

    a. rightward shift in the *LM* and *IS* curves

    b. rightward shift in the *LM* curve with the *IS* curve unaffected

    c. rightward shift in the *LM* curve and a leftward shift in the *IS* curve

    d. leftward shift in the *LM* curve and the *IS* curve

25. Prominent objections to the *ISLM* approach include which of the following?

    a. The possibility of sustained unemployment is ignored.

    b. It has no direct links to aggregate demand.

    c. Fiscal policy cannot be adequately illustrated.

    d. Monetary effects are presented in too narrow of a framework.

26. The aggregate demand schedule will shift to the right if

    a. fiscal policy is contractionary

    b. monetary policy is expansionary

    c. the *IS* curve shifts to the left

    d. the *LM* curve shifts to the right

    e. both (b) and (d)

    f. both (a) and (c)

27. The *ISLM* model can be used to derive the

    a. aggregate demand curve

    b. aggregate supply curve

    c. demand for loanable funds

    d. deposit expansion multiplier

28. When the *IS* curve shifts to the left, the aggregate demand curve

    a. shifts to the right

    b. shifts to the left

    c. is unaffected as long as the *LM* curve is unaffected

    d. becomes more elastic (flatter)

The following questions are based on the Appendix at the end of this chapter.

29. With a liquidity preference function of the form $L = f - h(R) + k(Y)$, the Keynesian liquidity trap occurs when

    a. $f = 0$

    b. $Y = 0$

    c. $k = $ infinity

    d. $h = $ infinity

30. The government spending multiplier is larger than the multiplier for a tax change in the *ISLM* framework as long as

    a. the economy is not in the liquidity trap

    b. the marginal propensity to consume is less than 1

    c. investment spending is positively related to the interest rate

    d. the velocity of money is constant

chapter 22

Monetarists and Keynesians in the *ISLM* World

Central Themes and Major Points

This chapter examines the debate between the Monetarists and the Keynesians using the *ISLM* model developed in the previous chapter.

The *ISLM* framework is a useful tool for examining the Monetarist-Keynesian debate, because both the Monetarist and the Keynesian positions can be presented in a single diagram. The positions of and the shifts in the *IS* and *LM* curves are then used to summarize either the Keynesian or the Monetarist view on the relative effectiveness of fiscal and monetary policies. It is important that you understand how the basic assumptions behind the Keynesian and the Monetarist positions are reflected in the *IS* and *LM* curves.

The extreme Monetarist position is represented by a vertical *LM* function, based on the assumption of fixed velocity. The extreme Keynesian position is characterized by a vertical *IS* curve and horizontal *LM* curve. Under the Monetarist assumptions, only monetary policy influences income. In the extreme Keynesian case, only fiscal policy has an impact on income. You should be able to work through each of these extreme cases and analyze the effects of relaxing the strict assumptions.

The chapter introduces the concept of the natural rate of interest. The natural rate of interest cannot be influenced by monetary policy, because it is determined by saving and investment at full employment. Monetary policy can affect nominal interest rates through influencing inflationary expectations. This result is essential for understand-

ing the debate over how inflationary expectations are formed, which is the subject of Chapter 24.

The *ISLM* framework also has its limitations. It does not lend itself to an exact representation of the extreme Monetarist position, and it cannot be used to examine some finer aspects of the Monetarist-Keynesian debate.

New Terms

Define and/or explain the following terms introduced in this chapter:

Comparative static analysis

Natural rate of interest

Essay Questions and Problems

1. Monetarism in the *ISLM* framework
   a. How should the *LM* curve be drawn in order to represent the extreme Monetarist position? Explain.
   b. Explain why a vertical *LM* curve does not fully convey the extreme Monetarist position on the effect of a change in the money supply on income. Draw a diagram to illustrate your answer.
   c. How should you draw the *IS* curve if you want to depict the extreme Monetarist position without introducing a Keynesian flavor? Illustrate your answer with the diagram you have drawn in your answer to question b.

*2. The Monetarist-Keynesian debate in the ***ISLM* framework** The following questions are based on Figure 22.1. The economy is initially at the general equilibrium point A with a level of interest rate of 7 percent, a level of income (GDP) of $2,000 billion, and a money supply of $400 billion. The marginal propensity to consume is 75 percent. Assume that the full employment level of income is $2,100 billion. This means that the GDP gap is $100 billion and the economy is experiencing a recession. Answer the following questions.

a. *The extreme Monetarist position*
  (1) In this case the *IS* curve is *IS* and the *LM* curve is LM_1. Explain.
  (2) Will fiscal policy (a shift in *IS* to *IS'*) bring the economy to its full employment level? Explain. What is the final equilibrium point and what are the levels of interest rate and income at this point?
  (3) You have just shown that fiscal policy is completely ineffective in raising GDP when the *LM* curve is vertical. It raises only the level of interest rate. The Monetarist position in this case is that only monetary policy can bring the economy to full employment. This can be implemented by shifting the *LM* curve from LM_1 to LM'_1. By how much should the money supply be increased to achieve this objective? *Note:* You should first determine the value of the velocity of money. What assumption about the velocity are you making in order to determine the change in the money supply?

b. *The extreme Keynesian position*
  (1) In this case the *IS* curve is still *IS* but the *LM* curve is LM_2. Explain.
  (2) Will monetary policy bring the economy to its full employment level? Explain. What is the final equilibrium point and what are the levels of interest rate and income at this point? If the equilibrium point remains at A, what has happened to the additional money supply?
  (3) You have just shown that monetary policy is completely ineffective in raising GDP and the level of interest rate when the *LM* is horizontal. The Keynesian position in this case is that only fiscal policy can bring the economy to full employment. This can be implemented by shifting the *IS* curve from *IS* to *IS'*. By how much should government expenditure be increased in order to achieve this objective? *Note:* You should first determine the value of the simple Keynesian multiplier. Does the method of financing government expenditures matter in this case?

c. *The normal case*
  (1) In this case both the *IS* and the *LM* curves are well behaved. The *IS* curve is still *IS*, but the *LM* curve is LM_3. Explain.
  (2) *Monetary policy.* The *IS* is fixed. The *LM* curve shifts from LM_3 to LM'_3 as a result of an increase in the money supply. What is the final equilibrium point in this case, and what are the equilibrium levels of interest rate and income? Using economic dynamics trace the path from the initial equilibrium point to the final equilibrium point. Identify on Figure 22.1 the liquidity effect and the income effect.

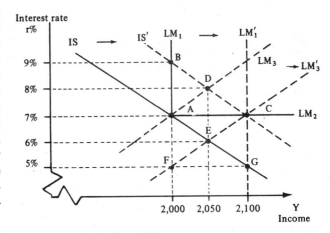

Figure 22.1

  (3) *Fiscal policy.* The *LM* is fixed at LM_3. The *IS* curve shifts from *IS* to *IS'* as a result of an increase in government expenditure financed by borrowing from the public. What is the final equilibrium point in this case, and what are the equilibrium levels of interest rate and income? Using economic dynamics trace the path from the initial equilibrium point to the final equilibrium point. Is crowding out complete in this case?

3. "Classical interest theory pops out of the Keynesian picture at full employment." Explain this statement.

4. Using the *ISLM* framework, explain why the *real* rate of interest is affected by shifts in the goods market (the *IS* curve) but is not affected by shifts in the money market (the *LM* curve) when the economy is at full employment. What happens when the economy operates at less than full employment?

*5. Using the *ISLM* framework, show the effects on income and the interest rate of an expansionary fiscal policy (increase in government expenditure) financed by borrowing from a banking system with excess reserves. Show that fiscal policy is more expansionary in this case than in the case where it is financed by borrowing from the nonbank public.

6. Using the *ISLM* diagram, show that when the economy is at the full employment level of income then

a. continuous rightward shifts in the *LM* curve will cause continuous inflation
b. continuous rightward shifts in the *IS* curve cannot cause continuous inflation

7. Using the *ISLM* diagram, show how an increase in the money supply does not always produce inflation.

The following problem is based on the Appendix to this chapter.

8. **Interest rates versus the money supply as targets of monetary policy** Review problem 3, Chapter 17, in the Essay Questions and Problems section. It deals with the same issue as the one raised in the Appendix to this chapter: what is the best operating target for the execution of monetary policy (interest rates or the money supply?) when the *IS* and *LM* curves shift unexpectedly?

SELF-TESTS

Completion Questions

Complete each of the following statements by entering the missing words and/or choosing the best alternative proposed.

1. A vertical (*LM/IS*) curve means that the demand for _____

    has a _____

    _____. It represents an extreme _____

    position. In this case _____

    is completely ineffective.

2. A horizontal (*LM/IS*) curve means that the demand for _____

    is in _____. It repre-

    sents an extreme _____ position. In this case _____

    _____ is completely ineffective

    and _____ is required.

3. A vertical *IS* curve means that the _____

    _____ has a _____

    _____. This is a case where _____

    _____ is completely ineffective and _____

    _____ is required.

4. A (*steeper/flatter*) (*IS/LM*) curve stabilizes the level of economic activity associated with a particular stock of money because the interest rate fluctuates (*more/less*).

5. The _____ rate of interest that prevails when the econ-

omy is at full employment is called the _____ rate of

interest.

6. When the economy is at its _____

level of income, the interest rate is determined by _____

and _____. In this case *(Classical/Keynesian)* interest

theory emerges from the *(Monetarist/Keynesian)* framework.

The following questions are based on the Appendix to this chapter.

7. The _____ and the ____

_____ are competing _____

_____ for monetary policy. Hitting a(n) _____

_____ target implies loss of control over the

money supply, while hitting a(n) _____

_____ target implies loss of control over the _____

_____.

8. According to the *(Monetarists/Keynesians)*, the most stable relationship in eco-

nomics is the _____.

The Keynesian _____ function is much less stable, and

therefore the major source of instability in GDP is the *(IS/LM)* curve. The Keyne-

sians argue that the _____

is unstable, and therefore the *(LM/IS)* curve is the major source of GDP instabil-

ity.

True and False Questions

For each of the following statements, circle the letter T if it is correct or the letter F if it is *partially* or totally incorrect.

T F 1. In order to do justice to the Monetarist position within the Keynesian *ISLM* framework, one should draw a horizontal *LM* curve and a vertical *IS* curve.

T F 2. Along an *LM* curve the velocity of money is always constant.

T F 3. Given a "normal" *IS* curve, the increase in income resulting from the same increase in the money supply will be smaller the flatter the *LM* curve.

T F 4. Moderate wings in the Monetarist camp assert that the *LM* is nearly vertical, whereas moderate wings in the Keynesian camp claim that it is quite flat.

T F 5. A steeper *LM* curve stabilizes the level of economic activity associated with a particular stock of money, because the interest rate fluctuates less.

T F 6. When the economy is operating near its full employment capacity, fluctuations in the price level help to stabilize the economy.

T F 7. As long as the *IS* curve is downward sloping, the equilibrium interest rate after an increase in the money supply will be below the old rate, because the income effect of the increased supply will not completely counter the initial liquidity effect.

T F 8. Crowding out occurs because higher levels of GDP are associated with higher levels of money demand.

T   F   9. Near full capacity, fluctuations in the price level provide a self-correcting stabilizing mechanism for the economy.

T   F   10. When the *LM* curve is upward sloping, an increase in government spending raises GDP by more than the full multiplier amount of the extreme Keynesian system.

T   F   11. When the economy is at full employment, the Keynesian economic system is essentially the same as the Classical-Monetarist model.

T   F   12. Monetary policy cannot change the real rate of interest; only fiscal policy can.

T   F   13. The natural rate of interest is synonymous with the real rate of interest.

T   F   14. Fiscal policy is most effective when liquidity preference is perfectly interest-sensitive and least effective when liquidity preference is perfectly interest-insensitive.

T   F   15. Crowding out is complete when the *LM* curve is vertical; it is partial when the *LM* curve is upward sloping; and it is absent when the *LM* curve is horizontal.

T   F   16. The real rate of interest cannot exceed the natural rate of interest.

T   F   17. The natural rate of interest is the rate that equates savings at full employment with investment.

T   F   18. Continuous rightward shifts in the *IS* curve unaccompanied by changes in the money supply will cause continuous inflation.

T   F   19. Even at full employment, increases in the money supply may not be inflationary in a growing economy.

The following questions are based on the Appendix to this chapter.

T   F   20. If the Federal Reserve knew the source of variation in income (a shift in the *IS* curve or a shift in the *LM* curve), it would have no problem in choosing the right target for conducting its monetary policy.

T   F   21. Under conditions of uncertainty, the Federal Reserve would minimize its errors in the execution of monetary policy if it monitored both the interest rate and the money supply.

T   F   22. According to the Monetarists, the source of variation in income is the

LM curve, whereas to the Keynesians it is the *IS* curve.

Multiple-Choice Questions

Answer the following multiple-choice questions by circling the best alternative.

1. The extreme Monetarist position within the *ISLM* framework is represented by an *LM* curve that has the following characteristic(s):
   a. It is vertical.
   b. It is perfectly interest insensitive.
   c. Velocity is constant along the *LM* curve.
   d. all of the above
   e. only (a) and (b)

2. In the *ISLM* framework, monetary policy will be completely ineffective if
   a. the *LM* curve is horizontal *and* the *IS* curve is vertical
   b. the *LM* curve is vertical *and* the IS curve is horizontal
   c. the *LM* curve is horizontal *or* the *IS* curve is vertical
   d. the *LM* curve is vertical *or* the *IS* curve is horizontal

3. Monetary policy has no effect on equilibrium income if
   a. the price level is constant
   b. velocity is constant
   c. saving is interest-insensitive
   d. investment is interest-insensitive

4. Fiscal policy has no effect on equilibrium income when the
   a. *LM* curve is vertical
   b. *IS* curve is vertical
   c. *IS* curve is horizontal
   d. economy is in the liquidity trap

5. In the *ISLM* framework, the expenditure multiplier is equal to that of the simple Keynesian system (without a financial sector) when the
   a. *LM* curve is vertical
   b. *LM* curve is horizontal
   c. *IS* curve is vertical
   d. *IS* curve is horizontal

6. The equilibrium rate of interest after an increase in the money supply may exceed the original equilibrium rate if
   a. the *IS* curve is slightly upward sloping
   b. the investment function has a zero interest-sensitivity
   c. the *IS* curve shifts far enough to the right as a result of an autonomous change in investment
   d. either (a) or (c)

7. Crowding out occurs because selling government bonds has a wealth effect that also raises
   a. consumption
   b. interest rates
   c. the money supply
   d. the saving rate

8. The natural rate of interest is the rate that equates
   a. saving and investment
   b. saving and investment at full employment
   c. the demand for money and the money supply at full employment
   d. the demand for money and the money supply

9. When inflationary expectations prevail, then
   a. the real rate of interest may exceed the nominal rate of interest
   b. the natural rate of interest may exceed the real rate of interest
   c. the natural rate of interest may exceed the nominal rate of interest
   d. both (a) and (c)
   e. none of the above

10. Given that the economy is operating at the full employment level of income, an increase in the money supply will
    a. lower the natural rate of interest
    b. lower the real rate of interest
    c. leave the real rate of interest unchanged
    d. raise both the natural and the real rate of interest

11. Fiscal policy is completely ineffective when
    a. the economy is in a liquidity trap
    b. the liquidity preference has a zero interest-sensitivity
    c. the investment function has a zero interest-sensitivity
    d. the *LM* curve is horizontal

12. The natural rate of interest is affected by shifts in
    a. the nominal *LM* curve
    b. the real *LM* curve
    c. the *IS* curve
    d. both (b) and (c)

13. Which of the following will produce inflation when the economy is at the full employment level of income?
    a. a rightward shift in the *LM* curve
    b. a rightward shift in the *IS* curve
    c. a leftward shift in the *IS* curve
    d. a leftward shift in the *LM* curve
    e. both (a) and (b)

14. Given that the economy is at the full employment level of income, a shift in the *LM* curve to the right will *not* affect
    a. real output

b. the money supply
c. the economy's GDP
d. all of the above
e. both (a) and (c)

15. Given that the economy is at the full employment level of income, a change in the rate of interest would result from
    a. a shift in the *LM* curve due to an increase in the money supply
    b. a shift in the *IS* curve due to an increase in government spending
    c. both (a) and (b) ·
    d. none of the above

16. As the *IS* curve moves to the right, inflation will not continue indefinitely if the money supply is held constant because
    a. a point will soon be reached where the entire money supply will be used for transaction balances
    b. a point will soon be reached where the velocity of money will attain its upper limit
    c. the *LM* curve will eventually have a zero interest-sensitivity
    d. all of the above
    e. only (b) and (c)

17. The economy is at the full employment level of income. Inflation will result if
    a. either the *IS* curve or the *LM* curve moves to the right
    b. either the *IS* curve or the *LM* curve moves to the left
    c. the *IS* curve moves to the right or the *LM* curve moves to the left
    d. the *IS* curve moves to the left or the *LM* curve moves to the right

The following questions are based on the Appendix to this chapter.

18. The Federal Reserve is faced with a dilemma on the issue of which target to specify for the execution of monetary policy because
    a. the source of the variation of the economy's GDP is uncertain
    b. the Keynesians and the Monetarists are pressuring the Fed to select opposite targets in the conduct of its monetary policy
    c. the economy is inherently unstable because of autonomous shifts in investment spending
    d. all of the above

19. Suppose that a decline in the economy's GDP is precipitated by an autonomous shift in the *IS* curve. In this case the correct monetary policy target would be
    a. the money supply
    b. excess reserves

c. the interest rate

d. both (a) and (b)

20. Suppose that a decline in the economy's GDP is precipitated by an autonomous shift in the *LM* curve. In this case the correct monetary policy target would be

a. the money supply

b. free reserves

c. monetary aggregates

d. the interest rate

21. The Monetarist-Keynesian debate as to whether the Federal Reserve should select a money supply target or an interest rate target hinges on

a. the claim that the demand-for-money function is far more stable than the consumption function according to the Keynesians

b. the claim that the consumption function is far more stable than the demand-for-money function according to the Monetarists

c. the claim that the demand-for-money function is more stable than the consumption function according to the Monetarists

d. the claim that the consumption function is far more stable than the demand-for-money function according to the Keynesians

e. both (c) and (d)

chapter 23

Monetarists and Keynesians: An Aggregate Supply and Demand Perspective

Central Themes and Major Points

This chapter examines various issues related to monetary theory and policy within the aggregate demand–aggregate supply framework and shows how Monetarists and Keynesians differ on these issues.

First we have the issue of whether the business or private sector of the economy is stable or not. If aggregate demand (same as aggregate spending or GDP) is affected by *exogenous shifts in business investment spending,* then the level of economic activity (GDP) will fluctuate considerably, and government intervention to stabilize the economy through monetary and fiscal policies may be justified. Monetarists tend to believe that aggregate demand is stable (given a fixed money supply). Keynesians, however, argue that aggregate demand is sensitive to exogenous shifts in business investment and that government intervention to stabilize the economy is therefore justified.

The second issue is how a change in the money supply affects aggregate demand and GDP. According to Monetarists, an increase in the money supply will raise the public's *cash balances*. These are then spent directly on real goods and services and that lifts up GDP. According to Keynesians the story is different. The increased money supply must first lower interest rates (this is called the *liquidity effect*), in turn stimulating business investment (this is called the *cost of capital* or *interest rate*

effect) and finally raising aggregate demand (GDP). This indirect mechanism is not reliable, and there are conditions under which it breaks down. In addition to the above transmission process the Keynesians have suggested two other links between the money supply and aggregate spending: the *credit availability effect* and the *wealth effect*.

A third issue is the nature of inflation. Monetarists argue that inflation is exclusively a monetary phenomenon, whereas Keynesians see other factors such as fiscal policy and private spending as potential sources of inflation. The Keynesians also emphasize a short-run trade-off between inflation and unemployment, depicted in the Phillips Curve. Keynesians argue that this trade-off exists because of lags in inflationary expectations, wages, and prices. The Phillips Curve implies that the short-run aggregate supply curve is positively sloped and neither vertical nor horizontal, as the extreme Keynesian and Monetarist positions would indicate.

Finally, Keynesians and Monetarists differ over whether monetary policy should be used to stabilize the economy. No, say the Monetarists, because they believe that the economy is inherently stable and that *discretionary countercyclical monetary policy* (easy money in recessions; tight money in booms) is not necessary and can be extremely harmful to the economy. Rather than stabilizing economic activity, monetary policy may actually destabilize the economy by amplifying the natural swings in the business cycle. Because of this destabilizing effect, extreme Monetarists led by Professor Milton Friedman have rejected discretionary countercyclical monetary policy altogether. Instead they propose to apply a *fixed rule* in the conduct of monetary policy: the Federal Reserve should increase the money supply at a constant rate regardless of the current state of the economy.

The Keynesians, however, argue that aggregate spending or GDP is *inherently unstable* because of *autonomous* shifts in investment. Hence intervention is recommended to stabilize GDP, preferably through fiscal policy, since the transmission process of monetary policy is, according to Keynesians, unreliable. To Monetarists, fiscal policy will be ineffective because any expansionary impact of such policy will be offset by rising interest rates, which would *crowd out* business investment.

New Terms

Define and/or explain the following terms introduced in this chapter:

Cost of capital effect	Stabilization policy
Credit availability effect	Countercyclical stabilization policy
Wealth effect	Countercyclical monetary policy
Instability of the private sector	Time lags in monetary policy
Autonomous or exogenous shifts in investment spending	Destabilizing monetary policy
Income effect	Discretionary monetary policy
Liquidity effect	Rules in monetary policy
Economic fine tuning	
Phillips Curve	
Inflationary expectations	

Essay Questions and Problems

1. **The Monetarist-Keynesian debate on the stability of the private sector** We have seen in the previous chapters that the level of investment spending undertaken by the business (same as private) sector is a major determinant of overall economic activity. Hence, it is important to know if the business sector is inherently stable or not. If it is unstable, then government intervention through monetary and fiscal policies to stabilize economic activity (aggregate demand) may be justified.
   a. What is the position of the Monetarists regarding the stability of the private sector and investment spending?
   b. How do Monetarists justify their position?
   c. What is the position of the Keynesians regarding the stability of the private sector and investment spending?
   d. How do Keynesians justify their position?

2. **The effects of changes in the money supply on aggregate demand (same as aggregate spending)** Do changes in the money supply affect aggregate demand? Again, Monetarists and Keynesians have different views on this issue.
   a. According to Monetarists, how do changes in the money supply affect aggregate demand?
   b. According to Keynesians, how do changes in the money supply affect aggregate demand? Distinguish between the basic effect (the cost of capital or interest rate effect) and the secondary effects (the wealth effect and the credit availability effect).

3. **The Monetarist-Keynesian debate on the effectiveness of fiscal policy** Monetarists argue that fiscal policy cannot change the level of aggregate spending unless it is accompanied by a change in the money supply.
   a. What is the position of the Monetarists regarding the effectiveness of fiscal policy?
   b. How do Keynesians explain the effectiveness of fiscal policy even when it is unaccompanied by a change in the money supply?
   c. Why do Monetarists still object to fiscal policy even if it is accompanied by a change in the money supply?

4. **The Phillips Curve and the Aggregate Supply Curve** What is the Phillips Curve? How can its existence be explained? What does it imply for stabilization policy? If a Phillips Curve exists, what does the aggregate supply curve look like?

5. **The response of interest rates to changes in the money supply** Some Monetarists have argued that the end product of an expansionary monetary policy is not lower interest rates, as Keynesians ordinarily maintain, but a higher interest rate than existed before the expansionary policy was undertaken. Explain the position of the Monetarists and that of the Keynesians regarding the effect of a change in the money supply on the level of interest rates.

*6. **The Monetarist view of money** The money supply is equal to $250 billion and aggregate spending (or aggregate demand) equal to $1,250 billion. Answer the following questions:

a. According to the simple version of Monetarism, the income velocity of money is a constant. What is the value of the velocity in this case?

b. Suppose that the Federal Reserve increases the money supply by $10 billion. This action makes the public more liquid. According to the Monetarists the public will try to get rid of this excess liquidity by increasing its spending on goods and services. By how much will spending on goods and services rise?

c. What is the percentage change in the money supply given in question b? What is the corresponding percentage change in spending? What can you therefore conclude?

7. **Time lags and countercyclical monetary policy**

a. Define countercyclical monetary policy.

b. In the absence of time lags, would monetary policy have a stabilizing effect on the course of economic activity? Why?

c. Carefully explain how time lags may render countercyclical monetary policy harmful to the economy. Use an example to illustrate your answer.

d. Under what conditions would time lags *not* act as destabilizers when countercyclical

monetary policy is used to direct the course of economic activity?

8. Monetarists consider the money supply the most important variable affecting the course of economic activity. Does this belief contradict the position taken by those Monetarists who consider monetary policy potentially hazardous?

9. **Alternative to discretionary countercyclical monetary policy** Discretionary countercyclical monetary policy has been rejected by some Monetarists, most notably Professor Friedman.

a. What do they propose instead and how does their proposal operate?

b. Explain why the economy would be more stable in this case.

10. According to House Congressional Resolution 133, which has been incorporated into the Federal Reserve Act, the Federal Reserve is instructed to "maintain long run growth of the monetary and credit aggregates commensurate with the economy's long run potential to increase production."

a. Would this be considered the same as Friedman's fixed rule in the conduct of monetary policy? Explain your answer.

b. Why is it difficult at the present time to justify legislation that would compel the Federal Reserve to follow a Friedman-type rule?

SELF-TESTS

Completion Questions

Complete each of the following statements by entering the missing words and/or choosing the best alternative proposed.

1. If the President of the United States and the Chairman of his Council of Economic Advisors were *(Keynesians/Monetarists)* they would spend considerable amounts of time pressing Congress for countercyclical *(monetary policy/tax and expenditure legislation).* If they were *(Keynesians/Monetarists)* they would first wait for things to get better by themselves; if they didn't they would then turn to *(Congress/the Federal Reserve).*

2. Monetarists tend to think that the aggregate demand curve is *(stable/unstable),* given a particular *(money supply/interest rate),* and that the aggregate supply curve is *(horizontal/vertical).* These conditions imply that exogenous shifts in

investment *(affect/do not affect)* real output. Keynesians argue that the aggregate demand curve is *(insensitive/sensitive)* to exogenous changes in investment and that the aggregate supply schedule *(is/is not)* vertical.

3. According to the Keynesians economic activity is inherently _____ because of fluctuations in *(endogenous/autonomous)* _____ spending. Therefore it is essential for the _____ to step in and _____ aggregate demand.

4. Monetarists have argued that *(an expansionary/a contractionary)* monetary policy will raise the level of interest rates and *(an expansionary/a contractionary)* monetary policy will lower the level of interest rates, just the reverse of standard *(Classical/Keynesian)* analysis. This will happen because the initial _____ _____ effect of monetary policy will be overwhelmed by the subsequent _____ effect of monetary policy.

5. If prices are currently stable and there are no *(inflationary expectations/rational expectations)*, then the _____ rate of interest should equal the _____ rate of interest.

6. The way *(monetary/fiscal)* policy is financed has *(monetary/fiscal)* implications.

7. According to *(Monetarists/Keynesians)*, any fiscal policy that is not accompanied by a change in *(income taxes/the money supply)* will be ineffective in changing aggregate *(supply/demand)*.

8. A decrease in prices *(raises/lowers)* aggregate demand (we are referring here to a movement along the aggregate demand curve, not a shift in the curve), because _____ balances increase when the price level falls.

9. The Keynesian basic view on how money affects _____ demand would go this way: a change in the _____ supply can only affect total spending if it first changes _____ _____, and then only if business _____ _____ is sensitive to those changes.

10. Two components of the Keynesian transmission mechanism of monetary policy besides the interest rate effect on investment spending are the _____ _____ and the _____. The first suggests that lenders are likely to make available more (or less) _____ _____ as the _____ is increased (or decreased) even if changes in the level of interest rates are minimal. The second suggests that a change in the level of _____

_____ affects the value of an in-

dividual's _____

which, in turn, may alter the individual's spending on _____

_____ and _____.

11. Monetarists view inflation as a _____ phenomenon,

    while Keynesians argue that inflation may result from _____

    _____ policy or other exogenous shifts in _____

    _____.

12. The Phillips Curve implies that there is a trade-off between _____

    _____ and _____.

13. _____

    _____ means easy money in recessions in order to get the economy on

    the move again and _____ money in _____

    _____ in order to *(accelerate/slow down)* the pace of _____

    _____.

14. The problem with countercyclical monetary policy is that it ignores the com-

    plications generated by _____.

15. Some of the reasons that led Friedman and some other Monetarists to give up

    countercyclical monetary policy are:

    a. _____

    b. _____

    c. _____

16. Under a Friedman-type rule the _____

    _____ is allowed to grow at a _____ rate

    regardless of _____

    _____.

True and False Questions

For each of the following statements, circle the letter T if it is correct or the letter F if it is *partially* or totally incorrect.

T F   1. The private sector of the economy is inherently unstable, say the Keynesians, and this instability will produce considerable fluctuations in the level of income.

T F   2. If the price level is constant and the money supply is raised, then real money balances increase.

T F   3. According to Keynesians, the transmission mechanism of the money supply to aggregate demand is reliable and quite powerful. An increase in real money balances is directly translated into increased spending on goods and services.

T F   4. The slope of the aggregate demand curve is flatter and the curve itself is more stable for Monetarists than for Keynesians.

T F   5. Although according to Keynesians the aggregate supply curve is upward sloping in the short run, they do not deny that this curve may be vertical in the long run. Hence in the long run both Keynesians and

Monetarists seem in agreement regarding the position of the aggregate supply curve.

T F 6. According to the Monetarists, if the central bank increases the money supply, the aggregate demand schedule shifts to the right, but according to Keynesians it will shift to the left.

T F 7. A reduction in the money supply shifts the aggregate supply curve to the left, according to both Monetarists and Keynesians. For the Keynesians, however, the shift will be less certain than for the Monetarists.

T F 8. Keynesians admit that a government deficit financed by money creation is more expansionary than one financed by bond sales to the public and that both are more expansionary than increased government spending financed by taxation.

T F 9. From the point of view of the Monetarists, a rise in aggregate spending that seems to be the result of a federal deficit is not the result of the deficit at all but of the way in which it was financed.

T F 10. The aggregate supply curve will be positively sloped if wages change at the same rate as the general price level.

T F 11. After all adjustments have taken place, including inflationary expectations and labor-business contractual agreements, the aggregate supply curve must be vertical.

T F 12. Keynesians emphasize that bank loans have more impact on spending than other sources of funds.

T F 13. An expansionary monetary policy will initially reduce interest rates, but the ultimate effect of that policy will be higher interest rates if that policy generates expectations among the public of a higher interest rate.

T F 14. One way in which an expansionary monetary policy may stimulate spending on goods and services is through the so-called income effect; that is, the increase in the value of financial assets that occurs as a result of the decline in interest rates generates additional income that the public spends on goods and services.

T F 15. According to the Monetarists, an increase in the money supply will be without effect on aggregate demand if that increase fails to reduce interest rates.

T F 16. Evidence indicates that a change in the inflation rate is almost immediately reflected in interest rates.

T F 17. In addition to other differences, Monetarists differ from Keynesians in that the former call for a less active or a more "hands off" policy by the government than do the latter.

T F 18. Many monetarists have abandoned countercyclical monetary policy and urged, instead, the use of cyclical monetary policy in order to avoid the complications bred by time lags.

T F 19. Because of time lags, countercyclical monetary policy must be destabilizing.

T F 20. Under a Friedman-type rule the money supply should remain constant.

T F 21. Under a Friedman-type rule the money supply is allowed to grow at a constant rate regardless of the state of the economy.

T F 22. Under a Friedman-type rule the money supply is allowed to grow at a constant rate regardless of the definition of money adopted.

T F 23. Under a Friedman-type rule the money supply is allowed to grow at a higher rate depending upon the broadness of the definition of money adopted.

T F 24. According to a provision of the Federal Reserve Act of 1977, the Federal Reserve must increase the money supply by a constant rate, which can be modified quarterly upon approval by Congress.

T F 25. Keynesians argue that in most circumstances the aggregate supply curve is upward sloping.

Multiple-Choice Questions

Answer the following multiple-choice questions by circling the best alternative.

1. In contrast to the Keynesians, who believe that aggregate demand will fluctuate considerably because of autonomous shifts in investment spending, the Monetarists have argued that aggregate demand will be relatively unaffected by these shifts. They claim all of the following *except*

a. the money supply and the velocity of money being fixed (at least in the short run), any exogenous decrease in investment must be automatically offset by an increase in either consumption or *endogenous* investment or both

b. business investment spending constitutes such a small percentage of aggregate spending that any autonomous shifts in investment will leave aggregate demand practically unchanged

c. an autonomous downward shift in investment will reduce the interest rate, in turn stimulating investment spending and consumption expenditure to counter the initial drop in investment

d. an autonomous downward shift in investment will create unemployment, and that will drive down prices and increase the *real* money supply, which in turn could stimulate spending and raise aggregate demand to its original level

2. The shape of the aggregate supply curve depends on whether one is a Keynesian or a Monetarist. Which of the following statements is correct?

a. Extreme Monetarists claim that the aggregate supply curve is horizontal, at least in the short run.

b. Extreme Keynesians claim that the aggregate supply curve is vertical.

c. Extreme Monetarists claim that the aggregate supply curve is vertical and extreme Keynesians claim it is horizontal, at least in the short run.

d. both (a) and (b)

3. If businessmen decide to invest less than they have been, then

a. aggregate demand will shift to the left, according to Keynesians

b. aggregate demand *may* be unaffected by the change in investment expenditure, according to Monetarists

c. prices will fall until aggregate economic activity is back to its full employment level, according to Monetarists

d. prices may fall somewhat but not enough to restore aggregate economic activity to its full employment level, according to Keynesians

e. all of the above

4. To Monetarists the crucial link between the money supply and aggregate demand is

a. the level of interest rates

b. the velocity of money

c. the marginal propensity to consume

d. the bank deposit multiplier

5. To Keynesians the crucial link between the money supply and aggregate demand is

a. the level of interest rates

b. the velocity of money

c. the marginal propensity to consume

d. the bank deposit multiplier

6. According to the Keynesians, which of the following effects does not play a role in the transmission process of monetary policy?

a. the liquidity effect

b. the wealth effect

c. the cost of capital effect

d. the credit availability effect

e. the fiscal effect

7. In the Keynesian system, increases in the money supply will raise GDP

a. by directly increasing the demand for goods and services

b. by increasing the demand for financial assets, thereby increasing their prices and lowering the level of interest rates, which in turn will stimulate investment

c. by indirectly increasing the demand for goods and services through a wealth effect

d. both (b) and (c)

8. In the Keynesian system, if monetary policy is to affect the economy's GDP it is *necessary* that

a. a change in the money supply affect the level of interest rates

b. a change in the level of interest rates affect real investment

c. both (a) and (b)

d. none of the above

9. According to the Keynesians, an expansionary fiscal policy unaccompanied by an increase in the money supply will still affect aggregate demand, essentially because

a. any initial reduction in private investment will be automatically reversed by the increase in government expenditure

b. the velocity of money will accelerate in response to higher interest rates

c. of a "wealth effect" resulting from the public's ownership of bonds, which induce the public to spend more

d. the velocity of money will slow down, thereby increasing the liquidity of the public and raising spending and aggregate demand

10. From the point of view of the Monetarists, a fiscal policy unaccompanied by a change in the money supply can only

a. change the level of interest rates

b. alter private investment by an amount equal

and opposite to a change in government expenditure

   c. change the composition but not the level of aggregate demand

   d. all of the above

   e. only (a) and (b)

11. According to the Keynesians, which of the following ways of financing a government deficit will be most expansionary?
   a. money creation
   b. bond sales to the public
   c. taxation
   d. either (b) or (c)

12. According to the Monetarists, fiscal policy is effective in changing aggregate demand only if government expenditures are financed by
   a. taxing the public
   b. borrowing from the nonbank public or banks with zero excess reserves
   c. borrowing from banks with excess reserves, borrowing from the Fed, or printing money
   d. either (a) or (c)
   e. none of the above

13. In the Monetarist system, any fiscal deficit unaccompanied by an increase in the money supply will fail to affect aggregate demand, because
   a. the "crowding out" effect will offset the initial increase in government spending
   b. the government will be unable to finance its expenditures without increasing the money supply
   c. consumers will reduce their spending in order to finance the deficit, thereby offsetting the initial increase in government expenditures
   d. taking a dollar from Peter to give it to Paula cannot increase the combined income of Peter and Paula

14. An expansion of the money supply has a more powerful short-run impact on the economy if it is associated with
   a. bank purchases of securities
   b. increased bank loans
   c. rising interest rates
   d. reductions in government spending

15. According to the Monetarists, inflation can be caused by all of the following *except*
   a. an expansion of the money supply when the economy is close to full employment
   b. government deficits financed by taxation
   c. government deficits financed by money creation
   d. both (a) and (c)

16. Which of the following movements in aggregate demand and supply will generate inflation?
   a. a rightward shift in the aggregate supply curve with a fixed aggregate demand curve
   b. a leftward shift in the aggregate demand curve with a fixed aggregate supply curve
   c. a leftward shift in the aggregate supply curve accompanied by a rightward shift in the aggregate demand curve
   d. a rightward shift in the aggregate supply curve accompanied by a leftward shift in the aggregate demand curve

17. Keynesians argue that lower rates of unemployment can be achieved only at the cost of some inflation, because
   a. money demand changes more slowly than money supply
   b. wages change more slowly than the price level
   c. investment is unstable
   d. saving is interest-sensitive

18. A vertical Phillips Curve indicates that there is
   a. a substantial trade-off between inflation and unemployment
   b. no trade-off between government deficits and private investment
   c. a substantial trade-off between government deficits and private investment
   d. no trade-off between inflation and unemployment

19. An expansionary monetary policy may raise the level of interest rates if
   a. the inflationary expectations of the expansionary monetary policy dominate the income effect of the increased monetary supply
   b. the inflationary expectations of the expansionary monetary policy dominate the liquidity effect of the increased money supply
   c. the income effect and the inflationary expectations of the expansionary monetary policy dominate the liquidity effect of the increased money supply

20. In the Monetarist-Keynesian debate on how to influence economic activity, the Keynesian position is that the best policy is
   a. no policy
   b. fiscal policy
   c. monetary policy conducted only for the purpose of controlling the money supply
   d. monetary policy conducted for the purpose of controlling credit conditions in the financial markets

21. Countercyclical monetary policy may be destabilizing because of

a. the uncertainty of economic forecasting
b. the unpredictability of time lags in monetary policy
c. the strength and speed of monetary policy
d. all of the above
e. only (a) and (b)

22. Under Friedman's fixed rule
   a. the rate of growth in the money supply depends on the definition of money adopted
   b. the rate of growth of the money supply must be equal to the rate of growth in productivity
   c. the rate of growth in the money supply is larger for M1 than for M2
   d. all of the above
   e. only (a) and (b)

23. House Congressional Resolution 133 instructed the Federal Reserve to
   a. maintain long-run growth of the monetary and credit aggregates commensurate with the economy's long-run potential to increase production
   b. report quarterly to Congress on its target monetary and credit growth rates for the upcoming twelve months
   c. increase the money supply at a constant growth rate equal to the long-term growth rate in the economy's real productive capacity
   d. both (a) and (b)
   e. both (b) and (c)

24. Monetarists argue against using monetary policy to fine-tune the economy because
   a. the Federal Reserve does not have sufficient tools to control the money supply
   b. velocity is unpredictable
   c. the private sector is inherently unstable
   d. monetary growth leads to inflation

25. Which of the following recommendations would be made by a Monetarist?
   a. a constant 3 percent annual growth in the money supply
   b. an aggressive counter-cyclical monetary policy
   c. a constant money supply
   d. price controls to prevent inflation

chapter 24

Rational Expectations: Theory and Policy Implications

Central Themes and Major Points

This chapter introduces the concept of *rational expectations*. Expectations are rational when people take into account all available information in forecasting the course of the economy. This simple statement has far-reaching consequences for the conduct of economic policy. Indeed, it is shown in the chapter that if wages and prices are completely flexible, then *anticipated* monetary policies have no effect on economic activity. In other words, *countercyclical* monetary policy, if fully anticipated by the public, will have no impact on the economy. The crucial assumption behind that statement, however, is that wages and prices are completely flexible. If contracts prevent wages and prices from being completely flexible, anticipated monetary policy can influence real output and employment.

The chapter examines the implications of rational expectations for the trade-off between inflation and unemployment (the so-called Phillips Curve trade-off) and concludes that in a rational expectations world there is no such trade-off even in the short run (assuming, again, completely flexible wages and prices). This suggests that it is feasible to develop a monetary policy that reduces inflation without increasing unemployment. However, to be effective, the policy must be credible to the public. Central bank credibility will play a critical role in bringing inflation under control for the emerging market economies of Eastern Europe.

Finally, the chapter looks at how rational expectations affect the relationship between changes in the money supply and the level of interest rates. Under rational expectations, the Federal Reserve cannot systematically influence the real interest rate.

New Terms

Define and/or explain the following terms introduced in this chapter:

Rational expectations
Adaptive expectations
Anticipated monetary policy
Efficient capital markets

Unanticipated monetary policy
The natural (full-employment) level of output

Essay Questions

1. **Rational expectations**
   a. Explain what rational expectations are.
   b. How do rational expectations differ from adaptive expectations?

2. **Anticipated versus unanticipated monetary policy**
   a. Explain why anticipated monetary policy will have no impact on economic activity according to rational expectations.

b. What is the crucial assumption behind the ineffectiveness of monetary policy in a rational expectations world?

c. Use the aggregate demand–aggregate supply framework to show how anticipated monetary policy will not affect economic activity in a rational expectations world.

3. **Rational expectations and stabilization policy**

a. What is the implication of rational expectations for the conduct of countercyclical monetary policy?

b. How should economic policy be conducted in a rational expectations world?

4. **Phillips Curve and rational expectations**

a. What is a Phillips Curve?

b. What is the Monetarists' view on the Phillips Curve?

c. How do rational expectations modify the Monetarists' view on the Phillips Curve?

5. **Rational expectations and Eastern Europe**

Using a rational expectations framework, how would you advise the monetary authorities in Eastern Europe as they work to establish a market economy? What are the critical elements necessary for effective anti-inflation policy?

6. **Interest rates and rational expectations**

a. Explain why an anticipated increase in the money supply leads to an immediate increase in interest rates.

b. Explain why an unanticipated increase in the money supply produces lower interest rates.

SELF-TESTS

Completion Questions

Complete each of the following statements by entering the missing words and/or choosing the best alternative proposed.

1. If people use *(some/all)* information to formulate expectations, then their expectations are said to be _____ expectations.

2. Extrapolations from recent price trends are often referred to as _____ _____ expectations.

3. Faster money supply growth leads to *(higher/lower)* output and *(more/less)* unemployment as long as wages go up more slowly than prices.

4. When money supply growth is *(anticipated/not anticipated)* it may lead to higher output and *(higher/lower)* unemployment.

5. The outcome of the rational expectations world is *(Keynesian/Classical-Monetarist)* rather than *(Keynesian/Classical-Monetarist)*. Because of this, rational expectations are sometimes referred to as the new _____ _____.

6. Under rational expectations, the Federal Reserve can reduce the inflation rate without causing an increase in the unemployment rate as long as monetary policy is _____ and _____.

7. When anticipated monetary policy is used in the rational expectations model, the liquidity effect _____ interest rates because inflationary expectations _____.

True and False Questions

For each of the following statements, circle the letter T if it is correct or the letter F if it is *partially* or totally incorrect.

T F 1. If people ignore information when making decisions, then expectations are not considered rational.

T F 2. If inflation has been on the rise, then adaptive expectations suggest that people expect inflation to go up.

T F 3. Adaptive inflationary expectations assume that people ignore the behavior of the monetary authority and the structure of the economy when they make predictions about inflation.

T F 4. Rational expectations implies that participants in financial markets can always accurately predict the inflation rate.

T F 5. Under rational expectations current securities prices reflect all available information and capital markets are said to be efficient.

T F 6. Combining rational expectations with the Classical world's assumption of completely flexible wages and prices, one can show that anticipated monetary policy has a powerful impact on economic activity.

T F 7. Under rational expectations only random acts by the central bank influence the money supply.

T F 8. Discussions on rules versus discretion in the conduct of monetary policy are irrelevant in a rational expectations world.

T F 9. According to rational expectations the Federal Reserve should be replaced by a robot since monetary policy is fully anticipated by the public.

T F 10. Because wages are generally set by contractual agreement they may very well lag behind prices even if expectations of inflation are formed rationally.

T F 11. The rational expectations model implies a vertical short-run Phillips Curve.

T F 12. Rational expectations push the Monetarists' long-run analysis into the short run by transforming a series of upward sloping aggregate supply curves into a vertical one.

T F 13. If wages and prices are rigid, whenever the Federal Reserve embarks on a countercyclical expansion in the money supply, the rightward shift in aggregate demand is met by a leftward shift in aggregate supply.

T F 14. In the Keynesian view, inflexible wages and prices mean that there is a trade-off between inflation and unemployment even if expectations are rational.

T F 15. The key to a successful monetary policy is credibility: only if the Federal Reserve announces its policy and the public is convinced that it will pursue it at all costs will the Federal Reserve achieve its objectives.

T F 16. The hyperinflations suffered by Germany, Austria, Poland, and Hungary in the aftermath of World War I were reversed at the cost of considerable reduction in real output as a result of tight monetary and fiscal policies.

T F 17. One way to establish central bank credibility in Eastern Europe would be to make the monetary authorities fully accountable to the parliament of each country.

T F 18. Keynesians have a long-run "liquidity" perspective when claiming that expansionary monetary policy lowers interest rates, while Monetarists have a short-run perspective when emphasizing that interest rates go up because of inflationary expectations.

Multiple-Choice Questions

Answer the following multiple-choice questions by circling the best alternative.

1. People are likely to formulate rational expectations because
   a. ignoring useful information is usually costly
   b. people are fundamentally rational
   c. they are educated to behave in a rational manner
   d. it increases their income
   e. it slows down the rate of inflation

2. Inflation is currently rising and the Federal Reserve is restricting the money supply. Rational expectations say that people would probably expect
   a. inflation to continue to rise
   b. inflation to go down rather than up
   c. inflation to remain the same

d. the Federal Reserve to expand the money supply

e. both (b) and (d)

3. According to rational expectations, anticipated monetary policy will have no impact on economic activity because
   a. workers recognize the connection between inflation and money supply growth
   b. workers fully anticipate future inflation
   c. workers make sure that wages move up simultaneously with prices
   d. all of the above
   e. only (b) and (c)

The economy is at the full-employment level of output and the price level is at P_1, the intersection between the aggregate demand and aggregate supply curves. Answer the following four questions (4–7).

4. Everything else being the same, an unanticipated increase in the money supply will
   a. shift the aggregate demand curve to the right
   b. shift the aggregate supply curve to the right
   c. shift the aggregate demand curve to the left
   d. shift the aggregate supply curve to the left
   e. both (a) and (d)

5. Everything else being the same, an anticipated increase in the money supply will
   a. shift the aggregate demand curve to the right
   b. shift the aggregate supply curve to the right
   c. shift the aggregate demand curve to the left
   d. shift the aggregate supply curve to the left
   e. both (a) and (d)

6. Under rational expectations the aggregate supply curve will shift in such a manner as to
   a. keep the economy at the full-employment level of output
   b. push the economy below its full-employment level of output
   c. pull the economy above its full-employment level of output
   d. none of the above

7. Under rational expectations the aggregate supply curve will shift in such a manner as to
   a. keep the price level at P_1
   b. pull the price level above P_1
   c. push the price level below P_1
   d. none of the above

8. If wages and prices are flexible and an increase in the money supply is fully anticipated, real wages will
   a. remain unchanged
   b. increase
   c. decrease along with nominal wages
   d. decrease but nominal wages will rise

9. The aggregate supply curve will have a positive, non-vertical slope even when expectations are rational if
   a. the economy is in the liquidity trap
   b. velocity is constant
   c. investment is interest-sensitive
   d. contracts prevent wage flexibility

10. As long as wages and prices are flexible, an anticipated increase in the money supply will lead to an increase in
    a. the price level
    b. velocity
    c. real wages
    d. the unemployment rate

11. According to the Monetarists, led by Milton Friedman, the long-run aggregate supply curve is
    a. horizontal, and hence no permanent trade-off is possible between inflation and unemployment in the long run
    b. vertical, and hence no permanent trade-off is possible between inflation and unemployment in the long run
    c. horizontal, and hence some trade-off is possible between inflation and unemployment in the long run
    d. vertical, and hence some trade-off is possible between inflation and unemployment in the long run
    e. none of the above

12. Under rational expectations, simultaneous shifts in the aggregate demand and aggregate supply curves produce a short-run effect identical to a
    a. horizontal aggregate demand curve
    b. vertical aggregate demand curve
    c. vertical aggregate supply curve
    d. horizontal aggregate supply curve

13. In order to be credible, a policy designed to fight hyperinflation should
    a. change the monetary unit
    b. introduce a truly independent central bank
    c. invoke severe fiscal restraint to balance the budget
    d. all of the above
    e. only (a) and (b)

14. Under rational expectations,
    a. anticipated increases in the money supply lead to immediate increases in interest rates
    b. unanticipated increases in the money supply produce higher interest rates
    c. unanticipated increases in the money supply produce lower interest rates
    d. anticipated increases in the money supply lead to immediate decreases in interest rates
    e. both (a) and (c)

15. According to the rational expectations model, which of the following policies will reduce unemployment in the short run?
    a. an expected increase in the money supply
    b. an expected decrease in the money supply
    c. an unexpected increase in the money supply
    d. an unexpected decrease in the money supply

16. Under rational expectations, an anticipated increase in the money supply leads to a
    a. short-term liquidity effect
    b. long-term liquidity effect
    c. double liquidity effect
    d. zero liquidity effect

chapter 25

Empirical Evidence on the Effectiveness of Monetary Policy

Central Themes and Major Points

Previous chapters have examined at length how monetary policy is transmitted from an initial change in the money supply (resulting from a change in bank reserves) to the final impact on spending (GDP). The effectiveness of monetary policy was examined in terms of parameters such as the interest-sensitivity of both the liquidity preference curve (the demand for money) and the investment function, without any reference to actual numbers or the time it would take for monetary policy actually to work itself through the economy and ultimately affect GDP.

The purpose of this chapter is to present some facts and figures on the behavior of *the velocity of money,* the demand for money, and the effectiveness of monetary policy.

First, the historical evidence indicates that the velocities of the monetary aggregates (M1, M2, and M3) are clearly not fixed and unchanging. The velocities of M2 and M3 have been fairly stable over time and, more importantly, predictable. The velocity of M1, however, has bounced around a great deal since the early 1980s. In 1986, therefore, the Fed abandoned setting a specific target range for M1. Studies indicate that the money-demand function is predictably related to key economic variables such as interest rates and income.

The following sections examine the effectiveness of monetary policy. The time dimension of monetary policy is discussed in terms of *the recognition lag*—the time it takes the Federal Reserve to recognize the need for action—and *the impact lag*—the time it takes for monetary policy to affect GDP. Figures on the impact of monetary policy on GDP and the time it takes for a change in the money supply to affect GDP are obtained from computer simulations using *econometric models of the economy.* For example, results derived from the Federal Reserve model indicate that a 1 percent increase in the money supply raises real GDP by about 1 percent after one year. Econometric models also indicate that an initial increase in the money supply will lower interest rates for six months to one year.

Figures are also presented on the comparative effectiveness of fiscal policy versus monetary policy. Finally, the Federal Reserve model reveals that monetary policy does not have the same influence on all categories of spending. Residential construction and construction expenditures by state and local governments appear to be particularly sensitive to the actions of the monetary authorities.

New Terms

Define and/or explain the following terms introduced in this chapter:

The velocity of M1, M2, and M3

Time lags in monetary policy:†
  The recognition lag
  The impact lag

Cash-management techniques

Econometric models of the economy

†These terms were first introduced in Chapter 23.

Essay Questions and Problems

1. **Velocity of money and monetary policy** Why is it necessary that the velocity of money be stable and that any changes be highly predictable in order for monetary policy to be effective?

2. **Historical behavior of the velocity of money** The velocity of M1 has tended to rise over the long term but fall during recessions. Can you explain this behavior? In recent years M1 velocity has fallen significantly even during economic expansions. Can you think of reasons for this change in behavior?

3. **Money demands** What does the evidence suggest regarding the interest-sensitivity of the demand for money and the stability of the demand for money? What are the implications of the above for the formulation and execution of monetary policy?

4. **Time lags in monetary policy**
   a. Carefully define the types of lags that policy makers confront when implementing monetary policy.
   b. Why do these lags exist?
   c. Why are they considered problematic?
   *d. Would it be possible to reduce their length? How?

*5. **The administrative lag** The recognition lag ends when the Federal Reserve has identified what the economy is actually doing and decides to take action, but the impact lag begins only at the time when the Federal Reserve starts using one of its tools of monetary policy. The time between the Fed's recognition of the need for action and the time when the Fed actually changes one of its tools of monetary policy is usually referred to as the "administrative" lag. How long do you expect this administrative lag would be? How long do you expect the administrative lag would be in the case of fiscal policy, which is implemented by the U.S. Treasury?

6. **Econometric models**
   a. What is an econometric model of the economy? What are the inputs required to build such a model?
   b. What are these models supposed to do?
   c. What are the two econometric models discussed in this chapter? Upon which type of theoretical model of the economy is each built?

7. **Differential impact of monetary policy** Monetary policy does not have an equal impact on all categories of spending. According to the Federal Reserve model, which categories of spending are most sensitive to monetary policy? Why?

SELF-TESTS

Completion Questions

Complete each of the following statements by entering the missing words and/or choosing the best alternative proposed.

1. If monetary policy is to alter GDP, it has to do it by changing the _____ _____ of households, the _____ _____ of business firms, or the expenditures of the _____, _____, or _____ governments.

2. The Monetarist-Keynesian debate hinges on the behavior of the _____

_____, the _____

contending that it is _____,

and the _____ arguing that these conditions are exag-

gerated.

3. The _____ of money is measured by dividing *(the econ-*

omy's GDP/the money supply) by the _____

_____.

4. Some of the factors that have contributed to the postwar rise in velocity are

a. _____

b. _____

c. _____

_____

5. The velocity of _____ and _____

____ have proven to be more stable than the velocity of _____

_____ over time.

6. Just about every statistical study has shown that money demand is influenced

by _____ and _____

_____.

7. The two components of the lag in the effect of _____

_____ on _____ activity are,

first, the _____ and,

second, the _____.

8. A mathematical-statistical representation that describes how the economy

behaves is called an _____

of the economy.

9. The two econometric models discussed in this chapter are the _____

_____ and the _____

_____ models. The former would be considered

(Keynesian/Monetarist) and the latter _____.

10. Some of the numerous factors that influence business investment spending are

a. _____

b. _____

c. _____

d. _____

True and False Questions

For each of the following statements, circle the
letter T if it is correct or the letter F if it is *partially*
or totally incorrect.

T F   1. Keynesians contend that the velocity
of money is quite stable and that its
changes are very predictable.

T F   2. The larger the size of the money supply, the greater will be the swings in the value of the economy's GDP resulting from a given miscalculation in the velocity of money.

T F 3. Historical movements in the velocity of money indicate that velocity is generally more stable when based on a narrower definition of money.

T F 4. The magnitude of the velocity of money increases when the velocity is measured using broader definitions of money.

T F 5. The velocity of money dropped in the period between the two world wars.

T F 6. When a larger volume of current spending flows from the same stock of money, the velocity of money must be rising.

T F 7. The postwar behavior of the velocity of money has been completely random and perverse.

T F 8. Higher interest rates tend to reduce the velocity of M1 because they encourage savings.

T F 9. Just about every statistical study has shown that the demand for money is influenced by the supply of money.

T F 10. The estimated interest-elasticity of the demand for money has generally been extremely high, thus supporting the Keynesian view on the demand for money and refuting the Monetarist view.

T F 11. If the demand for money jumps around for no apparent reason, then changes in the money supply will be useless predictors of economic activity.

T F 12. A key reason for the extensive use of currency for transactions purposes is the underground economy.

T F 13. The demand for M1 has been very stable since the mid-1970s.

T F 14. The two components of the lag in the effect of monetary policy follow each other. As soon as the impact lag ends, the recognition lag begins.

T F 15. Rough evidence regarding the recognition lag seems to support the contention that the Federal Reserve is more concerned with avoiding recession than with preventing inflation.

T F 16. One should expect the recognition lag to be much shorter under fiscal policy than under monetary policy.

T F 17. Econometric models are extremely

helpful in evaluating the length of the recognition lag in monetary policy.

T F 18. Modern computer technology has greatly expanded the capability of econometric models to simulate policy impacts on the economy.

T F 19. Our knowledge of how best to construct an econometric model of the economy has been refined to the point of an almost exact science.

T F 20. A Keynesian econometric model of the economy may differ from a Monetarist econometric model of the economy, because each type of model is based upon a different set of observations of the past behavior of the economy.

T F 21. All the econometric models of the economy indicate that interest rates decline and remain below their original levels for six months to a year after an expansionary monetary policy.

T F 22. Both the Federal Reserve and the St. Louis models show that a 1 percent change in the money supply increases GDP by about 1 percent after one year.

T F 23. According to the St. Louis econometric model of the economy, fiscal policy is ineffective. An increase in government spending leaves GDP unaffected after one year.

T F 24. Historical records indicate that interest rates and business investment spending are inversely related.

T F 25. Because a change in interest rates affects the current decision to invest, it affects business investment spending very quickly.

Multiple-Choice Questions

Answer the following multiple-choice questions by circling the best alternative.

1. Assume a money supply of $400 billion. The velocity is estimated to be somewhere between 5.95 and 6.05. This implies that the economy's GDP could be anywhere between
   a. $2400 billion and $2420 billion
   b. $2380 billion and $2420 billion
   c. $2380 billion and $2400 billion
   d. none of the above
2. The long-run rise in the velocity of M1 is attributed to the fact

a. that GDP has risen faster than the money supply, and since velocity is the ratio of GDP to the money supply it had to rise

b. that attractive yields on financial assets other than money have led the public to reduce their holding of idle cash by lending out part of it to borrowers who can use it for current purchases

c. that postwar consumer spending has risen steadily and at a faster rate than the money supply

d. all of the above

3. Over the long run the velocity of M2 has been
   a. stable
   b. highly predictable
   c. impossible to determine
   d. near 1 in recessions but around 5 during economic expansions

4. Which of the following would *not* increase the velocity of M1?
   a. financial intermediation
   b. efficient cash-management techniques
   c. the use of credit cards
   d. lower interest rates

5. Statistical studies generally indicate that the demand for money is affected by
   a. the level of interest rates
   b. the level of GDP
   c. the money supply
   d. all of the above
   e. only (a) and (b)

6. Empirical evidence regarding the interest-elasticity of the demand for money
   a. supports the extreme Keynesian case of perfectly elastic money demand
   b. supports the extreme Monetarist case of perfectly inelastic money demand
   c. indicates that it is generally quite low
   d. indicates that it is generally quite high
   e. is inconclusive

7. Which of the following factors have been responsible for the recent instability of the demand for money?
   a. the phenomenal growth of money market mutual funds
   b. automated transfers of funds
   c. the existence of money market instruments such as repurchase agreements
   d. all of the above
   e. only (a) and (b)

8. During the 1980s, the velocity of M1
   a. rose gradually
   b. rose sharply
   c. remained almost constant
   d. fell sharply

9. Growth of the underground economy has increased
   a. the demand for currency
   b. velocity of money
   c. the use of credit cards
   d. the money supply

10. The time between the Federal Reserve's realization of the need for action and the time when the Federal Reserve actually changes one of its tools of monetary policy is called
    a. the recognition lag in monetary policy
    b. the time lag in monetary policy
    c. the impact lag in monetary policy
    d. none of the above

11. Which of the following is not an ingredient required to construct an econometric model of the economy?
    a. mathematical expressions that formalize the interrelationships between economic variables
    b. a theory about how the economy functions and how economic agents interact
    c. data on past experience of the real world
    d. none of the above
    e. all of the above

12. Based on their respective views about the transmission mechanism of monetary policy
    a. Monetarists would predict a shorter recognition lag in monetary policy than Keynesians
    b. Keynesians would predict a shorter recognition lag in monetary policy than the Monetarists
    c. there should be no difference between the two schools in their respective predictions of the length of the recognition lag
    d. one cannot tell whether (a), (b), or (c) is correct

13. Econometric models of the economy are used to
    a. reduce the length of the impact lag in monetary policy
    b. decide whether monetary or fiscal policy should be selected to influence the course of economic activity
    c. predict the future course of economic activity
    d. all of the above
    e. only (b) and (c)

14. According to the St. Louis model, an increase of 1 percent in the money supply
    a. lowers GDP by 1 percent after one year
    b. raises GDP by 1 percent after one year
    c. lowers GDP by 2 percent after one year
    d. raises GDP by 2 percent after one year
    e. none of the above

15. Which of the following factors would *not* directly affect business investment spending?
    a. inflationary expectations
    b. sales expectations
    c. the marginal propensity to save
    d. the availability of internally generated funds
16. Which of the following is *not* considered a form of investment spending?
    a. the installation of new machinery
    b. the purchase of a new house
    c. the construction of a new plant
    d. none of the above
17. According to the Federal Reserve model, the following category of spending is *not* affected by monetary policy:
    a. federal government spending
    b. state and local government spending
    c. consumer spending
    d. investment spending
18. According to the Federal Reserve model, the category of spending most sensitive to changes in interest rates is
    a. residential construction
    b. business investment spending
    c. consumer spending
    d. state and local government spending
19. The St. Louis model indicates that
    a. fiscal policy is more powerful than monetary policy in affecting the economy's GDP
    b. monetary policy is less powerful than fiscal policy in affecting the economy's GDP
    c. fiscal policy has practically no effect on the economy's GDP one year after it is implemented
    d. fiscal and monetary policy are good substitutes in affecting the economy's GDP over very short periods of time
20. The Federal Reserve model indicates that
    a. an expansion in government spending, even with a fixed money supply, does not produce a complete crowding out of nominal GDP
    b. fiscal policy is most effective when it is accompanied by an increase in the money supply
    c. monetary policy has significant long-run impacts on economic activity
    d. all of the above
    e. only (a) and (c)

part V

Financial Markets and Interest Rates

chapter 26

Risk and Portfolio Choice

Central Themes and Major Points

What is the risk of an asset? How can this risk be measured? Given an amount of wealth, how much should be invested in each asset available in the market? This chapter provides answers to these questions.

To understand the nature of risk, it is useful to begin by examining a hypothetical world of certainty in which everything is perfectly predictable. In this case there is no risk in holding financial assets. Promised return will be paid. Furthermore, all assets with the same term to maturity will be identical to each other and will pay the same return.

Unfortunately perfect predictability does not exist. There is always a possibility that the promised interest and/or principal on a loan will not be repaid (*default risk*) or that a bond will be sold before its term to maturity at a price lower than its purchase price (*market risk*).

In an uncertain world the return on a risky asset is not known with any degree of certainty. Instead we have a set of possible alternative returns and their respective likelihood of occurrence, called a *probability distribution*. From this distribution we can obtain a measure of the *expected return* and the risk (the *standard deviation of return*) of an asset.

Risk averters will combine individual assets to form well-diversified *portfolios*. The fundamental proposition of *modern portfolio theory* is that an individual asset may be considered very risky when viewed in isolation (it may have a relatively high standard deviation of returns), but when it is combined with other assets, the risk of the portfolio may be substantially less, even zero if certain conditions are met. How this *diversification* effect works is explained in this chapter.

Finally, the portfolio selection problem is analyzed. Which portfolio should a risk averter hold? First the universe of all portfolios is divided into two groups: the set of *inefficient portfolios* and the set of *efficient portfolios*. No risk averter will ever hold an inefficient portfolio. The portfolio chosen will be from those that are efficient and will depend upon the degree of risk aversion specific to the individual decision maker.

New Terms

Define and/or explain the following terms introduced in this chapter:

Default risk	Probability distribution of returns
Market risk or capital uncertainty	
Holding period yield	Independence of returns
Modern portfolio analysis	Standard deviation
Risk aversion	Covariance
Risk averter	Perfectly negatively correlated returns
Expected return on a risky asset	Perfectly positively correlated returns
Risk loving	Efficient portfolio
Nonsystematic risk	Inefficient portfolio
Systematic risk	Index fund
Diversification	

Essay Questions and Problems

1. **Interest rates in a world of certainty**
   a. Would lending and borrowing take place in a world of certainty? If so, how would the rate of interest on loans be determined?
   *b. Explain why a unique interest rate would prevail in a world of certainty. Describe the mechanism that would bring all rates to equality, assuming that all interest-paying securities have the same term to maturity. Would the rate still be the same for two securities with different terms to maturity? Explain.

2. **Sources of risk under uncertainty** What are the two major sources of risk faced by a bondholder in a world of uncertainty? Explain carefully each of these two sources of risk and discuss how they could be reduced or completely eliminated.

3. **Alternative measures of the bond yield** Distinguish between (1) the promised yield on a bond and the actual yield on the same bond, (2) the holding period yield on a bond and the yield to maturity on the same bond, and (3) the nominal yield on a bond and the real yield on the same bond.

4. **Attitudes toward risk** Consider a riskless security paying 7 percent for certain and a risky security with an expected return of 7 percent. Answer the following questions:
   a. What does risk aversion mean?
   *b. Explain carefully why a risk-averse individual will *always* prefer the *riskless* security over the risky security.
   *c. What would be the choice of a risk lover? Explain.
   *d. How would you qualify an individual with no preference for one security over the other?

5. **How to determine an individual's attitude toward risk** What questions would you ask an individual if you wanted to determine if he was a risk averter or a risk lover?

6. **Measuring and defining risk** Under uncertainty all the possible returns that may be earned on a risky asset and their respective likelihood of occurrence are summarized in a probability distribution.
   a. Indicate how this probability distribution can be used to obtain a measure of the risk of this asset.
   b. In light of modern portfolio theory, would you consider this measure of risk satisfactory? Explain.
   c. Which other measure of risk would be relevant in the context of portfolio theory?

*7. **The number of covariances in a portfolio**
   a. Define covariance and distinguish between variance and covariance.
   b. How many distinct covariances does a two-security portfolio have?
   c. How many distinct covariances does a three-security portfolio have? How many variances? List these risk measures.
   d. How many distinct covariances does a four-security portfolio have? How many variances? List these risk measures.
   e. How many distinct covariances does a five-security portfolio have? How many variances? List these risk measures.
   f. What can you conclude when you compare the number of distinct covariances with the number of variances as the number of securities in the portfolio increases?

8. **Systematic versus nonsystematic risk** Distinguish between the systematic and the nonsystematic portions of the total risk of an asset. Explain why risk averters holding a risky security should receive an expected return above the risk-free rate that is in proportion only to the systematic risk of that security rather than to its total risk.

9. **Portfolio decision-making** Describe the two steps involved in portfolio decision-making.

*10. **Problem on portfolio selection** Suppose that the future state of the economy can be described as either expansionary or recessionary (this, of course, is an extremely simplified view of the future), with each state equally likely to occur. The distribution of the returns on two securities, A and B, is given in the table below.

State of the Economy	Probability of Occurrence	Return on Security A	Return on Security B
Expansion	½	+ 15%	− 1%
Recession	½	+ 3%	+ 11%

Answer the following questions:
   a. What is the expected return of security A and of security B? Which security would be considered "countercyclical" and which would be considered "cyclical"? Explain.

b. What is the risk (measured by the standard deviation) of security A and security B?

c. If a risk-averse individual had to make a choice between holding only security A or holding only security B (no combination allowed), which security would he or she choose? Explain.

d. Answer the same question as in (c) for the case of a risk-loving individual.

e. The investor is now allowed to hold portfolios combining security A and security B. He or she can now divide between security A and security B the amount of money to be invested in the portfolio. Suppose that three alternative portfolios can be formed: Portfolio 1 would have ¼ of the individual's money invested in security A and ¾ in security B.
Portfolio 2 would have ½ of the individual's money invested in security A and ½ in security B.
Portfolio 3 would have ¾ of the individual's money invested in security A and ¼ in security B.
Note that although these three portfolios contain the same two securities they are completely different portfolios, because of the different proportion of money invested in each security. This point is clearly demonstrated by determining the expected return and the risk of each portfolio. Proceed as follows. First determine the distribution of the returns of each portfolio and enter the return in the table below after showing your calculations. For example, if expansion occurs, then portfolio 1 (¼ of security A and ¾ of security B) will have a return of (¼) (15 percent) + (¾) (−1 percent) = 3 percent, since security A returns 15 percent and security B returns −1 percent in this case. (For further details see footnote 3 in Chapter 26 of the textbook.)

State of the Economy and Probability of Occurrence	Distribution of the returns on		
	Portfolio 1	Portfolio 2	Portfolio 3
Expansion (½)	3%	___	___
Recession (½)	___	___	___

Using the above distribution of returns and recalling that each return is equally probable, you can now easily calculate the expected return and the risk (standard deviation) of each of the three portfolios. Enter these results in the table below and show your calculations.

Characteristics	Portfolio 1	Portfolio 2	Portfolio 3
Expected returns	6%	___	___
Risk (standard dev.)	___	___	___

f. The investor now has a choice between five alternative investments: security A or security B held alone, portfolio 1, portfolio 2, or portfolio 3. (Note that other portfolios could have been formed simply by changing the proportions of money invested in each security.) Suppose that he or she is risk averse. Answer the following questions:

(1) Which of these five investments would be considered efficient, and which would be considered inefficient?

(2) Would the investor hold any inefficient investment? Explain.

(3) Which of the efficient investments would be selected by this risk-averse individual?

(4) If this person were a risk lover, which investment would he or she have selected? Why?

g. How could portfolio 2 be riskless, considering that it contains two risky assets? Would a risk averter choose portfolio 2 or a riskless bond paying 8 percent? What would a risk lover do in this case?

h. The reason why portfolio 2 is riskless is that security A and security B in this portfolio are perfectly, negatively correlated. In this case the correlation coefficient between the returns of security A and those of security B is equal to −1. This correlation coefficient can be computed according to:

$$\text{correlation coefficient} = \frac{\text{covariance between security A and security B}}{(\text{risk sec. A}) \times (\text{risk sec. B})}$$

where risks are measured as standard deviations. The covariance is calculated as follows: (1) compute the difference between the returns of each security and their respective expected return (the deviation from expected returns); (2) multiply the deviations obtained when expansion prevails and when recession prevails; (3) multiply these products by their probability of occurrence; (4) add up the end results to obtain the covariance. Using the above formula, show that the correlation coefficient is equal to minus one.

SELF-TESTS

Completion Questions

Complete each of the following statements by entering the missing words and/or choosing the best alternative proposed.

1. Under certainty there *(is a unique/are more than one)* level(s) of _____ _____ for loans with the same maturity.

2. Two major sources of risk in an uncertain world are _____ _____ and _____ _____.

3. *(U.S. government/Corporate)* bonds are free from *(default risk/market risk)*.

4. People who dislike risk are called _____ _____ and those who like risk are called _____ _____.

5. When uncertainty prevails, the set of all possible rates of return that could be earned on an asset and their corresponding likelihood of occurrence is called a _____. Using this information the _____ on the asset can be calculated by multiplying each possible outcome by its __ _____ and adding up all the products.

6. The risk of an asset by itself can be formally measured by a statistic called the _____.

7. The most fundamental proposition of modern portfolio analysis can be stated as follows: _____ _____ _____.

8. The interrelationship between the variability of two assets' returns is measured by their _____.

9. The _____ risk of a security is that portion of its *(total/ average)* risk that cannot be eliminated when that security is included in a _____.

10. The two characteristics of efficient portfolios are

a. _____

b. _____

True and False Questions

For each of the following statements, circle the letter T if it is correct or the letter F if it is *partially* or totally incorrect.

T F 1. In a world of certainty the level of interest rates never changes, since life is perfectly predictable.

T F 2. One can eliminate market risk by simply holding a zero-coupon bond until its maturity date.

T F 3. In the absence of risk the yield on securities is determined by consumption, saving, and real investment.

T F 4. Government securities, unlike the securities of individuals and corporations, have no market risk.

T F 5. Default risk is usually associated with dishonest individuals and corporations that refuse to pay borrowed funds at maturity.

T F 6. Only government bonds have real yields equal to their nominal yields, because of the government's power to tax and to create money.

T F 7. The price at which a bond can be sold before its maturity date is determined by the yields on similar bonds that have just been issued.

T F 8. In a riskless world there is only one optimal portfolio decision for all risk-averse individuals: hold one-half of your wealth in cash and the other half in the only security available in the market.

T F 9. An important assumption of modern portfolio analysis is that individuals are risk lovers.

T F 10. A risk-averse individual will always prefer a riskless bond that pays 5 percent for certain to a risky security that would pay either 3 percent or 7 percent with an equal probability of occurrence.

T F 11. The sum of the probabilities assigned to each possible outcome of a financial investment must be equal to unity.

T F 12. The expected return on a risky security is computed by taking the sum of all possible outcomes and then multiplying this sum by its probability of occurrence.

T F 13. The more risk averse an individual is, the higher the additional expected return required to compensate him for bearing one extra unit of risk.

T F 14. The risk of a portfolio of securities may be smaller than the risk of every individual security included in the portfolio.

T F 15. The variance is a statistic that measures the interrelationship between the variability of the returns of two securities.

T F 16. The standard deviation, which measures the risk of an individual security by itself, is always positive, whereas the covariance between the returns of two securities may be either positive or negative.

T F 17. A risk averter will never be indifferent between a riskless security and a risky security. He will always prefer the former over the latter.

T F 18. A probability distribution of returns is a summary of all possible returns on a financial investment, with their respective likelihood of occurrence.

T F 19. Given the probability distribution of returns on an asset (a security, a bond, or a portfolio of securities and bonds), one can compute the asset's expected return and risk (standard deviation).

T F 20. Evidence suggests that the probability distribution of security returns is symmetrical above and below the mean.

T F 21. The central problem of modern portfolio analysis is how to choose an efficient portfolio.

T F 22. An inefficient portfolio is one with more expected return and the same risk than another portfolio or one with less risk and the same expected return than another portfolio.

T F 23. The standard deviation of the returns on an individual asset is not the relevant measure of risk in a portfolio

T F 24. In order to determine the preferred efficient portfolio from the set of all available efficient portfolios, one must know the subjective trade-off between risk and return demanded by an individual.

T F 25. Systematic risk can be diversified away by holding a larger number of securities in a portfolio.

T F 26. With two different securities one can obtain an infinite number of different portfolios simply by varying the proportion of wealth invested in each security.

T F 27. Securities with returns that are independent of each other have zero covariance.

T F 28. Of two securities offering the same expected return but having different risks, a risk lover will prefer the security with the greatest risk because its potential for an extremely large capital gain is higher.

T F 29. In the portfolio selection problem, the final portfolio that is selected by the individual decision maker is called the efficient portfolio; all other portfolios are considered inefficient.

T F 30. An effective diversification strategy for investing in the stock market is to hold a number of "blue-chip" stocks.

Multiple-Choice Questions

Answer the following multiple-choice questions by circling the best alternative.

1. In a world of certainty in which all assets have the same maturity,
   a. the return on all securities is identical
   b. the price of all securities is the same
   c. all securities are perfect substitutes for each other
   d. all of the above
   e. only (a) and (c)

2. Default risk refers to
   a. the possibility that a borrower may be unable to repay the principal on his loan
   b. the possibility that a borrower may be unable to make the interest payments on his loan

   c. the possibility that a borrower may go bankrupt
   d. all of the above
   e. only (a) and (b)

3. Market risk is associated with
   a. fluctuations in the level of interest rates
   b. uncertainty about the inflation rate
   c. the failure of the borrower to repay the promised interest and/or principal on his loan
   d. the failure of the market mechanism to bring buyers and sellers together

4. U.S. government bonds are default-free because
   a. the government is trustworthy
   b. the government can always raise cash through taxes in order to pay back its creditors
   c. the government has always paid back whatever it borrowed in the past
   d. none of the above

5. If a bond is sold before maturity
   a. the bondholder will incur a capital loss because he or she will not be able to recover the initial investment outlay, which is paid back only at maturity
   b. the yield to maturity will be reduced
   c. the holding period yield may differ from the yield to maturity
   d. both (a) and (c)

6. Different bonds have different yields to maturity, because they may differ with respect to
   a. their term to maturity and/or their issuer
   b. the frequency of their coupon payments
   c. their face value
   d. all of the above
   e. only (a) and (b)

7. Portfolio theory assumes that people
   a. never take risks
   b. take risks only if they are risk lovers
   c. take risks only when they have incomplete or inaccurate information
   d. take risks only when there is sufficiently high expected yield

8. The most fundamental proposition of modern portfolio theory can be stated as follows:
   a. People are all risk averse.
   b. An asset may be very risky when viewed in isolation, but when combined with other assets the risk of the portfolio may be substantially reduced.
   c. Security returns are symmetrical above and below the mean, and consequently the standard deviation can be used as an adequate measure of risk.
   d. The returns on securities are interrelated,

and therefore a measure of their covariability must be used when combining securities in portfolios.

9. A risky security has two possible outcomes: it will pay either 6 percent or 10 percent, with each outcome equally probable to occur at the end of the investment period. The *actual* return that will be received from that security at the end of the investment period will be equal to
   a. 6 percent
   b. 8 percent
   c. 10 percent
   d. either (a) or (c)

10. If security A pays either 4 or 6 percent with equal probability and security B pays either 2 or 8 percent with equal probability, then
    a. security A and security B have the same expected return
    b. security A is riskier than security B
    c. security B is riskier than security A
    d. both (a) and (b)
    e. both (a) and (c)

11. Suppose that both Marci and Alana hold security A, which has an expected return of 6 percent and a risk (standard deviation) of 8 percent. Marci is willing to give up security A for a newly available security B, which has an expected return of 8 percent and a risk of 10 percent. Alana is not willing to give up security A for security B. It follows that
    a. Alana is more risk averse than Marci
    b. Marci is more risk averse than Alana
    c. Alana and Marci have the same degree of risk aversion
    d. one cannot tell from the above who is more risk averse, since nothing is said about the risk-return preference of these individuals

12. The standard deviation of returns is a good measure of risk when analyzing
    a. the risk of an individual security by itself
    b. the risk of an individual security as part of a portfolio of securities
    c. the systematic risk of a portfolio of securities
    d. the systematic risk of an individual security
    e. both (a) and (c)

13. An individual willing to take a fifty-fifty chance of doubling or losing his wealth is
    a. a risk-averse individual
    b. a risk-loving individual
    c. a diversifier
    d. both (a) and (c)

14. In order to determine the expected return on a portfolio of two securities, one must know
    a. the expected return on each individual security

b. the proportion of wealth invested in each one of the two securities
c. the covariance between the returns of the two securities
d. all of the above
e. only (a) and (b)

15. Consider a portfolio of three securities. How many distinct covariances exist between these three securities?
    a. one
    b. two
    c. three
    d. one cannot tell

16. In order to determine the risk on a portfolio of two securities, one must know
    a. the risk (standard deviation) on each individual security
    b. the proportion of wealth invested in each one of the two securities
    c. the covariance between the returns of the two securities
    d. all of the above
    e. only (a) and (b)

17. Consider a portfolio of four securities. How many distinct covariances exist between these four securities?
    a. four
    b. five
    c. six
    d. one cannot tell

18. An ideal asset to include in a portfolio of securities would have the following characteristic
    a. its returns should be independent of the returns on the securities already included in the portfolio—that is, the average covariance of this asset with the securities already included in the portfolio should be equal to zero
    b. its average covariance with the securities already included in the portfolio should be negative
    c. its average covariance with the securities already included in the portfolio should be positive
    d. the asset should be riskless

19. Consider a riskless asset paying 6 percent and a risky asset paying either 5 or 7 percent with an equal probability. The covariance between these two assets is
    a. zero
    b. positive
    c. negative
    d. cannot be calculated since the probability distribution of the first asset is not given

20. Consider the following three assets (securities or portfolios): asset A has an expected return of

10 percent with a risk of 6 percent, asset B has an expected return of 5 percent with a risk of 6 percent, and asset C has an expected return of 5 percent with a risk of 9 percent. It follows that

a. asset A is efficient and both asset B and asset C are inefficient
b. asset A and asset C are efficient and asset B is inefficient
c. asset A and asset B are efficient and asset C is inefficient
d. all three assets are inefficient
e. all three assets are efficient

21. Nonsystematic risk will be minimized by a mutual fund that specializes in
a. automobile industry stocks
b. small company stocks
c. blue-chip stocks
d. a wide variety of stocks

22. An efficient way to diversity a stock portfolio is to
a. purchase all the stocks you are aware of
b. ask a broker to develop a "balanced" portfolio for you
c. purchase an index fund
d. purchase blue-chip stocks

chapter 27

Flow of Funds Accounting: A Framework for Financial Analysis

Central Themes and Major Points

This chapter is an introduction to *flow of funds accounting*. In this system the economy is divided into sectors, such as the household sector, the business sector, the government sector, and the financial sector. By recording the payments each sector makes to other sectors and the receipts it receives from them, one can construct what is called a *flow of funds matrix* for the whole economy.

In order to construct this flow of funds matrix, it is first necessary to prepare a list of each sector's *uses* of funds and *sources* of funds. This is called a sector's uses and sources of funds statement.

Uses of funds are transactions that absorb funds from a sector. Sources of funds are transactions that generate funds to a sector. It is shown in this chapter that uses of funds consist of (1) investment, (2) lending, and (3) hoarding; and that sources of funds consist of (1) saving and (2) borrowing.

The sum of a sector's uses of funds must equal the sum of its sources. This fundamental equality is written:

$$\text{Investment} + \text{Lending} + \text{Hoarding} = \text{Saving} + \text{Borrowing}$$

A sector with saving in excess of investment is called a *surplus* sector. A sector with investment in excess of saving is called a *deficit* sector. For the economy as a whole, however, investment must equal saving, since the aggregate of all sectors cannot possibly have a collective deficit or surplus.

By putting together the sources and uses of funds statements of all the sectors that make up the economy, one can construct a flow of funds matrix for the whole economy. This is shown in the final section of the chapter.

New Terms

Define and/or explain the following terms introduced in this chapter:

Flow of funds accounting

A sector's income statement

Uses and sources of funds

Current expenditures and receipts

A sector's balance sheet

Assets, liabilities, and net worth

Flows versus stocks

Hoarding and dishoarding

Deficit sectors

Surplus sectors

Balance sectors

The flow of funds matrix

Essay Questions and Problems

1. **Flow of funds accounting**
   a. What is flow of funds accounting, and what is it used for?
   b. In what form are flow of funds data for the economy presented?

c. Who prepares this set of economic and financial information, and where is it published?

2. **The difference between a sector's net worth and the economy's net worth**

   a. Explain why a real asset must appear on only one sector's or unit's balance sheet, but a financial instrument always appears on the balance sheet of two different sectors or units.

   b. Show that the above implies that in the combined balance sheet of all the sectors in the economy all the financial instruments will cancel out and the economy's net worth must equal the sum of all its real assets.

   *c. To illustrate your answer to question b, consider a hypothetical economy made up of Alana, Marci, and a bank. Alana has $200 at the bank, a car worth $4,000, a $2,000 debt outstanding owed to the bank, and a $500 debt owed to Marci. Marci has $1,800 in deposit at the bank.
      (1) What are Alana's and Marci's net worths?
      (2) Draw the balance sheets for Alana, Marci, and the bank.
      (3) What is the economy's net worth?

   *d. Show why the net worth of all nongovernmental sectors (all sectors excluding the Treasury and the Federal Reserve) must equal the monetary base (bank reserves plus currency outside banks) plus publicly held government bonds plus real assets.

3. Explain why for the economy as a whole investment must equal saving, whereas for any sector or unit investment can differ from saving.

4. a. Consider an economy without money and financial markets.
      (1) Could any unit invest more than it saves?
      (2) Could it save more than it invests?

   b. Consider an economy with money but without financial markets.
      (1) Could any unit invest more than it saves?
      (2) Could it save more than it invests?

*5. In flow of funds accounting, why is the purchase of a new car considered an investment whereas the purchase of a new shirt is not?

*6. **The construction of the sources and uses of funds statement** At the bottom of the page is a hypothetical balance sheet for the household sector at year end in 1991 and 1992.

   a. Construct the sources and uses of funds statement for 1992.

   b. Was the household sector a surplus or a deficit sector in 1992?

   c. Now assume the economy consists of only two sectors, the household sector and the

---

Balance Sheets for the Household Sector

1991 (in billions of dollars)

Assets		Liabilities	
Cash and demand deposits	200	Residential mortgages	250
Consumer durables	300	Consumer credit	250
Residential construction	200	Other bank loans	100
Time and savings accounts	200	Other loans (including those	
Corporate equities	100	due loansharks)	50
Corporate bonds	250		
U.S. Treasury securities	150	Net worth	800
Federal Agency securities	50		

1992 (in billions of dollars)

Assets		Liabilities	
Cash and demand deposits	250	Residential mortgages	200
Consumer durables	450	Consumer credit	300
Residential construction	250	Other bank loans	50
Time and savings accounts	200	Other loans	50
Corporate equities	150		
Corporate bonds	275	Net worth	1,200
U.S. Treasury securities	125		
Federal Agency securities	100		

business sector. Could the sources and uses statement shown on the next page be that of the business sector? If not, why not?

Uses		Sources	
Investment	400	Borrowing	200
Hoarding	−50	Saving	500
Lending	350		

d. Could the sources and uses statement shown below be that of the business sector? If not, why not?

Uses		Sources	
Investment	500	Borrowing	450
Hoarding	−50	Saving	300
Lending	250		

e. Could the sources and uses statement shown above (right) be that of the business sector? If not, why not?

Uses		Sources	
Investment	600	Borrowing	325
Hoarding	−50	Saving	400
Lending	175		

*7. **The flow of funds matrix** Here is a hypothetical flow of funds matrix for the whole economy. Find W, X, Y, Z.

	Sector A	Sector B	Sector C
Saving	10	25	Y
Investment	W	20	10
Borrowing	20	15	Z
Lending	20	X	10
Hoarding	5	10	5

SELF-TESTS

Completion Questions

Complete each of the following statements by entering the missing words and/or choosing the best alternative proposed.

1. Flow of funds accounting is used to _____.

2. A sector's current receipts during a period of time are considered a *(source/use)* of funds and its current _____ are considered a _____ of funds.

3. In _____ accounting a _____ is a subdivision within a country's economy. Examples of these are _____, _____, and _____.

4. Saving of the government sector is called _____ and saving of the business sector is called _____ _____.

5. A sector's balance sheet is a list of the sector's _____ and _____. The difference between total _____ _____ and total _____ is defined as the sector's _____.

6. A sector's assets are divided into two broad categories: _____ assets and _____ assets. Examples of the former are _____ and _____. Examples of the latter are _____ in the case of the household sector and _____ in the case of the business sector.

7. A sector that *(saves/borrows)* an amount equal to its current _____ is called a _____ sector. If it _____ more than its current _____ it is called a _____ sector. If it _____ less than its current _____ it is called a _____ sector.

8. Any one of the following will constitute a "source" of funds: _____, _____, or _____.

9. Any one of the following will constitute a "use" of funds: _____, _____, or _____.

10. A surplus sector must dispose of its surplus by _____, _____, or _____ in an amount equal to its surplus.

11. A deficit sector must finance its deficit by _____, _____ _____, or _____ in an amount equal to its deficit.

12. For any given sector, the fundamental equality in flow of funds accounting is written as: _____ + _____ + _____ = _____ + _____ _____.

True and False Questions

For each of the following statements, circle the letter T if it is correct or the letter F if it is *partially* or totally incorrect.

T F   1. Flow of funds accounting is used to analyze a country's balance sheet.

T F   2. One sector's payments are another sector's receipts.

T F   3. A budget surplus is to the government sector what retained earnings are to the business sector.

T F   4. One major difference between an income statement and a balance sheet is the time dimension: the former shows accounting data at a point in time, whereas the latter shows accounting data between two points in time.

T F   5. Securities are financial assets to the issuer and liabilities to the holder and, therefore, appear on two different balance sheets.

T F   6. For every asset listed on the left-hand side of someone's balance sheet, there is a corresponding liability on the right-hand side of someone else's balance sheet.

T F   7. Capital expenditures, which are purchases of real assets with an expected useful life of one year or more, are not included in an income statement, since income statements are confined to current expenditures.

T F 8. Investment may refer either to a capital expenditure or to the purchase of financial assets.

T F 9. A change in the sector's net worth during a period of time is the same thing as "saving" on its income statement covering that time interval.

T F 10. A deficit sector is one that has an increase in real assets in excess of an increase in net worth.

T F 11. Borrowing is synonymous with an increase in outstanding liabilities.

T F 12. Lending is the same as an increase in the holdings of financial assets.

T F 13. A negative use of funds is actually a source of funds.

T F 14. Sources of funds consist of current receipts, any change in a liability, and any change in an asset.

T F 15. For a sector to be balanced, lending plus hoarding must equal borrowing.

T F 16. If a sector's saving exceeds its investment, then it must be a surplus sector.

T F 17. If a sector's investment equals its saving, then this necessarily implies that its financial sources of funds are equal to its financial uses of funds.

T F 18. A balanced sector has its investment equal to its saving and does not undertake any lending, hoarding, or borrowing.

T F 19. There cannot be any deficit or surplus sectors unless there exists a financial market.

T F 20. For the economy as a whole, saving must equal investment.

Multiple-Choice Questions

Answer the following multiple-choice questions by circling the best alternative.

1. A "uses and sources of funds" statement integrates a sector's
   a. income statement with its net worth
   b. balance sheet with its income statement
   c. net worth with its income statement
   d. none of the above

2. An income statement lists a sector's
   a. assets and liabilities
   b. changes in assets and liabilities
   c. current expenditures and current receipts
   d. capital expenditures and changes in net worth

3. A sector's excess of current receipts over and above its current spending is called
   a. saving
   b. net worth
   c. change in saving
   d. either (b) or (c)

4. Which of the following items does not appear on two different balance sheets?
   a. financial assets
   b. real assets
   c. liabilities
   d. both (a) and (c)

5. An example of a stock variable is
   a. wealth
   b. income
   c. the economy's GDP
   d. aggregate demand

6. Which of the following is *not* a use of funds?
   a. investment
   b. current expenditures
   c. the sale of a real asset
   d. hoarding
   e. lending

7. A sector's increase in money holdings is called
   a. lending
   b. borrowing
   c. hoarding
   d. saving

8. Which of the following is *not* a source of funds?
   a. the sale of a financial asset
   b. the purchase of a financial asset
   c. borrowing
   d. dishoarding

9. Uses of funds consist of all of the following *except*
   a. current receipts
   b. any increase in a financial asset
   c. any increase in a real asset
   d. hoarding
   e. any decrease in a liability item

10. Debt repayment is
    a. a use of funds
    b. a source of funds
    c. dishoarding
    d. none of the above

11. A sector can dispose of a surplus by
    a. dishoarding
    b. selling financial assets
    c. hoarding
    d. borrowing

12. For any sector the following equality must hold:
    a. investment + saving = lending + hoarding + borrowing
    b. investment + lending = saving + hoarding + borrowing

c. borrowing + saving = investment + lending + hoarding

d. hoarding + saving = investment + lending + borrowing

13. A sector is in deficit if
   a. its investment exceeds its savings
   b. its lending plus its hoarding exceed its borrowing
   c. its borrowing exceeds its lending plus its hoarding
   d. both (a) and (b)
   e. both (a) and (c)

14. For the economy as a whole
   a. lending plus hoarding must be equal to borrowing
   b. all sectors are balanced
   c. investment may differ from saving
   d. none of the above

15. For a balanced sector
   a. lending equals borrowing
   b. investment equals saving
   c. hoarding equals dishoarding
   d. all of the above

16. For a *surplus* sector
   a. saving + borrowing > investment + lending + hoarding
   b. saving + borrowing = investment + lending + hoarding
   c. saving + borrowing < investment + lending + hoarding
   d. none of the above

17. Which of the following is not an investment in flow of funds accounting?
   a. the purchase of a new car
   b. the purchase of a new house
   c. the purchase of legal services
   d. the purchase of a new plant

18. The flow of funds matrix shows
   a. aggregate supply and aggregate demand
   b. a categorical breakdown of aggregate expenditures
   c. interest rate levels for variations in risk
   d. financial relationships among all sectors

19. For which of the following purposes is the flow of funds accounting framework most useful?
   a. estimating the distribution of income
   b. projecting consumer spending
   c. determining surplus sectors in the economy
   d. predicting the inflation rate

20. The borrowing and lending relationships between and among all sectors in the economy are known as the
   a. total supply and demand
   b. GDP
   c. capital account
   d. flow of funds matrix

chapter 28

The Structure of Interest Rates

Central Themes and Major Points

In the preceding chapters any discussion on interest rates referred to only one rate—*the* interest rate. We all know, however, that there are many different rates out there, not just one.

This chapter recognizes this fact of life and explains why there are so many different interest rates on various types of financial instruments.

Several factors account for the observed yield differentials between securities. Two, however, are particularly significant: the term to maturity of the security and the credit risk of the issuer. To simplify the analysis of the *structure* of interest rates, it is convenient to examine the effect of the changes in one of these factors, holding the other constant.

The *term structure of interest rates* examines the relationship between the yield and the term to maturity for those securities that belong to the same risk class (for example, credit risk is held constant when one analyzes only government securities). This chapter shows how this is done by drawing *yield curves* and explains what determines their shape.

The *risk structure of interest rates* examines the relationship between the yield and the credit risk for those securities that have the same term to maturity (for example, long-term government bonds, long-term corporate bonds, and long-term municipal bonds). It is shown that, in general, the riskier a bond the higher its yield.

Other factors besides the term to maturity and credit risk are responsible for the observed yield differentials between securities. The chapter discusses three of these: (1) taxes (the special case of "flower bonds," lower taxes on capital gains than on coupon income, the tax-exempt status of municipal bonds); (2) the relative marketability of securities; and (3) the cash-flow uncertainty of mortgage securities.

The Appendix to this chapter introduces the concept of bond duration. It is a measure of the volatility of bond prices.

New Terms

Define and/or explain the following terms introduced in this chapter:

Term structure of
  interest rates
Yield curve
Expectations theory
Liquidity premium
Preferred habitat
  approach
Expected future
  short-term rates
Flower bonds
Risk structure of
  interest rates
Marketability

Credit rating services:
  Moody's
  Standard and
  Poor's
Municipal bonds
Tax-exemption of
  municipals
"Off the run" issues
"Current coupon
  issues"
"On the run" issues
Duration (Appendix)

Essay Questions and Problems

1. **Yield differential between securities** Securities available in the market have a wide range of yields.
   a. List all the factors that may explain a yield differential between securities.
   b. Why don't investors buy *only* the security that offers the highest yield?

2. **The yield curve**
   a. What is a yield curve, and how is it drawn?
   b. What determines the shape of yield curves? Briefly discuss how the segmented markets theory, the expectations theory, and the liquidity premium theory explain the shape of the yield curve. What should be the shape of the yield curve according to each theory?

3. **The yield curve as a forecasting tool** Describe how the yield curve can be used to forecast the economy. What is the yield curve likely to look like prior to a recession? Why?

*4. **The expectations theory of the term structure of interest rates** Suppose that the market for government securities consists of one-year Treasury bills and two-year Treasury notes.
   a. The bill rate is 6 percent and the note rate is 7 percent.
      (1) Draw the two-point yield curve.
      (2) According to the expectations theory, what is the expected yield on one-year bills to be issued at the end of the year?
   b. The bill rate is 7 percent and the note rate is 6 percent.
      (1) Draw the two-point yield curve.
      (2) According to the expectations theory, what is the expected yield on one-year bills to be issued at the end of the year?
   c. From your answers to (a) and (b), could you tell how the direction of change in short-run rates affects the shape of the yield curve?
   d. The bill rate is 6 percent and the note rate is 7 percent. According to the expectations theory investors should be indifferent between holding the 6 percent bill or the 7 percent note.
      (1) Explain why this statement is correct.
      (2) Suppose that an investor buys a 7 percent note and sells it at the end of the first year. Would the investor earn 7 percent instead of the 6 percent offered by one-year bills? How much would he or she earn and why?

5. **The risk structure of interest rates** Describe the market mechanism that will ensure that yields on lower quality bonds exceed the yields on higher quality bonds—other factors held constant.

6. **Variations in government bond yields** Explain the factors that cause differences in yields on U.S. government bonds. How did the Tax Reform Act of 1986 affect these differences?

7. **Duration (Appendix)**
   a. What is the definition of duration?
   *b. Calculate the duration of a two-year bond with $100 annual coupon payments, a principal of $1000, and a yield to maturity of 10 percent.
   c. Is this bond selling at par?
   d. How is duration related to yield to maturity?
   e. What would be the duration of the two-year bond cited above if it were a zero-coupon bond?

SELF-TESTS

Completion Questions

Complete each of the following statements by entering the missing words and/or choosing the best alternative proposed.

1. The relationship between yields on different maturities of the same type of security is called _____. This relation-
   _____. This relation-
   ship is depicted graphically by a _____.

2. The two major theories explaining the term structure of interest rates are the

_____ and the _____

_____. The _____ theory is a modifi-

cation of the _____ theory of term structure.

3. According to the _____ theory of term structure, the

   shape of the _____ curve depends on the _____

   _____

   _ rates. The key to this theory is that short- and long-term bonds are perfect

   _____ in the portfolios of investors.

4. The _____ is a reward

   for exposure to the capital uncertainty of long-term securities.

5. The relationship between yields on different risk classes of securities with the

   same _____ is called _____

   _____.

6. Credit rating _____ such as _____

   and _____ clas-

   sify corporate and municipal bonds in different _____

   _____. The yields on *(higher/lower)* rated bonds are

   lower than those on _____ rated bonds.

7. _____ bonds have a tax _____

   on _____.

8. Securities with the same maturity and credit risk may have different yields

   because of factors such as different _____ or different

   _____.

9. The most recently issued government bonds in each maturity range are often

   referred to as _____ is-

   sues. Older issues are known as _____

   issues.

10. Mortgages yield more than bonds of comparable _____,

    _____ and _____ because of

    _____.

True and False Questions

For each of the following statements, circle the letter T if it is correct or the letter F if it is *partially* or totally incorrect.

T   F   1. Yield curves are drawn at a point in time and not over a period of time. Thus, one can draw a yield curve for government securities on any given day by simply plotting the yield on government issues published daily in the financial pages of major newspapers.

T   F   2. According to the supply and demand for securities approach to term structure, the yield curve must be upward sloping.

T   F   3. As long as the expected future short-term rates are unchanged, changes in the relative supply of long- and short-term securities will not affect the shape of the yield curve.

T F 4. A rising yield curve (upward sloping) means that the price of short-term securities is higher than the price of long-term securities of the same issuer.

T F 5. According to the expectations theory, investors are indifferent between short-term government securities and long-term corporate securities.

T F 6. According to the liquidity preference theory, investors, on balance, will demand a premium for holding long-term securities.

T F 7. No evidence has ever been found that would suggest that liquidity premiums are actually embedded in long-term interest rates.

T F 8. When interest rates are high relative to what they have been, the yield curve should be downward sloping.

T F 9. The evidence indicates that short-term interest rates fluctuate more than long-term interest rates over the course of the business cycle.

T F 10. The fact that over long periods of time the yield curve tends to be upward sloping more often than it is downward sloping is consistent with the expectations theory of the term structure of interest rates.

T F 11. There is some evidence that in the very short run (a week or two) the relative supplies of securities may temporarily affect the shape of the yield curve.

T F 12. A negatively sloped yield curve is a sign of an impending recession.

T F 13. When the risk of default on municipal bonds becomes relatively high, the yield differential between government bonds and municipal bonds may disappear, even though interest on municipal bonds is tax-exempt.

T F 14. The yield on corporate bonds is smaller than the yield on government bonds, because the former are riskier than government bonds.

T F 15. Bonds with good marketability, other factors held constant, will have higher yields than bonds without this characteristic because bondholders like bonds that are easily marketable.

T F 16. The yield on higher rated bonds is higher than the yield on lower rated bonds—other factors held constant.

T F 17. Deep discount bonds will generally sell at lower yields than bonds with the same credit risk, marketability, and term to maturity.

T F 18. Flower bonds are bonds that are accepted at par in payment of real estate taxes if bought before the acquisition of property.

T F 19. Older, "off the run" issues tend to sell at higher yields than newer securities with similar coupon and term to maturity because they have more interest rate risk.

T F 20. Conventional mortgages yield slightly more than equivalent government insured mortgages, because they have a less active secondary market.

T F 21. Outstanding bonds on which the issuer has defaulted are called "on the run."

The following questions are based on the Appendix to this chapter.

T F 22. Government regulation has retarded the development of active secondary markets for mortgage-backed securities.

T F 23. For a zero-coupon bond, duration always equals maturity.

T F 24. In general, higher coupon payments increase duration.

T F 25. The duration of a bond is the inverse of its yield to maturity.

Multiple-Choice Questions

Answer the following multiple-choice questions by circling the best alternative.

1. Which of the following is held constant when the term structure of interest rates is analyzed?
   a. the credit risk of the issuers of the bonds
   b. the maturity of the bonds
   c. the market risk of the bonds
   d. the buyers of the bonds
   e. both (a) and (c)
2. According to the supply and demand for securities approach to term structure
   a. the shape of yield curves is determined by the supply of and the demand for securities of various maturities
   b. securities of various maturities are not good substitutes in the portfolios of investors
   c. some investors have preferences for securities of particular maturities

d. all of the above

e. only (a) and (b)

3. According to the expectations theory of the term structure
   a. securities of the same user are perfect substitutes
   b. the yield curve can take any shape
   c. the shape of the yield curve is determined by the future short-term rates anticipated by the market
   d. all of the above
   e. only (b) and (c)

4. If the market expects the future short-term rate of government issues to fall below the current short-term rate, then according to the expectations theory of the term structure, the yield curve for government securities must be
   a. upward sloping
   b. downward sloping
   c. flat
   d. one cannot tell

5. Suppose that two-year Treasury securities yield 8 percent and that one-year Treasury securities yield 6 percent. According to the expectations theory, the market expects next year's one-year Treasury securities to yield
   a. 8 percent
   b. 6 percent
   c. 10 percent
   d. 7 percent

6. Which of the following financial institutions will prefer short-term government securities to long-term government securities, all other things remaining the same?
   a. life insurance companies
   b. commercial banks
   c. pension funds
   d. both (a) and (c)

7. According to the liquidity premium theory of the term structure, the shape of the yield curve should be
   a. upward sloping (rising)
   b. downward sloping (declining)
   c. flat
   d. this theory has nothing to say about the shape of the yield curve

8. The yield curve on government securities is not a smooth curve because
   a. securities of the same maturity may have different credit ratings
   b. securities of the same maturity may have different coupon rates
   c. securities of the same maturity may have different tax treatment
   d. all of the above
   e. only (b) and (c)

9. Yield curves during economic expansions are usually
   a. negatively sloped
   b. positively sloped
   c. close to horizontal
   d. close to vertical

10. A good explanation for the reason why short-term interest rates tend to fluctuate more than long-term rates during a business cycle can be found in the
    a. expectations theory
    b. supply and demand for securities theory
    c. preferred habitat theory
    d. liquidity premium theory

11. Which of the following is held constant in analyzing the risk structure of interest rates?
    a. the issuer of the bonds
    b. the credit rating of the bonds
    c. the maturity of the bonds
    d. the risk of default on the bonds

12. If you pay 40 percent of your income in taxes and the coupon rate on a government bond is 8 percent, your after-tax yield is equal to
    a. 4 percent
    b. 4.8 percent
    c. 3.2 percent
    d. none of the above

13. Municipal bonds usually have lower yields than government bonds of the same maturity, because
    a. they are safer than government bonds
    b. interest on these bonds is tax-exempt
    c. they are less liquid than government bonds
    d. all of the above

14. The coupon rate on long-term government bonds is 8 percent and the coupon rate on long-term municipal bonds is 7 percent. You pay 20 percent of your income in taxes. In this case which bond should you buy if you consider municipals as practically risk-free?
    a. the government bond
    b. either the government bond or the municipal bond, with no preference
    c. the municipal bond
    d. neither the government bond nor the municipal bond since long-term corporate bonds pay 8 percent

15. The yields on GNMA mortgage securities are above those on government issues of the same maturity because they
    a. do not have organized secondary markets
    b. are riskier than government bonds, since they are liabilities of individuals with unknown credit ratings
    c. have uncertain cash flows
    d. both (a) and (b)

16. There are many different interest rates in the financial markets because
    a. securities have different terms to maturity
    b. securities have different credit ratings
    c. interest from securities may be taxed at different rates
    d. securities have different degrees of marketability
    e. all of the above
17. Which of the following bonds are rated by agencies such as Moody's and Standard and Poor's?
    a. government bonds
    b. FHA mortgages
    c. municipal bonds
    d. all of the above
    e. only (b) and (c)

The following questions are based on the Appendix to this chapter.

18. The duration of a bond is
    a. a measure of its "longness" that takes into account the fact that bondholders receive some of their money back before the maturity date
    b. a more comprehensive measure of a bond's maturity since it takes into account the timing of coupon as well as principal payments
    c. a measure of the volatility of bond prices
    d. all of the above
    e. only (a) and (c)
19. For a given change in yield
    a. a bond with longer duration has greater price volatility than a bond with shorter duration
    b. a bond with shorter duration has greater price volatility than a bond with longer duration
    c. a bond with longer maturity has greater price volatility than a bond with shorter maturity
    d. a bond with shorter maturity has greater price volatility than a bond with longer maturity
    e. both (a) and (c)
20. If the duration of a bond is eleven years and the yield to maturity rises from 10 percent to 10.50 percent, then the percentage drop in the price of the bond is

a. 0.5 percent
b. 5 percent
c. 50 percent
d. .05 percent
e. 10 percent

21. At a 20 percent yield to maturity, the duration of a 20 percent coupon bond which matures in two years is
    a. 2 years
    b. 1.83 years
    c. 1.91 years
    d. 1.50 years
22. The duration of a coupon bond is
    a. shorter than its maturity
    b. shorter when the yield to maturity is higher
    c. longer when the coupon rate is lower
    d. all of the above
    e. only (a) and (b)
23. Bond A matures in ten years and has a 10 percent coupon rate. Bond B matures in eleven years and has a 7 percent coupon rate. It follows that
    a. bond A has a longer duration than bond B
    b. bond A has a shorter duration than bond B
    c. bond B is riskier than bond A
    d. bond A is riskier than bond B
    e. both (b) and (c)
24. Bond A matures in eight years and has a 6 percent coupon rate. Bond B matures in seven years and has a 7 percent coupon rate. It follows that
    a. bond A has a longer duration than bond B
    b. bond A has a shorter duration than bond B
    c. bond B is riskier than bond A
    d. bond A is riskier than bond B
    e. both (a) and (d)
25. A zero-coupon bond
    a. is less volatile than a coupon-bearing bond with the same maturity
    b. is more volatile than a coupon-bearing bond with the same maturity
    c. has the same volatility as a coupon-bearing bond with the same maturity
    d. has a shorter duration than a coupon-bearing bond with the same maturity
    e. both (a) and (d)

chapter 29

The Structure and Performance of Securities Markets

Central Themes and Major Points

The importance of financial markets has been emphasized many times over in the preceding chapters. They play a crucial role in the Saving-Investment process, and they facilitate the exchange of financial assets. This chapter examines how financial markets are organized and how they should function. Three types of market organization are discussed: auction markets, brokered markets, and dealer markets.

A distinction is made between *primary* markets and *secondary* markets. The former are markets for newly issued securities. Investment bankers play a significant role in these primary markets. Secondary markets are those in which outstanding (existing) securities are traded. They may be *organized* markets such as the New York Stock Exchange or *over-the-counter* markets. This chapter examines the operation of both types of secondary markets.

A financial market, or any other market, that is *operationally efficient* should disseminate price information and trading interests (buying and selling orders) among market participants as fast as possible and at reasonable cost. It should also provide adequate facilities for the execution of transactions. In a market that is *allocationally efficient* the price of securities should fully reflect all publicly available information. In this case securities are neither overvalued nor undervalued. In this respect government regulation through the Securities and Exchange Commission plays an important role.

A key issue is how to measure the operational efficiency of markets. It is shown that the *bid-asked spread* (the difference between the price at which dealers are ready to sell a security and the price at which they are ready to buy the same security) is a useful quantitative measure of efficiency. A narrow spread indicates that transactions prices will be close to equilibrium prices. However, there is much more to good market performance than narrow bid-asked spreads.

New Terms

Define and/or explain the following terms introduced in this chapter:

Auction market
Brokered market
Dealer market
Brokers and dealers†
Specialists
Traders and market
　makers
Walrasian auction
Transactions prices
Equilibrium prices
Bid and asked prices
Bid-asked spread
Primary and
　secondary markets
Investment bankers†
Underwriting†

Syndicates
Organized stock
　exchanges
Over-the-counter
　markets (OTC)
National Association
　of Securities Dealers
Automated Quotation
　System (NASDAQ)
Breadth, depth, and
　resiliency of markets
Thin markets
Operational efficiency
　of markets
Allocational efficiency
　of markets

The efficient market hypothesis

Marketability

Underwriting spread

Round lot

Unregistered securities

Securities and Exchange Commission

National Association of Securities Dealers (NASD)

Globex

†These terms were first introduced in Chapter 9.

Essay Questions and Problems

1. **Functions of financial markets** What are the essential functions a market should perform?

2. **The price of a security** Distinguish between transactions prices and equilibrium prices.

*3. **Investment bankers** What role do investment bankers play in the capital markets? Are they brokers, dealers, both brokers and dealers, or none of these?

*4. **Specialists** What is the job of specialists in secondary equity markets? Are they brokers, dealers, both brokers and dealers, or none of these?

5. **Secondary markets**
   a. The price of new issues is determined in secondary markets. Explain this statement.
   b. Distinguish between organized exchanges and over-the-counter markets.

6. **The bid-asked spread** The table below gives the bid and asked prices quoted by dealers for a Treasury note, a Federal Home Loan bond, and shares of the XYZ corporation, an over-the-counter stock. Answer the following questions.
   a. What does the bid price indicate? What does the asked price indicate?
   *b. Compute the bid-asked spread for each issue and enter it in the next to the last column.
   *c. Compute and enter in the last column the cost of a $1,000 round trip. This is the cost of buying and immediately selling a note or a bond with a $1,000 face value or $1,000 worth of XYZ stock assuming an average price of $20 per share.
   *d. Which of the three issues is most liquid and which is least liquid? Explain.

*7. **More on the bid-asked spread** Consider the following: you can sell your antique car by getting in touch with an antique car dealer selling on consignment (you get your money only after the car is sold and there is no guarantee of a sale). The dealer's commission would be around 30 percent of the sale. You can immediately sell 100 of your shares in IBM by calling your stockbroker, whose commission would be less than 2 percent of the sale. What does the difference in commissions and the speed of the sale indicate?

8. **The efficiency of financial markets**
   a. Distinguish between the operational and the allocational efficiency of financial markets
   b. What is an efficient market in an allocational sense?
   c. What are the implications of the efficient markets hypothesis for the pricing and the trading of securities?

Type of Security	Bid Price	Ask Price	Spread	Cost of $1,000 Round Trip
Treasury note	$103^{18}\!/_{32}$	$103^{22}\!/_{32}$		
Federal Home Loan bond	$96^{26}\!/_{32}$	$97^{26}\!/_{32}$		
Stock of XYZ Corp.	$19\frac{1}{2}$	$20\frac{1}{2}$		

SELF-TESTS

Completion Questions

Complete each of the following statements by entering the missing words and/or choosing the best alternative proposed.

1. The role of financial markets is to _____ the exchange

   of _____ by bringing

   _____ and _____ together.

2. The price at which *(dealers/brokers)* stand ready to buy is called the _____ _____ price and the price at which they stand ready to sell is called the _____ price. The difference between the _____ _____ price and the _____ price is called the _____, which is the dealer's reward for _____.

3. _____ are financial institutions that specialize in _____ the securities of private corporations and the obligations of states and cities. They often band together to form a _____ for the purpose of _____ _____.

4. The difference between brokers and dealers is that the former act only as ____ _____ and are compensated by charging a _____ _____ for filling the _____ of their customers, whereas dealers _____ and _____ _____ securities for their _____ and are compensated by the _____ between the _____ _____ price and the _____ price.

5. Financial markets can be separated into primary markets and _____ _____ markets or into organized exchanges and _____ _____ markets or into capital markets and _____ markets.

6. A market that is able to absorb large trading volume without causing wild gyrations in transaction prices is said to have _____, _____, and _____. A market that lacks these characteristics is called a _____ market.

7. Commodities markets in the United States started an experiment in 1992 called _____ designed to conduct _____ _____ trading.

8. The _____ and _____ Commission was established in 1934 by an act of Congress to prevent _____ _____ and promote _____ _____.

9. According to the efficient markets hypothesis, the *(current/future)* price of a security reflects _____ _____.

True and False Questions

For each of the following statements, circle the letter T if it is correct or the letter F if it is *partially* or totally incorrect.

T F 1. The functions of financial markets are different from those of any other market because of the peculiar character of financial instruments.

T F 2. Equilibrium prices usually hover around the transactions price.

T F 3. A financial market that operates poorly is one that performs its functions slowly and at relatively high costs.

T F 4. Buyers and sellers meet at an open auction, with the highest bids selling and the lowest bids buying.

T F 5. Investment bankers are dealers in primary markets.

T F 6. One important function of secondary markets is that they help determine the required yield on new issues.

T F 7. Specialists act as brokers and as dealers in organized equity markets.

T F 8. The American Stock Exchange is the largest secondary market for equities in the United States.

T F 9. The activity of brokers is risky, because they hold inventories of securities, whereas the activity of dealers is riskless, since they act only as agents in executing orders.

T F 10. Virtually all U.S. government, federal agency, and municipal bonds are traded over-the-counter.

T F 11. The liquidity costs of a security are inversely related to the size of its bid-asked spread.

T F 12. Secondary markets in individual mortgage loans have been very active since their establishment in 1981.

T F 13. The bid-asked spread is equal to the bid price minus the asked price.

T F 14. The public auction occurring in organized exchanges cannot handle the large-sized trades of institutional investors.

T F 15. When new orders for a security pour in quickly in response to changes in the price of the security, the market for that security is said to be resilient.

T F 16. Unregistered securities cannot be traded on the New York Stock Exchange.

T F 17. The New York Stock Exchange has developed a reputation as an innovator of applications for new computer technology.

T F 18. If prices quickly incorporate all available information, it is impossible to earn above average returns by selling overvalued securities.

T F 19. According to the efficient markets hypothesis, the price of a security fully reflects all available information, and thus no extra profits can possibly be earned (and no losses avoided) by trading on nonpublic information.

T F 20. In an effort to promote more efficient stock prices, the U.S. government does not allow insider trading.

Multiple-Choice Questions

Answer the following multiple-choice questions by circling the best alternative.

1. One can distinguish three types of market organizations:
   a. spot, futures, and auction markets
   b. auction, option, and futures markets
   c. cash, futures, and brokered markets
   d. auction, dealer, and brokered markets

2. A direct relationship between buyer and seller in order to bargain over price is established in the
   a. equilibrium market
   b. auction market
   c. brokered market
   d. dealer market

3. Which of the following is not considered a market maker?
   a. a dealer
   b. a broker
   c. a specialist
   d. an investment banker
   e. none of the above

4. A highly liquid security will have a relatively
   a. narrow bid-asked spread
   b. wide bid-asked spread
   c. low marketability
   d. both (a) and (c)

5. Investment banks are
   a. dealers in primary markets
   b. financial institutions that make loans to corporations
   c. banks that specialize in the management of wealthy people's investments
   d. none of the above

6. The marketability of a security reflects the
   a. default risk of a security

   b. market value of a security
   c. type of market in which a security is sold
   d. relationship between the actual price of a security and its theoretical equilibrium price

7. The markets in which outstanding securities are traded are called
   a. primary markets
   b. secondary markets
   c. capital markets
   d. organized markets

8. The job of the specialist is to
   a. underwrite the securities of corporations
   b. specialize in the trading of securities within markets
   c. maintain orderly trading for the securities he is in charge of
   d. arbitrage away the price discrepancies of securities traded in more than one market

9. Which of the following prices should be the highest?
   a. the equilibrium price
   b. the bid price
   c. the asked price
   d. one cannot tell

10. Dealers' earnings come from
   a. the commission they charge their customers
   b. the bid-asked spread
   c. capital appreciation of their inventories of securities
   d. all of the above
   e. only (b) and (c)

11. Dealers will quote a narrow bid-asked spread for a particular issue if
   a. the volume of transactions in that issue is large
   b. the price volatility of that issue is low
   c. competitive pressures are high
   d. all of the above
   e. only (a) and (b)

12. The bid price on a Treasury note is $97^{10}/_{32}$ and the asked price is $97^{18}/_{32}$. The liquidity costs of this security for a $10,000 round trip are equal to
   a. $0.25
   b. $25
   c. $2.50
   d. none of the above

13. Which of the following is likely to have the lowest bid-asked spread?
   a. a General Motors corporate bond
   b. a municipal bond issued by the state of Arkansas
   c. a U.S. Treasury bond
   d. a U.S. Treasury note

14. If orders in a market exist in large volume, the market is said to have
   a. breadth
   b. depth
   c. resiliency
   d. all of the above

15. An efficient capital market is one in which
   a. security prices fully reflect all publicly available information
   b. there is no unexploited public information whose recognition would lead to superior investment performance
   c. there are no overvalued or undervalued securities
   d. all of the above

16. Which of the following may not be reflected in the stock price of ABD corporation, even in an efficient market?
   a. information on the historical price behavior of a share of ABD corporation
   b. information on past earnings performance and expected earnings of ABD corporation
   c. confidential information you have just received from an officer of ABD corporation on a very lucrative contract about to be signed by ABD corporation
   d. all of the above

17. The Securities and Exchange Commission was created in response to the
   a. insider trading scandals of the 1980s
   b. 1929 stock market crash
   c. inflation of the 1970s
   d. computer needs of the unregistered securities market

18. The primary argument supporting laws against insider trading is that such laws promote
   a. efficiency
   b. fairness
   c. economic growth
   d. profitability

chapter **30**

The Government Securities Market

Central Themes and Major Points

The largest amount of debt outstanding is that of the U.S. government. Part of this debt is in the form of marketable securities (U.S. Treasury bills, notes, and bonds) that can be bought or sold on the open market (secondary market). This market for government securities is very active and serves as a reference point for the pricing of other securities such as municipal securities and corporate debt securities.

The U.S. Treasury is also constantly issuing new securities (primary market) to raise fresh funds to finance its budget deficit and to pay interest on outstanding debt (this is called "servicing" the government debt). These financing requirements are important, because they affect the relative yield of securities and hence the shape of the yield curve.

The purpose of this chapter is to examine the nature and structure of the market for government securities (how they are priced, issued, and distributed) and to look at how the U.S. Treasury manages the government debt.

New Terms

Define and/or explain the following terms introduced in this chapter:

National debt
Marketable
   government issues
   (bills, notes, and
   bonds)
Nonmarketable

government issues
(savings bonds)
Treasury refinancing
   or refunding
   operations
Coupon stripping

Auction of Treasury
   bills
Competitive
   bidding
Noncompetitive
   bidding
Stop-out price
Discount yield

Coupon equivalent
   yield
Dutch auction
Debt management
Monetization of the
   public debt†
An "even keel" in the
   bond markets

†This term was first introduced in Chapter 18.

Essay Questions and Problems

1. **Government deficits and the debt** What is the difference between the federal government's debt and its deficit? Which of these has to be financed by the Treasury? Is the debt growing? Is the deficit growing?

*2. **Treasury bill auctions and yields** The following data pertain to a recent auction of three-month bills by the U.S. Treasury:

Amount applied for at auction	$12 billion
Amount scheduled to be sold	$5 billion
Sales by competitive bidding	$2 billion
High price paid at auction	$96,532
Average price paid at auction	$96,515
Low price paid at auction	$96,509

Answer the following questions:
   a. What amount of bills were sold to noncompetitive bidders?
   b. What was the stop-out price?
   c. At which price did noncompetitive bidders purchase the bills?
   d. Compute the discount yield and the coupon

equivalent yield, using the high price paid at the auction.

e. Compute the discount yield and the coupon equivalent yield, using the average price paid at the auction.

f. Compute the discount yield and the coupon equivalent yield, using the low price paid at the auction.

3. **Debt management**

a. What is debt management?

b. What are its objectives, and why are they often considered conflicting objectives?

c. Why should debt management be coordinated with fiscal policy and monetary policy?

SELF-TESTS

Completion Questions

Complete each of the following statements by entering the missing words and/or choosing the best alternative proposed.

1. The government debt outstanding is in two forms: _____ and _____.

2. An example of nonmarketable debt is _____ _____.

3. Treasury _____, _____, and _____ are marketable government issues that are traded in (primary/secondary) markets.

4. Three major buyers of U.S. government securities are _____ _____, _____, and _____ _____.

5. _____ is a technique used by government securities dealers to create _____ issues out of government securities by separating the _____ and _____ _____.

6. The technique used by the Treasury to sell securities is known as the _____ or _____ auction. Now, however, the Treasury is experimenting with the _____, which should have the effect of _____ bid prices.

7. The two objectives of debt management are

a. _____

b. _____

True and False Questions

For each of the following statements, circle the letter T if it is correct or the letter F if it is *partially* or totally incorrect.

T F 1. A reduction in the government deficit leads to an equal reduction in the size of the government debt.

T F 2. Treasury bills do not pay coupon income.

T   F   3. Most Federal Reserve open market operations involve thirty-year Treasury bonds.

T   F   4. If it weren't for heavy foreign purchases of government securities, U.S. interest rates would be considerably higher.

T   F   5. Treasury bills typically have original maturities of three months, six months, and one year.

T   F   6. One cannot purchase a Treasury bill with a two-month maturity in a secondary market, since the U.S. Treasury doesn't issue them.

T   F   7. Competitive bids on Treasury bills must be submitted at the Federal Reserve Bank of New York.

T   F   8. Competitive bidders buy their bills at different prices, whereas noncompetitive bidders pay the same price.

T   F   9. One can compute the yield on a Treasury bill either on a discount basis or on a premium basis.

T   F   10. When computing the discount yield on a Treasury bill, one should assume that the year has 365 days.

T   F   11. Three-month Treasury bills have an effective original maturity of 91 days, and six-month bills have an effective original maturity of 183 days.

T   F   12. Both the repo market and the federal funds market are overnight markets.

T   F   13. A Dutch auction should encourage more competitive bidding for Treasury securities than the current system used by the Treasury.

T   F   14. The objective of minimizing the interest cost of the debt dictates shortening the maturity structure of the debt during recession periods and lengthening the maturity structure during boom periods.

T   F   15. The monetization of the national debt refers to buying back outstanding government securities with newly printed money.

T   F   16. As fiscal agents for the Treasury, the Federal Reserve banks conduct regular bill auctions.

Multiple-Choice Questions

Answer the following multiple-choice questions by circling the best alternative.

1. Assume that the national debt is $6,000 billion at the end of 1995 and during 1996 the Treasury runs a $300 billion deficit which is financed by selling new securities. The national debt at the end of 1996 is
   a. $5,700 billion
   b. $6,300 billion
   c. $6,000 billion since the deficit is financed by selling new securities
   d. $300 billion
   e. the national debt in 1996 cannot be computed

2. At the end of 1991, the national debt amounted to
   a. $3,600 billion
   b. $3,600 million
   c. $360 billion
   d. $360 million
   e. $36 billion

3. What percentage of the national debt is in marketable securities?
   a. 5 percent
   b. 10 percent
   c. 20 percent
   d. 65 percent
   e. 30 percent

4. Which of the following government securities is nonmarketable?
   a. U.S. savings bonds
   b. U.S. Treasury notes
   c. U.S. Treasury bills
   d. U.S. Treasury bonds

5. Treasury notes are issued with an original maturity of
   a. three months
   b. six months
   c. one year
   d. all of the above
   e. none of the above

6. Coupon-bearing securities issued by the Treasury pay interest
   a. annually
   b. semi-annually
   c. quarterly
   d. monthly
   e. weekly

7. The longest bonds currently issued by the Treasury have an original maturity of
   a. ten years
   b. twenty years
   c. thirty years
   d. forty years
   e. fifty years

8. A newly issued ten-year Treasury bond can be "stripped" into
   a. ten separate zero-coupon securities
   b. twenty separate zero-coupon securities
   c. twenty-one separate zero-coupon securities

d. eleven separate zero-coupon securities

e. fifteen separate zero-coupon securities

9. Holders of marketable U.S. government securities include all of the following *except*

   a. the Federal Reserve

   b. the U.S. Treasury

   c. foreigners

   d. commercial banks

   e. mutual funds

10. Trading in government securities takes place

    a. on the New York Stock Exchange

    b. on the regional stock exchanges

    c. in the over-the-counter market

    d. at the Federal Reserve Bank of New York

    e. on the American Stock Exchange

11. Trading in government securities

    a. averages more than $100 billion a day

    b. is done around the clock, following the sun around the world

    c. involves forty or so government securities dealers

    d. all of the above

    e. only (a) and (b)

12. In a typical repurchase agreement, a government securities dealer

    a. sells government securities and agrees to repurchase them at a lower price the next day

    b. sells government securities and agrees to repurchase them at a higher price the next day

    c. buys government securities and agrees to resell them at a lower price the next day

    d. buys government securities and agrees to resell them at a higher price the next day

13. If the price paid at an auction of six-month Treasury bills is $93,843, then the bill's discount yield is equal to

    a. 12.280 percent

    b. 12.907 percent

    c. 12.112 percent

    d. 13.086 percent

    e. none of the above

14. The minimum denomination of a Treasury bill is

    a. $100

    b. $1,000

    c. $10,000

    d. depends on the original maturity of the bill: three-month bills usually have a lower denomination than either six-month or one-year bills

15. A competitive bidder who submitted a bid lower than the stop-out price

    a. receives a lower effective yield than the average yield

    b. receives a higher effective yield than the average yield

    c. receives a yield equal to the average yield

    d. does not receive any bills

    e. none of the above

16. The coupon equivalent yield on a Treasury bill

    a. is always higher than the discount yield

    b. is always lower than the discount yield

    c. is always higher than the discount yield as long as the bill has a maturity less than one year

    d. cannot be generally said to be related to the discount yield in a particular way

17. The difference between the coupon equivalent yield and the discount yield is that

    a. the former is based on 365 days and the latter on 360 days

    b. in computing the former one must divide the discount by the face value of the bill, whereas in computing the latter the discount is divided by the price paid for the bill

    c. in computing the former one must divide the discount by the price paid for the bill, whereas in computing the latter the discount is divided by the face value of the bill

    d. none of the above

    e. both (a) and (c)

18. The "winner's curse" has the effect of causing the Treasury to

    a. pay higher yields

    b. receive higher prices

    c. strip bonds

    d. reduce coupon payments

19. The two primary objectives of debt management policy are

    a. liquidity and rate of return

    b. maturity maximization and cost minimization

    c. stabilization and cost minimization

    d. profit maximization and cost minimization

20. If the primary objective of debt management policy is minimization of interest costs, the federal government should use

    a. monetary policy to expand the money supply

    b. monetary policy to reduce the money supply

    c. fiscal policy to reduce taxes

    d. fiscal policy to increase government spending

chapter 31

Other Fixed-Income Markets: Corporate Bonds, Municipals, and Mortgages

Central Themes and Major Points

The previous chapter examined the government securities market. This chapter is devoted to other fixed-income markets: corporate debt securities (corporate bonds and commercial paper), securities issued by state and local governments (municipal bonds and short-term municipals), and mortgages.

Corporate bonds differ according to features such as call provisions and conversion features. Most importantly they differ in terms of quality or risk. The riskiest bonds are called junk bonds. These bonds experienced very rapid growth in the 1980s. The key short-term market for corporations is the commercial paper market. Financial institutions are major borrowers in this market.

The municipal bond market is divided into general obligation bonds and revenue bonds. Revenue bonds, as some investors have painfully learned in recent years, are subject to default risk. An important feature of municipal bonds is their tax-free status with respect to federal income taxes.

Finally, the chapter briefly revisits the mortgage market. The focus here is on mortgage pools and the markets for pass-through securities.

New Terms

Define and/or explain the following terms introduced in this chapter:

Special features of bonds:
Tax-exempt bonds (tax exemption)
Callable bonds (call provisions)
Convertible bonds (convertible feature)
Quality of bonds:
Bond ratings
Investment grades
Junk bonds
Commercial paper:
Directly placed paper
Dealer-placed paper
Municipal securities = state and local

government securities:
General obligation bonds
Revenue bonds
Tax-anticipation notes (TANs)
Bond-anticipation notes (BANs)
Mortgage-backed securities:
GNMA pass-throughs
Collateralized mortgage obligations (CMOs)

Essay Questions and Problems

1. **Corporate fixed-income securities and market**
   a. How do corporations raise long-term funds in the financial markets? Describe the market for corporate long-term debt.
   b. How do corporations raise short-term funds in the financial markets? Describe the market for corporate short-term debt.

c. What is the difference between directly placed commercial paper and dealer-placed commercial paper? Which firms use the former and which use the latter? Why?

*2. **Corporate bonds** Corporate bonds can be *callable* or *noncallable, convertible* or *nonconvertible*.

a. Suppose that two bonds are identical in all respects except that one is callable and the other is not. Which one would you prefer? What would your choice imply regarding the return on the callable bond compared with that on the noncallable bond?

b. Suppose that two bonds are identical in all respects except that one is convertible and the other is not. Which one would you prefer? What would your choice imply regarding the return on the convertible bond compared with that on the nonconvertible bond?

3. **Junk bonds** What are junk bonds? What advantages do junk bonds offer investors? What are the risks? On average, how have junk bonds been as an investment over the years?

4. **Government versus municipal bonds**
*a. Since municipal bonds are of lesser quality than U.S. government bonds, they should have a higher return than U.S. government bonds in order to induce investors to hold them. The return on municipal bonds, however, is generally *lower,* not higher, than the return on U.S. government bonds. How could this be explained?

b. Why do municipal bonds have a much wider bid-asked spread than government securities?

5. **Municipal securities**
a. What are the differences between municipal revenue bonds and general obligation bonds?

b. What are tax-anticipation notes (TANs) and bond-anticipation notes (BANs)?

c. Where can you find information on municipal bond prices and yields?

6. **Mortgage-backed securities**
a. What are mortgage-backed securities (pass-through securities)?

b. What is prepayment risk? What type of security has been created to reduce this type of risk?

SELF-TESTS

Completion Questions

Complete each of the following statements by entering the missing words and/or choosing the best alternative proposed.

1. _____ bonds can be exchanged into the common stocks of the issuing companies.

2. _____ bonds can be paid off prematurely by the issuer.

3. _____ is to corporate bonds as Treasury bills are to _____.

4. Junk bonds are rated _____ by Moody's, and _____ _____ by Standard and Poor's.

5. Commercial paper is a form of *(secured/unsecured)* corporate borrowing which typically has an original maturity of between _____ and _____ days, with _____ days being the most common.

6. Most finance companies issue *(commercial paper/tax-anticipation notes) (directly/*

indirectly) to investors, whereas many other corporations go through *(brokers/ dealers)* who *(place/underwrite)* the issues.

7. State and local government securities are known as _____.

They are usually issued in *(sequential/serial)* maturity form as contrasted with the *(multiple/single)* maturity of government and corporate bonds.

8. It is important to distinguish between two kinds of municipal bonds. These are

_____ and _____

_____.

9. The two most popular short-term securities issued by state and local governments

are _____

_____ and _____

_____.

True and False Questions

For each of the following statements, circle the letter T if it is correct or the letter F if it is *partially* or totally incorrect.

T F 1. High-quality corporate bonds attract buyers because they usually yield more than government or municipal bonds and because they are safer than stocks.

T F 2. A major advantage of long-term corporate bonds is that they are immune to interest-rate risk.

T F 3. The price at which callable bonds can be called by the issuing corporation is usually set below the price at which the callable was issued.

T F 4. Corporate bonds that include a call provision can be exchanged into common stocks of the company that has issued them. This exchange is made at a predetermined price.

T F 5. Junk bonds have been used extensively to finance corporate mergers.

T F 6. Junk bonds have proved to be a poor investment over the years.

T F 7. Junk bonds are a good investment when combined with less risky assets into a diversified portfolio.

T F 8. Life insurance companies buy corporate bonds because they have a need for debt instruments that are liquid.

T F 9. Commercial paper sold to investors without any intermediary is called directly placed paper, and that sold through commercial paper dealers is called dealer-placed paper.

T F 10. Commercial banks are not allowed to underwrite commercial paper but they are allowed to "place" it as agents for corporate clients.

T F 11. The yield on municipal securities is lower than the yield on government securities because municipals are less risky than government securities.

T F 12. The denomination of single municipal bonds is usually $10,000 as compared to $5,000 for corporate bonds.

T F 13. Glass-Steagall prohibits banks from underwriting municipal general obligation bonds, but it allows them to underwrite municipal revenue bonds.

T F 14. General obligation bonds are usually considered riskier than revenue bonds.

T F 15. The bid-asked spreads on municipal bonds are much wider than they are on government bonds.

T F 16. Ginnie Mae is the most popular type of mortgage pool.

Multiple-Choice Questions

Answer the following multiple-choice questions by circling the best alternative.

1. Most outstanding corporate bonds are held by
   a. individuals
   b. foreigners
   c. life insurance companies and pension and retirement funds
   d. the Federal Reserve
   e. mutual funds

2. Which of the following is *not* a characteristic of corporate bonds?

a. Those of large corporations are often listed and traded on the New York Stock Exchange.
b. Most of them trade in the over-the-counter market.
c. They trade in highly liquid markets.
d. They are generally sold through underwriting syndicates of securities dealers.
e. both (a) and (d)

3. Investment banker Michael Milken was largely responsible for the widespread use of
a. mortgage-backed securities
b. commercial paper
c. convertible bonds
d. junk bonds

4. One can obtain bond ratings for all of the following debt instruments except
a. municipal bonds
b. corporate bonds
c. government bonds
d. bonds issued by the state and local governments

5. A bond that can be exchanged into shares of the issuing company's common stock at a predetermined price is called
a. a callable bond
b. a provisional bond
c. an exchangeable bond
d. a convertible bond
e. none of the above

6. When a bond issuer has the right to pay off part or all of the bond before the scheduled maturity date, the bond is said to have
a. a conversion feature
b. a call provision
c. a replacement value
d. a reduced maturity
e. none of the above

7. Consider two corporate bonds identical in all respects except that one is convertible and the other is not. The return on the convertible bond should be
a. higher than the return on the nonconvertible bond
b. lower than the return on the nonconvertible bond
c. the same as the return on the nonconvertible bond
d. not possible to compare with that on the nonconvertible bond

8. Consider two corporate bonds identical in all respects except that one has a call provision and the other has not. The return on the callable bond should be
a. higher than the return on the noncallable bond

b. lower than the return on the noncallable bond
c. the same as the return on the noncallable bond
d. not possible to compare with that on the noncallable bond

9. The ability of a bond issuer to service its debt refers to
a. the issuer's agreement to convert the bond into common stocks at the bondholder's request
b. the issuer's willingness to issue a new bond whenever an existing bond is either lost or destroyed
c. the issuer's readiness to fix the coupon rate whenever interest rates are falling
d. the capacity of the issuer to make timely interest payments and repay the bond's principal on the scheduled maturity date

10. Junk bonds are also known as
a. tax-exempts
b. convertibles
c. high-yield bonds
d. pass-through securities

11. Commercial paper is issued by
a. finance companies
b. individuals
c. corporations
d. money market mutual funds
e. both (a) and (c)

12. Commercial paper is bought by
a. finance companies
b. individuals
c. commercial banks
d. money market mutual funds
e. savings banks

13. Which of the following is *not* a characteristic of commercial paper?
a. It is usually sold in very large denominations ($1 million).
b. Its yield is usually slightly below the yield on Treasury bills of comparable maturity.
c. It is either directly placed paper or dealer-placed paper.
d. Until 1980, commercial banks had been barred from participating in the market for commercial paper.
e. There isn't much of a secondary market for commercial paper.

14. If the tax-free yield is 7 percent, then an individual who is in the 30 percent tax bracket is earning an equivalent taxable yield of
a. 23.33 percent
b. 10.00 percent
c. 4.90 percent

d. 2.10 percent

e. none of the above

15. The tax-free yield is 8 percent and the taxable yield is 10 percent. What is the tax rate at which an individual would be indifferent between the two yields?

    a. 10 percent

    b. 20 percent

    c. 25 percent

    d. 30 percent

    e. 40 percent

16. Which one of the following investors would not find it advantageous to purchase municipal bonds?

    a. commercial banks

    b. property and casualty insurance companies

    c. nonprofit organizations such as foundations and universities

    d. high-income individuals

    e. both (a) and (c)

17. Tax-anticipation notes (TANs) are

    a. long-term securities issued by corporations which will be repaid with future tax refunds

    b. short-term securities issued by municipalities which will be repaid with future tax receipts

    c. long-term securities issued by municipalities which will be repaid with future tax receipts

    d. short-term securities issued by municipalities which will be repaid with future tax refunds

    e. both (b) and (d)

18. Which of the following securities is a short-term municipal?

    a. tax-exempt commercial paper

    b. floating-rate issues

    c. bond-anticipation notes

    d. tax-anticipation notes

    e. all of the above

19. Municipal securities

    a. are issued by state and local governments

    b. pay interest that is exempt from federal income taxation

    c. pay interest that is exempt from state income taxation for holders who are residents of that state

    d. are backed either by the general taxing power of the issuing municipality or by the capacity of specific projects to generate future revenues

    e. all of the above

20. The largest municipal bond failure in U.S. history was that of

    a. the Washington Public Power Supply System

    b. the City of New York

    c. the Nuclear Power Plants Authority

    d. the State of Louisiana

21. Collateralized mortgage obligations were created to

    a. reduce the prepayment uncertainty and allow investors to get more stable cash flows

    b. provide investors with a collateral in case homeowners default on their mortgages

    c. increase the liquidity of the secondary market for mortgages

    d. all of the above

chapter 32

Equities, the Stock Market, and Interest Rates

Central Themes and Major Points

We have seen in Part IV how monetary policy affects the level of interest rates and the price of bonds. An increase in the money supply, at least in the short run, lowers the yield on bonds and raises their price. Clearly, monetary policy affects the bond market. But what about *stock* prices? Are they also affected by monetary policy? This chapter seeks an answer to this question and provides a description of the structure of the stock market.

The chapter begins by summarizing the structure of the stock market. It is important to recognize the impact of new communications technology on the market and how that technology has integrated markets throughout the country and the world. The over-the-counter market is also discussed in some detail. The chapter then turns to the relationship between monetary policy and stock prices.

First, the theory. An increase in the money supply not only raises bond prices but should also raise stock prices. Why? Because an expansion in the money supply increases the liquidity of the public, which uses part of this excess cash to buy stocks. This increases the demand for stocks relative to their supply and raises stock prices. Also, higher bond prices make them less attractive in comparison to stocks. This increases the demand for stocks relative to bonds and raises stock prices. But this is not all. The expansion in the money supply will eventually increase GDP and corporate profits, making stocks more attractive (they may bring higher dividends) and thus spur stock purchases and raise their prices.

Historically, changes in the money supply alone have not been a good guide to future stock market prices. Monetary policy in general, however, has exerted a major impact on overall stock market performance, particularly through its impact on interest rates and inflation. In recent years, the stock market has responded to changes in the yield curve, which the Fed affects through its monetary policy.

New Terms

Define and/or explain the following terms introduced in this chapter:

New York Stock Exchange	Listing
Ticker tape	Stockbroker
Specialists	To "churn" an account
Posts	Global trading
Floor traders	Margin requirement

Essay Questions and Problems

1. **Structure of the stock market** Contrast the operating procedures on the New York Stock Exchange with those of the over-the-counter market. How do these markets eliminate price discrepancies?

2. **From the money supply to stock prices** What are the various cause-and-effect hypotheses that are used to explain how a change in the

money supply affects the price of stocks? In your answer consider the following: (1) direct purchase of stocks, (2) initial purchase of bonds followed by a purchase of stocks, (3) purchase of capital goods, and (4) purchase of consumer goods and services. Indicate how these spending decisions are triggered and how they should lead to an increase in stock prices. Which of these transmission processes reflect Monetarist theory and which reflect Keynesian theory?

3. **The evidence**
   a. What does the evidence on the relationship between changes in the money supply and changes in stock prices indicate?
   b. Would a poor relationship between changes in the money supply and changes in stock prices mean that the transmission processes discussed in question 1 are inadequate or incorrect? Explain your answer.
   c. Would a good relationship between changes in the money supply and changes in stock prices mean that the transmission processes discussed in question 1 have necessarily been at work?

4. **Relationship of stock prices and bond prices** Why should the prices of bonds and

stocks move together? Describe the mechanism that will produce this coordinated movement.

5. **Margin requirements**
   a. What tool is currently available to the Federal Reserve to prevent speculative excesses in the stock market?
   b. How is it supposed to operate?
   c. Is it considered effective?

6. **Monetary policy and stock prices** Describe how overall monetary policy affects the stock market. What have investors focused on as a guide to monetary policy in recent years? Why?

7. **Monetary policy expectations** Monetary policy expectations seem to affect the price of stocks and bonds.
   a. Explain how these monetary policy expectations are formed.
   b. Show how they can be used to predict the future prices of stocks and bonds. Distinguish between predictions made in periods when there is no inflation and those made in periods when the rate of inflation is accelerating.
   *c. Show how monetary expectations can affect the *current* prices of stocks and bonds when stock market participants act on their predictions of future prices.

SELF-TESTS

Completion Questions

Complete each of the following statements by entering the missing words and/or choosing the best alternative proposed.

1. In recent years _____ investors consisting primarily of insurance companies, _____, and _____ have increased their share of stock ownership relative to the share held by _____.

2. The stock market refers to the _____ market for stocks. The distribution of _____ stocks operates through ___ _____ banks.

3. Advanced telecommunications prevents _____ discrepancies in the stock market by speeding up the process of _____ _____.

4. The minimum down payment imposed by the _____ _____ for the purchase of stocks is called a _____ _____.

5. Even though _____ has not been a good guide

to stock price movements, overall _____ has

clearly had a significant impact on stock prices.

True and False Questions

For each of the following statements, circle the letter T if it is correct or the letter F if it is *partially* or totally incorrect.

T F   1. Most of the increase in the total market value of all the publicly held shares of stock in existence represents price appreciation of existing shares.

T F   2. The stock market is the primary market for common stocks.

T F   3. The informal over-the-counter market is considered part of the stock market.

T F   4. The supply of newly issued equity by corporations has been growing very rapidly since the end of World War II.

T F   5. The stock market is dominated by individuals. According to the New York Stock Exchange, 35 million individuals own stocks in the United States.

T F   6. In terms of impact on overall stock prices, institutional investors have become increasingly important in recent years.

T F   7. Thanks to electronic communications, the various stock exchanges in the United States are effectively integrated, preventing the price of a stock with multiple listing to differ across exchanges.

T F   8. An increase in the money supply should lead to an increase in stock prices because the additional liquidity will raise the demand for stocks relative to the existing supply.

T F   9. If the additional liquidity resulting from an increasing money supply is not used by the public to purchase financial assets but instead goes to purchase real assets, then the price of stocks will not increase.

T F   10. When the level of interest rates drops, stocks become relatively more attractive than bonds.

T F   11. The evidence points to a strong relationship between changes in the money supply and changes in stock prices, particularly for the period between the two world wars.

T F   12. The comovement between the money supply and the price of stocks may be explained, in some instances, by assuming that both series have been reacting to a third causal force that pushed both series in the same direction.

T F   13. High margin requirements are not likely to help restrain speculation in stocks.

T F   14. The power of the Federal Reserve to set margin requirements was granted by Congress in the 1930s to prevent a repetition of the speculative wave that hit the market in 1928 and led to its fall in 1929.

T F   15. A 100 percent margin requirement means that no borrowing is permitted to purchase stocks.

T F   16. In theory, the prices of stocks and bonds should move together.

T F   17. In recent years, stock market participants have focused on M1 as a guide to monetary policy.

T F   18. Historically, stocks have been an excellent hedge against inflation.

T F   19. Monetary policy expectations affect the price of stocks but do not affect the price of bonds.

T F   20. A drop in the rate of inflation would stimulate higher stock prices.

Multiple-Choice Questions

Answer the following multiple-choice questions by circling the best alternative.

1. The stock market refers to
   a. the primary market for common stocks
   b. the over-the-counter market for equity
   c. the secondary market for common stocks
   d. the corporate market for equity
   e. the New York Stock Exchange

2. Shares of the largest and best-known corporations are traded on
   a. the primary market for common stocks
   b. the New York Stock Exchange
   c. the American Stock Exchange
   d. the over-the-counter market
   e. the Midwest Stock Exchange

3. The role of the specialists on the stock exchange is to

a. maintain orderly trading for the securities in their charge
b. match publicly tendered buy and sell orders submitted at the same price
c. prevent the sale of stocks below their average price
d. prevent unethical trading
e. both (a) and (b)

4. Smaller companies are generally listed on
   a. the New York Stock Exchange
   b. the American Stock Exchange
   c. the regional stock exchanges
   d. the Big Board
   e. both (b) and (c)

5. The over-the-counter market for equity
   a. has no single place of business where trading activity takes place
   b. is a market where smaller companies are traded
   c. is made up of a linkage of many dealers and brokers who communicate with one another via telephone and computer terminals
   d. all of the above
   e. only (b) and (c)

6. Stockbrokers are
   a. securities dealers
   b. account executives who act only as agents
   c. specialists in designated stocks
   d. securities traders
   e. floor traders

7. "Churning" a position refers to
   a. the practice of some stockbrokers who turn over their customers' accounts in order to generate brokerage commissions
   b. the practice of some mutual fund managers who turn over their portfolio in order to generate increased cash flow
   c. the practice of the specialist who buys against the trend in order to stabilize stock prices
   d. both (a) and (b)
   e. none of the above

8. An increase in the money supply should raise the price of stocks because
   a. the public, having more liquidity, will spend part of its excess cash buying a limited amount of stocks, thereby driving the average of stock prices up
   b. it will lower interest rates and raise bond prices, making them less attractive than stocks and hence expand the demand for and the price of stocks.
   c. the increase in the money supply will eventually raise GDP and corporate profits, making stocks more attractive and thus spur stock purchases and raise their price

d. all of the above
e. only (a) and (c)

9. Cyclical upswings in the economy are typically associated with a
   a. falling price level and rising stock prices
   b. rising money supply and rising stock prices
   c. falling money supply and falling stock prices
   d. falling money supply and rising stock prices

10. The facts about the relationship between changes in the money supply and changes in stock prices indicate that
    a. there is a strong positive relationship between the two series
    b. changes in the money supply lag behind changes in stock prices
    c. no definite relationship exists between these two series, although on some not-infrequent occasions over the past fifty years changes in stock prices were preceded or accompanied by changes in the rate of growth of the money supply in the same direction
    d. changes in the rate of growth of the money supply move concurrently with changes in the price of stocks
    e. none of the above

11. An increase in the price of bonds should
    a. reduce the yield on bonds
    b. trigger a substitution of bonds for stocks in the public's portfolio
    c. produce a price appreciation of stocks
    d. all of the above
    e. only (a) and (c)

12. Which of the following factors may explain the absence of a strong relationship between changes in the money supply and changes in stock prices?
    a. investors' expectations
    b. political developments
    c. crowd psychology
    d. all of the above
    e. only (b) and (c)

13. Under a system of margin requirements the Federal Reserve sets
    a. the level of interest rates that borrowers must pay to finance their purchase of stocks
    b. the maximum amount of funds that can be borrowed to purchase stocks
    c. the minimum amount of funds that can be borrowed to purchase stocks
    d. the maximum down payment required to purchase stocks
    e. none of the above

14. Everything else held constant, an increase in margin requirements should

a. raise stock prices, because it would increase the demand for stocks
b. lower stock prices, because it would decrease the demand for stocks
c. not affect stock prices, because the demand for stocks should not be affected by the value of the margin requirements
d. One cannot tell how stock prices would react to changes in margin requirements—even if one assumes every other factor is constant.

15. A 60 percent margin requirement means that
    a. one can borrow up to 60 percent of the price of the stock one wants to buy
    b. one can borrow up to 40 percent of the price of the stock one wants to buy
    c. one must put down at least 40 percent of the price of the stock one wants to buy
    d. none of the above

16. If an investor wishes to purchase $20,000 worth of stock and the margin requirement is 40 percent, the investor must put down at least
    a. $18,000
    b. $12,000
    c. $8,000
    d. $6,000

17. Which of the following factors is *not* expected to raise the price of stocks?
    a. an expansionary monetary policy
    b. a brighter outlook for corporate profits
    c. an increase in bond yields
    d. a substantial reduction in margin requirements

18. As a measure of monetary policy investors in recent years have focused on
    a. the budget deficit
    b. margin requirements
    c. the yield curve
    d. M1

19. Predictions on the future price of stocks that are derived from monetary policy expectations may be wrong because
    a. of difficulties in interpreting the weekly Federal Reserve statistics
    b. the Federal Reserve may have changed its money supply target, but the public will know it only one month after it has been modified
    c. both (a) and (b)
    d. neither (a) nor (b)

20. Fed watching is no quick and easy road to wealth because
    a. the Fed can't affect the money supply
    b. the Fed can't influence interest rates
    c. many things beyond the money supply have an impact on stock prices
    d. it is an unreliable exercise
    e. the Fed is not interested in what happens to stock prices

chapter 33

Financial Futures and Options

Central Themes and Major Points

This chapter covers in some detail the *futures* and *options* markets, which were first introduced in Chapter 3. Futures and options contracts are called *derivative financial instruments* because their value is determined by the *underlying asset* against which the contract is written. A buyer of a futures contract on a Treasury bond will *receive* Treasury bonds at a specified future date (*settlement* date) and will pay a price agreed upon today. A seller of a futures contract on a Treasury bond will *deliver* Treasury bonds at a specified future date and will receive a price agreed upon today. Options are different. The holder of a *call option* on a Treasury bond has the right to buy Treasury bonds at a price agreed upon today (the *exercise* price) but is not obligated to exercise that option. If the holder can purchase the bond in the open market for less than the agreed upon price, he or she will not exercise the option, which will expire unexercised.

This chapter explains how futures and options contracts are traded and how their price is determined. It also shows how individuals and financial institutions can use futures and options contracts to protect themselves against the price fluctuations of securities.

New Terms

Define and/or explain the following terms introduced in this chapter:

Derivative financial
  instruments:
  Futures contracts
  Options contracts
Trading in futures
  contracts:
  Trading pit
  Chicago Board of
  Trade (CBT)
  International
  Monetary Market
  (IMM)
Terms of futures
  contracts:
  Underlying asset
  Delivery date and
  place
  Settlement price
Underlying assets
  for futures
  contracts:
  Interest-bearing
  securities
  Stock market
  indexes
  Foreign currencies
Clearing corporation
Margin
Mark-to-market
  settlement

Price limits
Settlement by offset
Participants in futures
  and options
  markets:
  Hedgers
  Speculators
  Arbitrageurs
Cash market
Trading in options
  contracts:
  Chicago Board
  Options Exchange
  (CBOE)
Types of option
  contracts:
  Put options
  Call options
Option premium
Terms of options
  contracts:
  Underlying
  asset
  Expiration
  date
  Exercise or
  strike price
Intrinsic value of an
  option
Open interest

Essay Questions and Problems

1. **Financial futures contracts and markets**
   a. What are financial futures contracts?
   b. In which type of market are they traded? What are the names of the major institutions that sponsor trading in financial futures?
   c. What are the major forces that determine the prices of futures contracts?
   d. What is the relationship between the price of a security in the "cash" market and its price in the futures market? What is the role of arbitrageurs in this respect?
   e. What are the main advantages of trading in the futures markets for a security over trading in the "cash" market for that same security?

2. **Options contracts and markets**
   a. What are options contracts?
   b. In which type of market are they traded? What are the names of the major institutions that sponsor trading in financial futures?
   c. What are the factors that determine the price of a call option?

   d. What are the factors that determine the price of a put option?

3. **Hedging with futures**
   a. What is hedging, and how does it differ from speculation?
   b. Explain how a securities dealer can hedge his inventory using the futures market.
   c. Explain how, using futures markets, a pension fund manager who intends to buy bonds in one month can protect herself from an increase in the price of bonds in one month.

4. **Clearing corporation**
   a. What is a clearing corporation?
   b. How does a clearing corporation protect itself from credit risk?

5. **Hedging with options**
   a. Explain how a securities dealer can hedge his inventory using options contracts.
   b. What is the difference between hedging with futures contracts and hedging with options contracts?
   c. Explain why options are an expensive way to hedge against significant risk.

SELF-TESTS

Completion Questions

Complete each of the following statements by entering the missing words and/or choosing the best alternative proposed.

1. A _____ contract is a contractual agreement that calls

   for the delivery of a specific _____

   _____ at some future _____ at a price agreed

   upon *(now/in the future)*.

2. The following three categories of financial assets have futures contracts written

   on them:

   a._____

   b._____

   c._____

3. Futures contracts are traded *(over-the-counter/on organized exchanges)* such as

   the _____

   _____ and the _____

   _____.

4. The buyer of a futures contract has the *(right/obligation/right and obligation)* to

(deliver/receive) the underlying asset on the contract expiration date. The buyer of the contract is called *(short/long)* and is said to have a *(short/long)* position in the futures market.

5. The seller of a futures contract has the *(right/obligation/right and obligation)* to *(deliver/receive)* the underlying asset on the contract expiration date. The seller of the contract is called *(short/long)* and is said to have a *(short/long)* position in the futures market.

6. The _____ reduces the *(business/credit)* risk exposure associated with the future deliveries of underlying securities.

7. The *(auction/sale)* of futures contracts is conducted on a single location on the exchange floor, called the _____.

8. The activities of *(speculators/arbitrageurs)* will cause the price of a futures contract and the price of the underlying asset to *(converge/diverge)* on the *(delivery/purchase)* date.

9. The buyer of a call option has the *(right/obligation/right and obligation)* to *(sell/buy)* a given quantity of the underlying asset at the _____ _____ price at any time prior to the _____ date of the option.

10. The buyer of a put option has the *(right/obligation/right and obligation)* to *(sell/buy)* a given quantity of the underlying asset at the _____ _____ price at any time prior to the _____ date of the option.

11. The seller of a call option has the *(right/obligation/right and obligation)* to *(sell/buy)* a given quantity of the underlying asset at the _____ price at any time prior to the _____ date of the option.

12. The seller of a put option has the *(right/obligation/right and obligation)* to *(sell/buy)* a given quantity of the underlying asset at the _____ price at any time prior to the _____ date of the option.

13. The price paid for an option is called the option _____. An option's intrinsic value is equal to _____ _____ minus _____ _____.

True and False Questions

For each of the following statements, circle the letter T if it is correct or the letter F if it is *partially* or totally incorrect.

T F 1. Futures contracts are derivative financial instruments but options contracts are not.

T F 2. Futures and options contracts are major financial innovations as speculative tools but they are poor risk management tools.

T F 3. Futures and options contracts are traded in over-the-counter markets located primarily in Chicago.

T F 4. The similarities between options and futures contracts far outweigh their differences.

T F 5. There are financial futures contracts on bonds, on stock market indexes, and on foreign currencies.

T F 6. The most actively traded financial futures contract is the Standard and Poor's 500.

T F 7. The volume of trading in financial futures now exceeds that of trading in the more traditional agricultural commodities.

T F 8. A financial future's underlying asset can be either a specific security or the cash value of a group of securities.

T F 9. The standardization of contract terms on financial futures has reduced their liquidity and increased their transaction costs.

T F 10. Both the buyer and the seller of a futures contract must make a deposit with the clearing corporation. This deposit, called a margin, is a down payment on the price at which the contract will be eventually purchased or sold.

T F 11. Short hedgers offset inventory risk by buying futures, whereas long hedgers offset anticipated purchases of securities by selling futures.

T F 12. The price of futures contracts is determined by the buying and selling activities of hedgers and speculators.

T F 13. The "cash market" refers to the market where settlement for futures contracts is made in cash only.

T F 14. During the delivery period of a futures contract, the price of the contract and the price of the underlying security are one and the same.

T F 15. If the price of a futures contract is equal to the sum of the price of the underlying security and the cost of carrying the underlying security to the delivery date, then there will be no arbitrage opportunities between the cash market and the futures market.

T F 16. The main contribution of futures markets to the financial marketplace is the fact that futures contracts mirror the cash market, but with lower transaction costs.

T F 17. Option buyers have obligations, whereas option sellers have rights.

T F 18. The price paid for an option is called its intrinsic value.

T F 19. If on expiration the price of a call option is less than the price of the underlying asset, the option is worthless.

T F 20. The asymmetrical payoff on a put option means that a dealer can minimize downside risk by buying the put while retaining upside potential through inventory.

Multiple-Choice Questions

Answer the following multiple-choice questions by circling the best alternative.

1. Which of the following characteristics are common to futures and options contracts?
   a. They are both derivative financial instruments.
   b. They both trade on organized exchanges.
   c. They share similar arrangements for finalizing and clearing trades.
   d. They can both be used to hedge risk.
   e. all of the above

2. Financial institutions consider futures and options contracts a major tool for
   a. expanding customer base
   b. reducing taxes
   c. risk management
   d. expanding capital

3. Which of the following futures contracts is available on the various commodity exchanges in the United States?
   a. Federal Reserve stock
   b. foreign currencies of major countries
   d. individual stock of large corporations
   d. individual bonds of large corporations
   e. all of the above

4. The terms of a futures contract must specify
   a. the type of asset to be delivered
   b. the amount of asset to be delivered

c. the place where the delivery will take place

d. the date when the delivery will be made

e. all of the above

5. Which of the following are devices used by the clearing corporation to reduce its credit risk exposure?

a. requiring that buyers and sellers of contracts place a deposit with the clearing corporation

b. requiring that gains and losses be settled each day

c. imposing price limits on the amount that futures contracts can change each day

d. all of the above

e. only (b) and (c)

6. Which of the following is *not* an active trader in the futures and options markets?

a. hedgers

b. arbitrageurs

c. brokers

d. speculators

e. both (b) and (c)

7. In order to reduce their exposure to the risk produced by the price fluctuations of the underlying asset they hold, hedgers should

a. buy futures contracts on that underlying asset

b. sell futures contracts on that underlying asset

c. buy futures contracts and simultaneously sell an equal amount of the same contract

d. either (b) or (c)

e. none of the above

8. In order to reduce their exposure to the risk produced by the price fluctuations of the underlying asset they anticipate to buy in the near future, hedgers should

a. buy futures contracts on that underlying asset

b. sell futures contracts on that underlying asset

c. sell futures contracts and simultaneously buy an equal amount of the same contract

d. either (a) or (c)

e. none of the above

9. Assume that a futures exchange imposes a one-day price limit of $5 per $100 of security face value. In that case, the maximum that can be transferred into or out of an account on a $100,000 security is

a. $5.00

b. $5,000

c. $50

d. $50,000

10. A speculator expects interest rates to fall. To profit from that forecast the speculator should

a. buy Treasury bonds

b. sell Treasury bonds

c. buy Treasury bond futures contracts

d. sell Treasury bond futures contracts

e. either (a) or (c)

f. either (b) or (d)

11. A speculator expects interest rates to rise. To profit from that forecast the speculator should

a. buy Treasury bonds

b. buy Treasury bond futures contracts

c. sell Treasury bond futures contracts

d. either (a) or (b)

e. both (a) and (c)

12. The relationship between the price of an underlying asset and of a futures contract on that underlying asset is determined by

a. hedgers

b. speculators

c. arbitrageurs

d. all of the above

e. only (a) and (b)

13. The price of a futures contract and the price of the underlying asset on that contract

a. move in opposite directions

b. move in the same direction

c. are unrelated to each other

d. are independent of each other

e. are disconnected

14. Which of the following factors affect the value of an option?

a. the time to expiration of the option

b. the price of the underlying asset

c. the exercise price

d. the volatility of the underlying asset

e. all of the above

15. Which of the following implies a higher call value?

a. a lower price of the underlying asset relative to the exercise price of the call

b. a shorter time to expiration

c. a greater volatility of the underlying asset

d. both (a) and (c)

e. both (a) and (b)

16. Which of the following implies a higher put value?

a. a lower price of the underlying asset relative to the exercise price of the put

b. a shorter time to expiration

c. a greater volatility of the underlying asset

d. both (a) and (c)

e. both (a) and (b)

17. A call option for 100 shares of ABD corporation with a striking price of $32 per share expires three months from now, and a put option for 100 shares of ABD corporation with a strike price of $32 per share expires three months from now.

If the current price of a share of ABD corporation is $30, then

   a. the call option is worthless, since the strike price exceeds the current price of the stock

   b. the put option is worthless, since the strike price exceeds the current price of the stock

   c. neither the call nor the put option is worthless, because the price of a share of ABD corporation fluctuates, and there are still three months to go before either option expires

   d. both the call and the put option are worthless

18. A portfolio manager who wants to be certain of being able to buy Treasury bills at a fixed yield in three months should

   a. buy three-month put options on Treasury bills

   b. sell three-month call options on Treasury bills

   c. buy three-month Treasury bill futures contracts

   d. sell three-month Treasury bill futures contracts

   e. none of the above

19. A put option gives the owner the right to

   a. sell the underlying asset at a fixed price

   b. buy the underlying asset at a fixed price

   c. convert the underlying asset at a fixed price

   d. take delivery of the underlying asset at a fixed price

20. Suppose that you expect the price of the underlying asset to rise rapidly in the near future. Then you should

   a. buy a futures contract on the underlying asset

   b. sell a futures contract on the underlying asset

   c. buy a call option on the underlying asset

   d. both (a) and (c) could be profitable

21. Suppose that you expect the price of the underlying asset to fall sharply in the near future. Then you should

   a. buy a futures contract on the underlying asset

   b. sell a futures contract on the underlying asset

   c. buy a put option on the underlying asset

   d. both (b) and (c) could be profitable

22. Which of the following items would not be mentioned in an option contract?

   a. the nature of the underlying asset

   b. the current price of the underlying asset

   c. the period of time over which the option can be exercised

   d. the strike price

23. The option premium is

   a. the price at which an option writer agrees to sell an option

   b. the price at which an option writer agrees to buy an option

   c. the difference between the price of the underlying asset and the strike price

   d. none of the above

24. The largest potential loss to an options buyer is equal to the

   a. market value of the underlying asset

   b. premium paid for the options contract

   c. rate of return on the underlying asset

   d. price limit set by the Chicago Board of Trade

25. The simultaneous purchase of stock index futures and sale of the underlying asset to take advantage of price discrepancies is known as

   a. options contracting

   b. skimming the market

   c. program trading

   d. securitizing

part VI

International Finance

chapter 34

Foreign Exchange Rates

Central Themes and Major Points

The previous chapters dealt extensively with the role of money within the United States, ignoring the rest of the world. Countries, however, do not live in isolation. Goods produced in one country are often sold in another. Financial assets issued in one country are often purchased by foreigners.

These and other transactions among nations are recorded in their *national balance of payments*. A country's balance of payments, then, is an accounting record of all the payments it made to foreigners and all the funds it received from them in the course of a quarter or a year. This chapter briefly discusses the balance of payments. The next chapter will examine it in more detail.

If the citizens of one country want to purchase goods produced abroad or financial assets denominated in a *foreign* currency, they must first change their local currency into the currency of the foreign country from which they will make the purchase. These transactions—exchanging one currency for another, purchasing foreign-made goods or financial assets denominated in foreign currencies—raise two important questions. First, how is the *rate of exchange* between any two currencies determined? Second, what are the effects of these international transactions on the balance of payments of trading nations?

The answers to these questions will vary depending on the particular type of international monetary system linking nations together. This chapter examines the system of *floating* or *flexible exchange*

rates that is currently in effect. Under this system of freely fluctuating exchange rates, the *foreign exchange rate* is determined by the interaction of the demand for and the supply of *foreign exchange* (foreign money), and movements in foreign exchange rates will tend to eliminate both deficits and surpluses in the balance of payments. At the equilibrium exchange rate, the demand for and supply of foreign exchange are equal, and the balance of payments is in neither *deficit* nor *surplus*.

Alternative types of international monetary systems are examined in Chapter 35 (*fixed* exchange rates) and Chapter 37 (*gold standard*).

New Terms

Define and/or explain the following terms introduced in this chapter:

National balance of payments	Supply of foreign exchange
Deficits and surpluses	Flexible or floating exchange rates†
Imports and exports	
Foreign exchange = foreign money	Appreciation
	Depreciation
Foreign exchange market	Foreign exchange dealer
Foreign exchange rate	Fixed exchange rates†
Demand for foreign exchange	Currency exchange

†More on these terms in Chapter 35.

Essay Questions and Problems

1. **The balance of payments** The purpose of these questions is to clarify some basic principles regarding the balance of payments. In the next chapter we will examine the balance of payments in more detail.

   a. What is a country's national balance of payments? What is the meaning of (1) a balance of payments deficit? (2) a balance of payments surplus? (3) a balance or equilibrium in the balance of payments?

   *b. Give examples of transactions that are recorded in a country's balance of payments and indicate whether they involve a payment made to foreigners or a receipt of funds from foreigners.

   *c. Give examples of transactions that are *not* recorded in a country's balance of payments. Where would these transactions be recorded?

   *d. Is it possible for a country's balance of payments to show a surplus when it has imported more goods from abroad than it has exported to foreigners?

*2. **Foreign exchange and exchange rates** The purpose of these questions is to clarify the concept of foreign exchange and exchange rates. The next question deals with these concepts in detail.

   a. What are foreign exchanges? Here is a list of currencies issued by various countries:

Francs	(France)
Pounds	(Great Britain)
Marks	(Germany)
Dollars	(United States)
Yen	(Japan)

   In the United States, which of these currencies are considered foreign exchange? In Germany, which are considered foreign exchange? In Canada, which are considered foreign exchange?

   b. Distinguish between the foreign exchange market, the currency market, and the money market. In which market does the Federal Reserve conduct its open market operations?

   c. What is an exchange rate? You are in France and wish to change 50 U.S. dollars into French francs. A bank gives you 200 French francs for your 50 U.S. dollars. What is the French franc exchange rate (in terms of dollars)? What is the U.S. dollar exchange rate (in terms of French francs)?

   d. Exchange rates can be either fixed or flexible. Which type of exchange rate system prevailed from the end of World War II until the early 1970s? Which type of exchange rates characterizes the present international monetary system?

*3. **Freely floating exchange rates: A numerical analysis** Freely floating exchange rates are determined in the foreign exchange markets by the interplay of the demand for foreign exchange and the supply of foreign exchange.

   Consider the case of the French franc (FF). The purpose of this question is to illustrate how the exchange rate between the U.S. dollar and the FF is determined in the foreign exchange market. Recall that this foreign exchange rate is simply the dollar price of one FF.

   The hypothetical data in the table below give the quantity of FF that would be demanded (in billions of FF) at various exchange rates as well as the quantity of FF that would be supplied (in billions of FF) at various exchange rates. Note that there is no fundamental difference between the determination of the equilibrium foreign exchange rate (the equilibrium price of FF) resulting from the interaction of the demand for and the supply of FF and the determination of, say, the equilibrium price of potatoes resulting from the interaction of the demand for and the supply of potatoes.

   a. *The demand curve for French francs*
      This curve shows the amounts of FF that the market wishes to buy at any given exchange

Demand for French Francs (FF)		Supply of French Francs (FF)	
Exchange rate (price of a FF in $)	Quantity demanded (in billions of FF)	Exchange rate (price of a FF in $)	Quantity demanded (in billions of FF)
.30	4	.30	24
.25	9	.25	19
.20	14	.20	14
.15	19	.15	9
.10	24	.10	4

rate (price) during a specific time period (a day, a week, and so on).

(1) Construct the demand curve for FF in Figure 34.1.

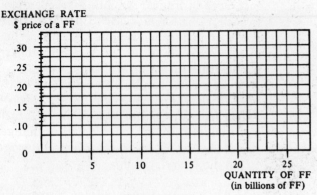

Figure 34.1
*Demand for and Supply of French Francs
Relative to the U.S. Dollar*

(2) Who are the demanders or buyers of FF, and for what purposes do they demand FF? What do they offer in exchange for the FF they wish to buy?

(3) What is the quantity demanded of FF if the exchange rate is 25 cents?

(4) Why does the quantity demanded of FF increase as the exchange rate falls (depreciates)?

(5) A change in the exchange rate causes the quantity of FF demanded to change in the opposite direction. This is represented by a movement along a *fixed* demand curve. It is also possible for the *entire* demand curve to shift to the left or to the right in response to a change in a factor other than the foreign exchange rate. Which factors would cause a shift in the supply curve to the right? to the left?

b. *The supply curve for French francs*
This curve shows the amounts of FF that the market is willing to sell at any given exchange rate (price) during a specified time period (a day, a week, and so on).

(1) Construct the supply curve for FF in Figure 34.1

(2) Who are the suppliers or sellers of FF, and for what purposes do they supply FF? What do they receive in exchange for the FF they are willing to sell?

(3) What is the quantity supplied of FF if the exchange rate is 25 cents?

(4) Why does the quantity supplied of FF increase as the exchange rate rises (appreciates)?

(5) A change in the exchange rate causes the quantity of FF supplied to change in the same direction. This is represented by movements along a fixed supply curve. It is also possible for the entire supply curve to shift to the left or to the right in response to a change in a factor other than the exchange rate. What factors would cause a shift in the supply curve to the right? to the left?

c. *The equilibrium foreign exchange rate*
The equilibrium rate is determined at the intersection between the demand curve for FF and the supply curve of FF. Refer to Figure 34.1.

(1) What is the equilibrium exchange rate between the U.S. dollar and the FF, and what is the equilibrium quantity of the FF? What is the FF price of the dollar at equilibrium?

(2) Suppose that the exchange rate is 22 cents. What are the quantities of FF demanded and supplied at this rate, and why is this rate not the equilibrium rate? Describe the market mechanism that will restore the exchange rate to its equilibrium level.

(3) Suppose that the exchange rate is 18 cents. Answer the same question as in question c(2) above.

(4) At an exchange rate of 22 cents, is the FF *overvalued* or *undervalued* relative to the dollar? At an exchange rate of 18 cents is the FF overvalued or undervalued relative to the dollar? Explain.

(5) Suppose that prices in the United States increase relative to prices in France. What will be the effect of this relative price change on the demand curve for FF, the supply curve of FF, the equilibrium exchange rate, and the equilibrium quantity of FF?

(6) Suppose that the market expects the future dollar price of FF will be lower. Answer the same question as in question c(5) above.

*4. Suppose that the exchange rate between the German mark (DM) and the U.S. dollar is $0.50 = 1 DM. If the mark appreciates by 10 percent relative to the dollar, is it correct to say that the U.S. dollar has depreciated by exactly 10 percent relative to the German mark?

SELF-TESTS

Completion Questions

Complete each of the following statements by entering the missing words and/or choosing the best alternative proposed.

1. A country's national _____

   _____ is an accounting record of all payments made by that country to

   _____ and the _____ of funds

   from them.

2. Examples of transactions involving payments by Americans to foreigners are

   a. _____

   b. _____

   c. _____

3. Examples of transactions involving receipts of funds by Americans from foreign-

   ers are

   a. _____

   b. _____

   c. _____

4. If a nation makes payments to foreigners in excess of the funds it receives from

   them, its _____ will

   show a _____. If the opposite holds true, its _____

   _____ will show a _____

   _____.

5. A country can pay for its imports by *(borrowing from/lending to)* _____

   _____ or by *(buying from/selling to)* _____

   domestically produced goods. The latter case is called *(importing/exporting)*.

6. An international monetary system under which exchange rates are determined

   by the demand for and the supply of _____

   _____ is called a system of _____

   _____. Under a system of

   _____

   _____, exchange rates are determined through international agree-

   ments under the sponsorship of agencies such as the _____

   _____.

7. When a country's currency *(appreciates/depreciates)* relative to other currencies,

   its value in terms of other currencies has increased and the *(exchange rate/*

   foreign exchange) between that currency and other currencies is now *(higher/*

lower), implying that foreign currencies are *(cheaper/more expensive)* than before.

8. Under a system of freely flexible exchange rates, a country with a temporary deficit in its _____ will see its _____ *(appreciate/depreciate)*. This mechanism should eventually *(eliminate/widen)* its balance of payments _____.

9. If the dollar price of a French franc is equal to $0.25, then the franc price of a U.S. dollar is equal to _____.

10. The dollar price of foreign money is called the _____ _____. If it is falling, then foreign money is *(depreciating/appreciating)* relative to the dollar.

11. Under a system of freely floating exchange rates, the _____ _____ is determined by the interplay of the _____ _____ and the _____ _____.

12. A surplus in the United States' balance of payments means that the *(supply of/demand for)* foreign exchange exceeds the _____ it, so the dollar price of foreign money should *(rise/fall)*.

True and False Questions

For each of the following statements, circle the letter T if it correct or the letter F if it is *partially* or totally incorrect.

T F   1. If Americans import more foreign *goods* than they export U.S. goods, then the United States' international balance of payments will necessarily show a deficit, because Americans would have made more payments to foreigners than they have received funds from foreigners.

T F   2. An increased supply of foreign exchange implies an increased demand for the domestic currency.

T F   3. The dollar price of Japanese yen is equal to the reciprocal of the yen price of dollars.

T F   4. Other factors held constant, a decrease in the supply of German marks will lower the dollar price of marks.

T F   5. An increase in the supply of British pounds accompanied by a decrease in the demand for British pounds will lower the pound price of dollars.

T F   6. A currency is said to be undervalued relative to another currency when its price in terms of that other currency is below the equilibrium rate of exchange that would prevail in a free market.

T F   7. If a currency is overvalued relative to another currency, then the latter is undervalued relative to the first.

T F   8. When the supply of Dutch guilders is larger than the demand for them, the demand for some other currency is smaller than its supply. This necessarily follows from the reciprocal value of foreign exchange transactions.

T F   9. Under a system of freely floating exchange rates, when a country's currency appreciates relative to other currencies, the other currencies are actually depreciating in terms of that country's currency.

T F   10. The term foreign exchange means foreign money, and the foreign exchange market refers to the market in which foreign currencies are traded.

T F   11. The exchange rate between the dollar and a foreign currency is the dollar price of one unit of foreign currency.

T F 12. Saying that there is an increase in the supply of British pounds on the foreign exchange market is the same as saying that there is an increase in the demand for foreign currencies, other than the pound, on the foreign exchange market.

T F 13. A country with a surplus in its balance of payments will see its currency depreciate in the foreign exchange markets, because the surplus will tend to depress the value of its currency relative to others.

T F 14. When a country's currency appreciates, the goods it exports become more expensive to foreigners and fewer goods will be exported, whereas the goods it imports become cheaper and more goods will be imported.

T F 15. When a country's currency depreciates in the foreign exchange market, its domestic prices (the prices of its home products in terms of the local currency) will immediately drop.

T F 16. If a dollar is worth four French francs, then one French franc is worth twenty cents.

T F 17. The foreign exchange rate is the domestic price of one unit of foreign currency.

T F 18. International finance currently operates under a fixed exchange rate system called the Bretton Woods System.

Multiple-Choice Questions

Answer the following multiple-choice questions by circling the best alternative.

1. Which of the following will be accompanied by an outflow of funds from the United States?
   a. foreigners buying U.S. Treasury bills
   b. lending by the U.S. government to a foreign country
   c. expenditures made by foreign tourists in the United States
   d. the construction of a German automobile plant in Pennsylvania

2. Which of the following will be accompanied by an inflow of funds to the United States?
   a. Americans buying foreign securities
   b. a U.S. company building a factory in Europe
   c. the sale of American-made goods to foreigners
   d. lending by the U.S. government to a foreign country

3. If an American dollar costs 25 Mexican pesos, then a Mexican peso costs
   a. $4
   b. $.04
   c. $0.25
   d. $0.40

4. An increase in imports from the United States to Mexico increases the
   a. demand for Mexican pesos
   b. supply of Mexican pesos
   c. supply of U.S. dollars
   d. Mexican inflation rate

5. If the price of a Swiss franc is 0.4 American dollars, then the price of an American dollar is
   a. 4 Swiss francs.
   b. 0.4 Swiss francs.
   c. 0.6 Swiss francs.
   d. 2.5 Swiss francs.

6. A currency exchange is
   a. foreign money
   b. a place where one can buy or sell foreign currencies
   c. foreign exchange
   d. the rate of exchange between two currencies
   e. both (a) and (c)

7. Other things the same, which of the following will raise the foreign exchange rate?
   a. an increase in domestic demand for foreign goods
   b. an increase in the demand for home-issued securities by foreigners
   c. an increase in foreign tourist expenditures in the home country
   d. an increase in foreign demand for domestically produced goods
   e. an increase in dividends received from abroad

8. The term *foreign exchange* is best defined by the following statement:
   a. It is the rate of exchange between two currencies.
   b. It is foreign money in the form of foreign currency or demand deposits denominated in foreign currency.
   c. It is the place in which foreign currencies are exchanged.
   d. It is synonymous with currency exchange.

9. Under a system of freely floating exchange rates, the value of a country's currency in terms of the currency of another country is determined by
   a. the International Monetary Fund
   b. international agreements between the two trading partners

c. supply and demand conditions for the currency of each country

d. trading activities in the money markets of each country

10. Under a system of freely floating exchange rates, the currency of a country with a temporary surplus in its balance of payments should
   a. depreciate relative to other currencies
   b. appreciate relative to other currencies
   c. devalue relative to other currencies
   d. revalue relative to other currencies
   e. both (a) and (d)

11. Other factors held constant, which of the following will *not* happen if the dollar depreciates?
   a. The currencies of other countries will appreciate.
   b. American exports will become cheaper to foreigners.
   c. Foreign goods will become more expensive to Americans.
   d. The dollar will become more expensive to foreigners.
   e. The dollar value of foreign currencies increases.

12. Other factors held constant, when a country's currency depreciates its domestic prices (the price of its home products in terms of local currency) will immediately
   a. increase
   b. decrease
   c. remain the same
   d. one cannot tell

13. When domestic prices in country A drop relative to domestic prices in country B, country A's imports decline because
   a. country B's goods are now more expensive for the citizens of country A, inducing country A to cut back on its imports
   b. country B's goods are now cheaper for the citizens of country A, inducing country A to cut back on its imports
   c. country A's goods are now cheaper for the citizens of country A, causing the citizens of country A to buy domestic products instead of foreign products (substitution effect) and thus decrease imports from country B
   d. country A's goods are now more expensive to the citizens of country A, causing the citizens of country A to buy foreign products instead of domestic products (substitution effect) and thus decrease imports from country B
   e. both (a) and (c)

14. Which of the following would cause the U.S. dollar to rise relative to the Japanese yen?
   a. an increase in the supply of yen
   b. a decrease in the demand for dollars
   c. an increase in the supply of dollars
   d. an increase in the demand for yen

15. Under the Bretton Woods system, fixed exchange rates were monitored by the
   a. Bank of America
   b. North Atlantic Treaty Organization
   c. International Monetary Fund
   d. United Nations

chapter 35

Fixed Versus Floating Exchange Rates

Central Themes and Major Points

From the end of World War II up until the early 1970s, international monetary relations were based on a system of fixed exchange rates. From 1973 to 1985, currency values were predominantly determined by a system of floating exchange rates. In 1985, the major industrial nations moved to a system of managed floating exchange rates. This system combines elements of both fixed and floating exchange rate systems.

Under the rules of the system of fixed exchange rates, countries with deficits in their balance of payments had to prevent their currency from depreciating by intervening in the foreign exchange market to buy their own currency in exchange for *international reserves*. If unable to defend the value of its currency, a deficit country had no choice but to *devalue* its currency. It is shown in this chapter how *speculation* may precipitate this devaluation.

The chapter examines the system of fixed exchange rates and compares it with the system of freely flexible or floating exchange rates, which was introduced in Chapter 34. One important aspect of this comparison is how domestic monetary and fiscal policies *(domestic stabilization policies)* are influenced or constrained by the type of exchange rate system that is in effect. To some extent, floating exchange rates provide countries more freedom and flexibility than fixed rates do.

In the case of a system of fixed exchange rates, a country's domestic stabilization policies may be constrained by the requirement that it maintain a fixed exchange rate relative to the currencies of other countries. Monetary policy may not be used as a domestic stabilization policy if a country sticks to the rules of a fixed exchange rate system.

With floating rates, things are different. Countries can adopt whatever domestic stabilization policies they want, because floating exchange rates will restore equilibrium to the balance of payments automatically *without* directly affecting the domestic money supply. It will be shown, however, that the automatic adjustment in the balance of payments does have a cost: deficit countries will experience a decline in their standard of living as their deficit shrinks.

In practice, the system of floating exchange rates failed to provide the automatic adjustment in nation's balance of payments. Strong demand for U.S. financial assets caused the U.S. dollar to continue rising in spite of mounting balance of payments deficits. Disillusionment with the system caused the G-5 (later G-7) nations to move toward a system of managed floating exchange rates.

New Terms

Define and/or explain the following terms introduced in this chapter:

International reserve
  assets
Devaluation
Revaluation

Speculative activities
  in the foreign
  exchange market
Chronic deficits

Discipline of the
  balance of payments
Intercountry interest
  rate differentials

Defending the dollar
Par rate of exchange
Managed floating

Essay Questions and Problems

*1. **International reserves** In general, one can say that international reserves are assets that are accepted in payment for international transactions.
a. What are these international reserve assets? Give an example of an asset that would qualify as an international reserve for Italy but not for the United States. Give an example of an asset that would qualify as an international reserve for both Italy and the United States.
b. Who are the holders of these international reserve assets and for what purposes are they held?
c. What is the role of international reserves in a system of floating exchange rates?

2. **Devaluation** Under the system of fixed exchange rates that prevailed from the end of World War II until the early 1970s, a country with a chronic deficit in its balance of payments eventually had to devalue its currency.
a. Define the word *devaluation*.
b. Why did countries with chronic deficits in their balance of payments have to devalue?
c. The United States played a key role in the system of fixed exchange rates, because its currency was used as an international reserve by most foreign countries. Why did the special position enjoyed by the United States allow it to run continual deficits up until the early 1970s *without* the necessity of devaluation?

3. **Speculation in the foreign exchange markets** Once the financial community senses that devaluation is a possibility under a fixed exchange rate system, it is likely to undertake actions that increase the probability of its occurrence.
a. Explain this statement.
b. What is speculation in the foreign exchange markets? Who are the speculators?
*c. Suppose that the official exchange rate between the British pound and the U.S. dollar is £1 = $2.50. If the market expects a depreciation of the pound to be announced next week, what would a speculator with £100,000 do? What would be his profit if Great Britain devalued by 10 percent?

4. **Independent domestic stabilization policies under fixed exchange rates**
a. How are balance of payments imbalances (surpluses and deficits) corrected under a system of fixed exchange rates, assuming that countries are playing by the rules of the game?
b. Under fixed exchange rates with central banks playing by the rules of the game, what freedom do individual nations have to pursue their own independent domestic stabilization policies?

5. **Independent domestic stabilization policies under floating exchange rates**
a. How are balance of payments imbalances corrected under a system of freely floating or flexible exchange rates?
b. Compare the balance of payments adjustment process under freely floating exchange rates with the same process under fixed exchange rates with central banks playing by the rules of the game.
c. What are the effects of the automatic adjustment process under freely floating exchange rates on the domestic economy of a deficit country?
d. Under freely floating exchange rates, do individual nations have the freedom to pursue their own independent domestic stabilization policies?
e. If a deficit country lets freely floating exchange rates take care of eliminating its balance of payments deficit, it will find its standard of living declining in the process. How do deficit countries attempt to forestall this painful adjustment, and what are the consequences of their actions?

*6. **Official intervention in the foreign exchange markets** Under fixed exchange rates the monetary authority of a country will intervene in the foreign exchange markets in order to maintain the par value of its currency.
a. Referring to Figure 35.1, suppose that the par value of the French franc is pegged at 1 FF = $0.20. Is this an equilibrium rate?
b. *Intervention points*
Actually, foreign exchange rates under a system of fixed rates are usually allowed to fluctuate within narrow bands. Under the system of fixed exchange rates that prevailed from 1944 up until late 1971, par rates were permitted under International Monetary Fund rules to fluctuate by 1 percent above or below their par value before a central bank was required to intervene to stabi-

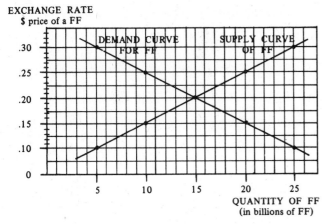

EXCHANGE RATE
$ price of a FF

DEMAND CURVE FOR FF — SUPPLY CURVE OF FF

QUANTITY OF FF
(in billions of FF)

Figure 35.1
*Government Intervention
in Foreign Exchange Markets*

lize the exchange rate of its currency. The upper limit of the band is called the upper intervention point, and the lower limit is called the lower intervention point. What are the intervention points for the FF? Draw in Figure 35.1 the band within which rates can fluctuate.

c. Suppose that the French demand for American-made goods increases. This will cause the supply curve of French francs to shift to the right. Assume that the shift is 2 billion FF at *every level of the exchange rate.*

(1) Why does the supply curve shift to the right in response to an increase in the French demand for American-made goods?

(2) Draw the new supply curve in Figure 35.1.

(3) Determine the new equilibrium exchange rate and the new equilibrium quantity of French francs. Has the FF depreciated or appreciated in this case? Why?

(4) Does the new equilibrium exchange rate require the intervention of the French central bank in the foreign exchange markets? Explain.

(5) What is the state of the balance of payments of France vis-à-vis the United States (deficit, equilibrium, or surplus)? Explain.

d. Suppose that the French demand for American-made goods increases and that the resulting shift in the supply curve of FF is 6 billion FF *at every level of the exchange rate.*

(1) Draw the new supply curve in Figure 35.1.

(2) What is the new exchange rate in this case?

(3) What keeps the new exchange rate from dropping to $.17, the point where the new supply curve intersects the demand curve for French francs?

(4) What is the state of the balance of payments of France vis-à-vis the United States?

Note: Under floating exchange rates central banks can still intervene in the foreign exchange markets in the same fashion as described for the case of fixed exchange rates. In this case floating exchange rates are called "managed" floats.

*7. **The link between the balance of payments and macroeconomic variables: The discipline of the balance of payments** From the end of World War II until the early 1970s, the world was under a system of fixed exchange rates. A nation with a persistent deficit in its balance of payments was supposed to pursue a domestic economic policy aimed at restoring equilibrium in its balance of payments and defend the value of its currency in the foreign exchange markets.

a. Which type of monetary policy should be pursued under those circumstances? What would be the impact of a change in the money supply on domestic prices, GDP, employment, and the level of interest rates? Explain.

b. What would be the effect of the changes in the domestic price level, GDP, employment, and the level of interest rates on imports, exports, and short-term capital movements? Explain.

c. Does this type of international monetary system insulate the domestic economic sector from disequilibrium in the balance of payments?

8. **Floating exchange rates: Success or failure?**

a. Why are floating exchange rates considered to be superior to fixed exchange rates in dealing with shocks such as oil price increases?

b. Explain why floating exchange rates did not produce a reduction of the U.S. balance of payments deficit during the early 1980s.

c. Describe the system that was developed to replace floating exchange rates.

9. Describe the framework you would use to forecast the value of the dollar against the German mark. What are some of the factors that have influenced this relationship in the recent past?

Do you think the dollar will depreciate or appreciate relative to the mark over the next year? Why?

SELF-TESTS

Completion Questions

Complete each of the following statements by entering the missing words and/or choosing the best alternative proposed.

1. Under a system of floating exchange rates, when a country runs a _____ _____ deficit, its money _____ _____ relative to other monies.

2. _____ are assets that are accepted in payment for (domestic/international) transactions. They include _____ and _____ _____.

3. With a system of _____ exchange rates, _____ _____ assets are used to intervene in foreign exchange markets whenever the value of a country's money starts to _____ _____ from its _____ value.

4. Under a system of fixed exchange rates, a country that officially lowers the ___ _____ value of its money is said to _____ its currency. A country that officially raises the _____ value of its money is said to _____ its currency.

5. _____ are international reserve assets to the United States but not to Germany; _____ _____ are international reserve assets to Germany but not to the United States, and _____ _____ is an international reserve asset to both countries.

6. Under a system of flexible exchange rates, a balance of payments deficit is corrected as follows. The currency of the deficit country will (appreciate/depreciate). Its domestic prices, however, will (increase/decrease/remain the same). As a result, the currency of the deficit country is now (less/more) expensive to foreigners and the (domestic/foreign) demand for the goods, services, and financial _____ _____ of the deficit country will (increase/decrease). Consequently, the deficit country's (imports/exports) will (expand/contract). Also, because foreign currencies are now (less/more) expensive for the citizens of the deficit coun-

try, this country's *(imports/exports)* will *(expand/contract)*. The combined effect is to *(narrow/widen)* the balance of payments _____.

7. A system of floating exchange rates without any government intervention is called a _____. When government intervenes in the _____ market the system is called a _____.

8. The G-7 nations consist of _____, _____, _____, _____, _____, _____, _____, and _____ _____.

9. Three key factors that influence the value of a currency relative to others are _____, _____, ____, and _____.

True and False Questions

For each of the following statements, circle the letter T if it is correct or the letter F if it is *partially* or totally incorrect.

T F 1. With floating exchange rates, when a country runs a temporary deficit in its balance of payments, the monies of other countries appreciate relative to the domestic money. This will expand other countries' imports and contract their exports to the country running the deficit.

T F 2. U.S. dollars are an international reserve asset to France but not to the United States, whereas French francs are an international reserve asset to the U.S. but not to France.

T F 3. From the end of World War II until 1973, international agreement dictated that a deficit country that saw its money start to depreciate had to step in promptly to stop the decline by selling its own money in the foreign exchange market.

T F 4. Under the Bretton Woods system, other nations acquired U.S. dollars when the United States ran deficits in its balance of payments. These dollars were then held as reserve assets.

T F 5. Under the Bretton Woods system of fixed exchange rates, the United States did not have to intervene constantly to keep its money from changing value relative to other monies. Only other countries had to.

T F 6. A major flaw in fixed exchange rate systems is that there is no self-correcting mechanism to eliminate balance of payments deficits.

T F 7. Under the system of fixed exchange rates, devaluations were caused by speculative activities in the foreign exchange markets.

T F 8. A speculator in the foreign exchange markets will sell a foreign exchange in anticipation of its short-term appreciation with the intent of buying it back at a profit after the expected appreciation has taken place.

T F 9. Under the Bretton Woods system, devaluation referred to a country's formally lowering the fixed ratio between its money and the U.S. dollar.

T F 10. Under the Bretton Woods fixed exchange rate system, all countries except the United States could devalue or revalue their money. This is so because all foreign monies were valued relative to the dollar.

T F 11. If you are convinced that a country has undertaken tight monetary policy, you would also conclude that the value of its currency will rise.

T F 12. A higher inflation forecast for the United States usually means a lower dollar forecast against other currencies.

T F 13. International capital movements refer to the international transfers of short-term funds in response to intercountry interest rate differentials and expectations with respect to exchange rate alterations.

T F 14. Short-term funds move out of countries with the lowest levels of interest rates into countries with the highest levels of interest rates and thereby contribute to balance of payments deficits and surpluses.

T F 15. Floating or flexible exchange rates are generally hailed as the one system that permits a country to pursue independent domestic policies, unhampered by external balance of payments considerations and irrespective of policies followed by other countries.

T F 16. Under a system of freely floating exchange rates, balance of payments imbalances are automatically corrected by a price adjustment. Domestic prices in the deficit country drop, and domestic prices in the surplus country rise. This will expand the deficit country's exports of goods and securities and contract its imports, thereby eliminating its deficit. The opposite will occur in the surplus country and thereby eliminate its surplus.

T F 17. Under flexible exchange rates, an automatic adjustment mechanism in the balance of payments does not imply that a country's standard of living will be left unaffected. Deficit countries will see their standard of living decline, and surplus countries will see theirs rise.

T F 18. Managed floats require government intervention in the foreign exchange markets in order to allow market forces to operate free of speculative activities.

T F 19. During the 1980s, the U.S. government strongly supported a system of freely floating exchange rates

T F 20. Under the current exchange rate system, central banks of major countries frequently intervene in foreign exchange markets.

Multiple-Choice Questions

Answer the following multiple-choice questions by circling the best alternative.

1. Which of the following assets would *not* qualify as an international reserve to Italy?
   a. U.S. dollars
   b. gold
   c. Italian lire
   d. Swiss francs
   e. German marks

2. Since the end of World War II and up until the early 1970s, most foreign countries held a substantial portion of their international reserves in the form of
   a. U.S. dollars
   b. gold
   c. silver
   d. special drawing rights
   e. foreign exchanges

3. Under the Bretton Woods system of fixed exchange rates, a country with chronic deficits in its balance of payments was expected to
   a. revalue its currency relative to the U.S. dollar, since the current par value could not be sustained
   b. let its currency depreciate, since it was clearly undervalued.
   c. devalue its currency relative to the U.S. dollar, since it was clearly undervalued
   d. devalue its currency relative to the U.S. dollar, since it was clearly overvalued
   e. let its currency appreciate, since it was clearly overvalued.

4. Which of the following will contribute to a worsening of a deficit in country A's balance of payments?
   a. a lower rate of inflation in country A than abroad
   b. a higher rate of inflation in country A than abroad
   c. a faster-rising level of income in country A than abroad
   d. flexible exchange rates
   e. both (b) and (c)

5. Suppose that under a system of fixed exchange rates the par value of the French franc is 25 U.S. cents. If the French franc is devalued by 20 percent, then all of the following occur *except*
   a. the post-devaluation exchange rate between the dollar and the French franc is $0.20 = 1 FF.
   b. the post-devaluation exchange rate between the French franc and the dollar is 5 FF = $1
   c. French goods are now more expensive to Americans
   d. fewer dollars are now required to buy 100 French francs

6. Speculative activities in the foreign exchange markets refer to
   a. the selling of a foreign exchange in anticipation of its short-term appreciation with the intent of buying it back at a profit
   b. the trading in a foreign exchange in accordance with expectations of a change in the

foreign exchange rate that will produce a short-term profit

   c. the buying of a foreign exchange in anticipation of its short-term depreciation with the intent of selling at a profit after the depreciation has occurred

   d. all of the above

   e. only (a) and (b)

7. Suppose that country A's rate of inflation exceeds that of other countries, then

   a. country A's currency is expected to depreciate relative to the currencies of other countries

   b. country A's currency is expected to appreciate relative to the currencies of other countries

   c. country A's balance of payments is expected to show a surplus

   d. country A's balance of payments will not be affected

8. Under a system of flexible exchange rates, a surplus country will see its surplus shrink because

   a. its domestic prices will rise, reducing its exports of goods and securities and increasing its imports

   b. its currency will depreciate, reducing its imports of goods and securities and increasing its exports

   c. its currency will appreciate, reducing its exports of goods and securities and increasing its imports

   d. its domestic prices will fall, reducing its imports of goods and securities and increasing its exports

   e. both (a) and (c)

9. Which of the following is likely to cause forecasters to raise their projections for the value of the dollar?

   a. increasing productivity of U.S. companies

   b. a lower U.S. inflation forecast

   c. tightening by the Federal Reserve

   d. all of the above

10. Under a system of fixed exchange rates, the central bank of a country with a chronic deficit in its balance of payments should take the following policy measures *except*

   a. raise the discount rate

   b. undertake an open market purchase of government securities

   c. intervene in the foreign exchange market to buy its money in exchange for foreign currencies.

   d. restrict short-term capital outflows and encourage short-term capital inflows

   e. stimulate exports and reduce foreign aid

11. External stability may require that a country forgo the use of an expansionary domestic monetary policy, because

   a. rising income at home would enlarge the country's balance of payments surplus

   b. rising interest rates at home would worsen the country's balance of payments deficit

   c. falling interest rates at home would worsen the country's balance of payments deficit

   d. falling income at home would worsen the country's balance of payments deficit

   e. falling income and rising interest rates would both worsen the country's balance of payments deficit

12. Which of the following international systems does *not* produce an automatic adjustment in the balance of payments of deficit and surplus countries?

   a. the system of flexible exchange rates

   b. the system of freely floating exchange rates

   c. the system of fixed exchange rates with monetary authorities playing by the rules of the game

   d. none of the above

   e. both (b) and (c)

13. Which of the following factors will cause a reduction in a country's imports?

   a. a decline in the country's income

   b. a decline in the income of other countries

   c. a depreciation of the country's currency in the foreign exchange markets

   d. all of the above

   e. only (a) and (c)

14. Faced with a chronic deficit in its balance of payments, country A must take deliberate internal measures to reduce its international payments imbalance. Which of the following should be implemented?

   a. an increase in bank reserves

   b. a lowering of the discount rate

   c. elimination of the restrictions on borrowing from abroad

   d. relaxation of foreign exchange restrictions

   e. reduction of the tax rates on imported goods

15. Up until the early 1970s the United States was in the unique position of being able to pursue independent domestic stabilization policies despite continual deficits in its balance of payments, because

   a. the par rate of foreign currencies was stated in terms of the dollar

   b. U.S. dollars were used as international reserves by the rest of the world

   c. the Federal Reserve conducted open market operations, which neutralized the effects on bank reserves of foreign exchange operations

d. U.S. dollars were convertible into gold at the fixed official price of gold

16. Under which of the following international monetary systems does a country have the most freedom to pursue its own independent domestic stabilization policies?
    a. flexible float
    b. managed float
    c. fixed exchange rates
    d. free float
    e. fixed exchange rates within a wide band

17. Which of the following best describes the present international monetary system?
    a. freely floating exchange rates
    b. flexible float
    c. fixed exchange rates within a wider band
    d. managed float

18. Which of the following would prefer to return to a system of fixed foreign exchange rates?
    a. the Federal Reserve

b. many bankers and business executives
c. the Congress of the United States
d. advocates of noninterference with market forces
e. none of the above

19. Freely floating exchange rates failed to function as expected because of
    a. high inflation in the United States
    b. large U.S. foreign trade deficits
    c. lack of cooperation among the major industrial nations
    d. heavy foreign demand for U.S. financial assets

20. The managed floating system calls for
    a. fixed exchange rates
    b. coordinated exchange rate intervention by major trading nations
    c. established ranges for each country's currency
    d. all major trading nations to achieve balance of payments equilibrium

chapter 36

Balance of Payments Accounting

Central Themes and Major Points

This chapter presents a detailed analysis of the accounting aspects of the balance of international payments. The principles behind this analysis are the same as those introduced in Chapter 27, where flow of funds accounting was covered. Actually, a country's balance of payments is nothing more than a sector sources and uses of funds statement, except that in this case the sector is a country and the flow of funds is between the country for which the balance of payments is drawn and the rest of the world. Also, for the case of the balance of payments, sources and uses of funds become *sources and uses of foreign exchange*. Before proceeding with this chapter it may be useful to review some of the basic principles introduced in Chapter 27.

What is a balance of payments deficit or surplus, and how is it measured? Recall that a sector's total sources must equal its total uses, but within the totals particular pairs might not match up. Deficits or surpluses occur only if one looks at a particular set of entries on the balance of payments. The total of all entries must balance.

There are six different frequently used measures of foreign account balance. Each of these measures has particular uses.

New Terms

Define and/or explain the following terms introduced in this chapter:

Uses of foreign exchange
Sources of foreign exchange
Trade balance
Goods and services balance

Current account balance
Basic balance
Net liquidity balance
Official settlements balance

Essay Questions and Problems

1. **The accounting of the balance of payments**
   The purpose of this question is to acquaint you with the accounting terms used in the balance of international payments and to show you how one can measure a deficit or a surplus in the balance of payments.
   a. What is the definition of a country's balance of payments, and what is the importance and usefulness of such a measure?
   b. Explain why a country's balance of payments is nothing more than a sector sources and uses of funds statement in disguise.
   *c. Identify the following transactions as sources or uses of foreign exchange for the United States and indicate the balance of payments account in which each of these transactions would be recorded. If a transaction is not recorded in the balance of payments, indicate why.

Note: An international transaction is entered in a country's balance of payments either as a source or as a use of foreign exchange. Sources of foreign exchange are usually called credits or *plus* items, and uses of foreign exchange are usually called debits or *minus* items.

(1) the purchase of an IBM computer by a British university

(2) an increase in foreign investment in the United States

(3) a reduction by an American multinational corporation of its investment in Argentina

(4) a deposit by a German firm of $100,000 in an American bank

(5) the purchase of a French-made machine tool by an American company

(6) $10 million in economic aid given by the United States to an African country

(7) the purchase of U.S. Treasury bills by a U.S. pension fund

(8) The purchase of U.S. equity by a Dutch investment company

d. Why does a balance of payments statement always balance?

e. If a balance of payments statement always balances, what does a deficit or a surplus in the balance of payments (a balance of payments imbalance or disequilibrium) mean?

f. What are the principal subsets of the overall balance of payments accounts that are used to measure an imbalance in the balance of payments? Define each measure and discuss its usefulness.

*g. How is a deficit in the official settlements balance financed?

h. Why did the Department of Commerce decide in 1976 that it would no longer publish figures on any of the measures used to indicate a surplus or a deficit in the U.S. balance of payments?

*2. **The balance of payments**   On the basis of the numerical values of the items given below, which pertain to the balance of payments of country A, answer the following questions.

1. Net military receipts	2
2. Net payments for foreign investment in country A	10
3. Imports	90
4. Net receipts from travel and transportation	4
5. Net transfer receipts	1
6. Net balance on long-term capital	2
7. Exports	85
8. Net balance on short-term private capital	1
9. Net balance on liquid private capital	2
10. Net increase in country A's liabilities to foreign official holders	2
11. Net decrease in the official reserve assets of country A:	
a. Gold	0
b. Convertible currencies	½
c. Other reserve assets	½

a. Calculate the merchandise trade balance. Does it show a deficit or a surplus?

b. Calculate the current account balance. Does it show a deficit or a surplus?

c. Calculate the basic balance. Does it show a deficit or a surplus?

d. Calculate the net liquidity balance. Does it show a deficit or a surplus?

e. Calculate the official settlements balance. Does it show a deficit or a surplus? If a deficit, how is it financed? Could you calculate the official settlements balance *without* the knowledge of items 1–9 listed above?

SELF-TESTS

Completion Questions

Complete each of the following statements by entering the missing words and/or choosing the best alternative proposed.

1. A country's source or receipt of funds means an *(inflow/outflow)* of *(local money/ foreign exchange)*; a country's use or _____ of funds means an _____ of _____ _____.

2. Give two examples of a country's sources of foreign exchange: _____

_____ and _____

_____.

3. Give two examples of a country's uses of foreign exchange: _____

_____ and _____

_____.

4. When Americans *(lend to/borrow from)* foreigners, they are actually importing financial assets, and their balance of international payments will show an *(inflow/outflow)* of foreign exchange.

5. The typical items that adjust to make the United States's balance of payments "balance" are increases and decreases in _____

_____ or _____

_____.

6. Balance of payments deficits and surpluses are usually measured by selecting different categories of transactions from the complete list of entries on the balance of payments accounts. List four of these measures, starting with the one that has the least amount of payments accounts (or balance of payments entries) and ending with the measure that has the most payments accounts: (1) _____

_____, (2) _____

_____, (3) _____

_____, and (4) _____.

True and False Questions

For each of the following statements, circle the letter T if it is correct or the letter F if it is *partially* or *totally* incorrect.

T F 1. The sources and uses of foreign exchange for the United States are the United States's balance of international payments.

T F 2. There is a fundamental difference between a country's balance of international payments and a standard sources and uses of funds for a sector in domestic trade.

T F 3. When a country borrows from abroad, its balance of international payments shows an outflow of foreign exchange.

T F 4. What is a source of foreign exchange for one country is a use of foreign exchange for another.

T F 5. A country's balance of payments is an accounting record of all the assets (real and financial) that the residents of the country have accumulated over the years.

T F 6. Gifts and grants between residents of one country and residents of other countries are not recorded in their respective balance of payments.

T F 7. American tourist spending in Japan is recorded in the balance of payments as a use of foreign exchange.

T F 8. The purchase by a French citizen of 100 shares of IBM stock will produce an outflow of foreign exchange from the United States, whereas the purchase by an American of 100 shares of Michelin stock (a French company) will produce an inflow of foreign exchange into the United States.

T F 9. If a country runs a balance of payments deficit, then some other country must be running a balance of payments surplus.

T F 10. A country's balance of payments is a flow variable and not a stock variable.

T F 11. The trade balance measures only merchandise trade.

T F 12. Transfer payment flows between countries are included in the goods and services trade balance.

T F 13. There is complete agreement between economists as to how one should go about measuring a balance of payments deficit or surplus. Although the basic balance would do a good job, the official settlements balance is usually preferred.

T F 14. Balance of payments deficits and surpluses are usually measured by selecting different categories of transactions from the complete list of entries on a balance of payments account. Six different measures are now published every quarter by the Department of Commerce.

T F 15. The different measures of an imbalance (a surplus or a deficit) in the balance of payments are cumulative. Starting with the trade balance, one must add additional international transactions to arrive at the next measure and so on until one gets to the official settlements balance.

Multiple-Choice Questions

Answer the following multiple-choice questions by circling the best alternative.

1. Which of the following is *not* a source of foreign exchange for the United States?
   a. foreign tourist spending in the United States
   b. the sale of an IBM computer to a research center in Germany
   c. dividends paid on foreign investment in the United States
   d. an increase in direct investment by foreign firms in the United States
   e. a sale of gold by the U.S. Treasury

2. Which of the following is a use of foreign exchange for the United States?
   a. the sale of a Westinghouse nuclear plant to Spain
   b. $10 million in economic aid given by the United States to a group of African countries
   c. a $100,000 increase in the demand deposit account of a German manufacturing company with its New York bank

   d. the purchase of U.S. Treasury bills by a private bank in Italy
   e. all of the above

3. Which of the following is *not* a source of foreign exchange for the United States?
   a. the purchase of U.S. Treasury notes by a British pension fund
   b. a sale of Japanese cars in the United States
   c. dividends earned from foreigners
   d. direct investment by Volkswagen in the United States
   e. none of the above

4. Which of the following is a source of foreign exchange for the United States?
   a. loans to foreigners
   b. reductions in foreign holdings of U.S. securities
   c. unilateral transfers from the United States
   d. all of the above
   e. none of the above

5. An imbalance in the balance of payments is usually measured by all of the following *except*
   a. the current account balance
   b. the trade balance
   c. the basic balance
   d. the long-term capital balance
   e. the net liquidity balance

6. The basic balance will necessarily show a deficit if
   a. the goods and services account is in deficit
   b. the current account is in deficit
   c. the long-term capital account is in deficit
   d. both (b) and (c)
   e. both (a) and (b)

7. The balance of payments always balances because
   a. any imbalance is always offset by an equal inflow or outflow of funds, since a sector's total sources must equal its total uses
   b. foreign exchange rates are allowed to fluctuate freely and thereby eliminate any imbalance in the balance of payments
   c. the International Monetary Fund will lend a country enough foreign exchange to restore the balance in its balance of payments
   d. none of the above. The balance of payments does not always balance. Some countries run deficits and surpluses in their balance of payments.

Questions 8–13 are based on the following information about the international accounts of country A in the year 19XX.

Exports	155
Increase in country A's holdings of foreign exchange	1

Net receipts from travel and
transportation 10
Net military payments 5
Increase in liabilities to foreign
official holders 6
Net long-term capital inflow 5
Net interest payments to
foreigners on investments in
country A 30
Imports 140

8. Country A's trade balance for the given year is equal to
   a. − 15, indicating a deficit
   b. + 15, indicating a surplus
   c. − 15, indicating a surplus
   d. + 15, indicating a deficit
   e. none of the above

9. Country's A's current accounts balance for the given year is equal to
   a. − 25, indicating a deficit
   b. + 25, indicating a surplus
   c. − 10, indicating a deficit
   d. + 10, indicating a surplus
   e. none of the above

10. Country A's basic balance for the given year is equal to
    a. − 5, indicating a deficit
    b. + 5, indicating a surplus
    c. − 5, indicating a surplus
    d. + 5, indicating a deficit
    e. none of the above

11. Country A's net overall surplus or deficit (the official settlements balance) for the given year is
    a. a surplus of 5
    b. a deficit of 5
    c. a deficit of 10
    d. in balance because the official settlements balance has been financed by a net change of 5 in liabilities to foreign official holders and holdings of foreign exchange
    e. it cannot be computed because of insufficient information

12. On the basis of the information about the international accounts of country A, one could infer that country A in the given year was a

a. net lender, meaning that country A was currently experiencing more long-term capital inflow than long-term capital outflow
b. net lender, meaning that country A was currently experiencing more long-term capital inflow than it was making interest payments to foreigners on investment in country A
c. net borrower, meaning that country A was currently experiencing more long-term capital outflow than inflow
d. net borrower, meaning that country A was currently experiencing more long-term capital inflow than outflow
e. none of the above

13. Under a system of freely flexible exchange rates, one should expect the currency of country A to
    a. remain at its equilibrium rate of exchange
    b. appreciate relative to a basket of currencies representing the rest of the world
    c. be undervalued relative to a basket of currencies representing the rest of the world
    d. depreciate relative to a basket of currencies representing the rest of the world
    e. none of the above, because under freely flexible exchange rates the balance of payments adjusts automatically

14. The least comprehensive measure of U.S. international transactions is the
    a. basic balance
    b. merchandise trade balance
    c. current account balance
    d. flow-of-funds international account

15. If a U.S.-based charitable organization makes a donation to a foreign organization, it will affect the U.S.
    a. export total
    b. import total
    c. merchandise trade balance
    d. current account balance

16. A Japanese bank's purchases of U.S. Treasury securities would affect the U.S.
    a. official settlements balance
    b. current account balance
    c. net liquidity balance
    d. merchandise trade balance

chapter 37

The Gold Standard

Central Themes and Major Points

This chapter provides answers to the following questions: What is the gold standard? How is it supposed to work? What is the probability that nations will return to a gold standard system in the foreseeable future?

The gold standard is a monetary system whereby a country links its money supply to gold. The result is that the country's money supply will change only if its gold stock changes.

To establish a *domestic* gold standard that works effectively, a country must adopt three requirements: (1) there must be a fixed ratio between its gold stock and its currency in circulation; (2) unlimited convertibility between gold and currency must be allowed; and (3) there must be an official fixed price of gold at which conversions between currency and gold can take place.

In order to establish an *international* gold standard, each nation must first adopt a domestic gold standard and then stand ready to buy or sell unlimited quantities of gold at the *official fixed price of gold*. It is shown in this chapter how the free movement of gold between nations will automatically eliminate any imbalance in their balance of payments and bring inflation under control. It is also pointed out that although the international gold standard has some clear theoretical advantages, it is quite difficult to implement in practice.

The conclusion examines why the gold standard is not a workable system and why it is unlikely that nations will reestablish it in the near future.

New Terms

Define and/or explain the following terms introduced in this chapter:

U.S. Gold Commission
The domestic gold standard
The international gold standard
Fractional gold reserves
Official price of gold

Par rate of exchange
Gold import point
Gold export point
Sterilization or neutralization of the monetary effects of gold flows

Essay Questions and Problems

1. **A domestic gold standard** Describe how a domestic gold standard could be established and how it would operate. What are the advantages of a domestic gold standard? What are the possible disadvantages?

2. **The international gold standard** The gold standard was in effect during the last half of the 1800s and the first few decades of the 1900s.
   a. State clearly all the conditions required for the gold standard to work effectively.
   *b. How would the balance of payments of a *surplus* country adjust under a gold standard system?
   *c. Under the gold standard, what freedom do individual nations have to pursue their own

independent domestic stabilization policies?

*d. Compare the international gold standard system to a system of fixed foreign exchange rates.

*3. **Gold export and gold import points** Suppose that the cost of shipping gold across the Atlantic in either direction is equal to 20 cents per ounce of gold. Under a gold standard system, the United States fixed 25 dollars an ounce as the official price of gold and France fixed 1,000 francs an ounce as the official price of gold. Answer the following questions.

a. What is the implication of the fact that the United States and France have set an official price for gold?

b. What is the par rate of exchange between the U.S. dollar and the French franc?

c. What is the gold export point (in dollars)? Explain.

d. What is the gold import point (in dollars)? Explain.

e. What are the limits within which the par exchange rate between the U.S. dollar and the French franc can fluctuate? Give your answer in U.S. dollars and French francs.

4. **The future of the gold standard** In 1981 and 1982 the U.S. Gold Commission, after long and hard deliberations, decided against a return to the gold standard. Why do you think the U.S. Gold Commission did not recommend that the gold standard be reestablished?

SELF-TESTS

Completion Questions

Complete each of the following statements by entering the missing words and/or choosing the best alternative proposed.

1. Under the _____ system there exists a fixed ratio between gold and _____ in circulation. In this case we have a banking system with _____ _____ reserves.

2. Under the _____ system there is a _____ rate of exchange between the currencies of two countries. This rate could not vary above or below the _____ _____ rate of exchange by more than _____ _____.

3. The upper and lower limits within which the rate of exchange between the currencies of two countries could vary under the _____ _____ system were called, respectively, the _____ _____ _____ and the _____ _____.

4. A gold *(inflow/outflow)* will raise a country's money supply. If the central bank wishes to offset this monetary effect, it must take action to *(increase/decrease)* the domestic _____ supply. This action by the _____ _____ bank is referred to as a _____ or neutralization of the monetary effects of _____ flows.

5. In general, when a country's money supply shrinks, the following is expected to take place: (a) domestic prices should *(fall/rise)*; (b) domestic income should *(fall/rise)*; (c) unemployment should *(fall/rise)*; (d) interest rates should *(fall/rise)*.

   The effect of (a), (b), and (c) *(increases/decreases)* imports and *(increases/decreases)* exports. The effect of (d) produces a short-term capital *(inflow/outflow)*. The combined effect of (a), (b), (c), and (d) *(widens/narrows)* the country's balance of payments deficit.

6. Under a gold standard system, a country with a balance of payments surplus will *(lose/gain)* gold and see its _____ supply *(expand/shrink)*, because the domestic _____ supply is _____ _____ rigidly to the country's _____ stock. The *(expanded/contracted)* money supply will *(lower/raise)* the level of domestic prices and employment and *(lower/raise)* the level of domestic short-term _____ rates relative to those of foreign _____ _____. This will *(increase/decrease)* the country's exports, *(increase/decrease)* its imports, and produce a _____ _____ capital *(inflow/outflow)*. The country's exports *(decrease/increase)* because domestic goods are now *(more/less)* expensive relative to foreign goods and hence *(more/less)* competitive in the world markets. The country's imports *(decrease/increase)* because *(higher/lower)* employment and income will *(raise/lower)* domestic spending on *(foreign/domestic)* goods. Finally, _____ _____ capital *(inflows/outflows)* will occur, because _____ _____ rates are now *(higher/lower)* abroad. The combined effect of all these changes *(reduces/enlarges)* the country's balance of payments surplus.

True and False Questions

For each of the following statements, circle the letter T if it is correct or the letter F if it is *partially* or totally incorrect.

T F   1. In 1981 and 1982 the U.S. Gold Commission recommended that the United States return gradually to a gold standard system.

T F   2. A domestic gold standard contains built-in safeguards against inflation.

T F   3. A domestic gold standard requires unlimited convertibility between currency and gold.

T F   4. Under a domestic gold standard, the money supply would be determined by the central bank.

T F   5. Inflation cannot take place under a domestic gold standard.

T F   6. Under a domestic gold standard, the money supply is determined by the public.

T F   7. Under the international gold standard, a devaluation is the same as raising the official price of gold.

T F   8. In March 1933 the United States abandoned the gold standard and Americans were not allowed to buy any more gold.

T F   9. In 1934 the U.S. dollar was devalued

and the official price of gold dropped from $35 an ounce to $20.67 an ounce.

T F 10. Under the gold standard system, the adjustment process in the balance of payments of deficit and surplus countries operates in large part through domestic instability.

T F 11. When a country gains gold, its money supply shrinks because its monetary authority accumulates gold and thus reduces the amount of money in circulation in that country.

T F 12. The reason why domestic prices rise in the country that gains gold and fall in the country that loses gold can be found in the quantity theory of money. A gain of gold means a larger money supply, which in turn implies higher domestic prices, according to the quantity theory of money. A loss of gold means a smaller money supply, which in turn implies lower domestic prices.

T F 13. Under the gold standard system, the par rate of exchange between two currencies is usually fixed at a rate equal or close to the rate that would prevail under a system of freely floating exchange rates.

T F 14. Under the gold standard system, the rate of exchange between currencies of any two countries could not exceed the gold import point or fall below the gold export point.

T F 15. Under the gold standard system, the adjustment mechanism that was supposed to restore equilibrium in a nation's balance of payments was essentially an automatic or "Classical" price mechanism.

T F 16. Under the gold standard system, the currency of a nation has a fixed value, which is expressed in terms of gold or in terms of another currency that has a fixed link to gold.

T F 17. Under the gold standard, a country could not continue to run a balance-of-payments deficit even if it had enough gold, simply because equilibrium in its balance of payments would be restored automatically no matter what this country chose to do.

T F 18. Suppose that the official price of gold is $50 an ounce; the French price is 250 francs, and the Japanese price is 300 yen. Then the exchange rate between the French franc and the Japanese yen must be 5 francs = 6 yen.

T F 19. Because the gold standard produces fairly stable exchange rates, it is similar to a system of fixed exchange rates but differs from a system of floating exchange rates.

T F 20. One of the strengths of the gold standard is that it has built-in safeguards against recessions and unemployment. One of its major weaknesses is that it is ineffective in fighting inflation.

Multiple-Choice Questions

Answer the following multiple-choice questions by circling the best alternative.

1. When was the United States officially on a gold standard?
   a. from 1900 to 1933
   b. over the second half of the last century
   c. after World War II
   d. the United States was never officially on the gold standard

2. Some of the conditions that ensure that the gold standard system will work effectively are
   a. a fixed ratio of each nation's gold holding to its money supply
   b. a fixed exchange ratio of one nation's money in terms of another's
   c. a fixed ratio of each nation's average wage rate to its level of income
   d. all of the above
   e. only (a) and (b)

3. Under a domestic gold standard, if the legal gold-to-currency ratio is 0.5 and the government holds $25 billion worth of gold, the currency the government can print is
   a. $12.5 billion
   b. $25 billion
   c. $50 billion
   d. $100 billion

4. With a 25 percent gold backing behind bank reserves and a reserve requirement of 20 percent against bank deposits, one dollar of gold would support a maximum volume of bank deposits equal to
   a. nine dollars
   b. twenty dollars
   c. sixteen dollars
   d. eight dollars
   e. none of the above

5. If the gold backing behind bank reserves is 25 percent and the reserve requirement against

bank deposits is 10 percent, then the gold-to-deposits multiplier is equal to

   a. 40
   b. 25
   c. 2.5
   d. 400
   e. none of the above

6. Under the domestic gold standard, the central bank of a country gaining gold from other countries should

   a. allow its domestic money supply to expand
   b. sell the gold in the open market in order to reduce its market price and discourage further gold inflows
   c. raise the price of gold in order to increase gold inflows
   d. take domestic policy measures to prevent the occurrence of an inflationary boom induced by gold gains
   e. both (a) and (b)

7. Assume there is a domestic gold standard. If the the gold-to-currency ratio is 0.25 and gold is set at $500 an ounce, 50 ounces of gold leads to a domestic money supply of

   a. $125
   b. $500
   c. $50,000
   d. $100,000

8. A domestic gold standard is least effective in preventing

   a. balance of payments deficits
   b. high interest rates
   c. inflation
   d. recessions

9. Suppose that the price of gold is fixed at 25 dollars an ounce in the United States and at 5 pounds an ounce in Great Britain; then the par rate of exchange between the dollar and the pound is

   a. 5 pounds for 1 dollar
   b. 4 pounds for 1 dollar
   c. 5 dollars for 1 pound
   d. 4 dollars for 1 pound

10. Under a system of fixed exchange rates, the doubling of the official price of gold will

   a. double the value of the dollar in terms of foreign currencies
   b. double the value of foreign currencies in terms of gold
   c. halve the value of foreign currencies in terms of gold
   d. halve the value of the dollar in terms of foreign currencies

11. The chief argument in favor of the international gold standard system is that

   a. gold is the only commodity that is universally accepted as a means of payment
   b. international trade can be regulated by controlling the volume of gold available for international payments
   c. adjustments in the balance of payments of deficit and surplus countries will be faster and smoother than under a different international monetary system
   d. countries can pursue an independent domestic economic policy and leave the adjustment in the balance of payments to the gold standard mechanisms
   e. none of the above

Questions 12 to 18 are based on the following information: the cost of shipping gold across the Atlantic in either direction is equal to 10 cents per ounce of gold. Suppose that the United States fixed 20 dollars an ounce as the official price of gold and that the par rate of exchange between the dollar and the British pound was 4 dollars to one pound.

12. The fixed value of the dollar in terms of gold is

   a. one dollar is worth 20 ounces of gold
   b. one dollar is worth one-twentieth of an ounce of gold
   c. one dollar is worth one-fifth of an ounce of gold
   d. one dollar is worth 5 ounces of gold

13. The price of one ounce of gold in terms of pounds is

   a. one ounce of gold is worth 4 pounds
   b. one ounce of gold is worth 20 pounds
   c. one ounce of gold is worth 5 pounds
   d. it cannot be computed because of insufficient information

14. The fixed value of the pound in terms of gold is

   a. one pound is worth a fifth of an ounce of gold
   b. one pound is worth a fourth of an ounce of gold
   c. one pound is worth 5 ounces of gold
   d. it cannot be computed because of insufficient information

15. The U.S. gold export point is equal to

   a. 4.01 dollars per pound
   b. 4.02 dollars per pound
   c. 3.98 dollars per pound
   d. 3.99 dollars per pound

16. The U.S. gold import point is equal to

   a. 4.01 dollars per pound
   b. 4.02 dollars per pound
   c. 3.98 dollars per pound
   d. 3.99 dollars per pound

17. The rate of exchange between the dollar and the pound could fluctuate within the limits of

   a. 3.98 dollars per pound to 4.02 dollars per pound
   b. 3.99 dollars per pound to 4.01 dollars per pound

c. 3.98 dollars per pound to 4.01 dollars per pound

d. 3.99 dollars per pound to 4.02 dollars per pound

18. From the preceding question one can conclude that the international gold standard produces
    a. floating exchange rates
    b. stable exchange rates
    c. flexible exchange rates
    d. managed exchange rates
    e. unstable exchange rates

19. Suppose that the public suspects that the government might soon devalue its currency. Then the public should
    a. sell gold immediately at the prevailing official price
    b. buy gold immediately at the prevailing official price
    c. buy gold only after the devaluation has taken place
    d. both (a) and (c)

20. Which of the following will take place if a country gains gold under the gold standard system?
    a. Its money supply shrinks.
    b. Its imports decline.
    c. Its rate of unemployment rises.
    d. The level of its domestic prices increases.
    e. The level of its interest rates rises.

21. Which of the following international systems does *not* produce an automatic adjustment in the balance of payments deficit and surplus countries?
    a. the gold standard system
    b. the system of freely floating exchange rates
    c. the system of fixed exchange rates with monetary authorities playing by the rules of the game
    d. none of the above
    e. both (b) and (c)

22. Despite their theoretical similarities, the gold standard and the fixed exchange rates system differ in that
    a. the link between the balance of payments and the money supply is far more rigid under the latter
    b. the link between the balance of payments and the money supply is far more rigid under the former
    c. under the gold standard the value of the currency of each country is stated in terms of gold, whereas under the fixed exchange rates system the value of each currency is stated in terms of the dollar
    d. under the fixed exchange rates system the par value of the currency of a country with a balance of payments disequilibrium can be altered by official devaluation or revaluation, whereas under the gold standard no devaluation or revaluation is possible

23. Under which of the following international monetary systems does a country have the most freedom to pursue its own independent domestic stabilization policies?
    a. gold standard
    b. managed float
    c. fixed exchange rates
    d. flexible float
    e. fixed exchange rates within a wide band

24. In order to sterilize (same as neutralize or offset) the domestic effect of a gold inflow, a country should
    a. increase its money supply
    b. reduce its money supply
    c. lower its discount rate
    d. increase bank reserves
    e. all of the above except (b)

25. It is unlikely that nations will soon return to a gold standard system, because
    a. it is practically impossible to establish a fixed relationship between a nation's gold stock and its money supply
    b. it is difficult to set an appropriate official price of gold
    c. the gold standard can produce severe recessions and extended periods of unemployment
    d. all of the above

Solutions

CHAPTER 1

Essay Questions and Problems

2. c. Money as a medium of exchange.

3. a. To avoid double counting. Suppose that a $10 bill is deposited in a checking account. This transaction should not affect the size of the money supply. The public is simply exchanging money in the form of a $10 bill for money in the form of a $10 demand deposit. If vault cash were counted as part of the money supply then the money supply would have risen by $10 ($10 vault cash minus the $10 in currency *not* held by the public plus $10 dollars of demand deposits equals a net increase of $10 dollars).

   c. Because it is the public that ultimately decides in which denomination it prefers to hold dollar bills. If the public does not want to hold $2 bills, the Federal Reserve and commercial banks have no way of forcing it to do so.

4. c. Yes, saving and investment can take place in a barter economy. Consider the case of a fisherman who wishes to increase his daily catch. In order to do so he must build a fishing net. The fishing net is an investment. While building the net the fisherman must feed himself. In order to do so he borrows food from a nearby farmer. This extra food the farmer has not consumed is saving that is lent out to the fisherman. When the fisherman increases his future catch he will be able to repay the farmer by giving him fish. Investment has taken place, because some member of the community had saved by refraining from consumption. Note that the community is now better off because it has more food available as a result of the increased productivity of the fisherman (economic growth).

5. a. Note that in a barter economy there will be saving and investment (see answer 4c). The point is that with money and financial markets there will be *more* saving and investment than in the case of a barter economy.

6. a. M1 = $450 billion; M2 = $1,850 billion; and M3 = $2,150 billion.

   b. (1) No change in M1, M2, or M3 (see answer 3a).
      (2) No change in M1, M2, or M3 (see answer 3a).
      (3) M1 is up $10 billion; M2 and M3 do not change. M1 is up $10 billion because there is a $10 billion demand deposit at commercial banks that did not exist before. M2 and M3 are unchanged because their total is the same; only their composition has changed.
      (4) M1 is unchanged; M2 and M3 are up by $10 billion. Recall that money market shares are part of M2 and M3 and that money market funds will first deposit the $10 billion at *their* banks.
      (5) M1 is reduced by $10 billion; M2 and M3 are unchanged.

Completion Questions

1. medium of exchange/store of value/standard of value
2. barter/medium of exchange
3. Federal Reserve System/Congress/Federal Reserve Banks/Board of Governors
4. Monetary/financial markets/fiscal/tax rates
5. intrinsic value/exchanged
6. Liquidity/currency/demand deposits
7. intermediaries / surplus funds / borrowers / investment/growth
8. Financial markets / separation / saving / investment
9. bonds/stocks (and mortgages)/borrowers/lenders
10. inflation/value

True and False Questions

1. F	2. T	3. F	4. F
5. F	6. F	7. F	8. F
9. T	10. T	11. F	12. T
13. F	14. T	15. T	16. T
17. F	18. T	19. T	20. F

Multiple-Choice Questions

1. d	2. e	3. b	4. a
5. e	6. a	7. e	8. d
9. b	10. e	11. a	12. c
13. c	14. d	15. d	16. c
17. f	18. c	19. d	20. e

CHAPTER 2

Essay Questions and Problems

5. a. Actual GDP = (Money Supply) × (Velocity)
   Actual GDP = (80 + 320) × (4) = $1,600 billion.
   b. GDP must be increased by $80 billion in order to reach its potential value of $1,680 billion. Since the velocity is 4, it follows that a $20 billion rise in the money supply (from $400 billion to $420 billion) will increase GDP by the needed $80 billion, since $20 billion times 4 equals $80 billion.
   c. Percentage change in GDP = $\frac{1,680 - 1,600}{1,600}$

   $$= .05 = 5 \text{ percent}$$

   Percentage change in money supply =
   $$\frac{420 - 400}{400} = .05 = 5 \text{ percent}$$

   Both GDP and the money supply increase by 5 percent. Velocity *must* remain constant in order for the percentage increase in GDP to be equal to the percentage increase in the money supply.

6. a. Debtors usually benefit from inflation at the expense of creditors if the rate of inflation is equal to or exceeds the rate of interest. In this case debtors repay loans with dollars that have a smaller purchasing power than the dollars they originally borrowed. Businessmen may benefit from inflation in the short run if the prices of goods and services they sell increase faster (because of inflation) than their costs of doing business.
   b. The benefits of inflation discussed above would not persist over a long period of time, because creditors would not accept rates of interest lower than the inflation rate over the long run. Likewise, workers would demand higher wages (a business cost) and obtain them if inflation continued. As a result the cost of doing business would eventually catch up with higher prices on goods and services, and businessmen would not benefit

from inflation anymore. All these effects assume a mild form of inflation. Under runaway hyperinflation everybody would be hurt.

Completion Questions

1. loans/buy/loans/sell
2. vault cash/deposit
3. excess reserves
4. liquid/liquidity/real assets/financial assets
5. higher/rise/less/reduce
6. velocity/money
7. money/few goods
8. hyperinflation/value/creeping
9. velocity
10. often

True and False Questions

1. T	2. F	3. T	4. T
5. F	6. T	7. T	8. F
9. F	10. F	11. F	12. T
13. F	14. T	15. F	16. T
17. T	18. T	19. T	20. T

Multiple-Choice Questions

1. d	2. a	3. c	4. b
5. a	6. e	7. b	8. d
9. e	10. a	11. e	12. b
13. a	14. d	15. d	16. a
17. e	18. c	19. a	20. b

CHAPTER 3

Essay Questions and Problems

3. Municipal bonds are tax-exempt. One should compare the *after-tax return* on government bonds to the return on municipal bonds. Suppose that a municipal bond of the highest quality pays a 7 percent tax-exempt coupon and a government bond with the same maturity pays a 10 percent taxable coupon. If investor's marginal tax rate is 40 percent, the *after-tax* return on the government bond is 6 percent (60 percent of 10 percent), which is lower than the 7 percent tax-exempt return on the municipal bond.

Completion Questions

1. saver-lenders/borrower-spenders
2. saver-lenders/borrower-spenders/borrower-spenders

3. borrowers / primary / lenders / financial institutions / lenders / direct / financial institutions / finance
4. federal income taxes
5. zero-coupon/perpetual/consol/lower than
6. interest (or coupon)/variable/floating
7. ownership/creditorship
8. variable/maturity
9. mortgage pools/pass-through
10. capital / money / stock / long-term bonds / U.S. Treasury bills/negotiable CDs

True and False Questions

1. T	2. F	3. F	4. F
5. F	6. T	7. F	8. T
9. F	10. F	11. T	12. F
13. T	14. F	15. F	16. T
17. T	18. F	19. F	20. T
21. T	22. F	23. T	24. T
25. F	26. T	27. T	28. F
29. T	30. F	31. F	32. T
33. T			

Multiple-Choice Questions

1. c	2. b	3. c	4. a
5. c	6. a	7. d	8. d
9. b	10. a	11. b	12. e
13. d	14. a	15. e	16. a
17. c	18. a	19. a	20. d

CHAPTER 4

Essay Questions and Problems

1. a. Note that financial intermediation is the same thing as indirect finance. Financial disintermediation is a movement away from indirect finance and into direct finance.
   b. (1) This transaction is neither direct nor indirect finance. It is not financial intermediation nor disintermediation. It involves the trading of existing securities, issued in the past. No lending or borrowing is taking place. Securities are just changing hands.
      (2) Direct finance. An ultimate lender-saver (Mr. Williams) buys the newly issued primary securities of the ultimate borrower-spender (IBM).
      (3) Indirect finance/financial intermediation. A financial intermediary (insurance company) buys the newly issued primary

securities of an ultimate borrower-spender (New York State).
      (4) Financial disintermediation. An ultimate lender-saver withdraws his funds from an intermediary (a savings bank or a commercial bank) and uses the proceeds to buy a primary security (a 91-day Treasury bill) of an ultimate borrower-spender (the U.S. government).
      (5) Indirect finance/financial intermediation. An intermediary (mutual fund company) buys the newly issued primary securities of an ultimate borrower-spender (IBM).
      (6) Indirect finance/financial intermediation. An ultimate lender-saver (Mrs. Smith) deposits funds in a financial intermediary (savings bank), which then uses the funds to extend a loan to an ultimate borrower-spender (the home buyer).
2. c. No. A broker is not a financial intermediary, because he does not issue securities to raise funds with which he can purchase direct securities. He is simply a go-between who facilitates the trade of existing securities.
   d. Yes. Federal Reserve banks can be considered financial intermediaries. They issue securities (currency and reserves) and acquire primary securities (government bonds).
6. d. When money market mutual funds use their funds to purchase negotiable bank CDs and U.S. Treasury bills, the money supply is reduced (at least initially in the case of negotiable CDs). To see this, consider the T-account for commercial banks that follows. The purchase of $100 million worth of CDs by a money market fund is represented by transaction (1). The purchase of $100 million of U.S. Treasury bills by a money market fund is represented by transaction (2). In both cases private demand deposits are reduced. Recall that government deposits are not part of the money supply.

Commercial Banks

(1) {		Private demand deposits	− $100
		Negotiable CDs	+ 100
(2) {		Private demand deposits	− 100
		Government demand deposits	+ 100

Completion Questions

1. intermediaries / ultimate saver-lenders / liabilities/assets/ultimate spender-borrowers
2. intermediaries/funds/lower/funds/acquired
3. savings and loan associations/mutual savings banks/credit unions
4. depository
5. long-term home mortgages/short- and medium-term savings deposits/short-term/long-term
6. Banking Act/Depository Institutions Deregulation and Monetary Control Act of 1980/NOW accounts (NOW = Negotiable Order of Withdrawal)/consumer
7. life insurance companies/pension and retirement funds/property and casualty insurance companies/sales and consumer finance companies/mutual funds
8. Life insurance companies/premiums
9. consumer/business
10. sales and consumer finance companies

True and False Questions

1. T	2. F	3. F	4. T
5. T	6. T	7. F	8. F
9. F	10. F	11. T	12. F
13. T	14. T	15. F	16. F
17. T	18. T	19. T	

Multiple-Choice Questions

1. b	2. a	3. c	4. c
5. b	6. e	7. e	8. c
9. c	10. d	11. e	12. e
13. c	14. c	15. e	16. c
17. a	18. c	19. d	

CHAPTER 5

Essay Questions and Problems

1. a. (1) Coupon rate is 4 percent.
(2) Annual coupon payment (income) is equal to $40 (4 percent of the $1,000 face value).
(3) Yes. You can tell that the current yield is higher than 4 percent, since current yield is the ratio of coupon payment to the current price of the bond. Since the price is less than $1,000, it means that the current yield is more than 4 percent.
(4) Current yield = ($40/980) = 4.08 percent (approximately).

(5) Current yield measures your income return per dollar of investment. You paid $980 for a security that returns $40 annually and hence earn 4.08 percent annually. It is not an adequate measure of your total annual return on the bond because, if the bond is held to maturity, you will receive $1,000 in one year. This represents a $20 capital gain (you paid only $980 for the bond), which is not taken into account by the current yield.

(6) The bond's yield to maturity will be higher than 4 percent, because if your $20 capital gain is taken into account you will earn more than 4 percent. Also, a capital gain means that the price of the bond is below its face value which, in turn, implies that the yield must be higher than 4 percent.

(7) $P = \dfrac{40 + 1,000}{(1 + r)}$ where r is the yield to maturity. Since P = $980 we have

$$980 = \frac{1,040}{(1 + r)} \text{ or } 980(1 + r) = 1,040$$

which gives r = .0612 = 6.12 percent (approximately).

(8) The bond's yield to maturity measures your annual average total return on the bond. It is an adequate measure only if the bond is held to maturity, because it assumes that the holder will receive a capital gain at maturity or incur a capital loss.

(9) No. You can use a bond table.

(10) The total return is 10.2%. Total return is limited because it does not discount for time.

(11) Real rate of return is a negative 1.88 percent (6.12 percent minus 8 percent).

b. (1) Higher than $1,000, because the yield to maturity is lower than the coupon rate.

(2)

$$P = \frac{90}{(1 + .08)^1} + \frac{90}{(1 + .08)^2}$$

$$+ \frac{90}{(1 + .08)^3} + \frac{1,000}{(1 + .08)^3} =$$

$$\frac{90}{1.080} + \frac{90}{1.166} + \frac{1,090}{1.260} =$$

$$83.33 + 77.19 + 865.08 = \$1,025.60$$

2. a. (2) The coupon payment is 6 percent of $1,000, or $60. At a yield of 4 percent, the price of the consol is ($60/.04), or $1,500. At 6 percent the price is $1,000, and at 8 percent it is $750. Conclusion: Bond prices and interest rates move in opposite directions.

b. (1)

r	Price of consol	Price of one-year bond
4%	$1,500	$1,019.23
6%	$1,000	$1,000.00
8%	$ 750	$ 981.48

(2) The consol rises in price by $500. The one-year bond rises in price by $19.23. Conclusion: Longer-term bonds increase in price more than short-term bonds in response to the same drop in the level of the interest rate.

(3) The consol drops in price by $250. The one-year bond drops in price by $18.52. Conclusion: Longer-term bonds decrease in price more than short-term bonds in response to the same increase in the level of the interest rate.

(4) The consol is riskier because its price fluctuates more than that of the short-term bond.

Completion Questions

1. coupon rate / current yield / yield to maturity / holding period yield (in any order)
2. drops
3. rises
4. short/drop/long
5. nominal rate of interest/expected rate of inflation

True and False Questions

1. T	2. T	3. T	4. F
5. F	6. T	7. T	8. F
9. F	10. T	11. F	12. F
13. F	14. F		

Multiple-Choice Questions

1. b	2. a	3. e*	4. c
5. e**	6. a	7. b***	8. b
9. c	10. a	11. b	12. b
13. a	14. a	15. d	16. b
17. c	18. e	19. d	

*$8/1000$ = 0.8 percent

**You know it exceeds 6 percent but you can't compute it because you do not know when the bond is due (maturity date).

***[(930 + 60) − 900]/900 = 10 percent

CHAPTER 6

Essay Questions and Problems

3. a. Interest rates should fall, since the supply of credit exceeds the demand for credit.
   b. See Figure 6.1. No, you need to know the interest-sensitivity of the demand and supply curves.
   c. Next year's interest rate should be 9 percent. Refer to Figure 6.1.

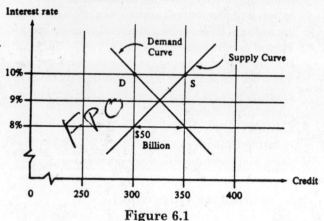

Figure 6.1

Completion Questions

1. price/lenders/borrowers
2. price/supply/demand/credit/loanable funds
3. Loanable/lenders/borrowers
4. upward/lenders/more/higher (or less/lower)
5. downward / borrowers / more / lower (or less / higher)
6. along/shift
7. business firms/households/state and local governments/federal government (in any order)
8. real assets
9. budget deficits
10. demand/right/higher
11. cyclical/secular

True and False Questions

1. T	2. F	3. T	4. T
5. F	6. T	7. T	8. F
9. F	10. F	11. T	12. F
13. F	14. F	15. T	16. F
17. F	18. F	19. F	20. F

Multiple-Choice Questions

1. e	2. b	3. b	4. d
5. b	6. a	7. c	8. c
9. b	10. d	11. a	12. b
13. b	14. a	15. a	16. c
17. a	18. e	19. a	20. e

CHAPTER 7

Essay Questions and Problems

5. e. Depositors with deposits of more than $100,000 in a failed bank would prefer the "assumption method," because under this method they would immediately recover the totality of their deposits. Under the "payoff method" they would receive only $100,000 initially, per deposit, and after liquidation of the failed bank they might get back only a fraction of any amount in excess of the insurance limit. This might also take several years.

Completion Questions

1. dual/federally/state-
2. Federal Reserve/Federal Deposit Insurance Corporation/Comptroller of the Currency
3. Insurance Corporation/commercial/mutual savings/savings and loan/$100,000/depositor/depository institution
4. National Credit Union Share Insurance Fund/unions
5. Banking Insurance Fund/Savings Association Insurance Fund
6. large/small

7. McFadden/Banking/national/state/state-chartered
8. Federal Home Loan Bank Board/ Office of Thrift Supervision
9. Veterans Administration/Federal Housing Administration
10. Regulation Q

True and False Questions

1. F	2. F	3. F	4. F
5. F	6. T	7. F	8. T
9. F	10. T	11. T	12. F
13. F	14. T	15. F	16. F
17. T	18. T	19. F	20. T
21. T	22. F	23. T	24. T
25. T	26. T	27. F	28. F
29. F	30. T		

Multiple-Choice Questions

1. c	2. d	3. d	4. e
5. c	6. a	7. b	8. c
9. a	10. d	11. b	12. b
13. e	14. b	15. a	16. a
17. c	18. b	19. b	20. c
21. b	22. a	23. b	24. e
25. d	26. c	27. d	28. d
29. c	30. c		

CHAPTER 8

Essay Questions and Problems

4. a.

Assets		Liabilities & Capital Accounts	
Cash	$110	Demand deposits	$310
Gov't securities	130	Time deposits	200
Loans	400	Negotiable CDs	90
		Equity capital	40
Total	$640	Total	$640

b. Risk assets = Total assets − Cash − Gov't securities.
Risk assets = 640 − 110 − 130 = $400 million.

c. Ratio of equity to risk assets = $(40/400)$ = 10 percent. This is higher than the average for the banking system and may be considered adequate (see your textbook).

5. b.

First National Bank

Demand deposits	− $10
Securities sold under agreement to repurchase	+ 10

(1) Required reserves decrease by $1.5 million. This is so because the reserve requirement ratio is 15 percent and thus the bank had to hold $1.5 million against the $10 million demand deposits. Once the deposit is converted into "securities sold under agreement to repurchase," $1.5 million of required reserves become free and move to the excess reserves category.

(2) Total reserves do not change because the repurchase agreement involves a customer of the bank.

(3) The bank was loaned up initially and its total reserves have not changed. This implies that it now has $1.5 million of excess reserves. Note that the bank was able to generate those excess reserves using a simple transaction with one of its larger customers. The excess reserves were obtained without going to an "outside" source of funds such as the federal funds market or the discount window. Also note that no other bank has lost excess reserves as a result of this transaction. There is a net increase in excess reserves of $1.5 million.

(4) The First National Bank can extend a loan by an amount equal to its excess reserves, or $1.5 million. Note that there is no multiple expansion of deposits in this case because we are looking at an individual bank, not the banking system.

(5) The effect of the above transaction is to reduce the size of the money supply by $1.5 million, since the $1.5 million of "securities sold under agreement of repurchase" are not counted as part of the money supply (M1).

8. a. Yes, it is possible for a bank to eliminate a reserve deficiency by selling CDs to its *own* depositors. This is so because the reserve requirement ratio against CDs is smaller than the reserve requirement ratio against demand deposits. Suppose a customer buys one dollar's worth of CDs. If the reserve requirement ratio against CDs is 5 percent and that against demand deposits is 15 percent, then the bank must only hold 5 cents of required reserves per dollar of CDs instead of 15 cents per dollar of demand deposits. This creates 10 cents of excess reserves per dollar of CDs sold.

b. Referring to the answer in (a) we showed that for every dollar of CDs sold banks get 10 cents of excess reserves. In order to eliminate a $100 million reserve deficiency, banks will have to sell $1 billion of CDs, since $1 billion worth of CDs will generate $100 million of excess reserves to cover the $100 million deficiency. Note that $1 billion is equal to $1,000 million.

14. d. To increase reserves, selling Treasury bills is the least costly alternative. To decrease reserves, selling federal funds is the most profitable alternative.

15. a. $3.39 million. Total amount of business time deposits is equal to $1,610 million. Average daily time deposits is equal to 1,610 divided by 14 days, which is $115 million. Required reserves are 3 percent of $113 million ($115 million minus $2 million reserve-free), which equals $3.39 million.

b. $7.35 million. Total amount of net demand deposits is equal to $1,120 million. Average daily net demand deposits is equal to 1,120 divided by 14 days, which is $80 million. Required reserves are 3 percent of the first $25 million plus 12 percent of $55 million (the rest), which equals $7.35 million.

c. $10.74 million, the sum of $3.39 million (answer to question a) and $7.35 million (answer to question b).

d. $1.5 million. Total amount of vault cash is equal to $21 million. Average daily vault cash is equal to 21 divided by 14 days, which is $1.5 million.

e. $9.24 million, the difference between $10.74 million (see answer to question c) and $1.50 million (see answer to question d).

f. From Thursday of Week 5 to Monday of Week 7, FNB held a daily average deposit with the Federal Reserve of $9 million ($108 million divided by 12 days). But FNB must hold over that two-week period a daily average deposit with the Federal Reserve of $9.24 million (see answer to question e). In order to bring its $9 million daily average up to $9.24 million by Wednesday of Week 7, FNB must hold $21.36 million with the Federal Reserve on Tuesday and Wednesday. It could hold one half on Tuesday ($10.68 million) and the other half on Wednesday or any combination that adds up to $21.36 million. This number is found as follows:

$$\frac{\$108 \text{ million} + X}{14 \text{ days}} = \$9.24 \text{ million}$$

where X is the amount of reserves FNB must hold on deposit with the Federal Reserve on Tuesday and Wednesday. Solving for X we get

$$X = (9.24 \times 14) - 108 = \$21.36 \text{ million}$$

Completion Questions

1. intermediaries/liabilities/assets/loans/securities/state/local
2. demand deposits/time deposits/large-size negotiable CDs
3. mortgage/business/consumer
4. time/demand/passbook/negotiable CDs
5. cash assets/securities/loans

6. cash assets/U.S. government securities/total assets
7. equity capital/risk assets
8. stocks/bonds/trusts/estates/pension plans/trust department/assets
9. liabilities/liquid
10. liquidity/profitability
11. safer/less
12. interest earned on loans/interest earned on securities/service charges and fees/trust department income
13. salaries and wages/interest paid on deposits/interest paid on other borrowed funds
14. management/liquidity/buying
15. Discretionary funds management/nondiscretionary / inflows / outflows / outflow / inflow / surplus/discretionary/assets and liabilities/outflow/inflow
16. monetary and fiscal policies/federal deposit insurance protection/the Federal Reserve

True and False Questions

1. F	2. F	3. T	4. F
5. T	6. T	7. T	8. F
9. T	10. T	11. F	12. T
13. F	14. T	15. T	16. T
17. F	18. T	19. T	20. T
21. T	22. F	23. T	24. F
25. T	26. F	27. F	28. T
29. F	30. T	31. F	32. F
33. T	34. T	35. T	36. F
37. F	38. F	39. T	40. F

Multiple-Choice Questions

1. a	2. a	3. b	4. b
5. a	6. c	7. b	8. b
9. c	10. b	11. d	12. d
13. c	14. a	15. a	16. d
17. c	18. d	19. b	20. c
21. a	22. c	23. b	24. b
25. d	26. c	27. c	28. c
29. b	30. c	31. a	32. c
33. e	34. b	35. e	

CHAPTER 9

Essay Questions

5. a. Securities brokers simply act as go-betweens. They do not purchase securities for their own account and do not issue securities. They are *not* financial intermediaries as defined in the question. Securities dealers and investment bankers are also *not* financial intermediaries. They do purchase the liabilities of ultimate borrowers, but this is usually a market-making activity. Furthermore, they do not obtain funds by selling their own liabilities to ultimate savers. Strictly speaking they are not intermediaries.

Completion Questions

1. stock companies/mutual associations
2. property and casualty insurance companies/states
3. whole life/term
4. Actuaries
5. vesting/funding
6. Employee Retirement Income Security Act/Pension Benefit Guaranty Corporation
7. Keogh Plans/Individual Retirement Accounts
8. Open-end/closed-end
9. Investment bankers/primary
10. Brokers/dealers
11. Glass-Steagall/investment/commercial
12. underwrite/trade/stock

True and False Questions

1. F	2. F	3. T	4. F
5. T	6. F	7. T	8. T
9. F	10. F	11. T	12. F
13. F	14. F	15. F	16. F
17. T	18. F	19. T	20. T

Multiple-Choice Questions

1. b	2. e	3. a	4. e
5. e	6. a	7. a	8. b
9. e	10. a	11. b	12. b
13. d	14. a	15. b	16. d
17. c	18. b	19. c	20. d
21. c	22. a	23. d	

CHAPTER 10

Essay Questions and Problems

Completion Questions

1. Edge Act Corporations
2. Edge Act / in the United States / McFadden Act's/branching
3. Eurodollar/outside the United States

4. dollar/an American bank/a foreign bank/U.S. dollars
5. shell/the United States
6. Eurobond
7. branches/subsidiaries/agencies/representative offices
8. in the United States/International Banking Act
9. market/currency/central bank

True and False Questions

1. F	2. F	3. F	4. T
5. F	6. T	7. T	8. T
9. F	10. F	11. T	12. F
13. F	14. F	15. T	16. T
17. F	18. F	19. T	20. T
21. T			

Multiple-Choice Questions

1. b	2. e	3. c	4. b
5. e	6. d	7. b	8. e
9. a	10. c	11. a	12. c
13. d	14. c	15. e	16. a
17. d	18. a	19. c	20. b

CHAPTER 11

Essay Questions and Problems

2. a. The return on the zero-coupon bond (Bond A) is 10 percent. We have (see Chapter 5):

$$1,000 = \frac{1,210}{(1 + r_A)^2}$$

and hence $(1 + r_A)^2 = 1,210/1,000 = 1.210$, which implies that $1 + r_A = \sqrt{1.210} = 1.10$, yielding $r_A = 10$ percent.

b. The return on the 10 percent coupon bond (Bond B) is also 10 percent. The first $100 of interest can be reinvested at 10 percent over the second year, to yield $110 at the end of the second year. The holder will also receive $1,100 at maturity ($100 of interest for the second year plus the $1,000 face value). In total, the holder of Bond B will end up with $1,210 ($110 + $1,100) at the end of year two. This represents a 10 percent annual return, the same as in the case of the zero-coupon bond (Bond A).

c. It is still 10 percent, since the holder gets his or her $1,210 at the end of the year two *regardless of the interest rate prevailing over year two*. The holder of the zero-coupon bond will achieve a 10 percent return no matter

what happens to the interest rate over the second year as long as he or she holds the bond until maturity to receive the promised $1,210.

d. It drops to 9.8 percent. It is less than 10 percent because the first $100 of interest can be reinvested at only 6 percent over the second year, to yield $106 at the end of the second year. The holder's total cash inflow at the end of year two will now drop to $1,206 ($106 plus $1,100) from $1,210 in the case where the interest rate over year two was 10 percent. The rate of 9.8 percent is found as follows:

$$1,000 = \frac{1,206}{(1 + r_B)^2}$$

and hence $(1 + r_B)^2 = 1,206/1,000 = 1.206$, which implies that $1 + r_B = \sqrt{1.206} = 1.098$, yielding $r_B = 9.8$ percent.

e. The zero-coupon bond (Bond A) returns 10 percent even if the rate of interest changes in the second year. This is not the case for the coupon-bearing bond (Bond B). Its return depends on the rate that will prevail in the second year.

Conclusion: The zero-coupon bond, if held to maturity, does not have any interest-rate risk, whereas the coupon-bearing bond, even if held to maturity, has some interest-rate risk because of the uncertainty surrounding the rate at which the first $100 coupon will be reinvested over the second year.

f. The zero-coupon bond still yields 10 percent. The coupon-bearing bond, however, now yields 10.23 percent, since total cash inflow at the end of year two is $1,215 ($115 + $1,100) and hence:

$$1,000 = \frac{1,215}{(1 + r'_B)^2}$$

yielding a value of $r'_B = 10.23$ percent.

Completion Questions

1. money market mutual funds
2. futures/options
3. money market deposit accounts *or* NOW accounts
4. governmental regulation/mutual funds/Regulation Q
5. Governmental National Mortgage Association (Ginnie Mae)/Department of Housing and Urban Development (HUD)/liquidity
6. IRAs/Keogh Accounts/voluntary
7. deductible/deferred/taxation

8. safety/flexibility
9. small/nonbank banks
10. automated teller/credit

True and False Questions

1. T	2. F	3. F	4. F
5. T	6. F	7. F	8. T
9. F	10. T	11. T	

Multiple-Choice Questions

1. b	2. d	3. b	4. d
5. a	6. e	7. a	8. e
9. d	10. c	11. d	12. d
13. d			

CHAPTER 12

Completion Questions

1. barter
2. bank/transfer (or shift)
3. correspondent balances
4. Fed Wire
5. CHIPS/international
6. credit cards/automated teller
7. point of sale (POS) terminals/checkout counters

True and False Questions

1. F	2. T	3. T	4. T
5. T	6. T	7. F	8. F
9. T	10. F	11. T	12. T

Multiple-Choice Questions

1. d	2. e	3. c	4. a
5. b	6. d	7. a	8. a
9. b	10. d	11. c	12. d

CHAPTER 13

Completion Questions

1. Federal Reserve
2. The chairman of the Board of Governors of the Federal Reserve System
3. Congress/1913
4. Board of Governors/regional Federal Reserve banks/member banks
5. Federal Open Market Committee
6. Board of Governors/president/Senate

7. Bank/bank directors
8. director / Bank / member banks / the Board of Governors
9. Board of Governors/Federal Reserve System/reserve requirements/discount rate/open market operations
10. Semi-independent/President/Congress
11. independent/lower

True and False Questions

1. F	2. T	3. F	4. T
5. T	6. T	7. F	8. F
9. T	10. F	11. F	12. F
13. F	14. T	15. F	16. F
17. F	18. T	19. F	20. F
21. F	22. F	23. F	24. T
25. F	26. F	27. F	28. F

Multiple-Choice Questions

1. b	2. a	3. c	4. d
5. e	6. b	7. e	8. a
9. d	10. d	11. b	12. e
13. c	14. b	15. b	16. b
17. a	18. a	19. a	20. b

CHAPTER 14

Essay Questions and Problems

2. c. See the solution to problem 14, Chapter 15 for the exhaustive list of all the alternatives available to an individual bank with a reserve deficiency. If we consider the banking system as a whole with a deficiency, then the elimination of this deficiency will be possible only if alternatives (1), (2), (3), (4), (5), and (7) are used.
Note: Alternative (8) can also be used. But this implies that the banking system as a whole will be able to sell stocks (equity capital) to the public by an amount equal to $50 million.

3. In the form of deposits at the Federal Reserve bank, reserves perform two functions: (1) they are a device used to facilitate the collection of checks among banks, and (2) they are a means available to the Federal Reserve to control the expansion and contraction of deposits (money) by banks, since banks would create deposits when they have excess reserves or destroy deposits when they have a reserve deficiency. In the form of vault cash, reserves are simply a source of liquidity with which banks can meet cash withdrawals by their depositors.

4. A reserve deficiency automatically leads to a deposit contraction, because banks must meet their reserve requirements. When banks have excess reserves, they do meet their reserve requirements. There is no penalty for holding excess reserves, and banks may therefore hold idle unused excess reserves. The implication of this asymmetrical behavior is that the Federal Reserve can implement a tight monetary policy (contraction in deposits) much more easily than an easy monetary policy (expansion in deposits).

5. To avoid double counting of deposits. If "cash items in process of collection" were not subtracted from total demand deposits outstanding, a $100 check deposited for collection would be counted as part of the money supply in addition to the deposit against which the check is drawn. This would "artificially" increase the money supply by $100 just because a $100 check is in the process of being collected.

6. The two differences are: (1) a reserve deficiency *must* cause a deposit contraction, but the existence of excess reserves *may* cause a deposit expansion (see the answer to question 4); and (2) a deposit contraction can conceivably take place in a single bank, but a deposit expansion involves a large number of banks, since an individual bank cannot lend or buy securities in an amount greater than its excess reserves.

7.   a. Banks buy $10 million of bonds from an insurance company:

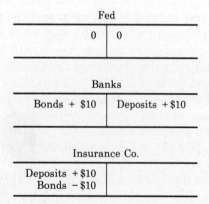

Fed	
0	0

Banks	
Bonds + $10	Deposits + $10

Insurance Co.	
Deposits + $10 Bonds − $10	

Note that $10 million of deposits are created in the process.

   b. Banks borrow $1 million from the Federal Reserve:

Fed	
Loans to banks + $1	Bank deposits + $1

Banks	
Reserves + $1	Debt to Fed + $1

Nonbank Public	
0	0

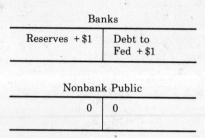

c. Mr. Williams deposits $100 at his commercial bank:

Fed	
0	0

Banks	
Reserves + $100	Deposits + $100

Mr. Williams	
Currency − $100 Deposits + $100	

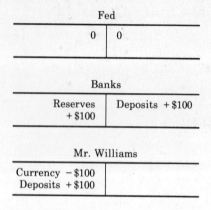

d. Mrs. Vega borrows $1,000 from her commercial bank:

Fed	
0	0

Banks	
Loan + $1,000	Deposits + $1000

Mrs. Vega	
Deposits + $1,000	Debt to bank + $1,000

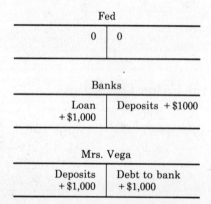

Note that $1,000 of deposits are created in the process.

e. Banks pay back a $1 million loan to the Federal Reserve:

Fed	
Loans to banks − $1	Bank deposits − $1

Banks	
Reserves − $1	Debt to Fed − $1

Nonbank Public	
0	0

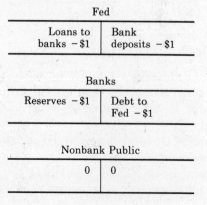

f. Mr. Chin writes a $20 check to Mr. Williams as a loan:

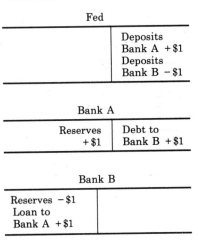

Banks	
	Deposits −$20
	Deposits +$20

Mr. Chin	
Deposits −$20	
Loan to Mr. Williams +$20	

Mr. Williams	
Deposits +$20	Debt to Mr. Chin +$20

g. Fed credits bank A by $1 million and debits bank B by $1 million as a result of a $1 million loan extended by bank B to bank A.

Fed	
	Deposits Bank A +$1
	Deposits Bank B −$1

Bank A	
Reserves +$1	Debt to Bank B +$1

Bank B	
Reserves −$1	
Loan to Bank A +$1	

h. An individual withdraws $100 in currency from his passbook savings account at his mutual savings bank:

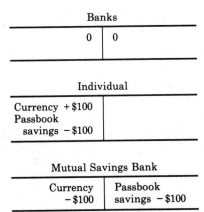

Banks	
0	0

Individual	
Currency +$100	
Passbook savings −$100	

Mutual Savings Bank	
Currency −$100	Passbook savings −$100

The balance sheet of the Federal Reserve is not affected.

i. A corporation writes a $20 million check to buy stocks issued by a newly founded bank:

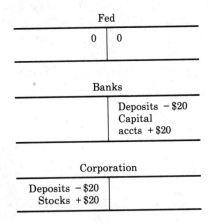

Fed	
0	0

Banks	
	Deposits −$20
	Capital accts +$20

Corporation	
Deposits −$20	
Stocks +$20	

j. A bank buys a $2 million building from a savings and loan association.

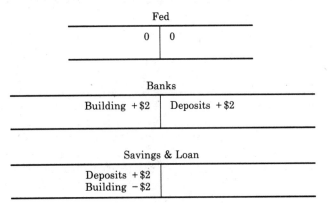

Fed	
0	0

Banks	
Building +$2	Deposits +$2

Savings & Loan	
Deposits +$2	
Building −$2	

Note that thrift institutions such as savings and loan associations hold deposits with commercial banks. In this respect they are not different from other members of the non-bank public.

8. a. (1) From City Bank to Federal Reserve Bank of New York and from Federal Reserve Bank of New York to Upstate Bank.

   (2) On the City Bank's balance sheet, reserves increase by $100 and A. Jones's deposit increases by $100. On the Federal Reserve Bank of New York's balance sheet, Upstate Bank's deposits increase by $100 and City Bank's deposits decrease by $100. On the Upstate Bank's balance sheet, reserves decrease by $100 and B. Jones's deposits decrease by $100.

   (3) The City Bank's balance sheet would have shown a decrease in cash by $100, accompanied by a decrease in A. Jones's deposit by $100, and the process would have stopped there.

b. (1) $612,000
   (2) $188,000
   (3) On the asset side of the Local National Bank's balance sheet, the "loans" item will increase by $75,000 and on the liability side the "demand deposits" item will increase by $75,000.
   (4) Reserves decrease by $75,000. Demand deposits decrease by $75,000.

b. (5)

Local National Bank

Assets		Liabilities & Capital Stock	
Reserves	$ 725,000	Demand deposits	$3,060,000
Gov't securities	1,100,000	Capital stock & surplus	440,000
Other securities	300,000		
Loans	1,375,000		
	$3,500,000		$3,500,000

   (6) The bank would lose reserves of $940,000. An individual bank cannot safely lend or buy securities in an amount greater than its excess reserves.
   (7) $188,000, the volume of excess reserves it has available.

c. (1) $200,000

Bank A (1)

Reserves	+ $200,000		
Gov't securities	− $200,000		

(2)

Bank A (2)

Loans	+ $200,000	Demand deposits	+ $200,000

(3)

Bank A (3)

Reserves	− $200,000	Demand deposits	− $200,000

Bank B (1)

Reserves	+ $200,000	Demand deposits	+ $200,000

(4) $160,000

(5)

Bank B (2)

Loans	+ $160,000	Demand deposits	+ $160,000

Bank B (3)

Reserves	− $160,000	Demand deposits	− $160,000

Bank C (1)		Bank D (1)	
Reserves + $160,000	Demand deposits + $160,000	Reserves + $128,000	Demand deposits + $160,000

Bank C (2)		Bank D (2)	
Loans + $128,000	Demand deposits + $128,000	Loans + $102,400	Demand deposits + $102,400

Bank C (3)		Bank D (3)	
Reserves − $128,000	Demand deposits − $128,000	Reserves − $102,400	Demand deposits − $102,400

(6) *Increase in Demand Deposits*

Bank A:	$200,000
Bank B:	160,000
Bank C:	128,000
Bank D:	102,400
Bank E:	81,920
Bank F:	65,536
Bank G:	52,429
Bank H:	41,943
Bank I:	33,554
Bank J:	26,843
Total	$892,625

(7) 1,000,000

(8) $DD = (1/r_{dd}) \times$ (excess reserves)
$DD = (5) \times (\$200,000) = \$1,000,000$

(9) With $r_{dd} = 25$ percent, the deposit multiplier (reciprocal of the reserve requirement ratio) is 4 instead of 5 and additional demand deposits would be $800,000. With $r_{dd} = 10$ percent, additional demand deposits would be $2,000,000.

(10) Demand deposits are considered money because they are a generally accepted means of payment. The banking system creates money by extending loans to the public and/or by buying bonds from the public.

(11) The final conclusion would be the same. Total excess reserves supplied to the banking system would still be $200,000.

9. a. The balance sheet of the banking system in billions of dollars is

Assets		Liabilities	
Total reserves	$ 20	Demand deposits	$100
Loans & securities	80		
Total assets	$100	Total liabilities	$100

b. Required reserves are equal to total reserves, since the banking system is in equilibrium (loaned up); that is, required reserves equal $20 million.

c. The reserve requirement ratio (r_{dd}) is the percentage of demand deposits the banking system must hold as required reserves. It is equal to the ratio of required reserves to demand deposits outstanding. We have $r_{dd} = (20/100) = 0.2 = 20$ percent. The deposit multiplier is equal to the reciprocal of the reserve requirement ratio, that is, $(1/20) = 5$.

d. (1) There is no initial change in the size of the money supply, just an equal exchange of currency for demand deposits. The bank has an additional $1 billion in cash (reserves) and $1 billion in new deposits.

(2) Total reserves are up by $1 billion, the amount deposited by the public, since cash in the vaults of banks is counted as part of their reserves. Thus total reserves are now $21 billion. Required reserves will increase by 20 percent of $1 billion, or $.2 billion. Total required reserves are now equal to $20.2 billion.

(3) Banks now have total reserves of $21 billion and required reserves of $20.2 billion. The difference is excess reserves of $.8 billion that can be used to expand deposits by five times (the deposit multiplier) the volume of excess reserves. We have: Additional deposits = (5) × (.8) = $4 billion. To each additional deposit corresponds a dollar of additional loan. This is how the deposits came into being in the first place, that is, through loan extension. Thus $4 billion of additional loans are extended by banks.

(4) The same as in answer 3, since banks can use their excess reserves either to extend loans or to purchase bonds from the public. The answer is $4 billion.

(5) The money supply increases by $4 billion. Recall that the initial effect was zero.

(6) The balance sheet in billions of dollars is now

Assets		Liabilities	
Total reserves	$ 21	Demand deposits	$105
Loans & securities	84		
Total assets	$105	Total liabilities	$105

Note that original deposits were $100 billion. To this we add the initial cash deposit of $1 billion and the subsequent $4 billion of created deposits resulting from loan extension and/or bond purchase. The grand total is $105 billion.

10. a. No change in M1.

b. The reserve deficiency created by the cash withdrawal is equal to $.75 billion. It is not equal to the amount withdrawn. This is so because the $1 billion withdrawal has reduced demand deposits by $1 billion. This reduction in demand deposits automatically reduces the volume of required reserves banks must hold. By how much do required reserves decrease? You must first figure out the value of the reserve requirement ratio. It is 25 percent, since the banking system is in equilibrium (loaned up) with $1,000 billion in deposits and $250 billion in reserves. With a 25 percent reserve requirement ratio, required reserves will decrease by $.25 billion as a result of the reduction in demand deposits by $1 billion. Now if required reserves decrease by $.25 billion, the deficiency created by the $1 billion cash withdrawal is only $.75 billion (1 billion minus $.25 billion) and not $1 billion.

c. The deposit multiplier is equal to 4 (the reciprocal of the reserve requirement ratio of 25 percent). Thus loans must contract by 4 times the reserve deficiency of $.75 billion, which is equal to $3 billion. The balance sheet of the BS in billions of dollars is

Assets		Liabilities	
Total reserves	$249	Demand deposits	$996
Loans & securities	747		
Total assets	$996	Total liabilities	$996

d. The final effect of the cash withdrawal on M1 is a decrease of $3 billion.

11. a. Total reserves of banks in group A = $25 billion.
Total reserves of banks in group B = $30 billion.
Loans and securities outstanding for group A = $75 billion.
Loans and securities outstanding for group B = $170 billion.

b. Yes, the merger will affect the money supply, because the merged banks will end up with a reserve deficiency under the new 20 percent reserve requirement ratio. To see this, note that the combined demand deposits are $300 billion and the combined total reserves are $55 billion. The required reserves with a 20 percent reserve requirement ratio are 20 percent of $300 billion, which equals $60 billion. Since the combined available reserves are only $55 billion, there is a reserve deficiency of $5 billion. With a deposit multiplier of 5 (the reciprocal of 20 percent), the merged banks will have to contract deposits (the money supply) by 5 times the $5 billion, which equals $25 billion. The money supply must be reduced by $25 billion in order for the merged banks to be in a position where they are in equilibrium (loaned up).

12. a. No, because required reserves are $20 billion, and actual reserves held are $19 billion. There is a $1 billion reserve deficiency.

b. Borrowing $1 billion from the Federal Reserve will bring the banking system to a position where it is in equilibrium. This transaction has no effect on deposits outstanding or on the money supply.

c. The deposit multiplier is 10, and hence $10 billion of bonds should be sold. The money supply will decrease by $10 billion as a result of this sale.

13. a. The multiplier would become less powerful because of leakages.

b. The Federal Reserve's control over the money supply is not as tight as in the case of the simple multiplier, because the leakages cannot be controlled by the Fed. They are determined by the behavior of the public. They are not set by the Federal Reserve. The Fed sets only reserve requirement ratios.

14. One reason is that the bank may want to have excess reserves available in case a good loan opportunity appears in the near future. The bank would have to turn it down if it had no excess reserves. It should be pointed out, however, that large banks usually do not turn down good loan opportunities for lack of excess reserves. They will most likely extend the loan and then go out and get the needed reserves to back the loan.

15. a. The monetary base equals total bank reserves plus currency in the hands of the nonbank public.

b. No. There is simply an exchange of one component of the monetary base (currency) for another component of the monetary base (reserves). This leaves the size of the monetary base unaffected.

c. No. A currency withdrawal from thrift institutions, for example, simply changes the ownership of the amount of the currency involved. Instead of being an asset to the thrift institution it becomes an asset to the public. Same for a deposit of currency.

d. Because the Fed cannot fully control bank reserves, since actions of the public affect bank reserves. The Fed can, however, better control the size of the monetary base, which is the sum of bank reserves and currency in the hands of the nonbank public.

16. a. Since the banking system is initially loaned up, the size of the reserve deficiency created by the loan repayment is equal to $200 million.

b. The deposit multiplier is equal to the inverse of the sum of the reserve requirement against demand deposits (0.14) plus the ratio of time deposits to demand deposits multiplied by the reserve requirement against time deposits (1.5 × .04 = .06) plus the ratio of currency to demand deposits (0.3), which add up to 0.5. The inverse of 0.5 is equal to 2, the value of the deposit multiplier.

c. The banking system will have to shrink demand deposits by an amount equal to the deposit multiplier times the initial reserve deficiency, that is, $400 million.

d. As demand deposits contract, the public deposits currency in the banking system (cash inflows for banks) in order to maintain the value of the ratio of currency to demand deposits constant. Since this ratio is .30, the public will deposit 0.30 × $400 million, that is, $120 million in currency into the banking system. Note that the opposite of a currency withdrawal (cash drain for banks) is occurring.

e. The money supply decreases by $520 million, the sum of $400 million of demand deposits contracted and $120 million of currency deposits at banks.

f. As demand deposits contract, the public transfers deposits out of time deposits and into demand deposits in order to maintain the value of the ratio of savings deposits to demand deposits constant. Since this ratio is 1.50, the public will reduce its holding of time deposits by 1.50 × $400, that is, $600 million. Note that the opposite of a transfer from demand to time deposits is taking place here.

g. From the balance sheet identity we know that the total decrease in assets must equal the total decrease in liabilities. Total decrease in liabilities equals $1,200 million, the sum of the loan repayment to the Fed ($200 million) and the contraction in both demand and time deposits ($1,000 million). Total decrease in assets equals the sum of the net decrease in total reserve by $80 million ($200 million due to the repayment of the loan minus $120 million of currency inflow) plus the dollar value of the bonds sold to the public (BONDS). We have:

$80 million + BONDS = $1,200 million and therefore BONDS = $1,120 million, which is the value of the bonds sold by the banking system to the pubic in order to return to a position in which it is loaned up.

h. From (g) it follows that the change in the balance sheet of the banking system is

Note that reserves drop by $80 million, an amount equal to the reduction in required reserves ($56 million reduction against demand deposits and $24 million reduction against time deposits), indicating that the banking system is back to a position in which it is loaned up.

17.

$$\text{Demand deposit multiplier} = \frac{1}{0.1 + 0.2 + 4(.05)} = 2$$

$$\text{M1 multiplier} = \frac{1 + 0.2}{0.1 + 0.2 + 4(.05)} = 2.4$$

Completion Questions

1. liabilities / commercial banks / assets / the nonbank public
2. liabilities/Federal Reserve Banks/assets/commercial banks
3. reserves/vault cash/deposits with their Federal Reserve Bank
4. gains / reserves / amount of the check / loses / reserves/amount of the check
5. total reserves held/required reserves
6. reserves/Federal Reserve/money
7. demand/multiple/reserves
8. the reciprocal of the reserve requirement ratio
9. collection/clearing
10. the amount of its excess reserves
11. base/total bank reserves/currency outside banks
12. currency withdrawals or deposits/transfers of funds between demand deposits and time and savings deposits/bank holdings of idle excess reserves/decrease/simple deposit

True and False Questions

1. F	2. F	3. T	4. T
5. T	6. T	7. F	8. F
9. T	10. T	11. T	12. F
13. F	14. T	15. T	16. F
17. F	18. F	19. T	20. T
21. T	22. F	23. T	24. T
25. F	26. T	27. F	28. F
29. F	30. F	31. F	32. F

Assets		Liabilities	
Decrease in total reserves	$ −200	Debt to the Fed	$−200
Currency inflow	+120	Decrease in demand deposits	−400
Net decrease in reserves	−80	Decrease in time deposits	−600
Decrease in value of bonds	−1,120		
Total decrease in assets	$ 1,100	Total decrease in liabilities	$1,100

33. F	34. F	35. F	36. F
37. T	38. F	39. F	40. T
41. F	42. F	43. T	44. T
45. T	46. F	47. F	48. T
49. T	50. F		

Multiple-Choice Questions

1. b	2. c	3. d	4. b
5. e	6. b	7. a	8. d
9. a	10. d	11. c	12. d
13. d	14. a	15. c	16. c
17. a	18. b	19. a	20. b
21. d	22. c	23. b	24. e
25. e	26. b	27. c	28. a
29. b	30. b	31. b	32. c

CHAPTER 15

Essay Questions and Problems

7. c. (1) No. In a country without financial markets there will be no lending and borrowing by means of issuing securities. There will be no government securities to buy and sell, and thus no open market operations could take place. Note that the existence of government securities may not be enough to enable the central bank to conduct its open market operations. These securities must also be traded actively in the financial markets for open market operations to be possible. If securities are held by the public until they are paid back by the government (the borrower), then open market operations in government securities cannot be undertaken by the central bank.

   (2) Yes. In principle the central bank can buy (and sell) any securities it wants. The effect on bank reserves and the money supply would be the same as if the central bank had purchased (or sold) government securities. The central bank in the United States trades exclusively in government securities.

   (3) Yes. There is always a price at which the Federal Reserve can buy or sell government securities if the Fed wants to trade.

8. a. The money supply decreases by only $400 million, the value of bonds purchased by insurance companies. This is so because the insurance companies are part of the nonbank public. They pay for the bonds by reducing

their demand deposits (DD) at commercial banks by $400 million. Unlike insurance companies, commercial banks pay the Fed for the bonds they purchase with reserves, and therefore the transaction involving commercial banks does not immediately affect the money supply. Note: *The money supply always decreases by the amount of the securities sold to the nonbank public.* In terms of T-accounts we have, in millions of dollars,

Federal Reserve

Bonds − $500	Bank Deposits − $500

Commercial Banks

Reserves − $100	
Bonds + $100	
Reserves − $400	DD − $400

Insurance Companies

DD − $400	
Bonds + $400	

b. Banks' total reserves decrease by the full $500 million, $100 billion as a result of their purchase of $100 billion worth of bonds from the Fed (see upper entries on T-account of commercial banks) and $400 million after the checks written by the insurance companies clear through the Fed (see lower entries on T-account of commercial banks). Note: *It does not matter who buys the bonds. Reserves will decrease by the total amount of securities sold by the Fed.* Banks' required reserves decrease by $80 million because the reserve requirement is 20 percent, so required reserves will decrease by an amount equal to 20 percent of $400 million, which is the volume of demand deposits commercial banks have lost. In other words, $400 million of demand deposits were destroyed when insurance companies paid for the bonds, and required reserves were reduced by 20 percent of $400 million, which equals $80 million.

c. Commercial banks must borrow from the Fed an amount equal to their reserve deficiency, which is equal to $320 million. This is found by observing that total reserves dropped by $500 million, but since required reserves were reduced by $80 million, this produced a deficiency in reserves of only $420 million. Recalling that the banking system had $100 million in excess reserves to begin with, the net deficiency in reserves is equal to $320 million.

d. Banks' portfolio of loans should be reduced by $1,600 million, since the deposit multiplier is equal to 5 ($\frac{1}{0.2}$) and the deficiency is $320 million, implying that loans worth 5 × $320 million must be called in.

e. The money supply decreases by an amount equal to the volume of demand deposits destroyed as a result of the reduction in the banks' portfolio of loans, that is, a decrease of $1,600 million.

f. The total effect is a decrease in the money supply by $400 million plus $1,600 million, that is, $2,000 million.

g. Changes in the balance sheet (in millions of dollars) are reported below:

COMMERCIAL BANKING SYSTEM
(in millions of dollars)

Assets			Liabilities		
Reserves		− $500	Demand Deposits		− $2,000
Required	− 80		Initial	− 400	
Deficiency	− 420		Additional	− 1,600	
Original Excess	+ 100				
Net Deficiency	− 320				
Bonds		+ 100			
Loans		− 1,600			
Total		($2,000)	Total		($2,000)

9. a. The money supply decreases by $400 million.

b. Bank reserves decrease by $500 million. Required reserves decrease by $80 million.

c. Borrowing of $420 million.

d. Loans should be reduced by $2,100 million.

e. The money supply decreases by $2,100 million.

f. The total effect on the money supply is a decrease of $2,500 million.

g. Changes in the balance sheet:

COMMERCIAL BANKING SYSTEM
(in millions of dollars)

Reserves	− $500	Demand	
Bonds	+ 100	deposits	− $2,500
Loans	− 2,100		
Total	($2,500)	Total	($2,500)

10. a. The money supply increases by $300 million.

b. Bank reserves increase by $500 million. Required reserves increase by $60 million.

c. No borrowing is needed in this case, since the banking system has excess reserves of $440 million, not a deficiency.

d. Loans should be increased by $2,200 million.

e. The money supply increases by $2,200 million.

f. The total effect on the money supply is an increase of $2,500 million.

g. Changes in the balance sheet:

COMMERCIAL BANKING SYSTEM
(in millions of dollars)

Reserves	+ $500	Demand	
Bonds	− 200	deposits	+ $2,500
Loans	+ 2,200		
Total	($2,500)	Total	($2,500)

11. a. The individual bank with a deficiency of $10 million (reserve requirement ratio = 20 percent)—and all other banks in the system in equilibrium (loaned up)—can take any of the following actions to eliminate its deficiency:

(1) Borrow $10 million from its Federal Reserve bank. We have

Reserves	+ $10	Debt to Fed	+ $10

(2) Call in $50 million in loans outstanding (recall that the multiplier is 5 and therefore $50 million of loans off the books means $50 million of deposits off the books which, in turn, means $10 million of required reserves are not needed anymore and can be used to cover the deficiency). We have

Loans	− $50	Demand deposits	− $50

Note that total reserves do not change. What happens is that $10 million of reserves are transferred from the required category to the excess category and then used to eliminate the deficiency.

(3) Sell $10 million worth of bonds to the Federal Reserve (assuming the Fed is buying). We have

Reserves	+ $10		
Bonds	− 10		

(4) Sell $50 million worth of bonds to its own depositors. This is similar to alternative (2). We have

Bonds	− $50	Demand deposits	− $50

Note that $50 million of bond sales are required in this case, instead of $10 million in alternative (3) when the sale is to the Fed. Alternative (4) means that all of the deposit contraction has taken place in the individual bank.

(5) Sell $10 million worth of bonds to depositors of other banks. In this case the bank gains $10 million of reserves, but other banks in the system have lost $10 million of reserves.

Reserves	+ $10
Bonds	− 10

Note that this alternative is similar to (3), although no additional reserves have been created here. When the Fed buys $10 million of bonds, additional reserves are created.

(6) Attract $12.5 million in new deposits from other banks. If our bank can attract $12.5 million in new deposits, it can eliminate its $10 million deficiency. This is so because $12.5 million of additional deposits will bring $12.5 million of additional reserves, $10 million to cover the deficiency, and $2.5 million as required reserves against the new $12.5 million of deposits (20 percent of $12.5 million = 2.5 million).

Reserves	+ $12.5	Demand deposits	+ $12.5

Note that in this case the $10 million deficiency has been transferred to another bank in the system.

(7) Sell $50 million of its own stock (capital accounts) to its own depositors. In this case $50 million are transferred from the demand deposit category, against which required reserves must be held, to the capital accounts, against which banks do not have to hold required reserves. This will release $10 million of required reserves to cover the deficiency.

	Demand deposits	− $50
	Capital accounts (stock)	+ 50

(8) Sell $10 million of its own stock (capital accounts) to depositors of other banks. This is similar to alternative (6) except that no additional required reserves (beyond the $10 million) are necessary in this case.

Reserves	+ $10	Capital accounts (stocks)	+ $10

Concluding remarks:
Alternatives (5), (6), and (8) will only shift the deficiency from one bank to another. Only alternatives (1) and (3) create new reserves that did not exist before, because they involve the Fed and only the Fed can create reserves. With alternatives (2), (4), and (7) the entire contraction takes place within the individual bank and does not involve other banks.

b. There exists one other possible source of reserves that this individual bank could have used to eliminate its deficiency. It could have borrowed $10 million of reserves from a bank with excess reserves. This possibility, however, is not available in this case, because we said that all other banks in the system are in equilibrium (loaned up).

12. d. Government securities, usually Treasury bills. No. See the answer to question 10 c (2) in this chapter.

f. No. See the answer to question 10 c (3) in this chapter.

Completion Questions

1. changes in the value of the reserve requirement ratios/changes in the discount rate/open market sales and purchases of government securities
2. discount/Federal Reserve/reserves/lending/depository institutions/Federal Reserve/discount rate
3. discount/initiative/Federal Reserve
4. Open market/buying/selling/Federal Reserve/alter the volume of bank reserves
5. reserve requirements/monetary control
6. zero
7. Banking Act/Garn–St. Germain Depository Institutions Act/all depository institutions/demand
8. lender/last resort
9. financial panics
10. announcement effect
11. follow/lead
12. prime rate
13. account manager/open market/monetary policy/Federal Open Market Committee/Washington
14. open market/trading/New York
15. open market/account/Board of Governors/Federal Reserve bank
16. the federal funds rate
17. federal funds

18. Repurchase agreements/a temporary/reverse repurchase agreements/a temporary/sale
19. matched sale-purchase agreements

True and False Questions

1. F	2. T	3. F	4. T
5. F	6. F	7. F	8. F
9. T	10. F	11. F	12. T
13. T	14. T	15. F	16. F
17. F	18. F	19. T	20. F
21. F	22. F	23. F	24. T
25. T	26. T	27. F	28. T
29. F	30. T	31. F	32. T
33. T	34. F	35. F	36. F
37. T	38. T	39. F	40. F
41. F	42. F	43. F	44. F
45. F	46. T	47. T	48. F
49. F	50. T	51. T	52. F

Multiple-Choice Questions

1. e	2. f	3. e	4. b
5. b	6. b	7. d	8. b
9. b	10. c	11. b	12. e
13. d	14. b	15. c	16. e
17. c	18. e	19. b	20. d
21. c	22. d	23. c	24. c
25. b	26. d	27. b	28. a
29. b	30. a	31. b	32. f
33. b	34. a	35. e	36. c
37. d	38. b	39. d	40. c
41. b	42. c		

CHAPTER 16

Essay Questions and Problems

1. a. Item 1 is a liability; item 2 is an asset; item 3 is an asset; item 4 is a liability; item 5 is a liability; item 6 is a liability; item 7 is an asset; item 8 is an asset; item 9 is a liability; item 10 is a liability; and item 11 is an asset. Refer to the textbook for a definition of these terms.
   b. Member bank deposits equal 50. We have the identity:

Member bank deposits = [gold certificates (20) + cash (1) + U.S. government and agency securities (155) + loans to member banks (4) + cash items in process of collection (20)] minus [Federal Reserve notes outstanding (120) + Treasury deposits (10) + foreign deposits (5) + deferred availability cash items (10) + capital accounts (5)] = [200] − [150] = 50.

d. The value of the gold stock held by the U.S. Treasury must equal 20, because the item "gold stock" (an asset to the Treasury) is always equal to the item "gold certificates" (an asset to the Fed), since the Treasury always issues a dollar of gold certificates to the Federal Reserve for every dollar of gold it holds in order to "monetize" its gold holdings.
e. The Federal Reserve float is the difference between the item "cash items in process of collection" (which equals 20) and the item "deferred availability cash items" (which equals 10). The float is therefore equal to 10.
f. Federal Reserve credit = (U.S. government and agency securities) + (loans to member banks) + (the float). Note that the two first items are Fed assets and the third is the difference between a Fed asset and a Fed liability. These three items are lumped together apart from the other items on the Fed's balance sheet, because any change in one of these three items is always accompanied by an equal change in "member bank deposits." That is, if "loans to member banks" increases then "member bank deposits" must increase by the same amount, everything else the same. The same is true for the float and U.S. government and agency securities. Note that this is not the case for "gold certificates" or "cash." An increase in these two items will first be accompanied by an equal increase in "Treasury deposits." The Federal Reserve credit is equal to 169.
g. One cannot determine bank reserves from the Fed's consolidated balance sheet because bank reserves include some Treasury currency in bank vaults for which no informa-

c.

Assets		Liabilities & Capital Accounts	
Gold certificates	$20	Federal Reserve notes outstanding	$120
Cash	1	Bank deposits	50
U.S. gov't & agency securities	155	Treasury deposits	10
Loans to member banks	4	Foreign deposits	5
Cash items in process of collection	20	Deferred availability cash items	10
		Capital accounts	5
Total assets	$200	Total liabilities & cap. accts.	$200

tion is given in the Fed's consolidated balance sheet.

2. a. *Currency in circulation* consists of coins and paper dollars in the hands of the nonbank public—that is, outside the Treasury, the Fed, and banks.

   Currency in bank vaults consists of coins and paper dollars held by banks in their vaults.

   Treasury cash consists of Treasury currency (coins and paper dollars) held by the Treasury.

   Treasury currency outstanding is the sum of all currency issued by the Treasury. It is equal to "Treasury cash" (Treasury currency with the Treasury) + "cash" (Treasury currency with the Fed) + Treasury currency in the vaults of member banks + Treasury currency held by the nonbank public.

   b. Bank deposits equal 50. Factors supplying reserves = 209 and factors absorbing reserves = 149 (see next answer). Thus "vault cash" (which equals 10) + "bank deposits" = (209 − 149) or 60 and "bank deposits" is therefore equal to 50.

   c. *Factors supplying reserves:*
   1. Gold stock 20
   2. Treasury currency outstanding 20
   3. Federal Reserve credit 169

   Minus factors absorbing reserves: 209
   1. Currency in circulation 127
   2. Treasury cash 2
   3. Treasury deposits 5
   4. Foreign deposits 10
   5. Capital accounts 5

   Equals bank reserves: 149
   1. Currency in bank vaults 10
   2. Bank deposits 50 60

   d. "Cash" is included in "Treasury currency outstanding" (see answer to question a) and "Federal Reserve notes outstanding" is included in "currency in circulation."

   e. The bank reserve equation provides an exhaustive list of the factors that affect bank reserves. By comparing the bank reserve equation at, say, the end of one week with the equation a week later, one can obtain a summary of the factors that have increased or decreased bank reserves over the week.

   f. Currency in circulation is the difference between all currency outstanding and currency held by the Treasury, the Fed, and deposit institutions. Currency in circulation = (Treasury currency outstanding + Federal Reserve notes outstanding) − (Treasury currency) − (cash) − (Treasury currency held by banks) − (Federal Reserve notes held by banks). The sum of the last two items is equal to "currency in bank vaults." Thus 127 = (20) + (120) − (2) − (1) − (currency in bank vaults) and therefore, "currency in bank vaults" must equal (137) − (127) = 10.

   g. The monetary base is the sum of "currency in circulation" plus "bank reserves." It is equal to 187 = (127 + 60) at the end of the year 19XX.

3. a.

Treasury's Balance Sheet			
Gold stock	− $50	Gold certificates	− $50

b.

Fed's Balance Sheet			
Gold certificates	− $50	Member bank deposits	− $50

c.

Banks' Balance Sheet			
Reserves	− $50	Demand deposits	− $50

d.

U.S. Public's Balance Sheet			
Demand deposits	− $50		
Gold	+ 50		

e. The money supply decreases by $50 million (see the liability side of banks' balance sheet).

f. The reserve deficiency created by the transactions described in answers a–d is equal to $40 million, since total reserves decrease by $50 million and required reserves decrease by $10 million (20 percent of $50 million). The deposit multiplier equals 5 (the reciprocal of 20 percent); therefore demand deposits will have to contract further by 5 times $40 million, which equals $200 million. Conclusion: The money supply initially decreases by $50 million and further contracts by $200 million. The total change in the money supply of a $50 million sale of gold by the U.S. Treasury to the U.S. nonbank public is a decrease of $250 million, assuming the reserve requirement ratio is 20 percent.

g. The balance sheet of the U.S. Treasury shows the same changes as in (a). The Fed's balance sheet shows the following changes:

Fed's Balance Sheet			
Gold certificates	− $50	Foreign deposits	− $50

The banks' balance sheet shows no change. The U.S. public's balance sheet shows no change.
The money supply is not affected.

4. a. If the returned Federal Reserve notes are frayed or worn out, the Federal Reserve destroys them; if they are still serviceable, they are stored along with the returned coins awaiting the day when banks will want them again.

b.

Fed's Balance Sheet			
Cash	+ $5	Federal Reserve notes outstanding	− $20
		Bank deposits	+ 25

c. Bank reserves have not changed in size. Banks have simply changed the composition of their reserves. They now have $25 million of additional deposits with the Federal Reserve and $25 million less in vault cash. They have exchanged one form of reserve for another.

5. They first get into the hands of the public when the public withdraws money from commercial banks in the form of coins. Commercial banks obtain these coins from their Federal Reserve banks, which in turn get these coins from the U.S. Treasury. When the U.S. Treasury sends the $100 million worth of coins to the Federal Reserve, the Fed's balance sheet shows:

Fed's Balance Sheet			
Cash	+ $100	Treasury deposits	+ $100

When banks request these $100 million worth of coins, the Fed's and the banks' balance sheet shows:

Fed's Balance Sheet			
Cash	− $100	Bank deposits	− $100

Banks' Balance Sheet			
Deposits with Fed	− $100		
Vault cash (coins)	+ $100		

When the public withdraws money in the form of coins, the banks' balance sheets show:

Banks' Balance Sheet			
Vault cash (coins)	− $100	Demand deposits	− $100

6. a. In the following T-accounts CIPC means "cash items in process of collection"; DACI means "deferred availability cash items"; BD means "bank deposits"; DD means "demand deposits"; TR means "total reserves"; NW

means "net worth"; A as a subscript indicates Alana's bank; and B as a subscript indicates Marci's bank.

Event	Fed		Alana		Marci		Bank A		Bank B	
1	0	0	0	0	0	0	0	0	0	0
2	0	0	0	0	DD +$100	NW +$100	0	0	CIPC +$100	DD +$100
3	CIPC$_A$ +$100	DACI$_B$ +$100	0	0	0	0	0	0	0	0
4	0	0	0	0	0	0	0	0	0	0
5	0	MBD$_B$ +$100 −$100	0	0	0 0		0	0	CIPC +$100	0
6	CIPC$_A$ −$100	MBD$_A$ −$100	DD −$100	NW −$100	0	0	TR −$100	DD −$100	0	0

(1) None of the balance sheets are affected by the writing of the check itself.

(2) Marci deposits the check. Her net worth increases by $100 with a corresponding increase in her demand deposit with Bank B (her bank). Bank B credits Marci's account with $100 and sends the check for collection. While the check is being collected, Bank B increases by $100 its asset item called "cash items in process of collection."

(3) The Fed credits DACI with $100 (liability side) for Bank B (the bank that will eventually gain reserves) and simultaneously credits CIPC with $100 (asset side) for Bank A (the bank that will eventually lose reserves).

(4) None of the balance sheets are affected by the fact that the Fed mails the check to Bank A.

(5) After two days Bank B gets its reserves (BD$_B$ + 100 and DACI$_B$ − 100), but Bank A has not yet lost any reserves. We have $100 of extra reserves in the system that did not exist before.

(6) After the third day Bank A loses reserves (DB$_A$ − 100 and CIPC$_A$ − 100), and the $100 of extra reserves are destroyed. The banking system had $100 of extra reserves for only twenty-four hours in this case. Once the check has cleared, Alana's net worth decreases by $100, the amount of the birthday present she gave to Marci.

b. No. See above.

c. The float is created by event 5 and destroyed by event 6. It lasts twenty-four hours and its size is $100, the amount of the check being cleared, which is also the difference between CIPC and DACI. Refer to event 5 and add up all items from event 1 to event 5. You get CIPC = + 100 and DACI = 0 and hence float = CIPC − DACI = 100 − 0 = $100. The float cannot be negative because it takes two days or more for banks against which checks are drawn to receive these checks from the Federal Reserve.

d. An increase in the float increases bank reserves. A decrease in the float decreases bank reserves.

e. In the case at hand the float would not have existed if the Fed had debited the reserve account of the bank losing reserves (Bank A) at the same time it credited the reserve account of the bank gaining reserves (Bank B).

f. If the Fed changed the reserve account of a bank without the bank's knowledge, the bank would be unable to keep track of the exact balance on its reserve account. The system currently enforced permits banks to know exactly when they are gaining or losing reserves. The bank that sends checks for collection knows that it will gain reserves in two days. The bank against which the checks are drawn knows that it will lose reserves only when the Fed sends to the bank the checks to be collected.

g. Examples of events outside the control of the Fed that may cause an unexpected increase in the size of the float are (1) a breakdown in the Fed's computer system, (2) bad weather that would slow down the delivery of checks, or (3) a mail strike. The Federal Reserve can prevent bank reserves from rising as a result of an increase in the float simply by carrying out an open market sale of securities, which will absorb reserve from the banking system.

7. a. Bank reserves *decrease* by $325 million [− (+ 100) − (+ 25) + (− 200)].

...y $150 million [+ (+
...)].
...y $200 million [− (−
...)].
...rves is positive, a fac-
...s is negative, any in-
... any decrease is nega-
... in a factor supplying
...eserves and a decrease
... reserves will *increase*

...ns

... agency securities/gold
... SDRs)
...otes outstanding/bank

...ocess of collection/liabili-
...ty cash items
...ital accounts/liabilities/

...rves/currency in circula-

...nd agency securities/loans
...at/assets/Federal Reserve
...ties

... certificates/increase/bank
deposits,... gold stock/increase/a liabil-
ity/gold certificates
8. bank reserve equation/U.S. government and
agency securities/currency in circulation
9. defensive/offsetting undesired changes in member bank reserves/dynamic/achieving a desired
monetary policy
10. Repurchase agreements/repurchase agree-
ments/defensive
11. outright/repurchase agreements

True and False Questions

1. F	2. F	3. T	4. F
5. T	6. F	7. F	8. T
9. T	10. F	11. T	12. F
13. F	14. T	15. F	16. F
17. T	18. F	19. F	20. T
21. T	22. F	23. F	

Multiple-Choice Questions

1. a	2. b	3. a	4. c
5. b	6. c	7. d	8. b
9. a	10. c	11. d	12. d
13. b	14. c	15. d	16. a
17. c	18. b	19. e	20. c
21. d	22. a	23. a	

CHAPTER 17

Essay Questions and Problems

3. Suppose that the Federal Reserve chooses the
federal funds rate as its operating target and
wishes to keep the rate at 8 percent. If the rate
falls below 8 percent, this means that the demand for federal funds is weak relative to the
available supply. In order to push the rate back
to 8 percent, the Fed steps in and absorbs reserves through open market sales of securities.
Reserves become relatively scarcer, and the federal funds rate moves up. If the rate rises above
8 percent, the Fed will have to supply reserves
through open market purchases of securities.
Reserves become relatively more abundant, and
the federal funds rate moves down. The point is
that while the Fed is successfully maintaining
the federal funds rate at 8 percent, it has lost
control over the volume of reserves. The Fed
cannot simultaneously control the federal funds
rate and the volume of reserves because it uses
the latter to control the former. A similar reasoning will show that if the volume of reserves is
chosen as the operating target, the Fed loses
control over the federal funds rate.

Completion Questions

1. monetary/FOMC directive
2. FOMC/aggregates/an annual/quarter/quarter/
year
3. federal funds
4. the economy's GDP/production/employment/
direct control
5. monetary/instruments/operating/intermediate
/ultimate
6. operating/bank reserves/the federal funds rate
7. Monetary aggregates/intermediate
8. operating/federal-funds-rate/reserve
9. contract/raise (or expand/lower)
10. contract/lower (or expand/raise)

True and False Questions

1. T	2. T	3. T	4. F
5. T	6. T	7. T	8. F
9. F	10. F	11. F	12. T
13. F	14. F	15. T	16. T
17. F	18. F	19. F	20. T
21. T			

Multiple-Choice Questions

1. c	2. c	3. a	4. c
5. b	6. e	7. d	8. a

9. c	10. c	11. b	12. b
13. e	14. c	15. a	16. d
17. c	18. b	19. a	20. d

CHAPTER 18

Essay Questions and Problems

1. a. The initial effects on bank reserves and the money supply are the same. The difference is that with borrowing the government will have to pay interest to the nonbank public and pay back the principal at maturity. Neither of these will happen in the case of taxation.

   b. They will be similar when banks are loaned up (zero excess reserves) and different when banks hold idle excess reserves.

   c. The answer will depend on whether the banking system is loaned up or holding idle excess reserves. If the banking system is loaned up, then bank reserves and the money supply are not affected by the fact that the public pays part of its taxes with funds borrowed from commercial banks. If the banking system holds idle excess reserves, then bank reserves are still not affected but the money supply will increase by an amount equal to the funds borrowed by the public from commercial banks to pay part of its taxes.

   The above conclusions are illustrated with the help of T-accounts. Suppose that the public borrows $100 from commercial banks to pay part of its taxes.

   (1) The commercial banking system is loaned up. Assume a reserve requirement ratio of 20 percent and hence a deposit multiplier of 5. In this case banks will have to sell bonds to the public (or call in loans) by an amount of $500 in order to release $100 of reserves that can be used to extend a $100 loan to the public. This is indicated by entry 1 in the T-account of commercial banks below. The extension of the loan is shown in entry 2. The payment of taxes by the public is shown in entry 3. When the government spends the $100, reserves increase by $100 and deposits by $500 after deposits expansion has taken place. This is indicated by entry 4 in the T-account.

Commercial Banks

1. Bonds	− $500	Demand deposits	− $500
2. Loans	+ $100	Demand deposits	+ $100
3. Reserves	− $100	Demand deposits	− $100
4. Reserves	+ $100	Demand deposits	+ $500

The net effect is no change in reserves or the money supply.

   (2) The commercial banking system has $100 of excess reserves. In this case there is no need to sell $500 of bonds to release reserves. Entry 1 in the T-account above should be ignored. Entries 2 and 3 are the same as in the case where banks had no excess reserves. The net effect of entries 2, 3, and 4 is no change in reserves (as in the previous case) and an increase in the money supply by an amount equal to the borrowing, or a multiple of the borrowing if the banking system uses its excess reserves to expand deposits.

2. Borrowing operations by the U.S. Treasury involve the sale of newly issued government bonds that did not exist before, whereas open market sales by the Federal Reserve involve selling already existing bonds that were issued by the U.S. Treasury in the past and were acquired by the Fed sometime in the past. There is no creation of additional bonds when the Fed sells. There is another fundamental difference. Borrowing by the U.S. Treasury from the nonbank public or commercial banks and the subsequent spending by the government does not affect bank reserves. Open market sales, however, reduce bank reserves by the amount of the sale. These two types of financial operations are somewhat related when the Federal Reserve purchases in the open market newly issued government bonds. In this case we are back to financing government spending by borrowing from the Federal Reserve.

3. a. The government is spending an amount smaller than the funds collected through taxation.

   b. The exact opposite effects of borrowing operations.

4. One of the differences is the same as answer 1a. The printing of currency does not involve the payment of interest and the repayment of a principal, which would be the case if there were a sale of securities to the Fed. Note, however, that the Federal Reserve usually transfers to the U.S. Treasury all interest income it receives on government bonds. The second, more important difference is that although the T-accounts of bond sales to the Federal Reserve and printing money by the Treasury are practically the same, the politics involved are not. Recall that the Federal Reserve has the option *not* to buy the bonds issued by the Treasury if it wishes to do so. If the Fed buys, new money is created and this is the same as printing money. If the Fed doesn't buy

but the public does, there is no effect on the money supply. Conclusion: The initiative lies with the Federal Reserve.

Completion Questions

1. finance/taxing the public/borrowing from the nonbank public/borrowing from banks/borrowing from the Federal Reserve/printing new money
2. sells/deficit
3. the nonbank public/banks/money supply/bank reserves/excess reserves/money supply/borrowing / bank reserves / Federal Reserve / printing money/money supply/bank reserves
4. fiscal/monetary
5. Treasury–Federal Reserve/peg
6. reserves/money/monetization of the public debt

True and False Questions

1. F	2. T	3. F	4. F
5. T	6. T	7. T	8. T
9. T	10. F	11. T	12. T
13. F	14. T	15. T	16. F
17. T	18. F	19. T	20. F
21. T			

Multiple-Choice Questions

1. b	2. c	3. a	4. b
5. a	6. d	7. c	8. d
9. b	10. b	11. d	12. a
13. b	14. e	15. c	16. a
17. a	18. c	19. b	20. a

CHAPTER 19

Essay Questions and Problems

11. a. M = \$400 billion.
   b. Y = 1,000. According to the income version of the equation of exchange, $MV = PY$ and therefore $Y = (MV)/P = (400 \times 5)/2 = 1,000$.
   c. The economy's GDP = $PY = 2 \times 1,000 = \$2,000$ billion.
   d. Real money supply = $M/P = 400/2 = \$200$ billion.
   e. $k = 1/V = 1/5 = 0.2$. Also according to the Cambridge version of the equation of exchange $M = kPY$ or $k = M/(PY) = 400/(2 \times 1,000) = 400/2,000 = 0.2$.
   f. T = 10,000. According to the transactions version of the equation of exchange, $MV = $

PT and therefore:
$T = (MV)/P = (400 \times 50)/2 = 20,000/2 = 10,000$.
T is larger than Y because it includes all transactions taking place in the economy over a given period of time, whereas Y includes only those transactions that involve the production of new goods and services over the given period of time.

12. a. The price level will increase by 0.2 to 2.2. Recall that according to the quantity theory of money an increase in the money supply raises only the price level. Since both the income velocity (V) and real output (Y) remain the same, we have: $\Delta M \times V = \Delta P \times Y$. Recall that Δ means "change in." Therefore the change in price $\Delta P = (\Delta M \times V)/Y = (40 \times 5)/1,000 = 0.2$. Alternatively, you can plug $M = 440$ in $MV = PY$ and get the corresponding value for P, which equals 2.2. Since the original price level is 2.0, the increase in the price level equals 0.2.
   b. By an amount proportionate to the increase in the money supply, since $\Delta P = 0.2$ and $\Delta M = 40$ are obviously different. The proportionality factor in $\Delta M = (Y/V) \times \Delta P$ is $(Y/V) = 200$, meaning that the increase in the money supply is 200 times larger than the increase in prices.
   c. The income velocity of money (V) is fixed, and the real output (Y) must be the full employment level of output and therefore Y is also fixed. This is why we were able to write $\Delta M \times V = \Delta P \times Y$.
   d. 10 percent, since the percentage change in the money supply equals $\Delta M/M = (40/400) = 0.1 = 10$ percent.
   e. Also 10 percent, since the percentage change in the price level equals $\Delta P/P = 0.2/2 = 0.1 = 10$ percent. Conclusion: *A given percentage change in the money supply produces the same percentage change in the price level, according to the quantity theory of money.*
   f. Real money supply = $M/P = (440/2.2) = \$200$ billion *after* the increase in the nominal money supply. It was also \$200 billion ($M/P = 400/2 = 200$) before the increase in the nominal money supply. Conclusion: *The real money supply does not change when the nominal money supply changes according to the quantity theory of money.*

13. a. GDP = $P.Y = 2 \times 1,500 = \$3,000$ billion.
   b. GDP at full employment = $P.Y_{FE} = 2 \times 1,650 = \$3,300$ billion.

c. $\Delta M = +\$50$ billion. The velocity is fixed. It is equal to 6 since $V = (GDP/M) = (3,000/500) = 6$. The desired increase in GNP is equal to $300 since $\Delta GDP = (3,300 - 3,000)$. It follows that $\Delta M = (\Delta GNP/V) = 300/6 = \$50$ billion. Alternatively, you can plug $P.Y_{FE} = 3,300$ in $MV = P.Y_{FE}$ and get the corresponding money supply at full employment, which equals $550 billion, meaning that M must increase by $50 billion.

d. $\Delta M = +\$77.5$ billion. The full employment GNP with a price level of 2.1 (2.1 represents a 5 percent increase in the price level) equals $Y_{FE} = 2.1 \times 1,650 = \$3,465$ billion. The desired increase in GDP is equal to $465 billion, which corresponds to an increase in the money supply of $\Delta M = (\Delta Y'_{FE}/V) = 465/6 = \$77.5$ billion.

Completion Questions

1. supply creates its own demand
2. Classical/Keynesian/John Maynard Keynes
3. Monetarists/Classical/Keynesian
4. Say's Law/Quantity Theory of Money
5. the public's saving/entrepreneurs' investment
6. full employment/full employment/full employment/flexible wage rates/flexible output prices/freely fluctuating interest rates that adjust firms' investment spending to households' saving
7. equation of exchange/transactions/income/Cambridge/cash-balance
8. equation of exchange/money supply/income velocity of money/price level
9. equation of exchange/money supply/transactions velocity of money/price level/transactions
10. quantity theory of money/money supply/a proportionate/price level
11. rational expectations/money supply

True and False Questions

1. F	2. F	3. F	4. T
5. T	6. F	7. F	8. F
9. T	10. F	11. T	12. F
13. T	14. F	15. T	16. F
17. F	18. F	19. T	20. T
21. F	22. F	23. F	24. F
25. F	26. T	27. T	28. T
29. F	30. F	31. T	32. F
33. T	34. T	35. T	

Multiple-Choice Questions

1. b	2. c	3. a	4. e
5. a	6. e	7. b	8. a
9. b	10. d	11. c	12. b
13. e	14. a	15. a	16. a
17. e	18. e	19. a	20. b
21. b	22. a	23. a	24. a
25. d	26. c	27. a	28. a
29. d	30. a		

APPENDIX TO CHAPTER 19

Essay Questions and Problems

6. b. No, because velocity is defined as the ratio of GDP to the money supply. You need GDP and the money supply to get the velocity of money.
   d. GDP = $C + I + G = 1,000 + 200 + 300 = 1,500$. With a money supply of 300, the velocity of money equals 1,500 divided by 300—that is, the velocity of money is equal to 5.

Completion Questions

1. Gross Domestic Product/national income
2. labor/land/capital/entrepreneurship/wages/rent/interest/profits
3. circular flow/real/money/households/business firms/government
4. consumer/investment/government
5. Desired/investment/actual/investment/always equal
6. desired/saving/taxes/desired/investment/government spending
7. consumers/business firms/government/money supply/velocity of money

True and False Questions

1. T	2. F	3. F	4. F
5. T	6. F	7. F	8. T
9. F	10. F	11. T	12. F
13. F	14. T		

Multiple-Choice Questions

1. a	2. d	3. a	4. b
5. e	6. a	7. c	8. b
9. c	10. c		

CHAPTER 20

Essay Questions and Problems

5. a. .8
   b. $440 billion

c. $450 billion. $S = -40 + 0.2\,Y = \$50$ billion $= I$

d. $1/0.2 = 5$

e. It would decline to $400 billion.

6. a. (1) Autonomous consumption = $50 billion

 (2) MPC =

$$\frac{\text{change in } C}{\text{change in } Y} = \frac{650 - 350}{800 - 400} = \frac{300}{400} = 0.75$$

Note that changes between any two points will yield the same result. The equation of the consumption function is:

$$C = 50 + 0.75\,Y$$

 (3) Savings $(S) = Y - C = Y - 50 - 0.75\,Y = -50 + 0.25\,Y$. Thus the equation of the saving function is $S = -50 + 0.25\,Y$ where MPS = 0.25. Note that MPC + MPS = 1

The saving schedule is:

$Y = 0; 40; 800; 1,200$

$S = -50; 50; 150; 250$

b. (1) These points indicate that total expenditures equal income—that is, the real sector of the economy is in equilibrium ($E = Y$).

 (2) $E = C + I + G = 50 + 0.75\,Y + 175 + 25 = 250 + 0.75\,Y$.

 (3) $Y_{eq} = \$1,000$ billion, the intersection point between the total expenditure line and the 45° line. Only at this point do we have $E = Y = \$1,000$ billion. See Figure 20.1.

 (4) $250 + 0.75\,Y_{eq} = .\,Y_{eq}$
 $250 = Y_{eq} - 0.75\,Y_{eq} = 0.25\,Y_{eq}$
 and $Y_{eq} = \dfrac{250}{0.25} = \$1,000$ billion

 (5) See Figure 20.2, in which $Y_{eq} = \$1,000$ billion.

c. (1) At $Y = 1,200$ we have $E = 50 + 0.75\,(1,200) + 175 + 25 = 1,150$. Thus total expenditures equal $1,150 billion when output is $1,200 billion. Output exceeds total expenditures.

 (2) At $Y = 1,200$, saving $(S) = Y - C = 1,200 - [50 + 0.75\,(1,200)] = \$250$ billion. Desired investment = Business investment spending + government investment spending = $175 + 25 = \$200$ billion. But with S at 250 actual I must be 250. Thus if actual $I = 250$ and desired $I = 200$, undesired investment in the form of accumulated inventories must be equal to the difference, or $50 billion. You could

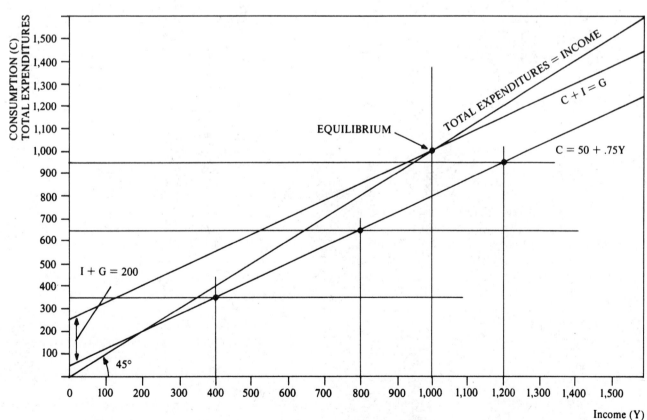

Figure 20.1
The Cross Diagram

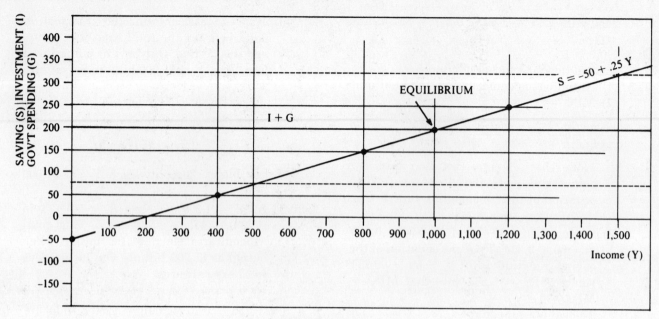

Figure 20.2
The Saving-Investment Diagram

have obtained this answer from Figure 20.2.

(3) Output will fall, because firms will cut back production next period in order to get rid of their accumulated inventories in the current period. Output will decline until the original equilibrium level of $1,000 billion is restored.

d. (1) Output gap = $1,200 - $1,000 = $200 billion. There is no natural tendency for the economy to bridge the gap automatically. Note that we have shown in question c (3) that if $Y = $1,200 the economy is not in equilibrium. It will return toward $Y = $1,000, the equilibrium output.

(2) Multiplier $k = \dfrac{1}{1 - \text{MPC}} = \dfrac{1}{1 - 0.75} = \dfrac{1}{0.25}$
= 4

Change in Income (ΔY) = Multiplier (k_y) × Change in government spending (ΔG). Since the desired ΔY is $200 billion (the output gap), then 200 = (4) × ΔG and therefore ΔG = $50 billion. Government spending should rise by $50 billion in order to raise output by $200 billion, since the multiplier is equal to 4.

e. (1) $C = 50 + 0.75 (Y - 50)$
$C = 50 + 0.75Y - 0.75(50)$
$C = 50 - 37.5 + 0.75Y$
$C = 12.5 + 0.75Y$

(2) After-tax autonomous consumption = $12.5 billion. Change in autonomous consumption (Δa) = 50 - 12.5 = $37.5 billion.

(3) $\Delta Y = k_y \times \Delta a$ = (4) × (37.5) = $150 billion. Output will drop by $150 billion as a result of the imposition of a lump sum tax of $50 billion.

(4) If the government spends $50 billion, output will rise by $200 billion [see question d (2)]. If the government simultaneously raises taxes by $50 billion to finance its spending, output will drop by $150 billion [see question e (3)]. The net effect of combined government spending and taxation of an equal size is to raise output by $50 billion. Note that output increases by an amount equal to G (and T). Thus to bridge the original $200 billion output gap the government should raise taxes and expenditures by $200 billion.

7. a. (1) Total Demand or Liquidity Preference (LP_1) in Table 20.1.
r = 13%; 11%; 9%; 7%; 5%; 3%; 1%
LP_1 = 150; 200; 250; 300; 350; 400; 450 or more

(2) When the level of interest rates is relatively high the public holds a higher proportion of bonds in its portfolio of assets and a smaller proportion of money. Thus the demand for money is smaller at relatively higher interest rates, and the LP curve will be downward sloping, as shown in Figure 20.3.

(3) At r = 1 percent. At this rate and below, any additional liquidity will be held as money and not invested in bonds. The public is said to hoard money when the

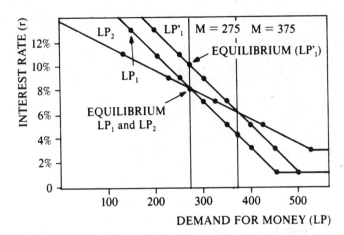

Figure 20.3
Liquidity Preference

economy is in a liquidity trap.

b. For *M* = \$275 billion, the interest rate (*r*) = 8 percent (see Figure 20.3).

c. (1) At 9 percent the public demands (wants to hold) \$250 billion but has \$275 billion, the amount made available by the Fed. The public will attempt to get rid of the undesired \$25 billion of liquidity by buying bonds. This will raise the price of bonds (more bonds demanded) and lower the rate of interest (the yield on bonds). The buying will stop when the interest rate is back to its equilibrium level at 8 percent.

(2) At 7 percent the public wants to hold \$300 billion but has available only \$275 billion. It will attempt to increase its holding of money by selling bonds. This will lower the price of bonds (less bonds are demanded) and raise the rate of interest (the yield of bonds). The selling will stop when the interest rate is back to its equilibrium level at 8 percent.

d. (1) For *M* = \$375 billion, the interest rate (*r*) = 4 percent (see Figure 20.3).

(2) A lower interest rate will stimulate investment (if investment spending is sensitive to changes in the rate of interest), which in turn will raise output.

e. (1) When the rate of interest drops by one percentage point (from 8 percent to 7 percent), the demand for money increases by \$25 billion (from \$275 billion to \$300 billion).

(2) New Liquidity Preference schedule LP_2:
r = 11%; 9%; 7%; 5%; 3%
LP_2 = 125; 225; 325; 425; 525 or more

(3) With the flatter LP_2 curve the demand for money increases by \$50 billion in response to the same one percentage drop in

the interest rate. The flatter LP_2 curve is *more* sensitive to a change in interest rates than the original LP_1 curve. In general the flatter the liquidity preference curve, the more interest-sensitive it is.

f. (1) By two percentage points (from 8 percent to 6 percent).

(2) With the original steeper LP_1 curve the interest rate drops by 4 percentage points (from 8 percent to 4 percent). The rate of interest drops *more* the *steeper* the *LP* curve. Thus monetary policy is more effective (it lowers the interest rate more) the steeper the *LP* curve.

(3) No, when the economy is in a liquidity trap monetary policy is completely ineffective since a change in the money supply will not affect the rate of interest in this case.

(4) Monetary policy will be more effective the more interest-sensitive the investment function is.

g. (1) The higher transactions demand for money may be the result of either an increase in the level of income or an increase in the fraction of income the public wants to hold in the form of transactions balances at the same level of income. In the former case, more income means that more money is needed to carry out an increased volume of transactions. In the latter case the fraction of income held by the public in the form of transactions balances increases, even though the level of income has not changed. For example, suppose that the transactions demand for money is equal to 20 percent of income. If income is 100, the transactions demand is 20. It will increase to 30 if income increases to 150 (20 percent of 150 = 30). It will also increase to 30 if the transactions demand for money increases to 30 percent of income and income remains at 100. In this respect see problem 7.

(2) The schedule of the new LP_1 function (LP'_1) is:

r = 13%; 11%; 9%; 7%; 5%; 3%; 1%
LP'_1 = 200; 250; 300; 350; 400; 450; 500 or more

It is drawn in the solution to Figure 20.3. With M = \$275 billion and LP'_1, the equilibrium interest rate is 10 percent. It has increased from its original level at 8 percent.

(3) The transactions demand for money has increased by \$50 billion (from \$100 billion to \$150 billion), but the total amount of money available is still \$275 billion. This means that the speculative demand for money must have dropped by \$50 billion (from \$175 billion to \$125 billion). Note that \$125 billion of speculative balances is exactly the amount consistent with the new higher interest rate of 10 percent (see Table 20.1), meaning that the money market is again in equilibrium.

8. a. increases k
   b. decreases k
   c. decreases k
   d. increases k
   e. does not affect k
   f. decreases k
   g. increases k
   h. decreases k

Completion Questions

1. equilibrium/ex ante or desired/saving/ex ante or desired/investment/Ex post or realized/saving/ex post or realized/investment
2. short/the economy's GDP or the level of income
3. desired/undesired changes in business inventories
4. inventories/cutting back production
5. marginal propensity to consume
6. total expenditure
7. consumption/investment/government spending
8. income/desired consumption
9. multiple/induced/consumer
10. multiplier/save
11. consumption/induced/investment/autonomous/investment/GDP
12. increase consumption/shift the consumption function upward

13. disposable income
14. liquidity preference/level of income/level of interest rates/transactions demand for money/speculative demand for money
15. level of interest rates/bonds/real investment/the level of income (GDP)/multiple/investment
16. liquidity trap/money supply/GDP/money supply/hoarded/monetary policy/the economy
17. flatter/liquidity preference/monetary policy
18. the level of interest rates/the timing of receipts and expenditures/the use of credit cards
19. money supply/demand for money or liquidity preference
20. rise/fall

True and False Questions

1. T	2. F	3. T	4. T
5. F	6. F	7. T	8. F
9. F	10. F	11. T	12. T
13. F	14. T	15. F	16. T
17. F	18. T	19. T	20. T
21. F	22. F	23. F	24. F
25. T	26. T	27. T	28. F
29. T	30. F	31. T	

Multiple-Choice Questions

1. a	2. b	3. c	4. b
5. d	6. a	7. d	8. e
9. b	10. a	11. c	12. b
13. c	14. b	15. b	16. b
17. c	18. b	19. d	20. b
21. b	22. a	23. c	24. a
25. d	26. c	27. c	28. b
29. c	30. b	31. a	32. e
33. d	34. b	35. b	36. c
37. a	38. e	39. a	40. c
41. c	42. a	43. a	44. e

CHAPTER 21

Essay Questions and Problems

1. a. (1)

Table 21.1

The Transactions Demand for Money (k = .10)

Income (Y)	Transactions Demand
\$ 250 billion	\$ 25 billion
\$ 500 billion	\$ 50 billion
\$ 750 billion	\$ 75 billion
\$1,000 billion	\$100 billion
\$1,250 billion	\$125 billion
\$1,500 billion	\$150 billion

Table 21.2

The Liquidity Preference (LP) for Various Levels of Income (in billions of dollars)

r	Y = 250	Y = 500	Y = 700	Y = 1,000	Y = 1,250	Y = 1,500
13%	75	100	125	150	175	200
11%	125	150	175	200	225	250
9%	175	200	225	250	275	300
7%	225	250	275	300	325	350
5%	275	300	325	350	375	400
3%	325	350	375	400	425	450
1%	375 +	400 +	425 +	450 +	475 +	500 +

(2) At higher levels of income the transactions demand for money is higher, and since the money supply is fixed, the speculative demand for money must be lower on an *LM* curve. Lower speculative demand for money is consistent with higher levels of interest rates. Hence higher levels of income are associated with higher levels of interest rates on an *LM* curve, and this curve must be upward sloping.

(3) The velocity of money is rising when one moves up along an upward sloping *LM* curve, because the money supply is fixed and income is rising.

(4) At point B the demand for money (*LP*) exceeds the available supply of money (*M* = $300 billion). This is so because at *r* = 8 percent demand equals supply only if *Y* = 1,250. If *Y* = 1,500 and *r* = 8 percent, then the transactions demand for money must be higher (a higher *Y* is associated with a higher transactions demand), and *LP* will exceed *M*. Alternatively, you can see that at *r* = 9 percent demand equals supply only if *Y* = 1,500. If *r* = 8 percent and *Y* = 1,500, then the speculative demand for money must be higher (a lower *r* is associated with a higher speculative demand), and *LP* will exceed *M*.

(2) Consider point B in Figure 21.1. We have shown in question a (4) that the demand

Table 21.3

The LM$_1$ Schedule: LP$_1$ Curves (Y in billions of dollars)

Y	250	500	750	1,000	1,250	1,500
r	4%	5%	6%	7%	8%	9%

Table 21.4

The Income Velocity of Money along LM$_1$

Y	500	750	1,000	1,250	1,500
V = Y/M	1.66	2.50	3.33	4.15	5.00

for money exceeds the supply at this point. At *Y* = 1,500 the interest rate must rise in order to reduce the demand for money and restore equilibrium. It is clear that the *more* interest-sensitive is the demand for money the *smaller* will be the *rise* in interest rate required to restore equilibrium. Hence the distance from point B to the relatively *more* interest-sensitive *LM* curve must be *shorter* than the distance from point B to the relatively *less* interest-sensitive *LM* curve. Consequently the relatively *more* interest-sensitive *LM* curve will be *flatter* than the relatively *less* interest-sensitive *LM* curve (see Figure 21.1).

b. (1)

Table 21.5

Liquidity Preference (LP$_2$) for Various Levels of Income (in billions of dollars)

r	Y = 250	Y = 500	Y = 750	Y = 1,000	Y = 1,250	Y = 1,500
11%	50	75	100	125	150	175
9%	150	175	200	225	250	275
7%	250	275	300	325	350	375
5%	350	375	400	425	450	475
3%	450 +	475 +	500 +	525 +	550 +	575 +

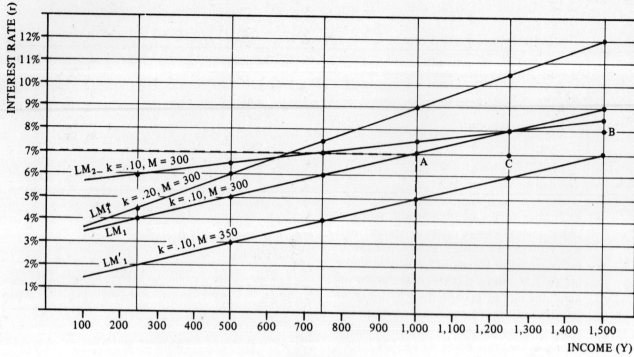

Figure 21.1
LM Curves

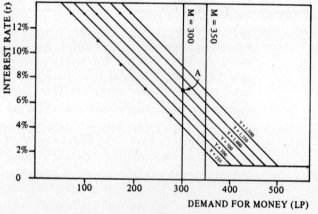

Figure 21.2
Liquidity Preference Curves (LP$_1$)

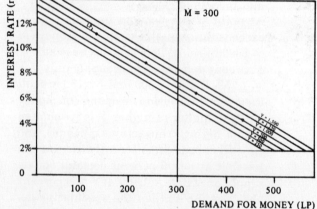

Figure 21.3
Liquidity Preference Curves (LP$_2$)

(3) The LM^*_1 curve corresponding to $k = .20$ and $M = \$300$ billion is drawn in Figure 21.1. The LM^*_1 schedule for $k = .20$ and $M = \$300$ billion is given below:

$Y = 250; 500; 750; 1,000; 1,250$

$r = 4.5\%; 6\%; 7.5\%; 9\%; 10.5\%$

(4) Consider the point C in Figure 21.1. The demand for money exceeds the supply at this point. At $r = 7$ percent the level of income must fall in order to reduce the demand for money and restore equilibrium. It is clear that the *more* income-

sensitive is the demand for money, the *smaller* will be the drop in income required to restore equilibrium. Hence the distance from point C to the relatively *more* income-sensitive LM curve must be *shorter* than the distance from point C to the relatively *less* income-sensitive LM curve. Consequently the relatively *more* income-sensitive LM curve will be *steeper* than the relatively *less* income-sensitive LM curve (see Figure 21.1).

c. (1) The LM'_1 curve corresponding to $k = 0.10$, and $M = \$350$ billion is drawn in

Table 21.6

Flatter LM₂ Schedule: Flatter LP₂ Curves

Y	250	500	750	1,000	1,250	1,500
r	6%	6.5%	7%	7.5%	8%	8.5%

LM'₁ Schedule

Y	500	750	1,000	1,250	1,500
r	3%	4%	5%	6%	7%

Figure 21.1. Its schedule is given below. An increase (decrease) in the money supply shifts the *LM* curve to the right (to the left).

(2) The horizontal distance Δ*Y* separating the two *LM* curves is equal to *k* times the change in the money supply, that is, Δ*Y* = *k*Δ*M*. For *k* = .10 and Δ*M* = $50 billion this distance equals $500 billion.

d. (1) See Figure 21.4, in which the investment function *I₁* is drawn. The interest payment on borrowed funds is a cost to borrowing firms. Higher interest rates mean that borrowed funds are costlier. This will reduce firms' demands for investment funds and result in a cutback in investment spending by firms. Thus higher rates of interest are associated with less investment, and the investment function is inversely related to the interest rate. The investment curve will be downward sloping.

(2) Lower (higher) interest rates resulting from an increase (decrease) in the money

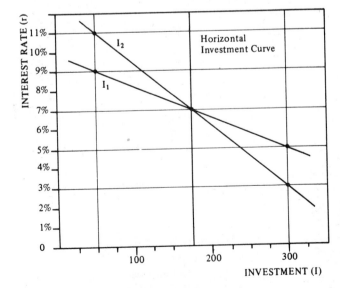

Figure 21.4
Investment Curve

supply stimulate (reduce) investment and thereby the economy's GDP.

(3) The investment function is completely insensitive to changes in the interest rate. Monetary policy is completely ineffective in this case.

(4) *I₂* is steeper and less interest-sensitive than *I₁*. Referring to Figure 21.4 note that a drop in interest rate from 9 percent to 7 percent will increase investment spending from $50 billion to $175 billion (an additional $125 billion) in the case of *I₁* and from $112.5 billion to $175 billion (an additional $62.5 billion) in the case of *I₂*. Thus *I₂* is less interest-sensitive than *I₁*.

e. (1)

Table 21.9

The IS₁ Schedule Corresponding to I₁ (in billions of dollars)

r	5%	7%	9%
Y	1,500	1,000	500

See Figure 20.2 (and problem 6) in the solution section of the previous chapter for details. The "new" investment lines are drawn as dashed lines. The *IS₁* curve is drawn in Figure 21.5. Algebraic determination of income: In equilibrium, total expenditure (*C* + *I* + *G*) equals income (*Y*). At *r* = 5%, *I₁* = 300 and hence: 50 + .75*Y*eq + 300 + 25 = *Y*eq.

Solving this equation gives $Y_{eq} = \frac{375}{.25} = 1,500$.

(2) At higher (lower) levels of interest rates, investment spending is lower (higher) and income must be lower (higher) in order for saving to be lower (higher) to match the lower (higher) investment. Hence higher (lower) levels of interest rates are associated with lower (higher) levels of income along an *IS* curve and this curve will be downward sloping.

f. (1)

Table 21.10

The IS₂ Schedule Corresponding to I₂ (in billions of dollars)

r	3%	7%	11%
Y	1,500	1,000	500

Note that the *Y* values are the same as for *IS₁*. Only the *r* values have changed. You don't have to repeat all the calcula-

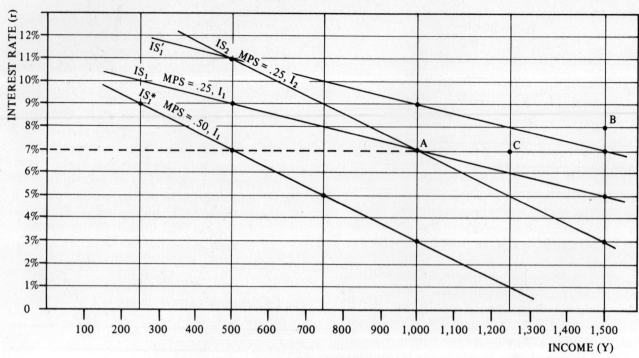

Figure 21.5
IS Curves

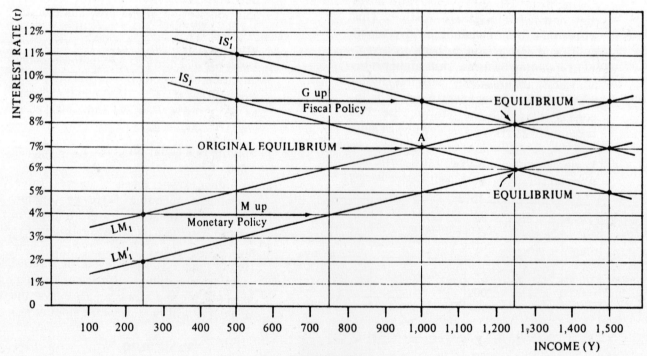

Figure 21.6
General Equilibrium:
Monetary and Fiscal Policies

tions to get IS_2. The IS_2 curve is drawn in Figure 21.5.

(2) IS_1 is flatter than IS_2. Recall that I_1 is more interest-sensitive than I_2. See Figure 21.5.

(3) Start from point B in Figure 21.5 and go through the same type of reasoning as in the answer to question b (2).

(4) See Figure 21.5, in which IS^*_1 is drawn.

(5) Start from point C in Figure 21.5 and go

through the same type of reasoning as in the answer to question b (4).

g. The IS'_1 Schedule:

r	7%	9%	11%
Y	1,500	1,000	500

The horizontal shift equals the income multiplier times the change in government spending or (4) × (125) = \$500 billion. See Figure 21.5. An autonomous increase (decrease) will shift the IS curve to the right (left).

h. (1) r_{eq} = 7 percent and Y_{eq} = \$1,000 billion (see Figure 21.6).

(2) Any other point would set forces in motion that lead to a change in both the interest rate and income.

i. (1) See Figure 21.6.

(2) r_{eq} = 6 percent and Y_{eq} = \$1,250 billion. With a contractionary monetary policy of a \$50 billion reduction in the money supply, r_{eq} = 8 percent and Y_{eq} = \$750 billion. A change in the money supply changes income in the same direction and the interest rate in the opposite direction.

j. (1) See Figure 21.6.

(2) r_{eq} = 8 percent and Y_{eq} = \$1,250 billion. With a contractionary fiscal policy of a \$125 billion reduction in government spending, r_{eq} = 6 percent and Y_{eq} = \$750 billion. A change in government spending changes income and the interest rate in the same direction.

(3) Y increases to \$1,250 billion instead of \$1,500 billion, because r has increased from 7 percent to 8 percent, thereby reducing investment spending and the level of income. The reduction in Y resulting from the rise in the interest rate is equal to \$250 billion.

2. a. (1) For r = 11%, L^* = 375 − 2,500 (0.11) = 375 − 275 = 100.
For r = 5%, L^* = 375 − 2,500 (0.5) = 375 − 125 = 250.

(2) $L + L^*$ = 0.1Y + 375 − 2,500r = 300 gives Y = −750 + 25,000r which is the equation of the LM_1 curve.

b. (1) For Y = 400, C = 50 + 0.75 (400) = 350.
For Y = 1,200, C = 50 + 0.75 (1,200) = 950.
For r = 5%, I_1 = 612.5 − 6,250 (.05) = 612.5 − 312.5 = 300.
For r = 9%, I_1 = 612.5 − 6,250 (.09) = 612.5 − 562.5 = 50.

(2) $C + I + G$ = (50 + 0.75Y) + (612.5 −

6,250r) + 25 = Y gives Y = 2,750 − 25,000r which is the equation of the IS_1 curve.

c. − 750 + 25,000r_{eq} = 2,750 − 25,000r_{eq} gives r_{eq} = 3,500/50,000 = .07 = 7%.
And Y_{eq} = 2,750 − 25,000 (.07) = 2,750 − 1,750 = \$1,000 billion.
Or Y_{eq} = −750 + 25,000 (.07) = −750 + 1,750 = \$1,000 billion.

d. (1) $L + L^*$ = .10Y + 375 − 2,500r = 350 gives Y = −250 + 25,000r which is the equation of the LM'_1 curve.

(2) −250 + 25,000r'_{eq} = 2,750 − 25,000r'_{eq} gives r'_{eq} = 3,000/50,000 = .06 = 6%.
Y'_{eq} = −250 + 25,000 (.06) = −250 + 15,000 = \$1,250 billion.

(3) Change in income $Y'_{eq} − Y_{eq}$ = 1,250 − 1,000 = + \$250 billion.
Change in interest rate = $r'_{eq} − r_{eq}$ = 6% − 7% = −1%.

e. (1) (50 + 0.75Y) + (612.5 − 6,250r) + 150 = Y gives Y = 3,250 − 25,000r which is the equation of the IS'_1 curve.

(2) − 750 + 25,000r'_{eq} = 3,250 − 25,000r'_{eq}.
r'_{eq} = 4,000/50,000 = .08 = 8%.
Y'_{eq} = 3,250 − 25,000 (.08) = \$1,250 billion.

(3) $\Delta Y = Y'_{eq} − Y_{eq}$ = 1,250 − 1,000 = + \$250 billion.
$\Delta r = r'_{eq} − r_{eq}$ = 8% − 7% = +1 percent.

(4) With no crowding out effect ΔY = (multiplier) (ΔG) with 4 × 125 = \$500 billion. Actual change ΔY_{eq} = \$250 billion. Therefore there is a reduction of \$250 billion in income due to the rise in the interest rate of 1 percent.

Completion Questions

1. interest rate/income level/demand for money (liquidity preference)/the money supply
2. equilibrium/money market
3. interest rate/income level/saving/investment/ total expenditure/output
4. equilibrium/goods market
5. the money supply
6. the interest-sensitivity of the demand for money/the income-sensitivity of the demand for money
7. autonomous spending (government, investment, or consumption)
8. the interest-sensitivity of the investment function/the marginal propensity to save
9. *IS* curve/*LM* curve/saving/investment/the demand for money/the money supply/goods/ money/equilibrium

10. prices and wages are sticky and inflexible/the economy is in a liquidity trap/investment is highly insensitive to the rate of interest
11. Crowding out
12. price level/real income

True and False Questions

1. T	2. F	3. F	4. T
5. F	6. F	7. F	8. T
9. T	10. F	11. F	12. F
13. F	14. F	15. T	16. F
17. T	18. T	19. F	20. F
21. T	22. T	23. T	24. F
25. T			

Multiple-Choice Questions

1. c	2. c	3. d	4. b
5. d	6. e	7. c	8. a
9. b	10. a	11. d	12. e
13. b	14. a	15. c	16. d
17. b	18. e	19. d	20. a
21. b	22. d	23. d	24. a
25. d	26. e	27. a	28. b
29. d	30. b		

CHAPTER 22

Essay Questions and Problems

2. a. (1) A vertical *LM* curve represents the extreme Monetarist position. Refer to the textbook.
   (2) No. Any shift in *IS* will change the interest rate but leave GDP unaffected at $2,000 billion. A shift in the *IS* curve from its initial position *IS* to its final position *IS'* will raise the interest rate from 7 percent to 9 percent and leave GDP at $2,000 billion.
   (3) The money supply must be increased by $20 billion. This is so because the velocity of money is equal to 5 (the ratio of a GDP of $2,000 billion to a money supply of $400 billion) and the GDP gap is equal to $100 billion. An increase in the money supply by $20 billion will raise GDP by $100 billion (20 × 5), the required amount to bridge the income gap. Note that when the *LM* curve is vertical, the velocity of money is constant along the *LM* curve. This is so because the money supply is constant ($400 billion) and GDP is constant ($2,000 billion).

b. (1) A horizontal *LM* curve represents the extreme Keynesian position. Refer to the textbook.
   (2) No. Any change in the money supply will leave the *LM* curve at the same position, LM_2. The equilibrium point will remain at point A. The interest rate will be at 7 percent and the level of income at $2,000 billion. The additional money supply is simply hoarded by the public and not spent. Recall that when the *LM* curve is flat, so is the liquidity preference curve (demand for money curve). The liquidity preference curve is in the "liquidity trap."
   (3) Government spending must be increased by $25 billion. This is so because the simple Keynesian multiplier is equal to 4 (the reciprocal of the marginal propensity to save, which equals 25 percent) and the GDP gap is equal to $100 billion. An increase in government spending by $25 billion will raise GDP by $100 (25 × 4), the amount required to bridge the income gap. The method of financing government expenditure matters in this case. Borrowing from the public may not be possible, since the public's liquidity preference is in a liquidity trap, meaning that the public wants to hold money and does not want to hold bonds. Government expenditure may have to be financed by printing money.

c. (1) When the *IS* curve is well behaved (the normal case), it is downward sloping. When the *LM* curve is well behaved, it is upward sloping. Refer to the textbook.
   (2) The final equilibrium point is point E. The equilibrium interest rate is 6 percent, and the equilibrium level of income is $2,050 billion. The immediate effect of an increase in the money supply is a decrease in the interest rate from 7 percent to 5 percent. This is the liquidity effect represented by the line AF. A lower interest rate stimulates investment, which in turn raises GDP from $2,000 billion to $2,050 billion. Higher income will also have the effect of increasing the demand for money, which will raise the interest rate from 5 percent to its final level at 6 percent (interest rate snaps back). This is the income effect represented by the line FE. The net effect of an expansionary policy is to raise GDP and lower the rate of interest.

(3) The final equilibrium point is point D. The equilibrium interest rate is 8 percent, and the equilibrium level of income is $2,050 billion. The initial effect of government spending is to raise GDP from $2,000 billion to $2,100 billion. Higher income increases the demand for money, which raises the interest rate from 7 percent to 8 percent. A higher rate of interest will, in turn, reduce investment and lower GDP from $2,100 billion to its final level at $2,050 billion.

The net effect of an expansionary fiscal policy is to raise GDP and the rate of interest. Note that the effect on GDP is the same as that of an expansionary monetary policy, but the effect on the rate of interest is the opposite.

Crowding out is not complete, since GDP did increase. Crowding out is only partial in this case. Complete crowding out would have occurred if the *LM* curve were vertical (the extreme Monetarist position). In this case the rate of interest jumps from 7 percent to 9 percent and GDP does not change.

5. An expansionary fiscal policy financed by borrowing from a commercial bank with excess reserves increases the money supply by an amount of the borrowing (see Chapter 18). The *IS* curve will shift to the right (expansionary fiscal policy), the *LM* curve will shift to the right (increase in the money supply), and GDP increases from Y_1 to Y_2. See Figure 22.1. Compare the above case with the same expansionary fiscal policy financed by borrowing from the nonbank public. The money supply is not affected, and the *LM* curve does not move. GDP increases from Y_1 to Y_3, which is a smaller increase than the previous case. See Figure 22.1.

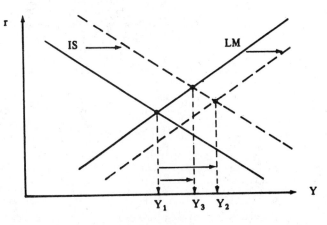

Figure 22.1

Completion Questions

1. *LM*/money/zero interest-sensitivity/Monetarist/ fiscal policy
2. *LM*/money/the liquidity trap/Keynesian/monetary policy/fiscal policy
3. investment function/zero interest-sensitivity/ monetary policy/fiscal policy
4. steeper/*LM*/more
5. real/natural
6. full employment/saving/investment/Classical/ Keynesian
7. interest rate/money supply/targets/interest rate/money supply/interest rate
8. Monetarists/demand for money/consumption/ *IS*/demand for money/*LM*

True and False Questions

1. F	2. F	3. T	4. T
5. F	6. T	7. T	8. T
9. T	10. F	11. T	12. F
13. F	14. T	15. T	16. F
17. T	18. F	19. T	20. T
21. T	22. F		

Multiple-Choice Questions

1. d	2. c	3. d	4. a
5. b	6. d	7. b	8. b
9. e	10. c	11. b	12. c
13. e	14. a	15. c	16. d
17. a	18. a	19. a	20. d
21. e			

CHAPTER 23

Essay Questions and Problems

6. a. Velocity = $(1,250/250)$ = 5
   b. Spending increases by $50 billion. The velocity is a constant at 5, therefore the change in spending is equal to 5 times the change in the money supply.
   c. Percentage change in the money supply = $(10/250)$ = 4%.
   Percentage change in spending = $(50/1,250)$ = 4%.
   Conclusion: *A percentage change in the money supply will produce an equal percentage change in spending in the simple version of Monetarism only because the velocity of money is assumed to be constant.*

Completion Questions

1. Keynesians/tax and expenditure legislation/ Monetarists/the Federal Reserve
2. stable/money supply/vertical/do not affect/ sensitive/is not
3. unstable/autonomous/investment/government/stabilize
4. an expansionary/a contractionary/Keynesian/ liquidity/income
5. inflationary expectations/nominal/real
6. fiscal/monetary
7. Monetarists/the money supply/demand
8. raises/real money or real cash
9. aggregate/money/interest rates/investment
10. credit availability effect/wealth effect/credit/ money supply/interest rates/portfolio of assets/ goods/services
11. Monetary/fiscal/aggregate demand
12. inflation/unemployment
13. Countercyclical monetary policy/tight/booms/ slow down/inflation
14. time lags
15. the precarious nature of economic forecasting/ the alleged length, variability, and unpredictability of the time lags/the fact that the economy is inherently stable
16. money supply / fixed / current economic conditions

True and False Questions

1. T	2. T	3. F	4. T
5. T	6. F	7. F	8. T
9. T	10. F	11. T	12. T
13. T	14. F	15. F	16. F
17. T	18. F	19. F	20. F
21. T	22. T	23. T	24. F
25. T			

Multiple-Choice Questions

1. b	2. c	3. e	4. b
5. a	6. e	7. d	8. a*
9. b	10. d	11. a	12. c
13. a	14. b	15. b	16. c
17. b	18. d	19. c	20. b
21. e	22. a	23. d	24. c
25. a			

*Note: It is not *necessary* that a change in the level of interest rates affect real investment for monetary policy to have an effect on the economy's GDP. This is so because of the wealth effect. A change in the level of interest rates will change the price of financial assets, and this change will create more or less spending on real goods and services even if investment spending is unaffected by the change in the level of interest rates.

CHAPTER 24

Completion Questions

1. all/rational
2. adaptive
3. higher/less
4. not anticipated/lower
5. Classical-Monetarist/Keynesian/Classical economics
6. announced/credible
7. has no effect on/respond immediately

True and False Questions

1. T	2. T	3. T	4. F
5. T	6. F	7. F	8. T
9. F	10. T	11. T	12. T
13. F	14. T	15. T	16. F
17. F	18. F		

Multiple-Choice Questions

1. a	2. b	3. d	4. a
5. e	6. a	7. b	8. a
9. d	10. a	11. b	12. c
13. d	14. e	15. c	16. d

CHAPTER 25

Essay Questions and Problems

4. d. The length of the recognition lag may be reduced if the Federal Reserve can improve its monitoring of the economy. The length of the impact lag could not be significantly reduced.
5. The administrative lag should be shorter for monetary policy than for fiscal policy. The Federal Reserve can act rapidly to affect bank reserves and money market conditions once it has recognized the need for action. The Federal Open Market Committee meets every four weeks, and the Account Manager who is responsible for the execution of open market operations is in constant contact with the Board of Governors. The administrative lag for fiscal policy is usually much longer, because Congress must approve any changes in the U.S. budget or the structure of tax rates.

Completion Questions

1. consumption spending/investment spending/federal/state/local
2. velocity of money/Monetarists/stable or highly predictable/Keynesians
3. velocity/the economy's GDP/money supply
4. attractive yields on financial assets other than money/imaginative new techniques of cash management/the growing use of credit cards
5. M2/M3/M1
6. interest rate/level of GDP
7. monetary policy/economic/recognition lag/impact lag
8. econometric model
9. Federal Reserve/St. Louis/Keynesian/Monetarist
10. sales expectations/changes in anticipated profitability/expectations regarding labor costs/competitive pressures

True and False Questions

1. F	2. T	3. F	4. F
5. T	6. T	7. F	8. T
9. F	10. F	11. T	12. T
13. F	14. F	15. F	16. F
17. F	18. T	19. F	20. F
21. T	22. T	23. T	24. F
25. F			

Multiple-Choice Questions

1. b	2. b	3. a	4. d
5. e	6. c	7. d	8. d
9. a	10. d	11. d	12. c
13. e	14. b	15. c	16. d
17. b	18. a	19. c	20. d

CHAPTER 26

Essay Questions and Problems

1. b. If two securities have different terms to maturity, they may not have the same rate of interest even in a world of certainty. To illustrate this point consider two consecutive periods of one year each. Suppose that the market-determined rate of interest is 6 percent for the first year and the market-determined rate of interest will be 8 percent for the second one-year period. What will be the rate of interest on a two-year bond in this case? It will be the average of the first one-year rate (6 percent) and the second one-year rate (8 percent), that is, 7 percent. Conclusion: One-year bonds currently pay 6 percent and two-year bonds pay 7 percent. However, all one-year bonds over the first one-year period pay 6 percent, all one-year bonds over the second one-year period pay 8 percent, and all two-year bonds pay 7 percent.

4. b. Because a risk-averse individual making a choice between securities with the same expected return will always select the one with the least amount of risk.

   c. The risk lover will select the risky security because although the expected return is the same as for the riskless security, the risky security has the potential for a higher return. By holding the risky security, the risk lover hopes to achieve a very large return, since the risky security has outcomes above 7 percent, whereas the riskless security has no potential for returns above 7 percent.

   d. Such an individual is called risk neutral or risk indifferent.

7. a. The covariance measures the direction and the strength of the co-movement between the returns of two securities. The covariance always involves a pair of securities. The variance measures the variability of a single security's returns around their mean value or expected return.

   b. One.

   c. Three covariances and three variances:

Covariances	Variances
Covariance between sec. 1 and sec. 2	Variance of sec. 1
Covariance between sec. 1 and sec. 3	Variance of sec. 2
Covariance between sec. 2 and sec. 3	Variance of sec. 3

   Note that the covariance between security 1's returns and those of security 2 are identical to the covariance between security 2's returns and those of security 1.

   d. Six covariances and four variances:

Covariances	Variances
Covariance between sec. 1 and sec. 2	Variance of sec. 1
Covariance between sec. 1 and sec. 3	Variance of sec. 2
Covariance between sec. 1 and sec. 4	Variance of sec. 3
Covariance between sec. 2 and sec. 3	Variance of sec. 4
Covariance between sec. 2 and sec. 4	
Covariance between sec. 3 and sec. 4	

   Note that you must list all the possible distinct pairs of securities.

   e. Ten covariances and five variances:

Covariances	Variances
Covariance between sec. 1 and sec. 2	Variance of sec. 1
Covariance between sec. 1 and sec. 3	Variance of sec. 2
Covariance between sec. 1 and sec. 4	Variance of sec. 3
Covariance between sec. 1 and sec. 5	Variance of sec. 4
Covariance between sec. 2 and sec. 3	Variance of sec. 5
Covariance between sec. 2 and sec. 4	
Covariance between sec. 2 and sec. 5	
Covariance between sec. 3 and sec. 4	
Covariance between sec. 3 and sec. 5	
Covariance between sec. 4 and sec. 5	

f. The number of covariances increases faster than the number of variances when the number of securities included in a portfolio increases. The number of variances is always equal to the number of securities included in the portfolio, but the number of covariances is larger than the number of securities for portfolios of four or more securities. If N is the number of securities, then it can be shown that $\frac{1}{2}N(N-1)$ is the corresponding number of distinct covariances.

10. a. Expected return of security A = $(\frac{1}{2})(15\%)$ $+ (\frac{1}{2})(3\%) = 9\%$. Expected return of security B = $(\frac{1}{2})(-1\%) + (\frac{1}{2})(11\%) = 5\%$. Security A is cyclical, since it has a high return under expansion and a low return under recession. It does well when the economy performs well and does poorly when the economy performs poorly. Security B is countercyclical for the opposite reason. It does well when the economy performs poorly and does poorly when the economy performs well.

b. Risk of security A = standard deviation of the returns on security A

$$= \sqrt{(.15 - .09)^2 \times (\tfrac{1}{2}) + (.03 - .09)^2 \times (\tfrac{1}{2})}$$

$$= \sqrt{(.0036) \times (\tfrac{1}{2}) + (.0036) \times (\tfrac{1}{2})}$$

$$= \sqrt{.0018 + .0018} = \sqrt{.0036} = .06 = 6\%$$

In order to obtain the standard deviation of the returns on security A you must subtract the expected return from each outcome, square the result, and multiply it by the probability of occurrence. You take the sum of all these items and then the square root of the sum. *Note:* Do not make your computation with returns expressed as percentage values. Convert returns into their decimal equivalent first. For example, do not enter 15 percent in the above formula, but .15. Risk of security B = standard deviation of returns on security B = 6 percent

c. He or she will choose security A because it has a higher expected return for the same level of risk as security B.

d. A risk-loving individual will also select security A. Recall that risk lovers prefer the

e.

State of the Economy and Probability of Occurrence	Distribution of the Returns on		
	Portfolio 1	Portfolio 2	Portfolio 3
Expansion ($\frac{1}{2}$)	3%	7%	11%
Recession ($\frac{1}{2}$)	9%	7%	5%

Expansion: Portfolio 1: $(\frac{1}{4})\cdot(15\%) + (\frac{3}{4})\cdot(-1\%) = 3\%$
Portfolio 2: $(\frac{1}{2})\cdot(15\%) + (\frac{1}{2})\cdot(-1\%) = 7\%$
Portfolio 3: $(\frac{3}{4})\cdot(15\%) + (\frac{1}{4})\cdot(-1\%) = 11\%$

Recession: Portfolio 1: $(\frac{1}{4})\cdot(3\%) + (\frac{3}{4})\cdot(11\%) = 9\%$
Portfolio 2: $(\frac{1}{2})\cdot(3\%) + (\frac{1}{2})\cdot(11\%) = 7\%$
Portfolio 3: $(\frac{3}{4})\cdot(3\%) + (\frac{1}{4})\cdot(11\%) = 5\%$

Characteristics	Portfolio 1	Portfolio 2	Portfolio 3
Expected returns	6%	7%	8%
Risk (standard dev.)	3%	0	3%

Expected returns: Portfolio 1: $(\frac{1}{2})\cdot(3\%) + (\frac{1}{2})\cdot(9\%) = 6\%$
Portfolio 2: $(\frac{1}{2})\cdot(7\%) + (\frac{1}{2})\cdot(7\%) = 7\%$
Portfolio 3: $(\frac{1}{2})\cdot(11\%) + (\frac{1}{2})\cdot(5\%) = 8\%$

Risk (Std. dev.): Portfolio 1: $[(.03 - .06)^2\cdot(\frac{1}{2}) + (.09 - .06)^2\cdot(\frac{1}{2})]^{\frac{1}{2}} = 3\%$
Portfolio 2: $[(.07 - .07)^2\cdot(\frac{1}{2}) + (.07 - .07)^2\cdot(\frac{1}{2})]^{\frac{1}{2}} = 0\%$
Portfolio 3: $[(0.11 - .08)^2\cdot(\frac{1}{2}) + (.05 - .08)^2\cdot(\frac{1}{2})]^{\frac{1}{2}} = 3\%$

security with the highest risk if they have the same expected return. Here the problem is different. The two securities have the same risk but different expected returns. Note that when choosing between two securities with the same risk, an individual will always prefer the one with the highest expected return regardless of his or her attitude toward risk.

f. (1) We have:

Characteristics	Sec. A	Sec. B	Port. 1	Port. 2	Port. 3
Expected returns	9%	5%	6%	7%	8%
Risk	6%	6%	3%	0	3%

An asset is inefficient if there exists another asset with the same risk but higher expected return. Applying this rule, we find that portfolio 1 is inefficient since there exists another portfolio, portfolio 3, with the same risk (3 percent) but higher expected return (8 percent rather than 6 percent). Similarly security B is inefficient since there exists another asset, security A, with the same risk (6 percent) but higher expected return (9 percent rather than 5 percent). Portfolio 2, portfolio 3, and security A are efficient since there are no other assets (securities or portfolios) with the same risk and higher expected returns than portfolio 2, portfolio 3, or security A. Conclusion:
Efficient investments: portfolio 2, portfolio 3, security A
Inefficient investments: portfolio 1, security B

(2) No investor, regardless of his or her attitude toward risk, will ever hold an inefficient investment, since another one with higher expected returns and the same risk can be obtained.

(3) One cannot tell without the knowledge of the degree of risk aversion specific to this individual decision-maker.

(4) The risk lover would select the investment with the highest expected return and the highest risk, that is, security A.

g. Portfolio 2 is riskless despite the fact that it contains two risky securities because the returns of the securities offset each other exactly. A risk averter will select the riskless bond paying 8 percent, because he or she can get more risk-free returns with the bond. The risk lover will also select the bond in this case. Remember, when risk is the same but expected returns differ, all investors (risk averters, risk-neutral individuals, or risk lovers) make the same decision: they pick the investment with the highest expected return.

h. The covariance between the returns of security A and security B
$$= (.15 - .09) \times (-.01 - .05) \times (\tfrac{1}{2}) + (.03 - .09) \times (0.11 - .05) \times (\tfrac{1}{2})$$
$$= (.06) \times (-.06) \times (\tfrac{1}{2}) + (-.06) \times (+.06) \times (\tfrac{1}{2})$$
$$= -.0018 - .0018 = -.0036$$

$$\text{Correlation coefficient} = \frac{-.0036}{(.06)(.06)}$$
$$= \frac{-.0036}{.0036}$$
$$= -1$$

Completion Questions

1. is a unique/interest rate
2. default risk/market risk
3. U.S. government/default risk
4. risk averters/risk lovers
5. probability distribution/expected return/probability of occurrence
6. standard deviation
7. An individual asset may be considered very risky when viewed in isolation, but when combined with other assets the risk of the portfolio may be substantially reduced
8. covariance
9. nonsystematic/total/well-diversified portfolio
10. they have the highest expected return for a given level of risk/they have the lowest risk for a given level of expected return

True and False Questions

1. F	2. T	3. T	4. F
5. F	6. F	7. T	8. F
9. F	10. T	11. T	12. F
13. T	14. T	15. F	16. T
17. F	18. T	19. T	20. T
21. T	22. F	23. T	24. T
25. F	26. T	27. T	28. T
29. F	30. F		

Multiple-Choice Questions

1. d	2. d	3. a	4. b
5. c	6. e	7. d	8. b

9. d 10. e 11. a 12. a
13. b 14. e 15. c 16. d
17. c 18. b 19. a 20. a
21. d 22. c

CHAPTER 27

Essay Questions and Problems

2. c. (1) Alana's Net Worth = (Total assets) − (Total liabilities) = (200 + 4,000) − (2,000 + 500) = \$1,700

Marci's Net Worth = (Total assets) − (Total liabilities) = (1,800 + 500) − (0) = \$2,300

Note: The \$500 debt owed to Marci is an asset to Marci (loan to Alana) and a liability to Alana (debt to Marci).

(2) Balance sheets of Alana, the Bank, and Marci:

Alana

Demand deposit: 200 Car: 4,000	Debt bank: 2,000 Debt Marci: 500 Net worth: 1,700
\$ 4,200	\$4,200

The Bank

Loans: 2,000	Demand deposits: 2,000
\$ 2,000	\$2,000

Marci

Demand deposits: 1,800 Loan to Alana: 500	Net Worth: 2,300
\$2,300	\$2,300

Note: The bank's balance sheet is very simplified. We have ignored cash items held by the bank and its net worth. These simplifying assumptions, however, do not modify the conclusions reached in (3) below.

(3) The economy's net worth is equal to \$4,000, the value of its real assets (the car). All other items have been canceled out. We have:

Economy's net worth = (Total assets for the whole country) − (Total liabilities for the whole country) = (200 + 4,000 + 2,000 + 1,800 + 500) − (2,000 + 500 + 2,000) = \$4,000

Note: All financial assets cancel out all liabilities. The only items left are real assets. In this case we are left with \$4,000, the value of the car, which is the only real asset.

d. To show this, consider the balance sheets of the banking system and the nonbank public.

Commercial Banks

Reserves (U.S. Bonds)$_B$ Loans to public	Demand deposits (Net worth)$_B$

Nonbank Public

Currency outside banks Demand deposits (U.S. Bonds)$_P$ Real assets	Debt to banks (Net worth)$_P$

The subscript B indicates that an item is on the banks' balance sheet and a subscript P indicates that an item is on the nonbank public's balance sheet.

Net worth of all nongovernmental sectors (banks + public) = [Total assets of banks and public] − [Total liabilities of banks and public] = [Reserves + (U.S. Bonds)$_B$ + Loans to public + Currency outside banks + Demand deposits + (U.S. Bonds)$_P$ + Real Assets] − [Demand deposits + Debt to banks] = Reserves + Currency outside banks + (U.S. Bonds)$_B$ + (U.S. Bonds)$_P$ + Real assets = Monetary base + publicly held U.S. Bonds + Real assets.

Note: Monetary base = Reserves + Currency outside banks

Publicly held U.S. bonds = (U.S. Bonds)$_B$ + (U.S. Bonds)$_P$

Demand deposits cancel out and loans to the public cancel out against debt to banks.

5. A new car is considered a consumer durable good (an investment in flow of funds accounting). The shirt is considered a nondurable consumer good.

6. a.

Uses		Sources	
Investment	200	Borrowing	−50
Hoarding	50	Saving	400
Lending	100		

Note: Investment = Change in consumer durables + change in residential construction.

Hoarding = Change in cash + change in demand deposits.

Lending = Change in all financial assets.

Borrowing = Change in all liabilities.
Saving = Change in Net Worth.

b. The household sector was a surplus sector in 1992 since it had saving (400) in excess of investment (200) or, alternatively, hoarding and lending (150) in excess of borrowing (-50).

c. No, because for the economy as a whole total investment *must* equal total saving, and total hoarding + lending *must* equal borrowing. This is not the case here.

Total investment $= 200 + 400 = 600$
Total saving $= 400 + 500 = 900$; that is, $I \neq S$

Total (hoarding + lending) $= 150 + 300 = 450$
Total borrowing $= -50 + 200 = 150$; that is, $(H + L) \neq B$

d. No, because, for the economy, hoarding plus lending is not equal to borrowing.

Total investment $= 200 + 500 = 700$
Total saving $= 400 + 300 = 700$; that is, $I = S$

Total (hoarding + lending) $= 150 + 200 = 350$
Total borrowing $= -50 + 450 = 400$; that is, $(H + L) \neq B$

e. Yes, because, for the economy, investment equals saving, and hoarding plus lending is equal to borrowing.

Total investment $= 200 + 600 = 800$
Total saving $= 400 + 400 = 800$
Total (hoarding + lending) $= 150 + 125 = 275$
Total borrowing $= -50 + 325 = 275$

7. $W = 5$ $X = 10$ $Y = 0$ $Z = 25$
Note: S = sources; U = uses
Since for a given sector all sources must equal all uses we get:
Sector A: $30 = 25 + W$ and $W = 5$.
Sector B: $40 = 30 + X$ and $X = 10$.
Sector C: $Y + Z = 25$. Can't solve this one yet.

Since for the economy as a whole investment must equal saving we get:
$W + 30 = 35 + Y$ but $W = 5$ and thus $Y = 0$.
If $Y = 0$ then $Z = 25$ (see sector C equation).

Completion Questions

1. analyze borrowing and lending in financial markets
2. source/expenditures/use
3. flow of funds/sector/the government/households/business
4. a budget surplus/retained earnings or additions to net worth
5. assets/liabilities/assets/liabilities/net worth
6. financial/real/bonds/money/cars and houses/plants and equipment
7. saves/investment/balanced/saves/investment/surplus/saves/investment/deficit
8. saving/borrowing/dishoarding
9. investment/lending/hoarding
10. lending/repaying debts/hoarding
11. borrowing/selling off financial assets/dishoarding
12. investment/lending/hoarding/saving/borrowing

True and False Questions

1. F	2. T	3. T	4. F
5. F	6. F	7. T	8. F
9. T	10. T	11. T	12. T
13. T	14. F	15. T	16. T
17. T	18. F	19. F	20. T

Multiple-Choice Questions

1. a	2. c	3. a	4. b
5. a	6. c	7. c	8. b
9. a	10. a	11. c	12. c
13. e	14. a	15. b	16. b*
17. c	18. d	19. c	20. d

*The equality always holds.

	Sector A		Sector B		Sector C		All Sectors	
	S	U	S	U	S	U	S	U
Investment		W		20		10		30 + W
Saving	10		25		Y		35 + Y	
Hoarding		5		10		5		20
Lending		20		X		10		30 + X
Borrowing	20		15		Z		35 + Z	
Total	30	25 + W	40	30 + X	Y + Z	25		

CHAPTER 28

Essay Questions and Problems

4. a. (1)

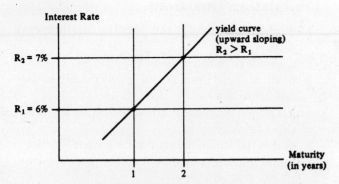

(2) The expected yield on one-year bills to be issued at the end of the first year is 8 percent. This is so because according to the expectation theory the yield to maturity of the two-year note (denoted R_2) is equal to the average yield on the current one-year bill (denoted R_1) and the expected yield on the future one-year bill (denoted r_1). Thus:

$$R_2 = \frac{R_1 + r_1}{2} \text{ or } 7\% = \frac{6\% + r_1}{2}$$

from which it follows that $r_1 = 8$ percent. Clearly, the average of 6 percent and 8 percent is 7 percent. Note that the yield curve plots only the yield on existing issues (the current one-year bill and the two-year note) and does not plot expected yields (the future one-year bill).

b. (1)

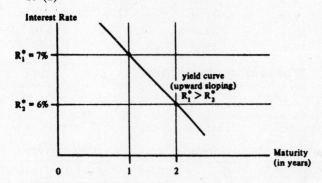

(2) The expected yield on the future one-year bill (denoted r^*_1) is 5 percent. We have:

$$R^*_2 = \frac{R^*_1 + r^*_1}{2} \text{ or } 6\% = \frac{7\% + r^*_1}{2}$$

which implies that $r^*_1 = 5$ percent.

c. Yes. You can make the following statement: "A rising (upward-sloping) yield curve indicates that the market expects short-term rates to increase. A declining (downward-sloping) yield curve indicates that the market expects short-term rates to decrease." When the yield curve is rising, long-term rates are higher than short-term and thus expected future short-term rates must be higher than current short-term rates, since according to expectation theory the long-term rate is the average of the short-term rates. The opposite argument will hold for the declining yield curve.

d. (1) Investors are indifferent because if they hold the 6 percent bill for one year they will receive the face value at maturity, which they can invest in a new one-year bill for the second year yielding 8 percent. Their average annual yield for holding two short-term issues is 7 percent. Alternatively, they can purchase the two-year note and earn an average annual return of 7 percent. Both average annual yields are equal to 7 percent. The investor should therefore be indifferent.

(2) No. Investors who purchase the two-year note and sell it at the end of the first year will not earn 7 percent but 6 percent, the yield on one-year bills. Why? Because 7 percent is the yield to maturity. To earn 7 percent the note must be held for two years. If the note is sold at the end of the first year, its price will be less than its face value, and the one-year holding return on the two-year note will be less than 7 percent, namely 6 percent, because of the capital loss incurred by the holders of two-year notes. According to the expectations theory, investors must earn the same return over equivalent holding periods. Why will the price of the two-year note be less than its face value at the end of the first year? Because the market rate for the next year is 8 percent and the note pays only 7 percent. The only way a holder of a two-year note could find a buyer at the end of the first year is to take a loss, that is, sell the note at a discount from face value.

7. b. Duration is equal to 1.909 years.

Completion Questions

1. the term structure of interest rates/yield curve

2. segmented markets theory/expectations theory/liquidity premium/expectations
3. expectations/yield/expected future short-term/substitutes
4. liquidity premium
5. maturity/the risk structure of interest rates
6. services/Moody's/Standard and Poor's/risk classes/higher/lower
7. municipal/exemption/interest income
8. marketability/tax treatment
9. current coupon/off-the-run
10. risk/maturity/marketability/cash flow uncertainty

True and False Questions

1. T	2. F	3. T	4. T
5. F	6. F	7. F	8. T
9. T	10. F	11. T	12. T
13. T	14. F	15. F	16. F
17. T	18. F	19. F	20. T
21. F	22. F	23. T	24. F
25. F			

Multiple-Choice Questions

1. a	2. d	3. d	4. b
5. c	6. b	7. a	8. e
9. b	10. a	11. c	12. b
13. b	14. c	15. c	16. e
17. c	18. d	19. a	20. b
21. b	22. d	23. e	24. e
25. b			

CHAPTER 29

Essay Questions and Problems

3. Investment bankers are dealers and brokers. They act as dealers when they purchase securities from the issuer (a corporation, for example) and resell them in the market (this is called a public offering). They act as brokers when they place the securities of an issuer with a large buyer. For example, an investment banker may arrange for a corporation to sell an entire issue of bonds to an insurance company (this is called a private placement). Note that in the second case the investment banker does not buy the securities but simply acts as a go-between.

4. Specialists are dealers and brokers. When they purchase and sell for their own accounts, they act as dealers. When they match a buying and selling order, they act as brokers.

6. b. and c.
   d. In decreasing order of liquidity: the Treasury note, the Federal Home Loan bond, and the stock of XYZ corporation.

7. Simply that shares of IBM are very liquid and that antique cars have very little liquidity.

Completion Questions

1. facilitate/financial assets/buyers/sellers
2. dealers/bid/asked/bid/asked/bid-asked spread/facilitating trading
3. Investment banks/underwriting/syndicate/sharing the risk of adverse price movements between the time an issue is bought from a corporation until it is sold in the market
4. agents / commission / orders / buy / sell / own accounts/spread/bid/asked
5. secondary/over-the-counter/money
6. breadth/depth/resiliency/thin
7. Globex/computer-based
8. Securities/Exchange/fraud/equitable and fair operations in securities markets
9. current/all publicly available information

True and False Questions

1. F	2. F	3. T	4. F
5. T	6. T	7. T	8. F
9. F	10. T	11. F	12. F
13. F	14. T	15. T	16. T
17. F	18. T	19. F	20. F

Multiple-Choice Questions

1. d	2. b	3. e	4. a
5. a	6. d	7. b	8. c
9. c	10. e	11. d	12. b
13. d	14. a	15. d	16. c
17. b	18. b		

Type of Security	Bid Price	Ask Price	Spread	Cost of $1,000 Round Trip
Treasury note	103¹⁸⁄₃₂	103²²⁄₃₂	⁴⁄₃₂ = $.125	$1.25
Federal Home Loan bond	96²⁶⁄₃₂	97²⁶⁄₃₂	$1	$10
Stock of XYZ Corp.	19½	20½	$1	$50

CHAPTER 30

Essay Questions and Problems

2. a. $3 billion
   b. $96,509
   c. $96,515
   d. Discount yield =

   $$\frac{100 - 96.532}{100} \times \frac{360}{91} = 13.720\%$$

   Coupon equivalent yield =

   $$\frac{100 - 96.532}{96.532} \times \frac{365}{91} = 14.410\%$$

   e. Discount yield = 13.787 percent
      Coupon equivalent yield = 14.483 percent
   f. Discount yield = 13.811 percent
      Coupon equivalent yield = 14.509 percent

Completion Questions

1. nonmarketable/marketable
2. U.S. savings bonds
3. bills/notes/bonds/secondary
4. the Federal Reserve/commerical banks/foreigners
5. Coupon   stripping/zero-coupon/principal/coupon payments
6. American/English/Dutch auction/increasing
7. the minimization of the interest cost of debt/the promotion of economic stability

True and False Questions

1. F	2. T	3. F	4. T
5. T	6. F	7. F	8. T
9. F	10. F	11. T	12. T
13. T	14. F	15. T	16. T

Multiple-Choice Questions

1. b	2. a	3. d	4. a
5. e	6. b	7. c	8. c
9. b	10. c	11. d	12. b
13. c	14. c	15. d	16. a
17. e	18. a	19. c	20. a

CHAPTER 31

Essay Questions and Problems

2. a. The noncallable bond should be preferred, since it does not carry the risk of being paid off before the scheduled maturity date. And since it is preferred, investors should accept a lower return on these bonds than on callable bonds. To put it differently, callable bonds, being less desirable, should have higher returns than noncallable bonds to induce investors to hold them instead of holding noncallable bonds.

   b. The convertible bond should be preferred, since it carries the attractive feature of being exchangeable into common stocks at a fixed conversion price. If the price of the common stock rises above the conversion price, the exchange will be profitable for the bondholder. This implies that bond buyers will accept a lower return on convertible bonds compared with similar nonconvertible bonds.

4. a. Municipal bonds are tax-exempt. One should compare the *after-tax return* on government bonds to the return on municipal bonds. Suppose that a municipal bond of the highest quality pays a 7 percent tax-exempt coupon and a government bond with the same maturity pays a 10 percent taxable coupon. If investor's marginal tax rate is 40 percent, the *after-tax* return on the government bond is 6 percent (60 percent of 10 percent), which is lower than the 7 percent tax-exempt return on the municipal bond.

Completion Questions

1. Convertible
2. Callable
3. Commercial paper/Treasury bonds
4. below Baa/below BBB
5. unsecured/5/270/30
6. commercial paper/directly/dealers/underwrite
7. municipals/serial/single
8. revenue bonds/general obligation bonds
9. tax-anticipation notes (TANs) / bond-anticipation notes (BANs)

True and False Questions

1. T	2. F	3. F	4. F
5. T	6. F	7. T	8. F
9. T	10. T	11. F	12. F
13. F	14. F	15. T	16. T

Multiple-Choice Questions

1. c	2. c	3. d	4. c
5. d	6. b	7. b	8. a
9. d	10. c	11. e	12. d
13. b	14. b	15. b	16. c
17. b	18. e	19. e	20. a
21. a			

CHAPTER 32

Essay Questions and Problems

7. c. Suppose that the market expects the future price of stocks and/or bonds to fall. In order to avoid a capital loss, market participants will sell now. This will lower the current price of stocks and/or bonds.

Completion Questions

1. institutional/pension funds/mutual funds/small investors
2. secondary/new/investment
3. price/arbitrage
4. Federal Reserve/margin requirement
5. the money supply/monetary policy

True and False Questions

1. T	2. F	3. T	4. F
5. F	6. T	7. T	8. T
9. F	10. T	11. F	12. T
13. T	14. T	15. T	16. T
17. F	18. F	19. F	20. T

Multiple-Choice Questions

1. c	2. b	3. e	4. e
5. d	6. b	7. a	8. d
9. b	10. c	11. d	12. d
13. b	14. b	15. b	16. c
17. c	18. c	19. c	20. c

CHAPTER 33

Completion Questions

1. futures/asset (a commodity or a security)/date/now
2. debt instruments/stock indexes/foreign currencies
3. on organized exchanges/Chicago Board of Trade/International Monetary Market
4. right and obligation/receive/long/long
5. right and obligation/deliver/short/short
6. clearing corporation/credit
7. auction/trading pit
8. arbitrageurs/converge/delivery
9. right/buy/exercise or strike/expiration
10. right/sell/exercise or strike/expiration
11. obligation/sell/exercise or strike/expiration
12. obligation/buy/exercise or strike/expiration
13. premium/the price of the underlying asset/exercise price

True and False Questions

1. F	2. F	3. F	4. F
5. T	6. F	7. T	8. T
9. F	10. F	11. F	12. T
13. F	14. T	15. T	16. T
17. F	18. F	19. F	20. T

Multiple-Choice Questions

1. e	2. c	3. b	4. e
5. d	6. c	7. b	8. a
9. b	10. e	11. c	12. c
13. b	14. e	15. c	16. d
17. c	18. c	19. a	20. d
21. d	22. b	23. a	24. b
25. c			

CHAPTER 34

Essay Questions and Problems

1. b. Exports: receipt of funds from foreigners
Imports: payments made to foreigners
Foreigners buying U.S. securities: receipt of funds from foreigners
Americans buying foreign securities: payments made to foreigners
   c. Americans buying newly produced U.S. goods: recorded in the Gross Domestic Product. Americans buying newly issued U.S. securities: recorded in the flow of funds matrix of the United States.
   d. Yes. Imports exceed exports, but foreigners may have purchased more U.S. securities than Americans have purchased foreign securities by an amount that covers and exceeds the deficit of imports over exports.

2. a. In the United States: all but dollars
In Germany: all but marks
In Canada: all currencies listed
   b. The first two are markets in which foreign exchanges are traded. The third is the market in which domestic short-term debt instruments are traded. The Federal Reserve conducts its open market operations in the money market when it trades in U.S. Treasury bills.
   c. French franc exchange rate: 1 FF = $0.25
U.S. dollar exchange rate: $1 = 4 FF

d. Fixed exchange rates prevailed from the end of World War II until the early 1970s. The present international monetary system is characterized by floating exchange rates.

3. a. (1) See Figure 34.1

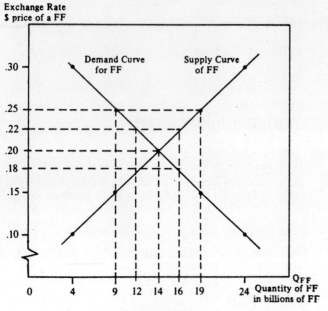

Figure 34.1

(2) Demanders or buyers of FF are nonresidents of France who need FF to purchase French goods and services; to make gifts and grants to residents of France; or to purchase French-issued securities. In exchange for the FF they wish to buy, demanders of FF offer foreign exchanges, in our case U.S. dollars.

(3) Nine billion FF are demanded if the exchange rate is 25 cents (see Figure 34.1).

(4) As the FF becomes cheaper (depreciates), more of it is demanded (other things the same) because French goods, services, and securities are becoming cheaper to holders of foreign exchanges (in this case U.S. dollars).

(5) The demand curve will shift to the *right* as a result of (1) an increase in real income in countries other than France, which will increase foreign demand for French goods as well as the demand for FF to buy these goods; (2) a fall in prices in France relative to other countries, which will increase the demand for French goods as well as the demand for FF to buy these goods; (3) an increase in the interest rate on French securities, which will increase the demand for French securities as well as the demand

for FF to buy these securities; (4) other factors such as expectations by nonresidents of France that the FF will appreciate, an increase in the taste for French goods by nonresidents of France, and so on. The demand curve will shift to the *left* as a result of a change in the opposite direction of any of the factors described above.

b. (1) See Figure 34.1.

(2) Suppliers or sellers of FF are residents of France who need foreign exchanges (in this case dollars) to purchase foreign goods, services, and securities, and to make gifts and grants to foreigners. In exchange for the FF they are willing to sell, suppliers of FF receive foreign exchanges (in this case U.S. dollars).

(3) Nineteen billion FF are supplied if the exchange rate is 25 cents (see Figure 34.1).

(4) As the FF becomes more expensive (appreciates), more of it is supplied (other things the same), because foreign goods, services, and securities are becoming cheaper to holders of FF. They must first exchange their FF into foreign exchanges (in this case U.S. dollars) before they can buy the now-cheaper foreign goods.

(5) The supply curve will shift to the *right* as a result of (1) an increase in real income in France, which will increase the demand by residents of France for foreign goods as well as their demand for foreign exchanges (in this case U.S. dollars) to buy these goods (recall that the demand for U.S. dollars by residents of France is identical to the supply of FF by the residents of France); (2) a fall in prices abroad relative to France, which will increase the demand for foreign goods by residents of France as well as their demand for foreign exchange (supply of FF) to buy these goods, and so on. You should notice that these are the same factors that affect the demand for FF discussed in the answer to question 3a(5). One must simply look at it from the foreigners' point of view.

c. (1) Equilibrium exchange rate: 1 FF = $0.20 (see Figure 34.1).
Equilibrium quantity of the FF: 14 billion FF (see Figure 34.1).
FF price of the dollar at equilibrium: $1 = 5 FF.

(2) At 1 FF = $0.22 the quantity of FF supplied (16 billion) exceeds the quantity of

FF demanded (12 billion). See Figure 34.1. This cannot be an equilibrium exchange rate, because supply and demand are not equal at this rate. The market mechanism that will restore the exchange rate to its equilibrium level operates as follows. Since supply exceeds demand, suppliers of FF will be unable to find buyers for all the FF they wish to sell. By lowering the dollar price of FF (exchange rate), they will increase the quantity of FF demanded. The exchange rate will drop until supply meets demand at the exchange rate that clears the market.

(3) At 1 FF = $.18 the quantity of FF demanded (16 billion) exceeds the quantity supplied (12 billion). See Figure 34.1. This cannot be an equilibrium exchange rate, because supply and demand are not equal at this rate. The market mechanism that will restore equilibrium is similar to that described in (2) above, except that it works in the opposite direction.

(4) At an exchange rate of 22 cents, the FF is *overvalued,* since the equilibrium rate is 20 cents. In a free market the FF will depreciate until it reaches its equilibrium rate. At an exchange rate of 18 cents, the FF is *undervalued,* since the equilibrium rate is 20 cents. In a free market FF will appreciate until it reaches its equilibrium rate.

(5) An increase in prices in the United States relative to prices in France will (1) shift the demand curve for FF to the right, since Americans will need FF to buy French goods, which are now a better buy than American goods; and (2) shift the supply curve of FF to the left, since residents of France will not need as many dollars as before (they will supply less FF), since they will now buy fewer American goods and more home-manufactured goods, which are relatively less expensive. The exchange rate will rise, meaning that FF will appreciate relative to the U.S. dollar. The equilibrium quantity of FF cannot be determined.

(6) The supply curve for FF will shift to the right, since foreigners will reduce their holding of FF; the demand curve for FF will shift to the left, since residents of France will postpone their buying of American-made goods; the foreign exchange will fall, meaning that the FF will depreciate relative to the U.S. dollar; the equilibrium quantity of FF cannot be determined.

4. No. When the DM appreciates by 10 percent relative to the dollar, the original exchange rate of $.50 = 1 DM changes to $.55 = 1 DM. Looking at the same thing from the viewpoint of the dollar, a 10 percent depreciation of the dollar relative to the DM means that the original exchange rate of $1 = 2 DM changes to $1 = 1.8 DM. You can see that $.55 = 1 DM is different from $1 = 1.8 DM, since the latter can be written (divide both sides by 1.8) $.5556 = 1 DM.

Completion Questions

1. balance of payments/foreigners/receipt
2. imports of foreign goods/purchases of foreign securities by Americans/lending to other countries
3. exports of U.S. goods/purchases of U.S. securities by foreigners/expenditures of foreign tourists in the United States
4. balance of payments/deficit/balance of payments/surplus
5. borrowing from/foreigners/selling to/foreigners/exporting
6. foreign exchange/freely floating or freely flexible exchange rates/fixed exchange rates/International Monetary Fund
7. appreciates/exchange rate/higher/cheaper
8. balance of payments/currency/depreciate/eliminate/deficit
9. 4 French francs
10. foreign exchange rate/depreciating
11. equilibrium rate of exchange/supply of foreign exchange/demand for foreign exchange
12. supply of/demand for/fall

True and False Questions

1. F*	2. T	3. T	4. F
5. F	6. T	7. T	8. F
9. T	10. T	11. T	12. T
13. F	14. T	15. F	16. F
17. T	18. F		

*The balance of payments is an accounting record of *all* international transactions. These include goods (exports and imports) *as well as* securities.

Multiple-Choice Questions

1. b	2. c	3. b	4. b
5. d	6. b	7. a	8. b
9. c	10. b	11. d	12. c
13. e	14. a	15. c	

CHAPTER 35

Essay Questions and Problems

1. a. The U.S. dollar. The Japanese yen.
    b. Countries' central banks. They are held in order to cover balance of payments deficits.
    c. Under a purely flexible exchange rate system, international reserves would play a minor role, since balance of payments would adjust automatically through changes in the exchange rates. International reserves, however, may still be needed by some countries to cover temporary balance of payments deficits.

3. c. A speculator with £100,000 should sell his pounds for U.S. dollars at the exchange rate of £1 = $2.50, hold on to the U.S. dollars for a week, and after the devaluation has taken place, buy devalued pounds with his dollars. With a 10 percent devaluation the speculator's profit will be equal to £11,111.11. This is so because the £100,000 will buy $250,000 a week before devaluation. If the 10 percent devaluation actually takes place the new exchange rate will be £1 = $2.25. The $250,000 can now buy

$$\frac{250{,}000}{2.25} = £111{,}111.11.$$

6. a. Yes. Supply equals demand at this exchange rate.
    b. Upper intervention point = .22 (.20 + 1% of .20). Lower intervention point = .18 (.20 − 1% of .20).
    c. (1) Residents of France develop a taste for American-made goods at the expense of French-made goods. Buying American-made goods requires the purchase of U.S. dollars, which are obtained by supplying FF. Note that the demand curve for FF is not affected by this shift in tastes.
        (2) See Figure 35.1.
        (3) New equilibrium exchange rate: 1 FF = $.19. The FF has depreciated relative to the U.S. dollar (see Figure 35.1).
        (4) No, because it is within the intervention band (see Figure 35.1).
        (5) Equilibrium. At 1 FF = $.19 supply meets demand. This equilibrium exchange rate guarantees equilibrium in the balance of payments of France vis-à-vis the United States (see Figure 35.1).
    d. (1) See Figure 35.1.
        (2) 1 FF = $.18 (see Figure 35.1).

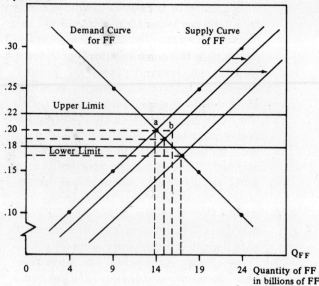

Figure 35.1

(3) The rate can't drop to 1 FF = $.17 because of official intervention by French monetary authorities in the foreign exchange markets. The French central bank will buy FF in exchange for U.S. dollars to prevent the exchange rate from dropping below 1 FF = $.18, the lower intervention point (see Figure 35.1).

(4) Deficit, since the equilibrium exchange rate that will clear the market is not allowed to be attained. Note that the deficit is equal to 2 billion FF, the difference between 18 billion FF and 16 billion FF, or the distance ab in Figure 35.1.

7. a. Restrictive monetary policy. Domestic prices, GDP, and employment should fall. The level of interest rates should rise.
    b. Lower domestic prices should stimulate exports, lower GDP should reduce imports (income is down and fewer imports are purchased), and higher interest rates should attract short-term foreign funds (capital inflow) and discourage outflow of short-term funds—all of which should reduce the size of the balance of payments deficit.
    c. No.

Completion Questions

1. balance of payments/depreciates
2. International reserves/international/gold/convertible foreign currencies (or foreign exchanges)
3. fixed/reserve/slide away/par

4. par/devalue/par/revalue
5. German marks/U.S. dollars/gold or any convertible foreign currency other than U.S. dollars and German marks
6. depreciate/remain the same/less/foreign/assets/ increase / exports / expand / more / imports / contract/narrow/deficit
7. free float/foreign exchange/managed float
8. U.S./Japan/Great Britain/Germany/France/ Canada/Italy
9. productivity/interest rates/inflation rates

True and False Questions

1. T	2. T	3. F	4. T
5. F	6. T	7. F	8. F
9. T	10. F	11. T	12. T
13. T	14. T	15. T	16. F
17. T	18. F	19. F	20. T

Multiple-Choice Questions

1. c	2. a	3. d	4. e
5. c	6. b	7. a	8. c
9. d	10. b	11. c	12. d
13. e	14. c	15. b	16. d
17. d	18. b	19. d	20. b

CHAPTER 36

Essay Questions and Problems

1. c. (1) source/Merchandise Trade balance
   (2) source/Basic balance
   (3) source/Basic balance
   (4) source/Goods and services balance
   (5) use/Merchandise Trade balance
   (6) use/Current Account balance
   (7) not recorded in the U.S. balance of payments/Domestic transaction
   (8) source/Basic balance
   g. By an increase in U.S. liabilities to foreign central banks and/or a decrease in U.S. reserve assets (international assets generally accepted in payment for international debt; more of this was in Chapter 35).
2. a. Merchandise trade balance $= -5$ (deficit)
   b. Current account balance $= -8$ (deficit)
   c. Basic balance $= -6$ (deficit)
   d. Net liquidity balance $= -5$ (deficit)
   e. Official settlements balance $= -3$ (deficit)
   Deficit is financed by a net increase in country A's liabilities to foreign central banks by 2 (country A owes foreign central banks 2)

and a decrease in the official reserve assets of country A by 1 (loss of reserves).

The official settlements balance could be calculated without knowledge of items (1) to (9). Looking at items (10) and (11) one can see that country A's debt to foreign central banks increased by 2 and that country A has lost 1 unit of reserves. This implies that country A had a deficit of 3 in its official settlements balance. Recall that the overall balance of payments (all items) is always in balance.

Completion Questions

1. inflow/foreign exchange/expenditure/outflow/ foreign exchange
2. merchandise exports/purchases by foreigners of domestic securities
3. merchandise imports/purchase of foreign securities
4. lend to/outflow
5. foreign holdings of U.S. dollars/short-term U.S. securities
6. the trade balance/any one of these: the goods and services balance; the current account balance; the basic balance/the net liquidity balance/the official settlements balance

True and False Questions

1. T	2. F	3. F	4. T
5. F	6. F	7. T	8. F
9. T	10. T	11. T	12. F
13. F	14. F	15. T	

Multiple-Choice Questions

1. c	2. b	3. b	4. b
5. d	6. d	7. a	8. b
9. c	10. a	11. b	12. d
13. d	14. b	15. d	16. a

CHAPTER 37

Essay Questions and Problems

2. b. See your answer to completion question 6. Note that in the case of a deficit the mechanism is exactly the opposite. All variables simply change in the opposite direction.
   c. If countries stick to the rules of the international gold standard, they cannot pursue their own independent domestic stabilization

policies. Domestic stabilization policies (monetary and fiscal) are dictated by the state of the balance of payments (surplus or deficit). For example, a deficit in the balance of payments will induce a contractionary monetary policy, and a surplus will create an expansionary monetary policy.

d. The two systems are very similar, at least in theory. Both are based on fixed exchange rates. Under the gold standard, however, the link between the money supply and the state of the balance of payments is rigid. It is not so under a system of fixed exchange rates.

3. a. The exchange rate between their currencies is fixed.

b. $1 = 40 FF (40 FF per dollar).
1 FF = $.025 ($.025 per French franc).

c. Gold export point = $.0252 = par rate of exchange ($.025) plus the cost of shipping $.025 worth of gold ($.0002). This is so because $.025 worth of gold weighs .001 ounce and the cost of shipping .001 ounce of gold is .001 × .20 = $.0002.

d. Gold import point = $.0248 = par exchange rate minus shipping cost.

e. The limits within which the par rate of exchange between the U.S. dollar and the French franc can fluctuate are the gold export point as the upper limit ($.0252) and the gold import point as the lower limit ($.0248). In French francs we have: gold export point = 39.683 FF (the reciprocal of $.0252) and gold import point = 40.323 FF (the reciprocal of $.0248).

Completion Questions

1. gold standard/currency/fractional gold
2. gold standard/fixed/par/the cost of shipping gold from one country to the other
3. gold standard/gold export point/gold import point
4. inflow / decrease / money / central / sterilization / gold
5. fall/fall/rise/rise/decreases/increases/inflow/narrows
6. gain/money/expand/money/tied/gold/expanded/raise / lower / interest / countries / decrease / increase / short-term / outflow / decrease / more / less/increase/higher/raise/foreign/short-term/outflows/short-term interest/higher/reduces

True and False Questions

1. F	2. T	3. T	4. F
5. F	6. T	7. T	8. T
9. F	10. T	11. F	12. T
13. F	14. F	15. T	16. T
17. F	18. T	19. T	20. F

Multiple-Choice Questions

1. a	2. e	3. c	4. b
5. a	6. a	7. d	8. d
9. c	10. d	11. e	12. b
13. c	14. a	15. b	16. c
17. a	18. b	19. b	20. d
21. d	22. b	23. d	24. b
25. d